Foundation GCSE M

Michael White

This book covers the material required for the GCSE Foundation Tier (grades C to G).

To allow for the range of abilities, each part of the book is written in 2 sections. The M exercises should be suitable for most students at this level. E exercises are generally more demanding. They may provide extension work following the M exercise or they may cover a related but more demanding topic.

Constant revisiting of topics is essential for exam success. Throughout this book, the author provides 'Can you still?' sections to encourage this continual reviewing process.

Each unit contains a functional 'Use your maths' section. There are also two additional units devoted to raising students' awareness of money matters.

The author does not refer specifically to 'QWC' (Quality of Written Communication) because it is assumed that all teachers encourage students to develop arguments logically and to use notation accurately.

Thanks are due to AQA, CCEA, Edexcel, OCR and WJEC for kindly allowing the use of questions from their past examination papers. The answers are solely the work of the author and are not ratified by the examining groups.

The author is indebted to the contributions from Hilary White and Peter Gibson.

First published 2010 by
Elmwood Press
80 Attimore Road
Welwyn Garden City
Herts AL8 6LP
Tel. 01707 333232

ISBN 9781 906 622 176

i

Contents

In this unit you will learn how to:

- understand place value in numbers
- round off numbers
- add and subtract whole numbers
- multiply whole numbers
- divide whole numbers
- add and subtract negative numbers
- multiply and divide negative numbers
- do calculations in the correct order
- USE YOUR MATHS! – win the premiership

Place value

There are 1423 students in the Blue School.

142<u>3</u> The 3 digit represents 3 students

1<u>4</u>23 The 4 digit represents 400 students

14<u>2</u>3 The 2 digit represents 20 students

<u>1</u>423 The 1 digit represents 1000 students

M1. 1

In Questions ① to ⑤ , write down the value of each digit of the number.

① There are 2541 students in High Grass College.

② There are 1384 students in King Arthur's School.

③ Forest Green School has 1279 pupils.

④ There are 865 pupils in Cragg High School.

⑤ Cleeve College has 3714 students.

6 What is the value of the underlined digit in each number below?

(a) 6<u>7</u>5   (b) 71<u>4</u>   (c) 137<u>8</u>   (d) <u>3</u>619   (e) 40<u>6</u>

(f) 5<u>7</u>14   (g) 37<u>8</u>1   (h) <u>5</u>369   (i) 5<u>1</u>8   (j) 3<u>6</u>72

(k) 372<u>6</u>   (l) <u>5</u>064   (m) 4<u>1</u>07   (n) 8<u>7</u>10   (o) 691<u>5</u>

7   6   8   3

(a) Using all the 3 cards above, what is the *largest* number you can make?

(b) Using all the 3 cards above, what is the *smallest* number you can make?

8   7   1   4

(a) Using all the 3 cards above, what is the *largest* number you can make?

(b) Using all the 3 cards above, what is the *smallest* number you can make?

Tenths, hundredths, thousandths

Key Facts

The digit after the decimal point shows tenths

0.<u>1</u> the 1 means $\dfrac{1}{10}$ 0.<u>6</u> the 6 means $\dfrac{6}{10}$ 27.<u>8</u> the 8 means $\dfrac{8}{10}$

The second digit after the decimal point shows hundredths

0.0<u>1</u> the 1 means $\dfrac{1}{100}$ 27.1<u>8</u> the 8 means $\dfrac{8}{100}$

The third digit after the decimal point shows thousandths

0.00<u>1</u> the 1 means $\dfrac{1}{1000}$ 0.00<u>6</u> the 6 means $\dfrac{6}{1000}$ 27.34<u>8</u> the 8 means $\dfrac{8}{1000}$

1 The 3 in the number 12.731 means $\dfrac{3}{100}$.

What is the value of the underlined digit in each number below:

(a) 0.8<u>2</u>   (b) 0.<u>9</u>13   (c) 0.<u>5</u>86   (d) 0.30<u>7</u>

(e) 0.<u>9</u>   (f) 0.51<u>7</u>   (g) 0.36<u>8</u>   (h) 0.4<u>2</u>8

(i) <u>7</u>.89   (j) 5.<u>2</u>38   (k) 2<u>8</u>.6   (l) <u>1</u>5.37

(m) 17.<u>8</u>26   (n) 26.10<u>8</u>   (o) <u>3</u>6.029   (p) 78.5<u>2</u>6

(q) 106.9<u>7</u>   (r) 2<u>7</u>1.638   (s) 386.59<u>1</u>   (t) 836.7<u>0</u>4

2 Which number is the larger: $\boxed{0.1}$ or $\boxed{0.01}$?

3 Which number is the larger: $\boxed{0.08}$ or $\boxed{0.7}$?

4 Which number is the largest: $\boxed{0.09}$ or $\boxed{0.5}$ or $\boxed{0.008}$?

5 $\boxed{A}$ $\boxed{B}$ $\boxed{\bullet}$ $\boxed{C}$ $\boxed{D}$ $\boxed{E}$

(a) Tom has 5 cards: $\boxed{7}$ $\boxed{3}$ $\boxed{8}$ $\boxed{4}$ $\boxed{6}$

Tom must place the cards on spaces $\boxed{A}$ $\boxed{B}$ $\boxed{C}$ $\boxed{D}$ $\boxed{E}$ above to make the *largest* number possible. Write down the number he makes.

(b) Tom must now place the cards on spaces $\boxed{A}$ $\boxed{B}$ $\boxed{C}$ $\boxed{D}$ $\boxed{E}$ above to make the *smallest* number possible. Write down the number he makes.

(c) Sasha has 6 cards: $\boxed{4}$ $\boxed{9}$ $\boxed{1}$ $\boxed{6}$ $\boxed{5}$ $\boxed{8}$

Sasha must place 5 of her cards on spaces $\boxed{A}$ $\boxed{B}$ $\boxed{C}$ $\boxed{D}$ $\boxed{E}$ above to make the *largest* number possible. Write down the number she makes.

(d) Sasha must now place 5 of her cards on spaces $\boxed{A}$ $\boxed{B}$ $\boxed{C}$ $\boxed{D}$ $\boxed{E}$ above to make the *smallest* number possible. Write down the number she makes.

People often round off numbers when giving information

THE PLANET

Around 100,000 people attended the Concert ..
....

Daily Times

Janet scoops just under £3 million on the Lottery....
....

Daily Herald

About 120 people feared dead.......

🔑 # Key Facts

Rounding to the nearest 10	Rounding to the nearest 100
Look at the units column. 5 or more, round up. Less than 5, round down. 49 rounds to 50 74 rounds to 70 65 rounds to 70	Look at the tens and units columns. 50 or more, round up. Less than 50, round down. 368 rounds to 400 327 rounds to 300 850 rounds to 900
Rounding to the nearest 1000	Rounding to the nearest whole number
Look at the hundreds, tens and units columns. 500 or more, round up. Less than 500, round down. 1361 rounds to 1000 2724 rounds to 3000 8500 rounds to 9000	Look at the tenths column (this is the first digit after the decimal point). 5 or more, round up. Less than 5, round down. 2.5 rounds to 3 7.38 rounds to 7 £6.65 rounds to £7

M1. 2

Round to the nearest 10

1 64	**2** 47	**3** 39	**4** 82	**5** 23
6 15	**7** 71	**8** 38	**9** 7	**10** 43
11 75	**12** 97	**13** 307	**14** 289	**15** 461
16 238	**17** 423	**18** 819	**19** 1324	**20** 6149

Round to the nearest 100

21 230   **22** 360   **23** 480   **24** 610   **25** 720

26 750   **27** 673   **28** 308   **29** 852   **30** 695

31 747   **32** 896   **33** 656   **34** 718   **35** 1350

36 2715   **37** 4582   **38** 1639   **39** 2193   **40** 5417

Copy the sentences in Questions **41** to **46**, writing the number to the nearest 1000

41 The van costs £ 16580

42 Jack flew 2813 miles to New York

43 Hale Brewery sold 16293 bottles of beer last week.

44 The 'Harry Potter' book has 678 pages.

45 Ramesh won £ 38625 last month.

46 482,301 people live in Bristol.

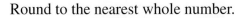

Round to the nearest whole number.

47 7.8   **48** 3.2   **49** 2.5   **50** 12.3   **51** 8.34

Round to the nearest pound.

52 £3.17   **53** £2.91   **54** £7.36   **55** £12.81   **56** £24.50

Round to the nearest kilogram.

57 7.2 kg   **58** 3.5 kg   **59** 14.3 kg   **60** 8.72 kg   **61** 23.26 kg

---

A headteacher says there are 800 students in Sand High School. This number is rounded off to the nearest 100.

Which of the numbers below could be the exact number of students in Sand High School?

820   701   791   752   861   850   831   750

Answer

820   791   752   831   750

are all possible answers.

Round off each number below to:

(a) the nearest 10   (b) the nearest 100   (c) to the nearest 1000

1   2317   **2**   4628   **3**   6278   **4**   4191

5   997   **6**   3283   **7**   8169   **8**   17451

9   A golf club has 600 members. This number is rounded off to the nearest 100.

Which of the numbers below could be the exact number of members of the golf club?

550   610   650   619   583   529   665

10   The table below shows the population (in millions) of some countries:

Population (millions)	
China	1131
India	871
USA	251
Brazil	153
Pakistan	126
Japan	124
Mexico	90

Write down each country and round off the number to the nearest 100.

11   The home of Chelsea football club is Stamford Bridge. One Saturday around 50,000 people watch a game at Stamford Bridge. This number is rounded off to the nearest 1000.

Which of the numbers below could be the exact number of people at Stamford Bridge?

50,351   50,564   49,681   50,018   49,394   50,500   49,499   49,899

12   Work out these answers with a calculator and then round off the answers to the *nearest whole number.*

(a) $5817 \div 57$ (b) 18.4×2.17 (c) $207 \div 0.7$ (d) $221 \div 19$

(e) 3.82×4.05 (f) $89.6 \div 5.3$ (g) $897 \div 17$ (h) 14.8×0.87

(i) $1.83 \div 0.07$ (j) $2725 \div 13$ (k) 63.3×2.9 (l) $83.4 \div 17$

Adding and subtracting whole numbers

4275 + 306

Line up units with units
Line up tens with tens
Line up hundreds with hundreds
and so on

867 − 248

```
  4275
+  306
  4581
     1
```

```
  8 ⁵6̸ ¹7
 −2 4 8
  6 1 9
```

Copy and complete.

1
```
   98
 + 64
```

2
```
  216
 + 71
```

3
```
  378
 + 214
```

4
```
  2587
 + 3179
```

5
```
  6781
 + 2194
```

6
```
   87
 − 48
```

7
```
   73
 − 29
```

8
```
  126
 − 71
```

9
```
  563
 − 148
```

10
```
  2847
 − 386
```

11
```
  893
 + 284
```

12
```
  527
 + 292
```

13
```
  376
 − 128
```

14
```
  829
 − 463
```

15
```
  3718
 + 587
```

16
```
  581
 − 273
```

17
```
  8172
 + 3218
```

18
```
  2160
 − 1317
```

19
```
  5863
 − 2194
```

20
```
  86148
 + 31683
```

21

Copy and complete the crossnumber using the clues.

Clues across	Clues down
1 737 + 187	**1** 382 + 576
4 471 − 228	**2** 561 − 137
5 1274 − 390	**3** 13872 + 9417
7 387 − 329	**6** 417 + 417
8 27383 + 36876	**7** 826 − 771

7

1 Find the sum of 318 and 187

2 Find the sum of the four numbers 49, 386, 172 and 563

> The *sum* of 51 and 38 means 51 + 38
>
> The difference of 51 and 38 means 51–38

3 Find the difference between 268 and 189

4 Find the difference between 637 and 476

5 What is the total of the three numbers 58, 124 and 186?

Copy and complete Questions **6** to **14** by writing the missing number in the box.

6 $220 + \square = 575$

7 $450 + \square = 610$

8 $785 - \square = 320$

9 $833 - \square = 525$

10 $864 + \square = 987$

11 $1238 - \square = 850$

12 $\square + 478 = 820$

13 $1650 - \square = 789$

14 $\square - 384 = 531$

Copy and complete the squares below:

15

+	38	87		66
109	147			
326		571		
				229
				512

16

+		148	516	
384	827			
		400		
87			331	
226				

17 Joe has £ 383. He needs to save £ 760 to buy a laptop. How much more money does he need?

18 Tina has collected the following money from a sponsored run: £ 22, £ 39, £ 21, £ 6, £ 18, £ 54, £ 31, £ 28, £ 42. How much money has she collected in total?

19 Sparrow Electrical Goods sell the following:

(a) What is the total cost of all 5 items?

(b) How much more does the Dishwasher cost than the Freezer?

(c) What is the difference in the prices of the Fridge and the Microwave?

Washing machine	£ 389
Fridge	£ 225
Dishwasher	£ 412
Microwave	£ 87
Freezer	£ 149

8

20 The table below shows how many students were absent from school one week.

Year	Monday	Tuesday	Wednesday	Thursday	Friday
7	11	12	7	13	16
8	3	7	6	4	9
9	10	13	13	7	11
10	17	13	14	19	21
11	16	14	21	22	18

(a) How many students in total were absent on Monday?

(b) How many students in total were absent on Wednesday?

(c) What is the difference in the total number of students absent on Wednesday compared to Monday?

(d) What is the difference in the total number of students absent on Friday compared to Tuesday?

21 A rock concert was supposed to be watched by 80,000 people maximum. One night the Police estimate that 112,350 people have managed to watch the concert. How many *extra* people were able to see the concert that night?

22 Sid's car shows 52,487 miles on the milometer at the start of the year. At the end of the year it shows 68,279 miles. How many miles did Sid's car cover during that year?

Multiplying and dividing by 10, 100 and 1000

$586 \times 10 = 5860$	$\times 10$	digits move 1 place to the left
$586 \times 100 = 58600$	$\times 100$	digits move 2 places to the left
$586 \times 1000 = 586000$	$\times 1000$	digits move 3 places to the left
$79000 \div 10 = 7900$	$\div 10$	digits move 1 place to the right
$79000 \div 100 = 790$	$\div 100$	digits move 2 places to the right
$79000 \div 1000 = 79$	$\div 1000$	digits move 3 places to the right

Write the answers only.

1 769 × 10

2 31 × 1000

3 268 × 1000

4 416 × 100

5 24 × 100

6 3861 × 10

7 6300 ÷ 10

8 81700 ÷ 10

9 397000 ÷ 10

10 418000 ÷ 1000

11 527000 ÷ 100

12 4800 ÷ 100

13 51600 ÷ 100

14 31600 × 10

15 530 × 100

16 417000 ÷ 100

17 684000 ÷ 1000

18 5370 × 1000

19 Ned earns £ 100 each week. How much money does he earn in one year (52 weeks)?

20 Molly does a sponsored swim. Her total sponsorship money is £ 13 for each length of the swimming pool. How much money does Molly get if she swims 100 lengths?

21 A factory makes 110,000 sweets during one week. The sweets are packed equally into 1000 boxes. How many sweets are there in each box?

Copy and complete.

22 ⬚ × 10 = 8930

23 ⬚ × 100 = 46000

24 ⬚ ÷ 100 = 218

25 ⬚ ÷ 1000 = 49

26 ⬚ ÷ 10 = 8410

27 ⬚ × 100 = 9300

28 621 × ⬚ = 62100

29 480000 ÷ ⬚ = 480

30 710 × ⬚ = 71000

31 ⬚ ÷ 100 = 3820

32 ⬚ ÷ 10 = 9240

33 87600 ÷ ⬚ = 8760

34 316 → × 10 → ⬚ → × 100 → ⬚ → ÷ 10 → ⬚ → ÷ 100 → ⬚

35 ⬚ → × 100 → 864000 → ÷ 100 → ⬚ → ÷ 10 → ⬚

(a) $3 \times 2\underline{0}$

$= 3 \times \overbrace{2 \times 10}$

$= 6 \times 10$

$= 6\underline{0}$

(b) $3\underline{0} \times 2\underline{0}$

$= 3 \times 10 \times 2 \times 10$

$= 3 \times 2 \times 10 \times 10$

$= 6 \times 10 \times 10$

$= 60 \times 10$

$= 6\underline{00}$

(c) $5\underline{0} \times 7\underline{00}$

$= 5 \times 10 \times 7 \times 100$

$= 5 \times 7 \times 10 \times 100$

$= 35 \times 10 \times 100$

$= 350 \times 100$

$= 35\underline{000}$

(d) $80 \div 20$ is the same as $8 \div 2$ which equals 4

Before dividing 2 numbers you may divide *both* numbers by 10, 100 or 1000 which will make the division easier

(e) $280 \div 40$ is the same as $28 \div 4$ which equals 7

(f) $36000 \div 6000$ is the same as $36 \div 6$ which equals 6

E1. 4

Work out

1 6×30

2 8×50

3 40×7

4 3×90

5 60×6

6 70×30

7 80×50

8 9×400

9 30×400

10 60×800

11 700×20

12 800×200

13 300×90

14 800×700

15 400×600

16 20 people each save £ 400. How much do they save in total?

17 A school buys 30 boxes of drawing pins. Each box contains 200 drawing pins. How many drawing pins are there in total?

Work out

18 $120 \div 30$

19 $360 \div 40$

20 $540 \div 60$

21 $180 \div 90$

22 $400 \div 50$

23 $4800 \div 600$

24 $7200 \div 900$

25 $5600 \div 800$

26 $32000 \div 4000$

27 $27000 \div 9000$

28 $48000 \div 8000$

29 $4200 \div 70$

30 $8100 \div 90$

31 $21000 \div 700$

32 $32000 \div 800$

11

33 60 people share a Lottery win of £300 000. How much does each person get?

34 720 000 packets of crisps are packed equally into 8000 boxes. How many packets of crisps are in each box?

Copy and complete

35 ☐ × 30 = 150   **36** ☐ × 40 = 1200   **37** ☐ × 700 = 14000

38 ☐ × 800 = 56000   **39** ☐ × 60 = 3000   **40** ☐ ÷ 30 = 50

41 ☐ ÷ 500 = 70   **42** 25000 ÷ ☐ = 500   **43** 7000 × ☐ = 210000

44 20 → × 40 → ☐ → × 30 → ☐ → ÷ 600 → ☐ → ÷ 10 → ☐

45 300 → ÷ 10 → ☐ → × 50 → ☐ → × 30 → ☐ → ÷ 90 → ☐

Can you still?

Can you still?

1A **Round off numbers**

Round to the nearest 100.

1. 771   **2.** 850   **3.** 1723   **4.** 2198

Round to the nearest 10.

5. 18   **6.** 73   **7.** 449   **8.** 251

Round to the nearest whole number.

9. 8.9   **10.** 6.7   **11.** 3.16   **12.** 6.5

Round to the nearest 1000.

13. 8312   **14.** 7900   **15.** 28184   **16.** 53582

Work out these answers *WITH A CALCULATOR* and then round off the answers to the *nearest whole number*.

17. 4.9 × 3.61   **18.** 2142 ÷ 38   **19.** 1.97 ÷ 0.03   **20.** 17.6 × 31.8

1 Copy and complete the grids below. Time yourself on the first grid. Try to improve your time on the second grid.

×	7	2	10	8	6	3	11	9	4	5
7	49									
2										
10										
8										
6			48							
3					9					
11										
9										
4										
5										

×	2	9	6	3	5	11	0	8	7	4
2										
9										
6										
3										
5										
11										
0										
8										
7										
4										

Work out

2 31
 × 3

3 34
 × 4

4 61
 × 4

5 39
 × 5

6 89
 × 7

7 26
 × 8

8 416
 × 4

9 325
 × 5

10 513
 × 3

11 245
 × 7

12 216
 × 6

13 137
 × 4

14 436
 × 8

15 309
 × 7

16 154
 × 6

17 328 × 6

18 208 × 5

19 9 × 246

20 6 × 3152

21 6384 × 7

22 One night 73 people watch a film at the cinema. They each pay £ 7. How much money do they all pay in total?

23 Ralph likes collecting fossils. Each month he collects 8 new fossils. How many fossils will Ralph collect in 3 years (36 months)?

24 Sandra and her 5 friends are going to Spain on holiday. They each have to pay £ 418. How much do Sandra and her friends have to pay in total?

25 A fast-food restaurant sold 326 'special meals' at £ 4 each. How much money did they get for all 326 'special meals'?

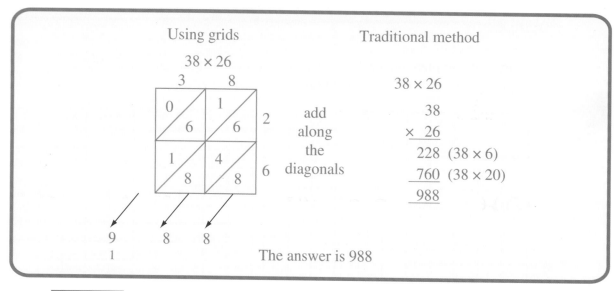

Using grids

38 × 26

add along the diagonals

The answer is 988

Traditional method

38 × 26

```
        38
    ×   26
       228   (38 × 6)
       760   (38 × 20)
       988
```

E1. 5

Work out

1 23 × 16   **2** 16 × 35   **3** 93 × 27   **4** 68 × 46

5 76 × 52   **6** 59 × 34   **7** 64 × 28   **8** 417 × 76

9 398 × 59   **10** 68 × 409   **11** 623 × 67   **12** 518 × 43

13 28 × 338   **14** 81 × 716   **15** 543 × 728

16 64 people each pay £ 724 to go on a holiday in the USA. How much do the 64 people pay in total?

17 On average, a person in the UK laughs 15 times each day. How many times will a person laugh in one year (52 weeks)?

18 A person sheds 18 kg of skin in his or her lifetime. How much skin would be shed by 500 people over their lifetimes?

19 In 2003, single men in the UK spent an average of £ 186 on a first date. How much in total would 73 single men have spent on their first dates?

20

| TV | £ 527 |
| CD player | £ 218 |

How much will 34 televisions and 19 CD players cost in total?

Short division

(a) $625 \div 5$

$$\begin{array}{r} 1\,2\,5 \\ 5\overline{)6^1 2^2 5} \end{array}$$

(b) $936 \div 4$

$$\begin{array}{r} 2\,3\,4 \\ 4\overline{)9^1 3^1 6} \end{array}$$

(c) $3073 \div 7$

$$\begin{array}{r} 0\,4\,3\,9 \\ 7\overline{)3^3 0^2 7^6 3} \end{array}$$

M1. 6

Part One

Copy and complete the following division problems.

1 $6 \div 3 = ?$
2 $8 \div 4 = ?$
3 $48 \div 8 = ?$
4 $88 \div 11 = ?$

5 $16 \div 2 = ?$
6 $10 \div 2 = ?$
7 $49 \div 7 = ?$
8 $90 \div 9 = ?$

9 $20 \div 5 = ?$
10 $99 \div 11 = ?$
11 $50 \div 5 = ?$
12 $96 \div 12 = ?$

13 $24 \div 6 = ?$
14 $14 \div 7 = ?$
15 $54 \div 6= ?$
16 $100 \div 10 = ?$

17 $28 \div 4 = ?$
18 $15 \div 3 = ?$
19 $0 \div 7 = ?$
20 $5\frac{1}{2} \div 5\frac{1}{2} = ?$

Part Two   Work out

1 $3\overline{)99}$
2 $2\overline{)42}$
3 $4\overline{)48}$
4 $7\overline{)84}$

5 $5\overline{)65}$
6 $6\overline{)72}$
7 $7\overline{)847}$
8 $9\overline{)558}$

9 $8\overline{)128}$
10 $9\overline{)729}$
11 $2\overline{)678}$
12 $6\overline{)3372}$

13 $3\overline{)729}$
14 $5\overline{)725}$
15 $4\overline{)1028}$
16 $8\overline{)1856}$

17 $6\overline{)1296}$
18 $7\overline{)343}$
19 $9\overline{)6561}$
20 $6\overline{)2796}$

21 $8\overline{)2056}$
22 $5\overline{)1025}$
23 $6\overline{)7776}$
24 $7\overline{)5082}$

25 $3050 \div 10$
26 $1387 \div 1$
27 $38199 \div 7$
28 $14032 \div 8$

29 $31386 \div 6$
30 $3490 \div 5$
31 $28926 \div 9$
32 $15638 \div 7$

(a) How many teams of 5 can you make from 113 people?

Work out 113 ÷ 5 $\quad \dfrac{0\ 2\ 2}{5\overline{)1^11^13}}$ remainder 3

Here we round *down*. You can make 22 teams and there will be 3 people left over.

(b) An egg box holds 6 eggs. How many boxes do you need for 231 eggs?

Work out 231 ÷ 6 $\quad \dfrac{3\ 8}{6\overline{)23^51}}$ remainder 3

Here we round *up* because you must use complete boxes. You need 39 boxes altogether.

E1. 6

Write the answers with a remainder.

1 $2\overline{)432}$ **2** $4\overline{)716}$ **3** $6\overline{)895}$ **4** $3\overline{)164}$

5 $8\overline{)514}$ **6** $9\overline{)375}$ **7** $5\overline{)2642}$ **8** $2\overline{)7141}$

9 $1079 \div 7$ **10** $2132 \div 5$ **11** $4014 \div 8$ **12** $235 \div 6$

13 $657 \div 10$ **14** $8327 \div 10$ **15** $85714 \div 6$ **16** $4826 \div 9$

17 $2007 \div 7$ **18** $9998 \div 9$ **19** $6732 \div 11$ **20** $84563 \div 7$

In the Questions below, round the answer up or down, depending on which is more sensible.

21 There are 27 children in a class. How many teams of 4 can be made?

22 Tickets cost £ 7 each. I have £ 100. How many tickets can I buy?

23 Tins of spaghetti are packed 8 to a box. How many boxes are needed for 943 tins?

24 Five people can travel in one car. 83 people are to be transported. How many cars are needed?

25 A tennis coach has 52 tennis balls. A box holds 4 tennis balls. How many boxes does the tennis coach have?

16

You can divide large numbers in the same way as you do short division.

$962 \div 26$

Write out the 26 times table by adding on 26 each time.

The most you will need are 9 numbers.

Write out the division leaving a space between each digit in 962.

26
52
78
104
130
156
182
208
234

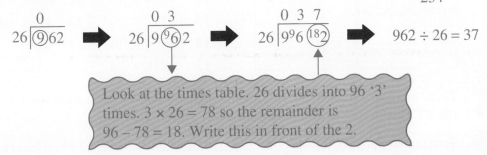

$$26\overline{)9\!\!\;62} \qquad 26\overline{)9\!\!\;9\!\!\;62}^{\;0\;3} \qquad 26\overline{)9\!\!\;9\!\!\;6\!\!\;182}^{\;0\;3\;7} \qquad 962 \div 26 = 37$$

Look at the times table. 26 divides into 96 '3' times. $3 \times 26 = 78$ so the remainder is $96 - 78 = 18$. Write this in front of the 2.

M1. 7

Work out

1. $504 \div 14$
2. $513 \div 19$
3. $400 \div 16$
4. $552 \div 24$
5. $559 \div 13$
6. $408 \div 17$
7. $704 \div 22$
8. $625 \div 25$
9. $798 \div 21$
10. $812 \div 28$
11. $884 \div 34$
12. $851 \div 37$
13. $630 \div 35$
14. $972 \div 27$
15. $702 \div 39$

16. To change months into years, we divide by 12. Find the age in years of each person below:

Charlie
348 months

Tessa
516 months

Ron
984 months

Teresa
180 months

17. 840 packets of crisps are packed into 24 boxes. How many packets of crisps are there in each box?

1 Copy and complete the crossnumber using the clues.

1			2		3
		4			
5	6		7	8	
	9				
10			11		
	13				
14				15	

	Clues across		Clues down
1	$874 \div 23$	**1**	$5372 \div 17$
2	$9504 \div 18$	**2**	$7436 \div 13$
4	$1598 \div 34$	**3**	$9493 \div 11$
5	$3536 \div 52$	**6**	$9828 \div 12$
7	$3888 \div 16$	**8**	$5978 \div 14$
9	$1152 \div 64$	**10**	$6540 \div 15$
10	$2058 \div 42$	**11**	$2871 \div 87$
11	$4836 \div 13$	**12**	$6318 \div 26$
13	$2117 \div 29$	**13**	$4788 \div 63$
14	$8764 \div 14$		
15	$3818 \div 46$		

2 There are 380 children in a school. How many classes of 31 children can be made? How many children would be left over?

3 Tom has to put 1000 bottles into crates. One crate will take 24 bottles. How many crates will Tom need?

4 How many 27p stamps can I buy with a £20 note?

5 A party of 17 people are going on holiday to Greece. The total holiday bill is £7191. How much does each person have to pay?

Can you still?

1B **Add and subtract**

Can you still?

Work out

1. $573 + 64$

2. $937 + 418$

3. $561 - 38$

4. $572 - 419$

5. $4174 + 629$

6. $6834 - 458$

7. $3218 + 4627$

8. $6134 - 816$

9. $7428 - 2917$

Copy and complete Questions (10) to (15) by writing the missing number in the box.

10. $371 + \boxed{} = 518$ 11. $523 + \boxed{} = 741$ 12. $681 - \boxed{} = 251$

13. $\boxed{} + 334 = 620$ 14. $1369 - \boxed{} = 817$ 15. $\boxed{} - 265 = 306$

Adding and subtracting negative numbers

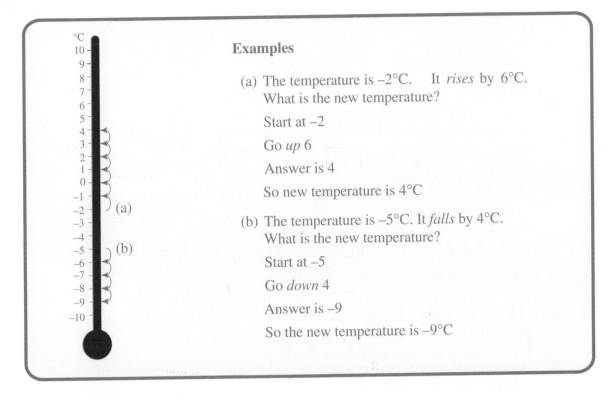

Examples

(a) The temperature is –2°C. It *rises* by 6°C.
What is the new temperature?

Start at –2

Go *up* 6

Answer is 4

So new temperature is 4°C

(b) The temperature is –5°C. It *falls* by 4°C.
What is the new temperature?

Start at –5

Go *down* 4

Answer is –9

So the new temperature is –9°C

M1. 8

1 Copy and complete the table below by moving up or down the thermometer to find the new temperature.

Temperature °C	Change °C	New temperature °C
4	falls by 5	
1	falls by 6	
–3	rises by 2	
–6	falls by 3	
–4	rises by 7	
–9	rises by 6	
5	rises by 3	
0	falls by 7	
–2	falls by 3	
6	falls by 10	

In questions **2** to **4** put the numbers in order, smallest first:

2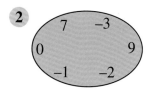

3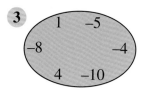

4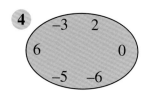

5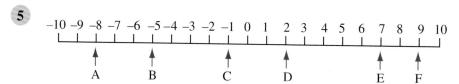

The *difference* in temperature between C and D is 3°C. Give the difference in temperature between:

(a) E and F

(b) B and C

(c) D and E

(d) A and B

(e) A and C

(f) B and E

6 The temperature in Birmingham at midday is 15°C. During the night it falls by 16°C. What is the new temperature?

7 One night the temperature in Plymouth is 1°C and the temperature in Newcastle is −3°C. How much colder is Newcastle than Plymouth?

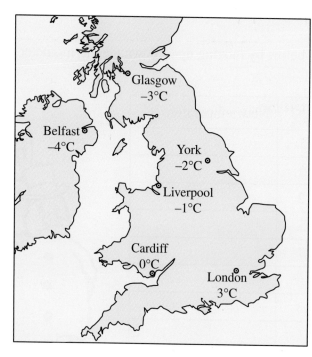

8 Which city has the highest temperature?

9 Which city has the lowest temperature?

10 What is the difference in temperature between York and London?

11 What is the difference in temperature between Belfast and Liverpool?

12 During the day, the temperature in Glasgow rises by 10°C. What is the new temperature?

13 During the day, the temperature in Liverpool rises by 15°C and the temperature in Belfast rises by 17°C. Which city now has the higher temperature, Liverpool or Belfast?

14 Work out

(a) $3 - 6$ (b) $-5 - 1$ (c) $-5 + 1$ (d) $-3 + 3$

(e) $-8 + 5$ (f) $3 - 9$ (g) $2 - 10$ (h) $-4 - 5$

(i) $-8 + 6$ (j) $-10 + 6$ (k) $-7 - 2$ (l) $-6 + 5$

15 Copy and complete the table below:-

Old temperature $^\circ$C	Change $^\circ$C	New temperature $^\circ$C
-2	rises by 7	
	rises by 3	2
	falls by 6	-4
-8	falls by 2	
	rises by 7	0
-6		-2
-12	rises by 8	
	rises by 3	-1
	falls by 5	-7
-10		-14

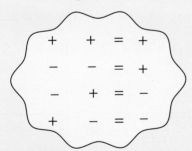

🔑 Key Facts

Two signs together

$8 - -5$ can be read as '8 take away negative 5'. This is sometimes written as $8 - (-5)$.

It is possible to replace two signs next to each other by one sign as follows:

+	+	=	+
−	−	=	+
−	+	=	−
+	−	=	−

'same signs: +'

'different signs: −'

When two signs next to each other have been replaced by one sign in this way, the calculation is completed using the number line as before.

Examples

(a) $-6 + -2$
$= -6 - 2$
$= -8$

(b) $3 - -4$
$= 3 + 4$
$= 7$

(c) $-4 + -2$
$= -4 - 2$
$= -6$

21

1   Work out

(a) $3 + -1$ (b) $8 + -5$ (c) $-4 - 2$ (d) $-2 + -3$

(e) $8 + -3$ (f) $4 - -2$ (g) $-3 + -4$ (h) $-2 - -1$

(i) $7 - 10$ (j) $4 + -6$ (k) $-6 - 3$ (l) $-8 - -4$

(m) $7 - -1$ (n) $5 - -4$ (o) $-1 + -6$ (p) $-12 + 5$

2   John is overdrawn at the bank by £70 (This means he owes the bank £70). If John pays in £100, how much money will he have in the bank?

3   Cassie is overdrawn at the bank by £60. How much money will she have in the bank if she:

(a)   pays in £100   (b)   pays in £70   (c)   pays in £140?

4   Todd has £36 in his bank account. He buys some clothes for £150 with his bank card. How much money does he now owe the bank?

5   Lola wants to buy a pair of shoes for £60. She has £12 in her bank account. The bank will allow her to go up to £50 overdrawn. Can she use her bank card to buy the shoes?

6   Work out

(a) $-4 + 3$ (b) $-9 - 1$ (c) $4 - -7$ (d) $-8 - -2$

(e) $6 + -4$ (f) $-3 + -8$ (g) $7 - 13$ (h) $-9 + 5$

(i) $-9 - 5$ (j) $-9 - -5$ (k) $-4 - -10$ (l) $-5 - 6$

(m) $3 + -10$ (n) $-6 + 2$ (o) $-3 - -4$ (p) $-8 + 4 - 3$

(q) $-7 - 2 + 10$ (r) $-5 - -1 - 6$ (s) $4 - 7 + -2$ (t) $-8 + -5 - -5$

Copy and complete the boxes below:

7
$-6 + 4 = -2$
$\square - 2 = -3$
$-8 - -7 = \square$
$-6 + 1 = \square$
$\square - -2 = 7$

8
$7 + -3 = \square$
$\square + -4 = -2$
$\square - 7 = -8$
$6 - \square = -1$
$-3 + \square = 1 - 10$

9
$-3 - -2 = \square$
$-9 + -3 = \square$
$\square - -7 = -2$
$-8 - \square = -2$
$\square + -6 = -12$

10   **Check** your answers to Questions **6** to **9** by *using a calculator*. Make sure your teacher shows you the correct button to use for negative numbers.

Key Facts

When a positive number is multiplied by a negative number the answer is negative.

When two negative numbers are multiplied together the answer is positive.

For division, the rules are the same as for multiplication.

Examples

$$-3 \times (-7) = 21 \qquad 5 \times (-3) = -15 \qquad -12 \div 3 = -4$$

$$20 \div (-2) = -10 \qquad -40 \div (-20) = 2 \qquad -1 \times (-2) \times (-3) = -6$$

M1. 9

Work out

1 (a) 3×-5 (b) 6×-3 (c) -4×-6 (d) -3×-7

2 (a) -8×-4 (b) -7×6 (c) -2×-6 (d) 4×-9

3 (a) 5×-6 (b) 3×-1 (c) -9×-5 (d) -4×-4

4 (a) $-10 \div 5$ (b) $-28 \div 4$ (c) $-25 \div -5$ (d) $30 \div -6$

5 (a) $-60 \div -10$ (b) $-42 \div 7$ (c) $21 \div -7$ (d) $-18 \div -3$

6 (a) $48 \div -8$ (b) $-24 \div -4$ (c) $-35 \div -7$ (d) $-49 \div 7$

Copy and complete the squares below:

7

×	−3	−6	8	−2
7	−21			
−5				
−4				
9				

8

×	−7	4	−3
4	−28		−32
	42		
		15	
			−56

23

Work out

9   (a) $45 \div -9$ (b) $-120 \div -10$ (c) $-81 \div -9$ (d) $-63 \div 7$

10   (a) 12×-13 (b) -24×-16 (c) -17×14 (d) -23×-34

11   (a) -2×-2 (b) $-2 \times -2 \times -2$ (c) $-2 \times -2 \times -2 \times -2$

12   (a) $-3 \times -3 \times -3$ (b) $-4 \times 2 \times -4$ (c) $-10 \times -1 \times 3 \times -2$

13   **Check** your answers to Questions **7** and **8** by *using a calculator*. Make sure your teacher shows you the correct button to use for negative numbers.

E1. 9

Each empty square contains either a number or an operation $(+, -, \times, \div)$. Copy each square and fill in the missing details. The arrows are equals signs.

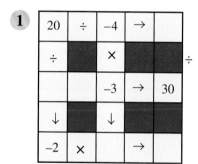
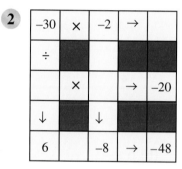

1

20	÷	−4	→	
÷		×		
		−3	→	30
↓		↓		
−2	×		→	

2

−30	×	−2	→	
÷				
	×		→	−20
↓		↓		
6		−8	→	−48

3

−8	÷		→	4
3	×	−6	→	
↓		↓		
−24		12	→	−2

4

−8	+	−4	→	
−		+		
2		12	→	−10
↓		↓		
	+		→	

5

−11	−	−1	→	
+				
6		8	→	−2
↓		↓		
	−	7	→	

6

−10	−		→	−8
−		−		
−4		7	→	3
↓		↓		
	−		→	

7

−10	÷	5	→	
×		−		
−2			→	−18
↓		↓		
		−4	→	−5

8

30	÷		→	−6
−				
40		−8	→	−5
↓		↓		
	×	3	→	

9

−16	+		→	−12
		×		
−8	−		→	
↓		↓		
2		−24	→	−48

24

Key Facts

Everyone has agreed to work out problems in the same order so that there is only one correct answer.

The table below shows the order.

Brackets	( )	do first	'B'
O			'O'
Division	÷	do this pair next	'D'
Multiplication	×		'M'
Addition	+	do this pair next	'A'
Subtraction	–		'S'

Remember the word
'BODMAS'
(The 'O' is just used
to make a word)

(a) $14 - 6 \div 2$

$= 14 - 3$

$= 11$

(b) $(14 - 6) \div 2$

$= 8 \div 2$

$= 4$

(c) $14 \times 2 + 3 \times 5$

$= 28 + 15$

$= 43$

M1.10

Work out the following: Show every step in your working.

1 $5 + 3 \times 2$

2 $7 + 4 \times 4$

3 $28 \div 7 + 6$

4 $20 \div 4 + 5$

5 $(5 + 3) \times 3$

6 $(6 + 2) \times 5$

7 $36 \div (5 + 1)$

8 $40 \div (4 + 4)$

9 $24 \div 4 + 8$

10 $42 \div 7 + 3$

11 $8 \times (3 + 4)$

12 $3 \times 10 + 4$

13 $40 \div (7 + 3)$

14 $3 \times 8 + 9$

15 $5 \times (8 + 3)$

16 $6 + 2 \times 4 + 3$

17 $(6 + 2) \times (4 + 3)$

18 $(6 + 2) \times 4 + 3$

19 $(7 + 13) \div 5 + 4$

20 $10 + 24 \div (6 + 2)$

21 $(8 + 7) \div (2 + 1)$

22 $35 - 3 \times 5$

23 $8 + 9 + 10 \div 2$

24 $(3 + 8 + 9) \div 4$

25 $5 + 3 \times 4 \div 2$

26 $5 + 21 \div 3 + 6$

27 $8 + 4 \times 7 + 2$

28 $49 \div 7 + 3$

29 $(6 + 4) \div 2 + 3 \times 3$

30 $9 + 8 \div 2 + 4 \times 5$

31 $12 + 12 \div 3 + 3$

32 $(3 + 8 + 9) \div 10$

33 $5 + 7 + 8 \div 2$

34 $(5 + 7 + 8) \div 2$

35 $3 \times 12 \div 3 + 1$

36 $(11 + 24) \div (10 - 3)$

37 $15 + 5 \div 5$

38 $(15 + 5) \div 5$

39 $(12 - 3) \div (2 + 3 + 4)$

E1. 10

Work out the following, show every step in your working.

1 $8 + 2 \times 4$

2 $12 - 2 \times 3$

3 $(8 - 3) \times 4$

4 $15 \div 3 - 1$

5 $17 + 9 \div 3$

6 $4 + 39 \div 13$

7 $15 + 4 \times 10$

8 $50 - 11 \times 3$

9 $48 \div (20 - 8)$

10 $(14 + 3) \times 2$

11 $7 + 7 \times 7$

12 $32 - 5 - 11$

13 $9 + 3 \times 3 - 4$

14 $16 - (8 \times 1) + 3$

15 $3 + 15 \div (9 - 6)$

16 $(6 \times 5) - (12 \div 3)$

17 $100 - (88 \div 4)$

18 $(100 + 3) \div (104 - 101)$

19 $8 + 32 \div 4 - 5$

20 $40 \div 8 - 24 \div 8$

21 $3 \times (4 \times 5 - 1)$

Copy each question and write brackets so that each calculation gives the correct answer.

22 $3 + 2 \times 5 = 25$

23 $7 + 4 \times 4 = 44$

24 $5 \times 2 + 3 = 25$

25 $8 + 3 \times 6 = 26$

26 $5 \times 9 - 4 = 25$

27 $6 \times 15 - 6 = 54$

28 $40 - 25 \times 3 = 45$

29 $63 - 7 \div 8 = 7$

30 $42 \div 6 + 1 = 6$

31 $18 - 12 \div 12 \div 4 = 2$

32 $16 + 14 \div 2 = 15$

33 $7 + 25 \div 4 = 8$

34 $7 + 3 \times 8 - 5 = 30$

35 $13 + 2 \times 4 = 60$

36 $3 + 8 + 19 \div 3 = 10$

37 $5 + 6 \times 10 - 4 = 66$

This table shows the positions of the top four football teams in the premiership during one season.

> goal difference = 'goals for' – 'goals against'

Team	Games played P	games won W	games drawn D	games lost L	goals scored for the team F	Goals scored against the team A	Points total Pts
Chelsea	31	20	8	3	70	23	68
Manchester United	30	20	5	5	72	26	65
Liverpool	31	19	7	5	61	27	64
Arsenal	32	18	10	4	58	25	64

If teams are level on points, the team with the higher goal difference is placed above the other team.

Liverpool goal difference = 61 – 27 = 34
Arsenal goal difference = 58 – 25 = 33
So Liverpool are above Arsenal.

Points scored
3 points for a win
1 point for a draw
0 points for a loss

Task A

The season ends when each team has played 38 games. Each team's final results are shown below:

Liverpool: 5 wins, 0 draws, 2 losses, 14 goals for, 8 goals against.

Manchester United: 7 wins, 0 draws, 1 loss, 18 goals for, 6 goals against.

Arsenal: 5 wins, 1 draw, 0 losses, 10 goals for, 5 goals against.

Chelsea: 5 wins, 2 draws, 0 losses, 15 goals for, 7 goals against.

Draw a final full table to show the positions of these four teams.

Task B

Draw a full table to show the positions of these four teams at the end if their final results are as shown below:

Manchester United	Arsenal	Chelsea	Liverpool
Man Utd 3v1 Sunderland	Arsenal 3v2 West Ham	Chelsea 3v2 Man City	Liverpool 2v1 Fulham
Man Utd 2v0 Spurs	Arsenal 3v0 Fulham	Chelsea 1v0 Everton	Liverpool 2v1 Birmingham
Man Utd 1v1 Chelsea	Arsenal 2v1 Hull	Chelsea 1v1 Man Utd	Liverpool 0v0 Aston Villa
Man Utd 2v0 Stoke City	Arsenal 1v0 Spurs	Chelsea 4v2 Sunderland	Liverpool 1v1 West Ham
Man Utd 2v1 Aston Villa	Arsenal 1v2 Chelsea	Chelsea 2v1 Arsenal	Liverpool 4v3 Everton
Man Utd 4v0 Portsmouth	Arsenal 3v1 Wolves	Chelsea 3v0 Hull	Liverpool 2v1 Spurs
Man Utd 2v2 Liverpool		Chelsea 2v1 Aston Villa	Liverpool 2v2 Man Utd
Man Utd 1v0 Fulham			

TEST YOURSELF ON UNIT 1

1. Understanding place value

What is the value of the underlined digit in each number below?

(a) 419

(b) 4621

(c) 0.79

(d) 12.68

(e) 31.827

2. Rounding off numbers

Round the numbers below to   (i) the nearest 10

(ii) the nearest 100

(iii) the nearest 1000

(a) 3289   (b) 5614   (c) 12324   (d) 22831

(e) Round off 3.5 to the nearest whole number.

(f) Round off 7.82 to the nearest whole number.

3. Adding and subtracting whole numbers

Work out

(a) 39 + 53

(b) 67 + 248

(c) 3617 + 2394

(d) 86 – 49

(e) 263 – 146

(f) 5126 – 3811

4. Multiplying whole numbers

Work out

(a) 7×8

(b) 70×80

(c) 243×4

(d) 384×6

(e) 46×27

(f) 39×78

(g) 27×419

(h) 362×53

5. Dividing whole numbers

Work out

(a) $684 \div 4$ (b) $984 \div 3$ (c) $2282 \div 7$

(d) $864 \div 16$ (e) $1608 \div 24$ (f) $3286 \div 62$

(g) 289 children are going on an ice-skating trip. One coach holds 48 children. How many coaches are needed for this trip?

6. Adding and subtracting negative numbers

(a) The temperature in Sydney is 34°C. The temperature in Moscow is –12°C. What is the difference in the temperatures?

(b) The temperature in Moscow in part (a) rises by 9°C. What is the new temperature in Moscow?

Work out

(c) $7 - 10$ (d) $-8 + 4$ (e) $-6 - -2$ (f) $7 + -3$

(g) $-3 - -4$ (h) $-8 - 4$ (i) $-7 - -5$ (j) $-4 + -3$

7. Multiplying and dividing negative numbers

Work out

(a) 8×-3 (b) -4×-6 (c) -7×4 (d) $-20 \div 10$

(e) $-40 \div -5$ (f) -9×8 (g) $-48 \div 6$ (h) $-63 \div -9$

8. Doing calculations in the correct order

Work out

(a) $5 + 2 \times 4$ (b) $20 - (7 + 4)$ (c) $(9 + 7) \div 4$

(d) $(6 + 10) \div (10 - 2)$ (e) $12 + 8 \div 2$ (f) $(7 - 2) \times 9$

Remember: 'BODMAS'

Copy the Questions for parts (g) and (h) then write brackets so that each calculation gives the correct answer.

(g) $7 \times 4 + 5 = 63$ (h) $10 - 7 \times 8 + 2 = 30$

29

Mixed examination questions

This machine multiplies all numbers by 7 then subtracts 2.

1 In → ×7 → −2 Out →

   (a) Complete this table

In	Out
5	33
2	
7	

   (b) 26 comes **out** of the machine. What was put **in**?   (AQA)

2 The map shows the positions and heights of six mountains.

   (a) Write the names of the six mountains in order of height. Put the highest mountain first.

   (b) Helvellyn is added to the list of mountains in part (a). It is fourth in the list. What can be said about the height of Helvellyn?   (OCR)

3 (a) Write the number forty six thousand six hundred and two in figures.

   (b) Write your answer to part (a) to the nearest thousand.

4 Work out   (a) 563×78 (b) $793 \div 26$ (EDEXCEL)

5 As a gas cools it eventually turns to liquid. Radon gas turns to liquid at $-62°C$. Argon gas turns to liquid at $-186°C$.

   (a) What is the difference between the two temperatures?

   (b) In each of the statements below, write a possible temperature. (Temperatures below $-273°C$ are not possible.)

   (i) At ...... °C radon is a gas.

   (ii) At ...... °C argon is a liquid.   (OCR)

6 Nick fills a van with large wooden crates.

   The weight of each crate is 69 kg.

   The greatest weight the van can hold is 990 kg.

   Work out the greatest number of crates that the van can hold.   (EDEXCEL)

7 (a) (i) Write down the number **fifty two thousand six hundred and two** in figures.

   (ii) Write down **fifty two thousand six hundred and two** to the nearest thousand.

   (b) (i) Write down 20 387 in words.

   (ii) Write down 20 387 to the nearest hundred.

8 These maps show the temperatures at midday and at midnight on a certain day in five different places.

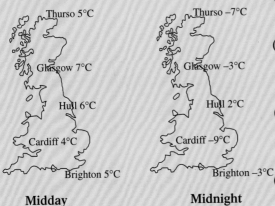

Midday   **Midnight**

   (a) Which place was the warmest at midday?

   (b) How much colder was Cardiff than Glasgow at midnight?

   (c) Which place had the greatest drop in temperature from midday to midnight?

   (d) Which place had the least difference in temperature from midday to midnight?

(AQA)

9 In this question you must **NOT** use a calculator.

You must show **ALL** your working.

Asif buys 37 ovens at £412 each.

Work out the total cost.

10 A first class stamp costs 26p.

(a) What is the greatest number of first class stamps you can buy for £2?

Jean buys 10 first class stamps.

She pays with a £5 note.

(b) How much change should she get?   (EDEXCEL)

11 A gardener buys 375 trays of plants. There are 54 plants in a tray.

How many plants is this altogether?   (CCEA)

NUMBER 2

2

In this unit you will learn how to:

- square and square root numbers
- cube and cube root numbers
- use powers
- find factors and prime numbers
- find multiples and the Lowest Common Multiple (LCM)
- find the Highest Common Factor (HCF)
- break down numbers into prime factors
- find equivalent fractions
- cancel fractions
- put fractions in order of size
- convert between fractions and decimals
- order decimals
- USE YOUR MATHS! – wages – overtime

Square numbers

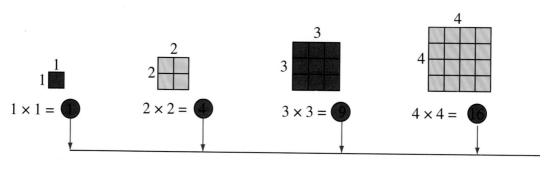

$1 \times 1 = 1$ $2 \times 2 = 4$ $3 \times 3 = 9$ $4 \times 4 = 16$

When a whole number is multiplied by itself, we get a *square number*

$3 \times 3 = 9$ We write this as 3^2 (3 squared)

so $5^2 = 5 \times 5 = 25$

A *calculator* has a button for squaring $\boxed{x^2}$. Use this button with your teacher to make sure you know how to use it correctly.

Key Facts

The square root of a number n is the number which is multiplied by itself to give that number n.

The square root of 36 is **6** because **6 × 6** = 36

The symbol for square root is $\sqrt{}$ so $\sqrt{36} = 6$

$\sqrt{49} = 7$ because $7 \times 7 = 49$

A calculator has a button for finding square roots $\boxed{\sqrt{}}$ or $\boxed{\sqrt{x}}$. Use this button with your teacher to make sure you know how to use it correctly.

M2. 1

1 $1(1 \times 1)$ and $4(2 \times 2)$ are the first two square numbers. Write down the first 12 square numbers.

2 'In your head', find the value of

   (a) 4^2 (b) 8^2 (c) 9^2 (d) 10^2 (e) 20^2

Work out

3 $10^2 + 7^2$ **4** $8^2 - 5^2$ **5** $8^2 - 6^2$

6 $7^2 + 4^2$ **7** $3^2 + 5^2$ **8** $(7 - 3)^2$

9 $10^2 - 4^2$ **10** $(20 - 11)^2$ **11** $1^2 + 2^2 + 3^2 + 4^2$

12

length

length

If you multiply the length of one side of a square by itself, you will find the area of the square

   (a) What is the length of one side of a square if the area is 9?

   (b) What is the length of one side of a square if the area is 49?

   (c) What is the length of one side of a square if the area is 100?

13 Write down the square root of 64.

14 Work out

(a) $\sqrt{1}$ (b) $\sqrt{25}$ (c) $\sqrt{81}$ (d) $\sqrt{4}$ (e) $\sqrt{16}$

15 Work out

(a) $\sqrt{100} - \sqrt{64}$ (b) $\sqrt{81} + \sqrt{49}$ (c) $\sqrt{(47 - 11)}$ (d) $\sqrt{25} + \sqrt{9}$

You may **use a calculator** for the rest of the questions.

16 Work out

(a) 17^2 (b) 28^2 (c) 114^2 (d) 0.4^2 (e) 3.8^2 (f) 0.1^2

17 Work out

(a) $\sqrt{289}$ (b) $\sqrt{576}$ (c) $\sqrt{2500}$ (d) $\sqrt{1681}$ (e) $\sqrt{8.41}$ (f) $\sqrt{0.09}$

18 Work out

(a) $\sqrt{0.16}$ (b) $\sqrt{0.25}$ (c) $\sqrt{0.36}$ (d) $\sqrt{0.49}$ (e) $\sqrt{0.64}$

(f) Can you write down the value of $\sqrt{0.81}$ without using a calculator?

19 Find a pair of square numbers which give a total of:

(a) 65   (b) 10   (c) 29   (d) 73   (e) 61

20 Work out   (a) $\sqrt{(10^2 - 6^2)}$ (b) $\sqrt{(13^2 - 12^2)}$ (c) $\sqrt{(100^2 - 80^2)}$

Cube numbers

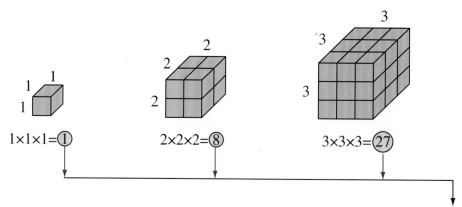

$1 \times 1 \times 1 = ①$ $2 \times 2 \times 2 = ⑧$ $3 \times 3 \times 3 = ㉗$

when a whole number is multiplied by itself 3 times, we get a *cube number*

$2 \times 2 \times 2 = 8$ we write this as 2^3 (2 cubed)

so $1^3 = 1 \times 1 \times 1 = 1$ (this is 1 cubed. Sometimes we say 1 to the *power* 3)

34

 **Key Facts**

The cube root of a number n is the number which is multiplied by itself 3 times to give that number n.

The cube root of 8 is **2** because **2 × 2 × 2** = 8

The symbol for cube root is $\sqrt[3]{}$

so $\sqrt[3]{8}$ = 2

$\sqrt[3]{1}$ = 1 because 1 × 1 × 1 = 1 (1^3 = 1)

A *calculator* has a button for finding cube roots $\boxed{\sqrt[3]{}}$ or $\boxed{\sqrt[3]{x}}$. The power button $\boxed{x^y}$ or root button $\boxed{\sqrt[y]{x}}$ can also be used. Use these buttons with your teacher to make sure you know how to use them correctly.

E2. 1

1
$1^3 = 1 \times 1 \times 1 = 1$
$2^3 = 2 \times 2 \times 2 = 8$
$3^3 = 3 \times 3 \times 3 = ..$
$4^3 = ... = ..$

Copy and complete this list of cube numbers down to 10^3.

2
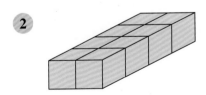
Can all these small cubes be used to make one large cube? If yes, draw the large cube made from the small cubes.

3 Can all these small cubes be used to make one large cube? If yes, draw the large cube made from the small cubes.

4 What number multiplied by itself 3 times will give an answer of 27?

5 Work out

(a) $\sqrt[3]{27}$ (b) $\sqrt[3]{8}$ (c) $\sqrt[3]{125}$ (d) $\sqrt[3]{64}$ (e) $\sqrt[3]{216}$

(Use your answer to Question **1** to help you)

You may **use a calculator** for the rest of the questions

6 Work out

(a) 14^3 (b) 21^3 (c) 1.5^3 (d) 0.1^3 (e) 0.2^3

7 Evaluate (this means 'work out the value of')

(a) $\sqrt[3]{3375}$ (b) $\sqrt[3]{13824}$ (c) $\sqrt[3]{64000}$ (d) $\sqrt[3]{0.027}$ (e) $\sqrt[3]{0.064}$

8 Work out

(a) $\sqrt[3]{(2 + 5^2)}$ (b) $\sqrt[3]{(3 + 5^2 + 6^2)}$ (c) $\sqrt[3]{(11^2 + 9^2 + 4^2 - 2)}$

9 Evaluate

(a) $\sqrt{(5^2 + 3^2 + 2)}$ (b) $(\sqrt{25} - \sqrt{9})^3$ (c) $(\sqrt[3]{343} - \sqrt{4})^3$

10 Work out

(a) $\sqrt{(2 \times 2 \times 3 \times 3)}$ (b) $\sqrt{(3 \times 3 \times 5 \times 5 \times 6 \times 6)}$

(c) $\sqrt[3]{(3 \times 3 \times 3 \times 5 \times 5 \times 5)}$

Powers

 Key Facts

3×3 is written as 3^2 ← power 2

$3 \times 3 \times 3$ is written as 3^3 ← power 3

$3 \times 3 \times 3 \times 3$ is written as 3^4

the power 4 means multiply 4 lots of 3 together

For 3^4 we say '3 to the power 4'

'3 to the power 5' is 3^5 which means $3 \times 3 \times 3 \times 3 \times 3$

Numbers written using powers are said to be in index form.

81 written in *index form* is 3^4 (because $3 \times 3 \times 3 \times 3 = 81$)

20 written in *index form* is $2^2 \times 5$ (because $2 \times 2 \times 5 = 20$)

2^4 means $2 \times 2 \times 2 \times 2$

Copy and complete the following:

1 8^4 means _ _ _ _ _ _ _

2 6^5 means _ _ _ _ _ _ _

3 10^4 means _ _ _ _ _ _ _

4 12^2 means _ _ _ _ _ _ _

5 7^5 means _ _ _ _ _ _ _

6 3^7 means _ _ _ _ _ _ _

7 8^6 means _ _ _ _ _ _ _

8 2^8 means _ _ _ _ _ _ _

Write the following in index form

9 $4 \times 4 \times 4 \times 4 \times 4$

10 $2 \times 2 \times 2 \times 2 \times 2 \times 2$

11 $5 \times 5 \times 5$

12 $3 \times 3 \times 3 \times 3 \times 3 \times 3 \times 3 \times 3$

13 $10 \times 10 \times 10 \times 10 \times 10$

14 $6 \times 6 \times 6 \times 6$

15   Which is larger? 2^4 or 3^3

16   Which is larger? 4^3 or 2^6

Work out the value of the following:

17 $3^2 \times 5$ **18** $2^3 \times 3$ **19** $2^4 \times 3$ **20** $6^2 \times 2$

21 $5^2 \times 2^2$ **22** $3^3 \times 2$ **23** $4^2 \times 2^2$ **24** $4^2 \times 2^3$

25   Copy and complete this table, *using a calculator* when needed.

We say	We write	We work out	Answer
3 to the power 4	3^4	$3 \times 3 \times 3 \times 3$	81
2 to the power 5		$2 \times 2 \times 2 \times 2 \times 2$	
7 to the power 3	7^3		
8 to the power 4			
	4^7		
9 to the power 5			
10 to the power 6			

2A **Add and subtract negative numbers (see Unit 1)**

1 The temperature in Toronto is –1°C. It falls by 6°C. What is the new temperature?

2 The temperature in Oslo is –8°C. The temperature in Athens is 23°C. What is the difference in temperature?

3 Work out

(a) –2 – 5   (b) –3 + 5   (c) –6 + 1   (d) 3 – 6

(e) 2 – –4   (f) 2 – 4   (g) –4 – –2   (h) –6 – –1

(i) –6 – 1   (j) 5 – 6   (k) –5 – –6   (l) –4 – 3

4 Copy and complete the boxes below:

(a) $\boxed{}$ – 4 = –6   (b) 3 – $\boxed{}$ = 5   (c) –4 – $\boxed{}$ = –9

Factors and prime numbers

A *factor* is a number which divides exactly into another number (there will be no remainder).

If 2 divides into a number exactly, that number is an *even* number (2, 4, 6, 8, …).

If 2 does *not* divide into a number exactly, that number is an *odd* number (1, 3, 5, 7, …).

A *prime* number can only be divided by two different numbers (these are the numbers 1 and itself). The first four prime numbers are 2, 3, 5, 7, …

M2. 3

Reminder: All the factors of 10 are $\boxed{1, 10}$ $\boxed{2, 5}$ so the factors of 10 are 1, 2, 5, 10.

Write down all the factors of the following numbers:

1 8 (4 factors)   **2** 16 (5 factors)   **3** 11 (2 factors)   **4** 15 (4 factors)

5 24 (8 factors)   **6** 19   **7** 35   **8** 28

9 40 **10** 23 **11** 30 **12** 42

13 17 **14** 26 **15** 50

16 Write down the numbers given in Questions **1** to **15** which are *odd* numbers.

17 Write down the numbers given in Questions **1** to **15** which are *even* numbers.

18 Write down the numbers given in Questions **1** to **15** which are *prime* numbers (remember: this means they have *2 factors only*).

19 1, 2, 4, 5, 10 and 20 are all the factors of which number?

20 1, 2, 11 and 22 are all the factors of which number?

21 Harry picks his National Lottery numbers by choosing the first six prime numbers. The winning numbers are drawn as below:

5   **42**   **1**   **13**   **40**   **6**

Does Harry win a small prize for picking 3 correct numbers?

22 Which numbers between 20 and 30 have 7 as a factor?

23 Write down the next 4 odd numbers after 49.

24 Add together all the prime numbers less than 20.

Multiples and the Lowest Common Multiple

🔑 # Key Facts

Multiples are the numbers in a multiplication table. 6, 12, 18, 24, 30, ... are multiples of 6.

The *Lowest Common Multiple* (LCM) of two or more numbers is the smallest number which each of these numbers will divide into.

Here, for example, we find the LCM of 4 and 10.

The multiples of 4 are 4, 8, 12, 16, ⓞ20ⓞ, 24, ...

The multiples of 10 are 10, ⓞ20ⓞ, 30, ...

The *lowest* number in both lists is 20

The LCM of 4 and 10 is 20.

Copy and complete the first 10 multiples of the number in the first box:

1 | 4 | 8 | 12 | 16 | | | | | | |

2 | 7 | 14 | | | | | | | | |

3 | 8 | | | | | | | | | |

4 | 30 | | | | | | | | | |

5 | 16 | | | | | | | | | |

Copy and draw a circle around the numbers which are *not* multiples of:

6 | 5 | 11 25 35 54   **7** | 9 | 36 22 38 91   **8** | 6 | 23 18 54 42

9 Here are the first six multiples of 6 and 10

$\underline{6}$: 6 12 18 24 30 36

$\underline{10}$: 10 20 30 40 50 60

Write down the Lowest Common Multiple (LCM) of 6 and 10 (ie the lowest number which is in both lists).

10 Copy and complete the first five multiples of 4 and 6

$\underline{4}$: 4 8 ☐ ☐ ☐

$\underline{6}$: 6 ☐ ☐ ☐ ☐

Write down the LCM of 4 and 6.

11 Find the Lowest Common Multiple of each of these pairs of numbers:

(a) 3 and 10   (b) 3 and 7   (c) 5 and 9   (d) 10 and 7

(e) 3 and 6   (f) 8 and 20   (g) 12 and 15   (h) 12 and 20

12 In the game of 'Fizzbuzz', people take it in turns to count up one number at a time. When a multiple of 3 is reached, the person must say 'Fizz'. When a multiple of 5 is reached, the person must say 'Buzz'. If a multiple of both 3 and 5 is reached, the person says 'Fizzbuzz'.

Write down the first 2 numbers when the person would have to say 'Fizzbuzz'.

Highest Common Factor

All the factors of 21 are 1, 3, ⑦, 21

All the factors of 28 are 1, 2, 4, ⑦, 14, 28

The highest factor in both lists is 7

This is called the Highest Common Factor (HCF)

1 Copy and complete the sentences below:

(a) All the factors of 12 are 1, 2, 3, ▢, ▢, ▢

(b) All the factors of 18 are 1, 2, 3, ▢, ▢, ▢

(c) The Highest Common Factor of 12 and 18 is ▢

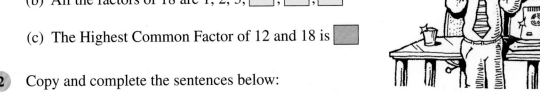

2 Copy and complete the sentences below:

(a) All the factors of 20 are 1, 2, ▢, ▢, ▢, ▢

(b) All the factors of 30 are 1, 2, ▢, ▢, ▢, ▢, ▢, ▢

(c) The HCF of 20 and 30 is ▢

3 (a) List all the factors of 32

(b) List all the factors of 40

(c) Write down the HCF of 32 and 40

4 (a) List all the factors of 24

(b) List all the factors of 36

(c) Write down the HCF of 24 and 36

5 Find the Highest Common Factor of

(a) 8 and 10   (b) 10 and 40   (c) 15 and 35   (d) 15 and 40

(e) 12 and 20   (f) 16 and 40   (g) 11 and 13   (h) 16 and 48

6 Find the HCF of

(a) 4, 6 and 12   (b) 10, 20 and 45   (c) 24, 48 and 60

41

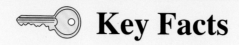

Key Facts

Factors of a number which are also prime numbers are called prime factors.

We can find these prime factors by using a 'factor tree' or by dividing by prime numbers again and again.

Example

Find the prime factors of 36.

Method 1

Factor tree

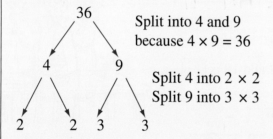

Split into 4 and 9 because $4 \times 9 = 36$

Split 4 into 2×2
Split 9 into 3×3

Stop splitting when all numbers are prime numbers

We can say $36 = \underline{2 \times 2 \times 3 \times 3}$
$\qquad\qquad$ prime factors

Method 2

Dividing by prime numbers

Divide by any prime number

$$
\begin{array}{c|c}
2 & 36 \\
2 & 18 \quad\leftarrow 36 \div 2 = 18 \\
3 & 9 \quad\leftarrow 18 \div 2 = 9 \\
3 & 3 \quad\leftarrow 9 \div 3 = 3 \\
& 1 \quad\leftarrow 3 \div 3 = 1
\end{array}
$$

$\qquad$ Stop when you get 1

These are the prime factors.

We can say $36 = 2 \times 2 \times 3 \times 3$

The product of prime factors

When we write $36 = 2 \times 2 \times 3 \times 3$, the prime factors 2, 2, 3 and 3 are multiplied together. This is called a *product*.

$2 \times 2 \times 3 \times 3$ is the *product of its prime factors*.

Index form

$2 \times 2 = 2^2 \qquad\qquad 3 \times 3 = 3^2$

so $36 = 2 \times 2 \times 3 \times 3$ can be written as $2^2 \times 3^2$

The answer written like this using powers is said to be in *index form*.

1 Work out

    (a) $2 \times 2 \times 5$ (b) $2 \times 3 \times 5$ (c) $3 \times 3 \times 5$

    (d) $2 \times 3 \times 7$ (e) $3 \times 5 \times 11$ (f) $2 \times 2 \times 5 \times 5$

2 Copy and complete these factors trees:

    (a) 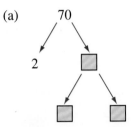   (b)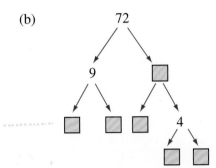

$70 = 2 \times \square \times \square$ $72 = \square \times \square \times \square \times \square \times \square$

3 Copy and complete the boxes below:

    (a) 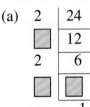   (b)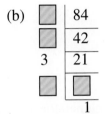

$24 = \square \times \square \times \square \times \square$ $84 = \square \times \square \times \square \times \square$

4 Using any method, write the following numbers as products of prime factors:

    (a) 18   (b) 28   (c) 22   (d) 32   (e) 48   (f) 50

    (g) 81   (h) 96   (i) 200   (j) 120   (k) 196   (l) 392

5 Copy the numbers below and put a circle round all the common factors for each pair of numbers.

    (a) $180 = 2 \times 2 \times 3 \times 3 \times 5$

        $120 = 2 \times 2 \times 2 \times 3 \times 5$ Write down the HCF of 180 and 120.

    (b) $720 = 2 \times 2 \times 2 \times 2 \times 3 \times 3 \times 5$

        $600 = 2 \times 2 \times 2 \times 3 \times 5 \times 5$ Write down the HCF of 720 and 600.

    (c) $3850 = 2 \times 5 \times 5 \times 7 \times 11$

        $140 = 2 \times 2 \times 5 \times 7$ Write down the HCF of 3850 and 140.

2B **Multiply and divide negative numbers (see Unit 1)**

1   Work out

(a) 2×-3 (b) 4×-5 (c) -6×-2 (d) -5×6

(e) $-8 \div 2$ (f) $15 \div -3$ (g) $-24 \div -3$ (h) $-42 \div -7$

(i) $-9 \div 3$ (j) -10×8 (k) $-30 \div -6$ (l) $20 \div -5$

2   Copy and complete the boxes below:

(a) $-3 \times \boxed{} = 12$ (b) $5 \times \boxed{} = -45$ (c) $\boxed{} \times -4 = -20$

(d) $10 \div \boxed{} = -5$ (e) $\boxed{} \div 4 = -9$ (f) $\boxed{} \times -5 = 40$

3   Work out

(a) $(-3)^2$ (b) $(-5)^2$ (c) $(-9)^2$ (d) $-1 \times -1 \times -1$ (e) $2 \times -4 \times 2$

Equivalent fractions

Cancelling Fractions

We often like to make the numerator (top number) and denominator (bottom number) as small as possible by dividing the numerator and denominator by the same number.

This is called 'cancelling down the fraction'.

$\dfrac{2}{8}$ is the same as $\dfrac{1}{4}$ $\dfrac{2}{8}$ $\overset{\div 2}{\overbrace{\dfrac{2}{8}}} = \dfrac{1}{4}$
$\underset{\div 2}{}$

M2. 5

Write the equivalent fractions shown by the blue areas in each pair of diagrams.

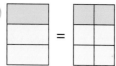   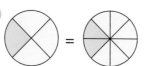   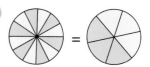

      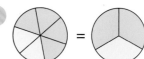

7 **8** **9**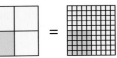

Copy and complete these equivalent fractions by filling in the box.

$$\left(\text{Example: } \frac{7}{10} = \frac{\square}{30} \quad \Rightarrow \quad \overset{\times 3}{\overset{\frown}{\frac{7}{10} \underset{\times 3}{=} \frac{21}{30}}}\right)$$

10 $\dfrac{1}{6} = \dfrac{\square}{12}$ **11** $\dfrac{7}{8} = \dfrac{\square}{16}$ **12** $\dfrac{1}{2} = \dfrac{\square}{8}$ **13** $\dfrac{3}{5} = \dfrac{\square}{20}$

14 $\dfrac{4}{5} = \dfrac{\square}{20}$ **15** $\dfrac{5}{6} = \dfrac{\square}{12}$ **16** $\dfrac{5}{8} = \dfrac{\square}{24}$ **17** $\dfrac{4}{7} = \dfrac{\square}{21}$

18 $\dfrac{3}{4} = \dfrac{\square}{20}$ **19** $\dfrac{8}{9} = \dfrac{\square}{45}$ **20** $\dfrac{3}{10} = \dfrac{\square}{60}$ **21** $\dfrac{2}{5} = \dfrac{8}{\square}$

22 $\dfrac{4}{9} = \dfrac{12}{\square}$ **23** $\dfrac{1}{2} = \dfrac{9}{\square}$ **24** $\dfrac{3}{8} = \dfrac{15}{\square}$ **25** $\dfrac{7}{10} = \dfrac{\square}{80}$

26 $\dfrac{3}{20} = \dfrac{24}{\square}$ **27** $\dfrac{5}{7} = \dfrac{30}{\square}$ **28** $\dfrac{7}{9} = \dfrac{\square}{54}$ **29** $\dfrac{4}{11} = \dfrac{24}{\square}$

30 $\dfrac{2}{9} = \dfrac{20}{\square}$ **31** $\dfrac{6}{7} = \dfrac{\square}{42}$ **32** $\dfrac{9}{100} = \dfrac{\square}{300}$ **33** $\dfrac{4}{25} = \dfrac{32}{\square}$

E2. 5

Copy the Questions below and fill in each box.

1 $\dfrac{6}{8} = \dfrac{\square}{4}$ **2** $\dfrac{2}{10} = \dfrac{\square}{5}$ **3** $\dfrac{3}{9} = \dfrac{1}{\square}$ **4** $\dfrac{9}{12} = \dfrac{3}{\square}$

5 $\dfrac{6}{10} = \dfrac{\square}{5}$ **6** $\dfrac{9}{15} = \dfrac{\square}{5}$ **7** $\dfrac{9}{24} = \dfrac{\square}{8}$ **8** $\dfrac{4}{8} = \dfrac{\square}{2}$

9 $\dfrac{25}{30} = \dfrac{\square}{6}$ **10** $\dfrac{3}{24} = \dfrac{\square}{8}$ **11** $\dfrac{8}{10} = \dfrac{\square}{5}$ **12** $\dfrac{8}{12} = \dfrac{\square}{3}$

13 $\dfrac{10}{30} = \dfrac{1}{\square}$ **14** $\dfrac{6}{18} = \dfrac{1}{\square}$ **15** $\dfrac{12}{24} = \dfrac{\square}{2}$ **16** $\dfrac{30}{40} = \dfrac{3}{\square}$

17 Cancel each fraction below to its lowest terms.

(a) $\dfrac{8}{20}$ (b) $\dfrac{4}{10}$ (c) $\dfrac{7}{21}$ (d) $\dfrac{4}{18}$

(e) $\dfrac{4}{12}$ (f) $\dfrac{20}{30}$ (g) $\dfrac{12}{18}$ (h) $\dfrac{20}{24}$

(i) $\dfrac{32}{36}$ (j) $\dfrac{6}{15}$ (k) $\dfrac{14}{42}$ (l) $\dfrac{18}{30}$

(m) $\dfrac{27}{45}$ (n) $\dfrac{28}{36}$ (o) $\dfrac{45}{90}$ (p) $\dfrac{44}{66}$

(q) $\dfrac{24}{60}$ (r) $\dfrac{18}{72}$ (s) $\dfrac{75}{100}$ (t) $\dfrac{54}{81}$

18 Which of the fractions below are the same as $\dfrac{5}{8}$?

(a) $\dfrac{15}{25}$ (b) $\dfrac{45}{80}$ (c) $\dfrac{10}{16}$ (d) $\dfrac{20}{40}$ (e) $\dfrac{30}{48}$ (f) $\dfrac{40}{64}$

19 Which of the fractions below are the same as $\dfrac{4}{7}$?

(a) $\dfrac{12}{21}$ (b) $\dfrac{24}{48}$ (c) $\dfrac{40}{70}$ (d) $\dfrac{20}{35}$ (e) $\dfrac{12}{28}$ (f) $\dfrac{36}{65}$

20 Find the fractions in the table which are equivalent to the given fraction. Rearrange the letters to make a word using the clue. The first Question is done for you.

(a) Find fractions = $\dfrac{1}{2}$

Clue: country

$\frac{3}{4}$	P	$\frac{2}{4}$	G
$\frac{1}{3}$	U	$\frac{4}{7}$	H
$\frac{5}{10}$	E	$\frac{6}{12}$	E
$\frac{3}{5}$	Y	$\frac{3}{6}$	C
$\frac{8}{16}$	E	$\frac{21}{42}$	R

The fractions equivalent to $\dfrac{1}{2}$ are:

$$\dfrac{5}{10} \quad \dfrac{8}{16} \quad \dfrac{2}{4} \quad \dfrac{6}{12} \quad \dfrac{3}{6} \quad \dfrac{21}{42}$$

E   E   G   E   C   R

Now rearrange the letters to make the name of a country:

GREECE

(b) Find fractions = $\frac{1}{10}$ (c) Find fractions = $\frac{3}{4}$ (d) Find fractions = $\frac{1}{4}$ (e) Find fractions = $\frac{2}{3}$

Clue: country   Clue: fruit   Clue: school subject   Clue: sport

$\frac{8}{80}$	N
$\frac{6}{50}$	P
$\frac{5}{60}$	U
$\frac{4}{20}$	Y
$\frac{2}{20}$	A
$\frac{9}{90}$	I
$\frac{8}{24}$	M
$\frac{3}{30}$	C
$\frac{5}{50}$	H
$\frac{9}{108}$	U

$\frac{6}{8}$	R
$\frac{9}{12}$	E
$\frac{7}{14}$	T
$\frac{8}{24}$	I
$\frac{5}{7}$	X
$\frac{5}{12}$	B
$\frac{15}{20}$	P
$\frac{9}{15}$	M
$\frac{25}{50}$	C
$\frac{75}{100}$	A

$\frac{8}{20}$	T
$\frac{2}{8}$	G
$\frac{5}{20}$	E
$\frac{6}{25}$	F
$\frac{3}{12}$	H
$\frac{4}{16}$	N
$\frac{4}{7}$	A
$\frac{25}{100}$	L
$\frac{20}{80}$	I
$\frac{12}{48}$	S

$\frac{14}{22}$	N
$\frac{18}{21}$	A
$\frac{20}{30}$	O
$\frac{4}{6}$	Y
$\frac{32}{49}$	B
$\frac{60}{90}$	K
$\frac{16}{24}$	E
$\frac{12}{18}$	C
$\frac{16}{25}$	R
$\frac{14}{21}$	H

Can you still?

2C **Do calculations in the correct order – BODMAS (see Unit 1)**

Can you still?

Work out

1. $3 + 8 \times 2$

2. $28 \div (3 + 4)$

3. $(6 + 2) \times 5$

4. $9 \times (6 - 4)$

5. $(8 + 1) \times (7 - 5)$

6. $30 \div 5 + 4$

7. $(5 - 1) \times 5 + 7$

8. $(8 + 4) \div (5 - 2)$

9. $25 - 3 \times 4$

10. $22 + 8 \div 2$

11. $36 \div 4 + 8$

12. $36 \div (4 + 8)$

13. $20 - 20 \div 4$

14. $(8 - 3) \times 3$

15. $(9 + 1) \div (7 - 2)$

16. $6 + 8 \div 2 + 4$

Copy each question below and write brackets so that each calculation gives the correct answer.

17. $7 + 4 \times 3 = 33$ 18. $25 - 20 \times 4 = 20$ 19. $9 + 21 \div 6 = 5$ 20. $7 - 2 \times 5 + 1 = 30$

 **Key Facts**

Get the denominator the same for each fraction so that you can easily compare the fractions.

Place $\frac{3}{4}$, $\frac{5}{8}$ and $\frac{4}{5}$ in order, smallest first.

Get the denominators the same for each fraction. 4, 8 and 5 all divide exactly into 40.

$$\frac{3}{4} \overset{\times 10}{\underset{\times 10}{=}} \frac{30}{40} \qquad \frac{5}{8} \overset{\times 5}{\underset{\times 5}{=}} \frac{25}{40} \qquad \frac{4}{5} \overset{\times 8}{\underset{\times 8}{=}} \frac{32}{40}$$

Put the fractions in order, smallest first: $\quad \dfrac{25}{40} \quad \dfrac{30}{40} \quad \dfrac{32}{40}$

$$\downarrow \qquad \downarrow \qquad \downarrow$$

so the answer is $\quad \dfrac{5}{8} \quad \dfrac{3}{4} \quad \dfrac{4}{5}$

M2. 6

1 Write down the larger fraction:

(a)

$\frac{3}{8}$ or $\frac{1}{2}$

(b)

$\frac{2}{5}$ or $\frac{3}{10}$

2 $\quad \dfrac{1}{2} = \dfrac{\square}{6} \qquad \dfrac{1}{3} = \dfrac{\square}{6}$

Which is larger, $\dfrac{1}{2}$ or $\dfrac{1}{3}$?

3 $\dfrac{3}{4} = \dfrac{\square}{8}$ Which is larger, $\dfrac{3}{4}$ or $\dfrac{7}{8}$?

4   Write down the *larger* fraction:

(a) $\dfrac{1}{4}$ or $\dfrac{1}{3}$ (b) $\dfrac{1}{10}$ or $\dfrac{1}{5}$ (c) $\dfrac{3}{8}$ or $\dfrac{3}{4}$

(d) $\dfrac{3}{4}$ or $\dfrac{2}{3}$ (e) $\dfrac{2}{5}$ or $\dfrac{7}{20}$ (f) $\dfrac{4}{7}$ or $\dfrac{3}{5}$

5   Place in order, *smallest first*:

(a) $\dfrac{1}{3}, \dfrac{1}{2}, \dfrac{1}{6}$ (b) $\dfrac{1}{2}, \dfrac{3}{8}, \dfrac{3}{4}$ (c) $\dfrac{1}{6}, \dfrac{2}{3}, \dfrac{7}{12}$

(d) $\dfrac{3}{10}, \dfrac{1}{2}, \dfrac{2}{5}$ (e) $\dfrac{7}{10}, \dfrac{4}{5}, \dfrac{13}{20}$ (f) $\dfrac{3}{4}, \dfrac{11}{16}, \dfrac{5}{8}$

6   Write down the *smaller* fraction:

(a) $\dfrac{3}{5}$ or $\dfrac{11}{20}$ (b) $\dfrac{7}{10}$ or $\dfrac{13}{20}$ (c) $\dfrac{3}{4}$ or $\dfrac{13}{16}$

(d) $\dfrac{8}{9}$ or $\dfrac{9}{10}$ (e) $\dfrac{5}{6}$ or $\dfrac{4}{7}$ (f) $\dfrac{7}{40}$ or $\dfrac{1}{5}$

Can you still?

2D   **Use squares, square roots, cubes and cube roots (see Unit 2)**

Can you still?

Work out

1. 3^2 **2.** 8^2 **3.** $\sqrt{36}$ **4.** $\sqrt{81}$ **5.** 10^2 **6.** $\sqrt{400}$

7. Which is larger,   (a) 2^2 or $\sqrt{100}$ (b) $\sqrt{81}$ or 4^2

8. Write down the first 3 cube numbers.

Work out

9. $\sqrt[3]{8}$ **10.** $\sqrt[3]{1}$ **11.** 3^3 **12.** 4^3 **13.** 2^3

14. $9^2 - 3^2$ **15.** $\sqrt{64} + \sqrt{16}$ **16.** $(4 + 2)^2$ **17.** $\sqrt{(61 - 52)}$

18. Find two square numbers which add up to 41.

Key Facts

Changing decimals into fractions.

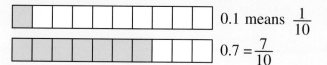 0.1 means $\frac{1}{10}$

0.7 = $\frac{7}{10}$

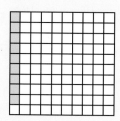 $0.09 = \frac{9}{100}$

If you change a decimal into a fraction, *cancel* the fraction if you can.

$$0.2 = \frac{2}{10} \overset{\div 2}{\underset{\div 2}{=}} \frac{1}{5} \qquad\qquad 0.34 = \frac{34}{100} \overset{\div 2}{\underset{\div 2}{=}} \frac{17}{50}$$

Changing fractions into decimals.

If you can find an equivalent fraction with the denominator (bottom part) equal to 10, 100 or 1000, it will be easier to find the decimal value.

$$\frac{3}{5} \overset{\times 2}{\underset{\times 2}{=}} \frac{6}{10} = 0.6 \qquad \frac{7}{20} \overset{\times 5}{\underset{\times 5}{=}} \frac{35}{100} = 0.35 \qquad \frac{101}{200} \overset{\times 5}{\underset{\times 5}{=}} \frac{505}{1000} = 0.505$$

Change denominator to **10**　　Change denominator to **100**　　Change denominator to **1000**

Note.

If you cannot easily change the denominator into 10, 100 or 1000, divide the numerator (top part) by the denominator (bottom part), as shown below.

(a) Change $\frac{1}{3}$ to a decimal

We work out $1 \div 3$　　$3\overline{\smash)1.{}^10{}^10{}^10{}^10\ldots}$ 　 $0.3\,3\,3\,3\ldots$

We write $\frac{1}{3} = 0.\dot{3}$

We say 'nought point three recurring'

(the 3 carries on forever!)

Write True or False for each of the following statements.

1 $0.3 = \dfrac{3}{10}$ **2** $0.07 = \dfrac{7}{100}$ **3** $0.08 = \dfrac{1}{8}$

4 $0.5 = \dfrac{1}{2}$ **5** $0.049 = \dfrac{49}{100}$ **6** $0.079 = \dfrac{79}{1000}$

7 $0.4 = \dfrac{2}{5}$ **8** $0.25 = \dfrac{1}{4}$ **9** $0.217 = \dfrac{217}{1000}$

10 $0.7 = \dfrac{1}{7}$ **11** $0.75 = \dfrac{3}{4}$ **12** $0.81 = \dfrac{81}{100}$

Change the following decimals to fractions in their most simple form.

13 0.11 **14** 0.04 **15** 0.9 **16** 0.6

17 0.002 **18** 0.37 **19** 0.012 **20** 0.8

21 0.35 **22** 0.015 **23** 0.08 **24** 0.45

25 0.008 **26** 0.36 **27** 0.125 **28** 0.375

29 Which is larger 0.43 or $\dfrac{41}{100}$?

30 Which is larger 0.7 or $\dfrac{3}{5}$?

Copy Questions **31** to **36** below and fill in the boxes.

31 $\dfrac{4}{5} = \dfrac{\square}{10} = 0.\square$ **32** $\dfrac{3}{20} = \dfrac{\square}{100} = 0.\square\square$

33 $\dfrac{7}{25} = \dfrac{\square}{100} = 0.\square\square$ **34** $\dfrac{17}{50} = \dfrac{\square}{100} = 0.\square\square$

35 $\dfrac{9}{25} = \dfrac{\square}{100} = \square$ **36** $\dfrac{11}{200} = \dfrac{\square}{1000} = \square$

Convert the fractions below to decimals.

37 $\dfrac{1}{20}$ **38** $\dfrac{9}{20}$ **39** $\dfrac{2}{5}$ **40** $\dfrac{1}{25}$

41 $\dfrac{3}{25}$ **42** $\dfrac{21}{25}$ **43** $\dfrac{29}{100}$ **44** $\dfrac{3}{200}$

45 $\dfrac{1}{4}$ **46** $\dfrac{21}{200}$ **47** $\dfrac{1}{8}$ **48** $\dfrac{73}{200}$

49 $\dfrac{7}{8}$ **50** $\dfrac{3}{4}$ **51** $\dfrac{119}{1000}$ **52** $\dfrac{17}{20}$

Change the following fractions to decimals by dividing the numerator by the denominator.

53 $\dfrac{2}{3}$ **54** $\dfrac{5}{11}$ **55** $\dfrac{2}{9}$

56 $\dfrac{7}{9}$ **57** $\dfrac{1}{6}$ **58** $\dfrac{5}{6}$

To change $\dfrac{3}{11}$ to a decimal we work out $3 \div 11$

$$\begin{array}{r} 0.\,2\ 7\ 2\ 7\ 2\ 7\ldots \\ 11\overline{)\,3.^30^80^30^80^30^80\ldots} \end{array} \qquad \dfrac{3}{11} = 0.\overset{..}{2}\overset{}{7}$$

Ordering decimals

Key Facts

Write the set of decimals in a line with the decimal points in a column.

Fill in any empty spaces with zeros. This makes it easier to compare the decimals.

Arrange 0.29, 0.209, 0.09 and 0.2 in order, starting with the smallest.

Write in column	Put in zeros	Arrange in order
0.29	0.290	0.09
0.209	0.209	0.2
0.09	0.090	0.209
0.2	0.200	0.29

In Questions **1** to **10**, answer True or False.

1 7.2 is less than 7.02

2 0.03 is more than 0.003

3 0.8 is equal to 0.800

4 0.51 is more than 0.15

5 0.004 is more than 0.04

6 3 is equal to 3.00

7 0.83 is less than 0.847

8 0.08 is less than 0.083

9 0.2 is less than 0.028

10 0.71 is less than 0.089

> means 'more than'   < means 'less than'

Copy and complete questions **11** to **18** by writing >, < or = in the box.

11 0.7 ☐ 0.73

12 0.18 ☐ 0.2

13 0.81 ☐ 0.82

14 0.6 ☐ 0.60

15 0.09 ☐ 0.83

16 3.1 ☐ 3.06

17 5.17 ☐ 5.2

18 0.187 ☐ 0.3

19 Here is a pattern of numbers based on 4.

Write a similar pattern based on 3 and extend it from 30000 down to 0.0003. Write the numbers in figures and in words.

four thousand	4000
four hundred	400
forty	40
four	4
nought point four	0.4
nought point nought four	0.04

In Questions **20** to **34**, arrange the numbers in order of size, smallest first.

20 0.08, 0.8, 0.008

21 0.4, 0.41, 0.042

22 0.72, 0.702, 0.73

23 0.832, 0.83, 0.85

24 0.06, 0.61, 0.063

25 0.52, 0.503, 0.053, 0.51

26 0.014, 0.017, 0.1, 0.107

27 0.03, 0.303, 0.31, 0.32, 0.034

28 0.81, 0.806, 0.812, 0.087, 0.82

29 0.061, 0.06, 0.064, 0.603, 0.61

30 0.107, 0.11, 0.121, 0.13, 0.015

31 3.6, 3.16, 3.04, 3.2, 3.18

32 8.1, 8.13, 8.021, 8.14, 8.019

33 0.51, 5.02, 0.53, 5.1, 5.17

34 1.72, 1.07, 1.16, 1.03, 0.19

35 Here are numbers with letters.

Put the numbers in order, smallest first. Write down just the letters. Write out the sentence clearly.

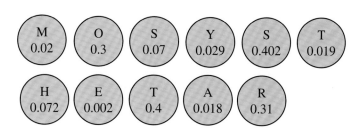

36

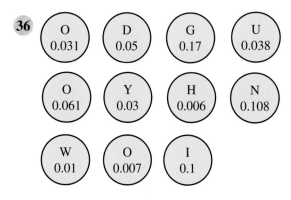

Here are numbers with letters.

Put the numbers in order, smallest first. Write down just the letters. Write out the sentence clearly.

37 Here we have fractions and decimals.

Write the numbers in order to find a word.

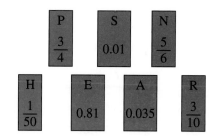

USE YOUR MATHS! – Wages – overtime

Overtime is money paid for working more than the agreed number of hours each week.

Overtime is often paid at a different rate such as 'time and a half' or 'double time' (for example, evening work is often paid at 'time and a half' and weekend work is often 'double time').

Note

The average UK salary (in 2008) was £24,900 = £12.97 per hour (based on a 48 week year and a 40 hour week).

Jess the mechanic is paid £8 per hour and overtime at 'time and a half'.

One week, Jess works for 40 hours plus 5 hours overtime. How much will Jess earn that week?

pay for 40 hours is 40 × £8 = £320

('time and a half' pay rate = £8 × 1.5 = £12)

pay for 5 hours overtime = 5 × £12 = £60

total pay = £320 + £60 = £380

TASK

1 Andy is paid £ 5 per hour for a 40 hour week.

   Overtime is paid at time and a half.

   How much will he be paid for a full week plus two hours overtime?

2 Jane is paid £ 6 per hour for a 40 hour week.

   Overtime is paid at time and a half.

   How much will she be paid for a full week plus 5 hours overtime?

3 Sid is paid £ 9 per hour for a 35 hour week.

   Overtime is paid at double time.

   How much will he be paid for a full week plus 6 hours overtime?

4

Pay Rate:
£ 6 per hour
Overtime paid at time and a half

Work out how much the following people are paid for one week's work:

(a) Emma: 30 hours plus 4 hours overtime.

(b) Billy: 35 hours plus 6 hours overtime.

(c) Jack: 32 hours plus 7 hours overtime.

(d) Sarah: 40 hours plus 10 hours overtime.

(e) Ashley: 40 hours plus 8 hours overtime.

5   Arnie is paid £4.50 per hour for 20 hours plus 5 hours overtime at time and a half. How much was he paid?

6   Tamsin is paid £5.20 per hour for 30 hours plus 8 hours overtime at time and a half. How much was she paid?

7   Sophie is paid £5.30 per hour for 40 hours plus 4 hours overtime at *double time*. How much was she paid?

8   Max is paid £7.40 per hour for 35 hours plus 4 hours overtime at time and a half. How much was he paid?

9   Work out the amount of pay for each part below:

(a) £6.80 per hour. 30 hours plus 6 hours overtime at time and a half.

(b) £4.70 per hour. 40 hours plus 5 hours overtime at double time.

(c) £5.60 per hour. 32 hours plus 6 hours overtime at time and a half.

(d) £6.90 per hour. 38 hours plus 4 hours overtime at time and a half.

10

BRIDGE MOTORS
Pay rate: £8.50 per hour
Saturday overtime: time and a half
Sunday overtime: double time

Jake works at Bridge Motors. He works for 40 hours then does 4 hours on Saturday and 3 hours on Sunday. How much money does Jake earn?

11 Tamsin works at Bridge Motors. She works for 36 hours then does 3 hours on Saturday and 6 hours on Sunday. How much money does Tamsin earn?

12 Jenny earns £5.40 per hour.

Simon earns £5.20 per hour.

Jenny works for 35 hours plus 6 hours overtime at time and a half.

Simon works for 35 hours plus 7 hours overtime at time and a half.

Who earns the most money and by how much?

TEST YOURSELF ON UNIT 2

1. Square and square root numbers

Work out

(a) 7^2 (b) 5^2 (c) $\sqrt{16}$ (d) $\sqrt{9}$ (e) $4^2 - 3^2$

(f) Which of these are square numbers?

8   1   15
    26
36   81

2. Cube and cube root numbers

Work out

(a) 2^3 (b) 4^3 (c) $\sqrt[3]{64}$ (d) $\sqrt[3]{8}$ (e) 5^3

(f) Which of these are cube numbers?

4   1   49
    25
27   8

3. Using powers

Copy and complete the following:

(a) 3^4 means $\cdots\cdots\cdots$ (b) 2^5 means $\cdots\cdots\cdots$

Write the following in index form:

(c) $6 \times 6 \times 6$ (d) $5 \times 5 \times 5 \times 5$ (e) $3 \times 3 \times 3 \times 3 \times 3 \times 3$

(f) Work out the value of 2^6

4. Finding factors and prime numbers

Write down all the factors of   (a) 18   (b) 32

(c) Which of these are prime numbers?

6   3   10
    12   5
17   7

5. Finding multiples and the Lowest Common Multiple (LCM)

(a) Write down the first five multiples of 6.

(b) Write down two multiples of 7 which lie between 40 and 50.

(c) Write down any multiple of 4 which lies between 22 and 30.

Find the Lowest Common Multiple of each of these groups of numbers:

(d) 5 and 3   (e) 8 and 12   (f) 3, 4 and 8.

6. Finding the Highest Common Factor (HCF)

(a) List all the factors of 15

(b) List all the factors of 20

(c) Write down the Highest Common Factor of 15 and 20

Find the Highest Common Factor of:

(d) 16 and 24   (e) 21 and 35   (f) 8, 12 and 20

7. Breaking down numbers into prime factors

Write the following numbers as products of prime factors:

(a) 12   (b) 36   (c) 54   (d) 100   (e) 144

8. Finding equivalent fractions

Copy and complete these equivalent fractions by filling in the box.

(a) $\dfrac{7}{8} = \dfrac{\square}{24}$ (b) $\dfrac{5}{9} = \dfrac{\square}{36}$ (c) $\dfrac{2}{7} = \dfrac{10}{\square}$

(d) $\dfrac{2}{3} = \dfrac{\square}{27}$ (e) $\dfrac{20}{25} = \dfrac{\square}{5}$ (f) $\dfrac{9}{30} = \dfrac{3}{\square}$

9. Cancelling fractions

Cancel each fraction below to its lowest terms.

(a) $\dfrac{6}{10}$ (b) $\dfrac{9}{24}$ (c) $\dfrac{15}{40}$ (d) $\dfrac{12}{28}$ (e) $\dfrac{42}{56}$ (f) $\dfrac{24}{72}$

Write down the larger fraction:

(a) $\dfrac{1}{5}$ or $\dfrac{1}{4}$ (b) $\dfrac{2}{3}$ or $\dfrac{3}{5}$ (c) $\dfrac{5}{7}$ or $\dfrac{5}{9}$

Place in order, *smallest first*:

(d) $\dfrac{2}{5}, \dfrac{1}{4}, \dfrac{3}{8}$ (e) $\dfrac{5}{6}, \dfrac{3}{4}, \dfrac{2}{3}, \dfrac{7}{12}$

11. Converting between fractions and decimals

Change the following decimals to fractions in their most simple form:

(a) 0.37   (b) 0.08   (c) 0.8   (d) 0.028   (e) 0.42

Convert the fractions below to decimals:

(f) $\dfrac{7}{20}$ (g) $\dfrac{3}{5}$ (h) $\dfrac{2}{25}$ (i) $\dfrac{19}{25}$ (j) $\dfrac{5}{9}$ (k) $\dfrac{7}{11}$

12. Ordering decimals

(a) Which is larger, 0.04 or 0.3?

(b) Which is larger, 0.028 or 0.17?

In the Questions below, arrange the numbers in order of size, smallest first:

(c) 0.7, 0.071, 0.07

(d) 0.062, 0.064, 0.63, 0.6

(e) 0.32, 0.318, 0.034, 0.331

(f) 2.83, 2.183, 2.318, 2.14, 2.714, 2.049

1 Here are two fractions $\frac{3}{5}$ and $\frac{2}{3}$.

Explain which is the larger fraction.

You may use the grids to help with your explanation.

(EDEXCEL)

2 Write the following fractions in order of size with the smallest first.
Show your working.

$$\frac{3}{5} \qquad \frac{1}{2} \qquad \frac{5}{8}$$

(CCEA)

3

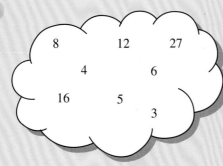

Using only the numbers in the cloud, write down

(i) all the multiples of 6,

(ii) all the square numbers,

(iii) all the factors of 12,

(iv) all the cube numbers. (EDEXCEL)

4 (a) Work out

(i) 10^3 (ii) $\dfrac{2^5}{4^2}$

(b) 21   22   23   24   25   26   27   28   29

From these numbers choose one which is

(i) a cube number,

(ii) a prime number.

(OCR)

5 (a) Write 0.35 as a fraction. Give your answer in its simplest form.

  (b) Write $\dfrac{3}{8}$ as a decimal.   (EDEXCEL)

6 (a) Write down all the factors of 10.

  (b) Write down all the prime numbers between 20 and 30.

  (c) Work out the cube of 6.   (EDEXCEL)

7 (i) Write 45 as a product of prime factors.

  (ii) What is the lowest common multiple of 45 and 75?   (AQA)

8 Write these five fractions in order of size. Start with the smallest fraction.

  $\dfrac{3}{4}$ $\dfrac{1}{2}$ $\dfrac{3}{8}$ $\dfrac{2}{3}$ $\dfrac{1}{6}$ (EDEXCEL)

9 (i) p and q are prime numbers.

   Find the values of p and q when $p^3 \times q = 24$.

  (ii) Write 18 as a product of prime factors.

  (iii) What is the lowest common multiple of 24 and 18?   (AQA)

GEOMETRY 1

3

In this unit you will learn how to:

– identify acute, obtuse, reflex and right angles

– label angles

– find angles on a straight line and angles at a point

– find vertically opposite angles and angles in a triangle

– use isosceles and equilateral triangles

– find alternate and corresponding angles

– use reflection symmetry and rotational symmetry

– recognise planes of symmetry

– find angles in polygons

– find angles in quadrilaterals

– recognise common quadrilaterals

– ⟨USE YOUR MATHS!⟩ – pitch the tent

Acute, obtuse, reflex and right angles

🔑 Key Facts

An **acute** angle

is **less** than a
$\frac{1}{4}$ turn (90°)

A **right** angle

is a $\frac{1}{4}$ turn
(90°)

An **obtuse** angle

is **more** than a
$\frac{1}{4}$ turn (90°) and

less than a

$\frac{1}{2}$ turn (180°)

A **reflex** angle

is **more** than
a $\frac{1}{2}$ turn

(180°)

1　Which of these angles are acute?

2　Which of these angles are obtuse?

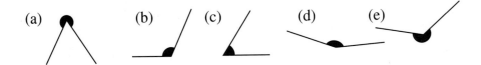

3　Which of these angles are reflex?

4　For each of these angles say whether they are acute, obtuse or reflex:

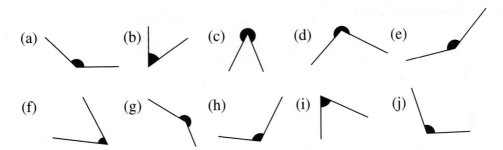

5　For each shape, say whether the angles marked are acute, obtuse or reflex:

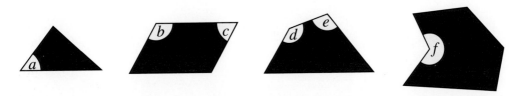

6　(a) Draw a triangle with an obtuse angle:

　　(b) Draw a quadrilateral (a shape with 4 sides) with a reflex angle.

　　(c) Can you draw a triangle with a reflex angle inside it?

This is called angle *BCD* or angle *DCB*.
We write this as $B\hat{C}D$ or $D\hat{C}B$.

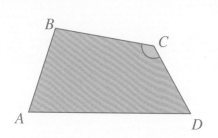

E3. 1

Name the shaded angles below:

1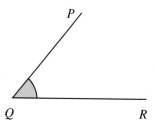

2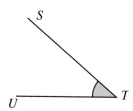

3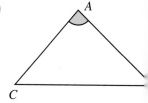

4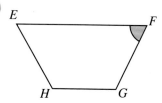

5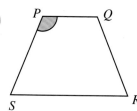

6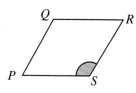

7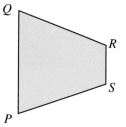

Is angle *PSR* acute or obtuse?

8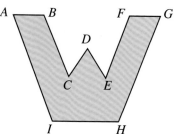

(a) Name 3 acute angles

(b) Name 3 obtuse angle

(c) Is $G\hat{H}I$ acute or obtus

(d) Is $B\hat{A}I$ acute or obtus

Write down the size of each angle stated below:

9

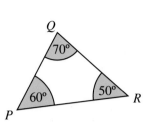

(a) $P\hat{R}Q$ (b) $Q\hat{P}R$

10

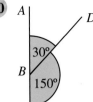

(a) $D\hat{B}C$ (b) $A\hat{B}D$

11

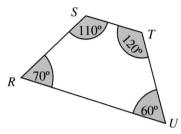

(a) $T\hat{S}R$ (b) $T\hat{U}R$

Angles on a straight line and angles at a point

🔑 # Key Facts

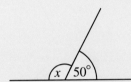

$$x + 50° = 180°$$
$$x = 130°$$

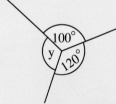

$$y + 100° + 120° = 360°$$
$$y = 140°$$

The angles on a straight line add up to 180°.

The angles at a point add up to 360°.

M3. 2

Find the angles marked with the letters.

1

2

3

4

5

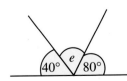

6

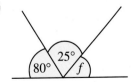

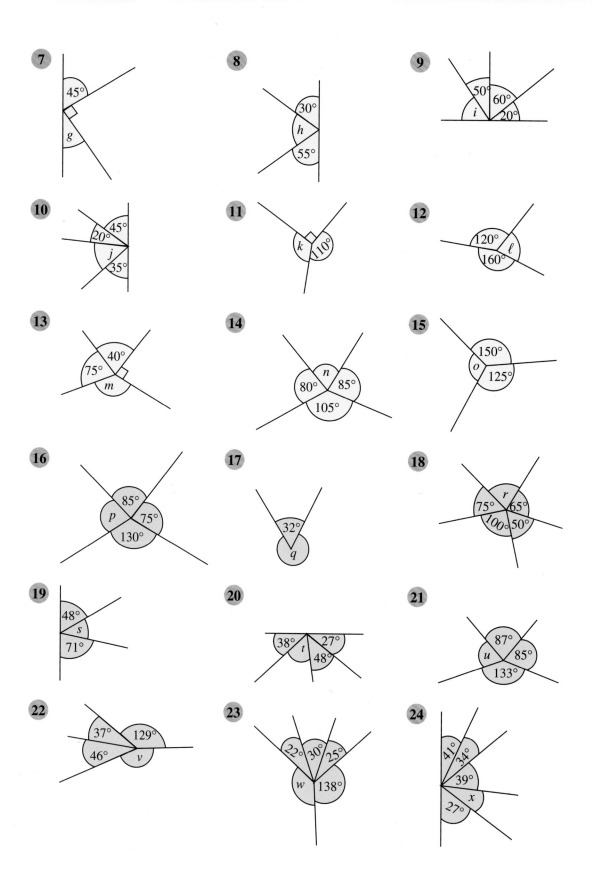

Key Facts

$x = 42°$
When 2 lines intersect the opposite angles are equal.
ie. vertically opposite angles are equal.

$y + 80° + 60° = 180°$
$y = 40°$
The angles in a triangle add up to 180°.

Lines which cross or meet at right angles are called **perpendicular** lines.

E3. 2

Find the angles marked with the letters.

1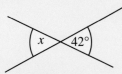

2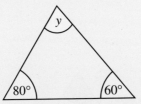

3

4

5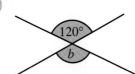

6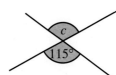

7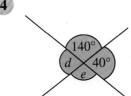

8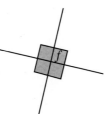

9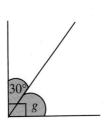

10

11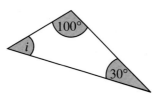

12

13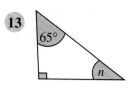

14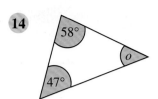

15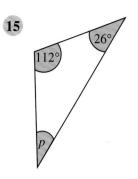

16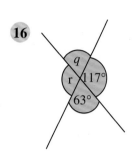

17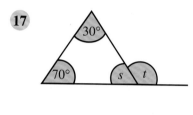

18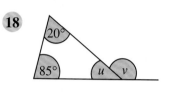

19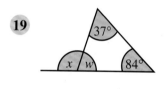

20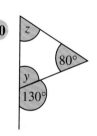

21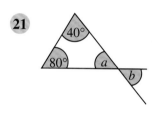

22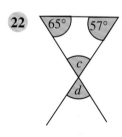

23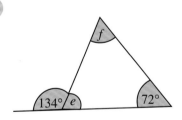

24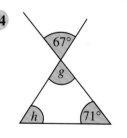

25 Which two lines are perpendicular?

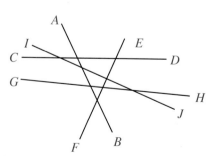

Isosceles and equilateral triangles

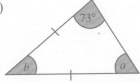

(a)

$a = 73°$ (isosceles triangle)
$b + 73° + 73° = 180°$ (angles in a triangle
add up to 180°)

$b = 34°$

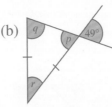

(b)

$p = 49°$ (vertically opposite)
$q = p = 49°$ (isosceles triangle)
$r + 49° + 49° = 180°$ (angles in a triangle
add up to 180°)

$r = 82°$

M3. 3

Find the angles marked with letters.

1

2

3

4

5

6

7

8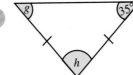

9

10

11

12

13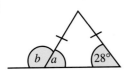

14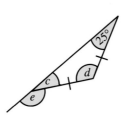

15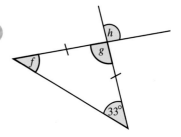

16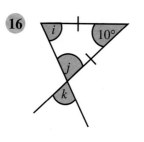

17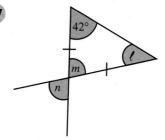

18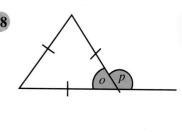

19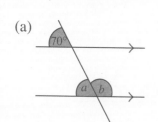

20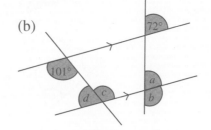

🔑 Key Facts

Many people think of alternate angles as 'Z' angles.

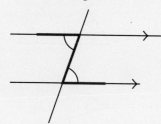

Alternate angles are equal

Many people think of corresponding angles as 'F' angles.

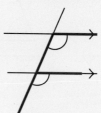

Corresponding angles are equal

(a)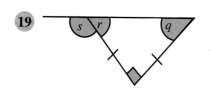

$a = 70°$ (corresponding angles)

$b = 110°$ (*a* and *b* are angles on a straight line which add up to 180°)

(b)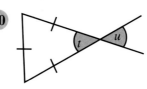

$a = 72°$ (corresponding)

$b = 108°$ (angles on a straight line add up to 180°)

$c = 101°$ (alternate)

$d = 79°$ (angles on a straight line add up to 180°)

Find the angles marked with letters.

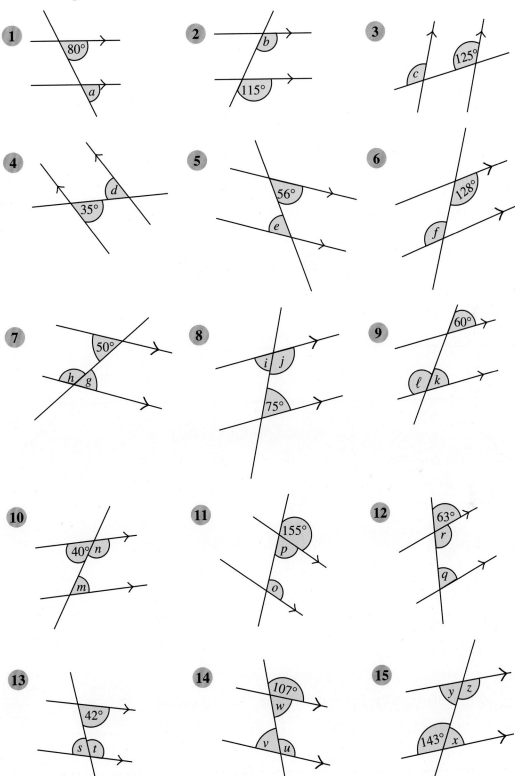

16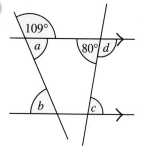

17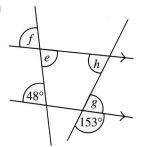

18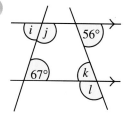

19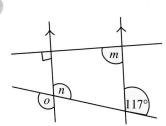

20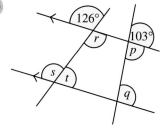

21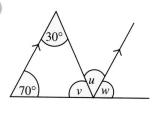

22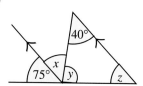

23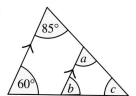

24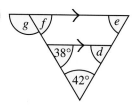

3A **Factors and Multiples (see Unit 2)**

1. Write down all the *factors* of:

   (a) 10   (b) 25   (c) 24

2. Which numbers below have 4 *factors* only?

   (15)   (7)   (16)   (22)

3. Which of the numbers below are *multiples* of 6?

   (17)   (12)   (22)   (30)   (19)   (42)

4. (a) Write down the first six *multiples* of 7

   (b) Write down the first eight *multiples* of 5

   (c) Write down the Lowest Common Multiple of 5 and 7

5. Find the Lowest Common Multiple of each of these pairs of numbers:

   (a) 4 and 7   (b) 6 and 9   (c) 8 and 6

Key Facts

A shape has a line of symmetry if one side is a reflection of the other along the line. One side folds exactly onto the other along the line.

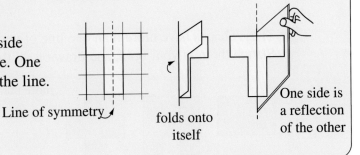

Line of symmetry

folds onto itself

One side is a reflection of the other

M3. 4

1 Which of these road signs have one or more lines of symmetry?

(a)   (b)   (c)   (d)   (e)   (f)

2 Which of these signs have a line of symmetry?

(a)   (b)   (c)   (d)   (e)   (f)

3 Copy this shape into your book.

Shade one more square so that the shape has a line of symmetry.

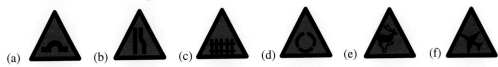

Copy this shape into your book.

Shade two more squares so that it has a line of symmetry.

4

5 Each of these shapes have a line of symmetry

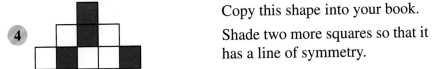

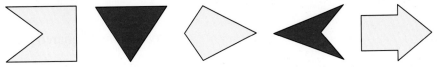

Copy them into your book and draw on a dotted line to show the line of symmetry.

6 Sketch these shapes in your book.
Draw on their line of symmetry using a dotted line.

Hint: Turn them
around to help see
their line of
symmetry

7 These shapes have more than one line of symmetry.
Sketch them in your book and draw on all the lines of symmetry.

more than 3   more than 4

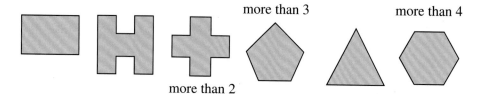

more than 2

8 Copy these shapes. Mark on all their lines of symmetry.

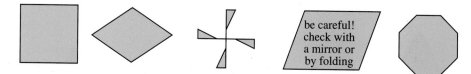

be careful!
check with
a mirror or
by folding

9

10

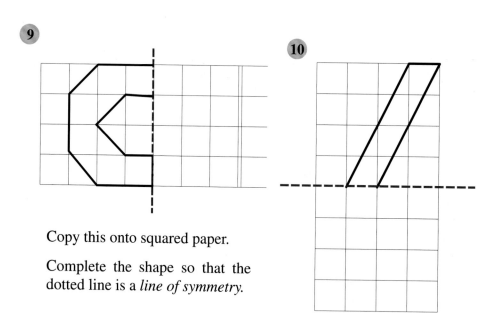

Copy this onto squared paper.

Complete the shape so that the
dotted line is a *line of symmetry*.

Copy this onto squared paper.

Complete the shape so that the
dotted line is a *line of symmetry*.

 # Key Facts

A shape has **rotational symmetry** if it fits onto itself when rotated (turned) before it gets back to its starting position.

The shape A fits onto itself three times when rotated through a complete turn. It has rotational symmetry of **order three**.

A

If a shape can only fit onto itself in its starting position, it has rotational symmetry of **order one**.

E3. 4

For each shape write down the order of rotational symmetry (use tracing paper if you wish).

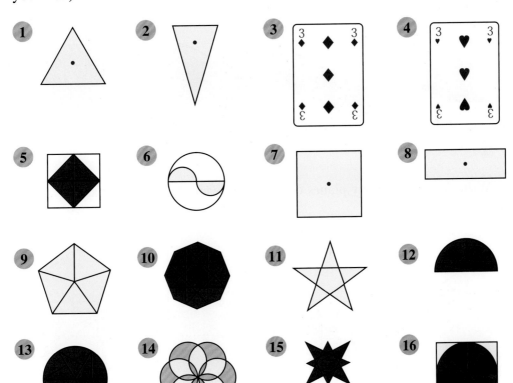

1

2

3

4

5

6

7

8

9

10

11

12

13

14

15

16

Key Facts

A plane of symmetry divides a 3-D shape into two identical halves. One half must be the mirror image of the other half.

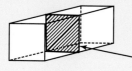

A plane of symmetry must be shown fully as a clear slice through the 3-D shape. Each half of the cuboid on each side of the plane of symmetry is symmetrical.

Note: a 3-D shape may have more than one plane of symmetry.

M3. 5

1 Draw each shape below and show one plane of symmetry.

(a)   (b)   (c)   (d)

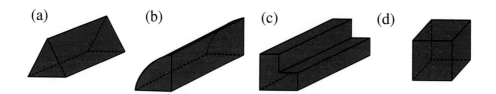

2 Write down how many planes of symmetry each shape below has.

(a)   (b)   (c)

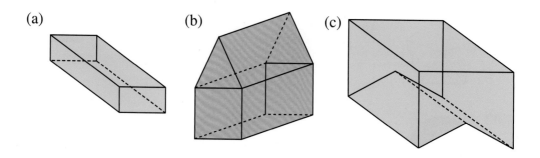

3B **Prime Factors and Highest Common Factors (see Unit 2)**

1. Copy and complete these factor trees:

(a)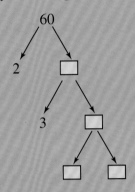

(b)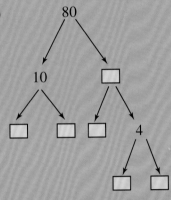

$60 = 2 \times \square \times 3 \times \square$

$80 = \square \times \square \times \square \times \square \times \square$

2. $20 = \underbrace{2 \times 2 \times 5}$

'a product of its prime factors'

Using any method, write the following numbers as products of prime factors:
(a) 30   (b) 36   (c) 50   (d) 144

3. (a) List all the factors of 28

(b) List all the factors of 21

(c) Write down the Highest Common Factor of 21 and 28

4. Using any method, find the Highest Common Factor of:

(a) 24 and 60   (b) 45 and 75   (c) 135 and 81

Quadrilaterals – Four sided shapes

M3. 6

You will need some punched strips and tracing paper.

1 Which of these shapes is a quadrilateral?

2 The diagram shows a square.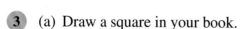

  (a) What is special about its angles?

  (b) What is special about its sides?

3 (a) Draw a square in your book.

  (b) Use dashes to show equal sides and little squares to show right angles.

4 (a) Draw a square in your book and use dotted lines to show all the lines of symmetry.

  (b) Copy and complete: A square has .... lines of symmetry.

5 (a) Does the square have rotational symmetry?

  (b) Trace the square. How many times does it fit into itself when you turn it?

  (c) Copy and complete: A square has rotational symmetry of order ...

6

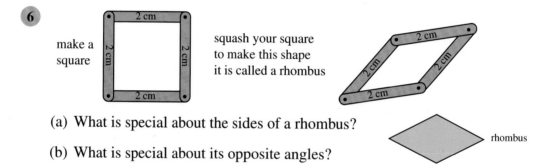

make a square

squash your square to make this shape it is called a rhombus

rhombus

  (a) What is special about the sides of a rhombus?

  (b) What is special about its opposite angles?

7 (a) Draw a rhombus in your book.

  (b) Use dashes to show equal sides and curves to show equal angles.

8 (a) How many lines of symmetry does a rhombus have?

  (b) Draw another rhombus in your book. Show its lines of symmetry using dotted lines.

9 (a) Does the rhombus have rotational symmetry?

  (b) Trace the rhombus. How many times does it fit into itself when you turn it?

  (c) Copy and complete: A rhombus has rotational symmetry of order ....

10 Which of these shapes are rhombuses?

11

(a) Draw a rectangle in your book.

(b) Mark any equal sides using dashes.

(c) Mark any parallel lines using arrows.

(d) Mark any right angles using little squares.

12 (a) Draw a rectangle in your book. Show its lines of symmetry with dotted lines.

(b) Copy and complete: A rectangle has .... lines of symmetry.

13 (a) Does a rectangle have rotational symmetry?

(b) Trace the rectangle. How many times does it fit into itself when you turn it?

(c) Copy and complete: A rectangle has rotational symmetry of order ....

14

make a rectangle.

squash your rectangle to make this shape. It is called a parallelogram.

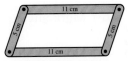

(a) Copy this parallelogram into your book.

(b) Why do you think it is called a parallelogram?

(c) Mark any parallel sides with arrows.

(d) Mark any equal angles with curves.

15 (a) How many lines of symmetry does a parallelogram have?

(b) Trace the parallelogram. Cut it out. Try and fold it onto itself.

(c) Copy and complete: A parallelogram has ... lines of symmetry.

16 (a) Does the parallelogram have rotational symmetry?

(b) Trace the parallelogram. How many times does it fit into itself when you turn it?

(c) Copy and complete: A parallelogram has rotational symmetry of order ...

17 Which of these shapes are parallelograms?

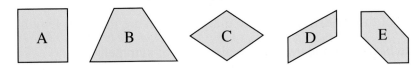

18 Copy and complete each shape below to make a parallelogram

19 Take the parallelogram from Question **14** apart.

Take the same four strips.

Make a quadrilateral which is not a parallelogram and not a rectangle.

This shape is called a kite.

20 (a) Draw a kite in your book.

   (b) Mark any equal sides with dashes.

   (c) Mark any equal angles with curves. (check with a protractor!)

21 (a) Draw another kite in your book using dotted lines to show any lines of symmetry.

   (b) Copy and complete: A kite has . . . line of symmetry.

22 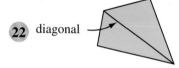 This line across from one corner to another is called a **diagonal**.

Copy this **square**.
Draw on both its diagonals. What angle do they meet at?

23 Trace these special **quadrilaterals.**

Draw the diagonals on each shape.

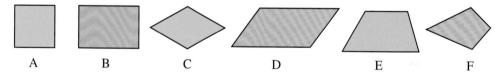

A   B   C   D   E   F

(a) Which of the quadrilaterals have diagonals that meet at right-angles:

(b) Which of the quadrilaterals have diagonals that are the same length?

(c) Which have diagonals which are also lines of symmetry?

E3. 6

Find the angles marked with letters.

1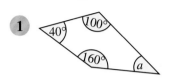

2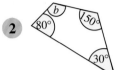

3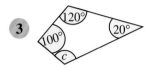

4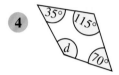

5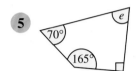

6

7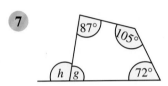

8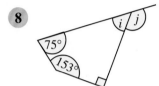

9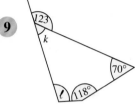

10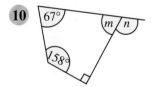

11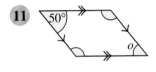

12

13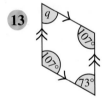

14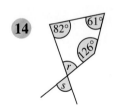

15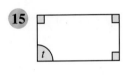

16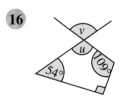

17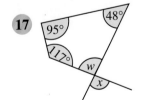

18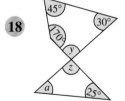

19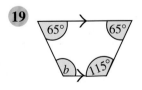

20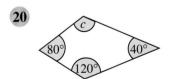

21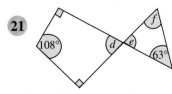

22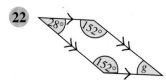

23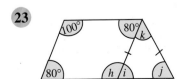

24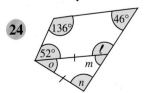

(3C) Fractions (see Unit 2)

In Questions **1** to **8**, copy and fill in the empty box:

1. $\dfrac{1}{3} = \dfrac{\square}{12}$

2. $\dfrac{2}{5} = \dfrac{\square}{30}$

3. $\dfrac{3}{10} = \dfrac{\square}{40}$

4. $\dfrac{2}{3} = \dfrac{10}{\square}$

5. $\dfrac{5}{9} = \dfrac{15}{\square}$

6. $\dfrac{4}{7} = \dfrac{\square}{35}$

7. $\dfrac{12}{15} = \dfrac{\square}{5}$

8. $\dfrac{20}{28} = \dfrac{\square}{7}$

Cancel each fraction below to its lowest terms:

9. $\dfrac{5}{20}$

10. $\dfrac{3}{9}$

11. $\dfrac{10}{40}$

12. $\dfrac{12}{20}$

13. $\dfrac{16}{24}$

14. $\dfrac{30}{50}$

15. $\dfrac{20}{45}$

16. $\dfrac{30}{42}$

17. $\dfrac{21}{56}$

18. $\dfrac{72}{88}$

19. Which of the fractions below are the same as $\dfrac{3}{4}$?

$$\dfrac{12}{50} \qquad \dfrac{15}{20} \qquad \dfrac{12}{16} \qquad \dfrac{30}{45} \qquad \dfrac{24}{32}$$

20. Which of the fractions below are the same as $\dfrac{2}{9}$?

$$\dfrac{6}{27} \qquad \dfrac{20}{90} \qquad \dfrac{25}{100} \qquad \dfrac{16}{72} \qquad \dfrac{18}{63}$$

Mixed angle problems

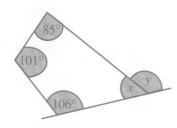

Find angles x and y

$x = 68°$ (angles in a quadrilateral add up to 360°)

$y = 112°$ (angles on a straight line add up to 180°)

Find the angles marked with letters (Exam Questions often want reasons. Ask your teacher if you must write down all the reasons)

1. 35°, 75°, a

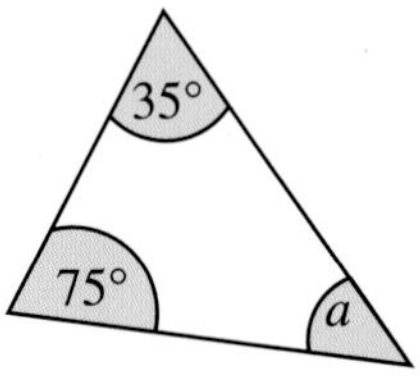

2. 106°, b, c, 38°

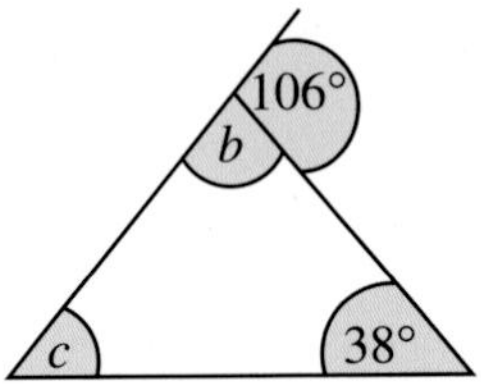

3. 74°, d, 82°, e

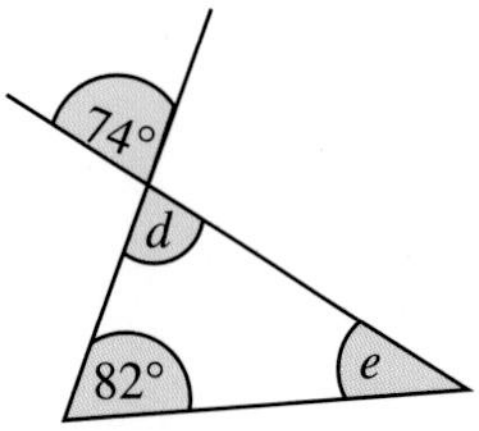

4. 40°, f, g

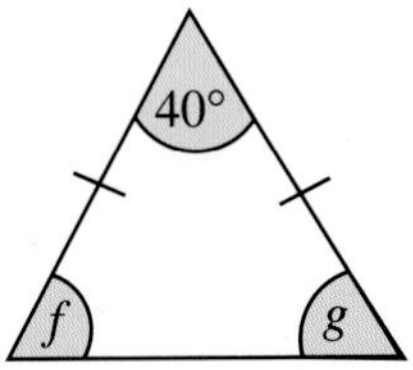

5. 40°, h, i

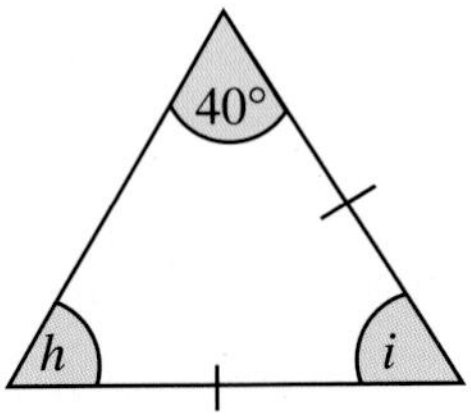

6. 112°, j

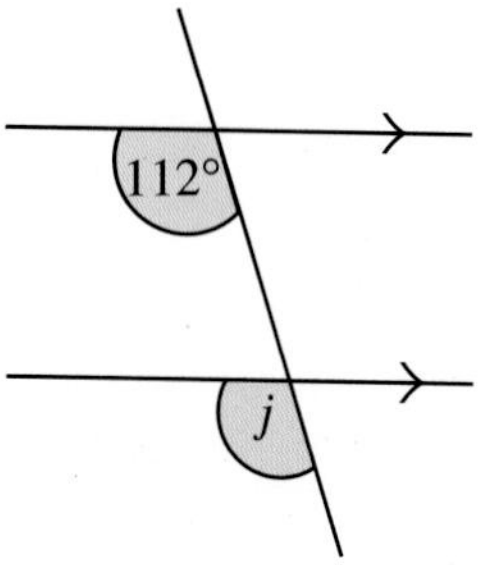

7. 108°, l, k

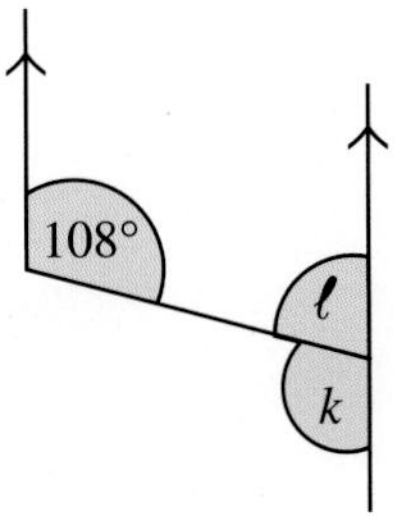

8. 82°, 125°, m, 131°

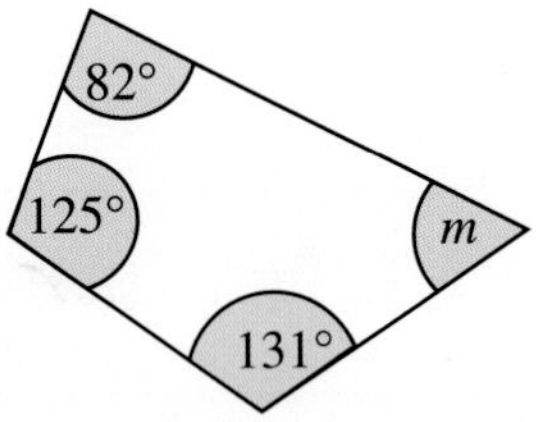

9. 76°, P, n, 85° o

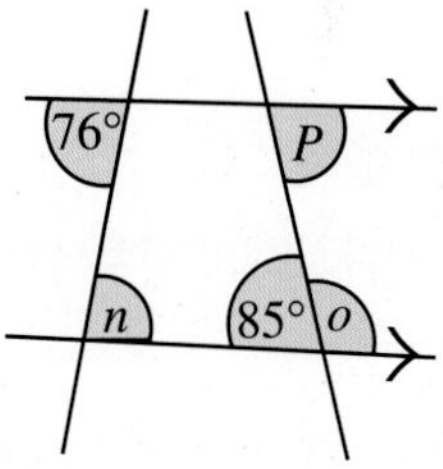

10. 100°, q

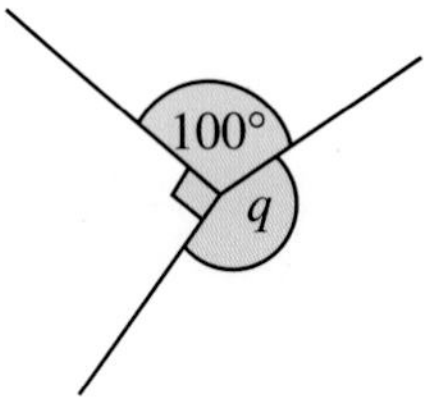

11. 80°, 72°, 147°, r, s

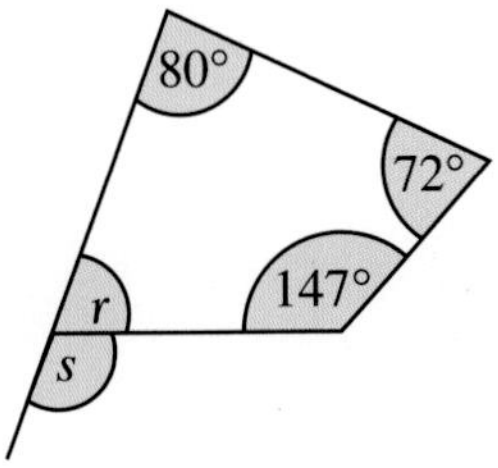

12. t

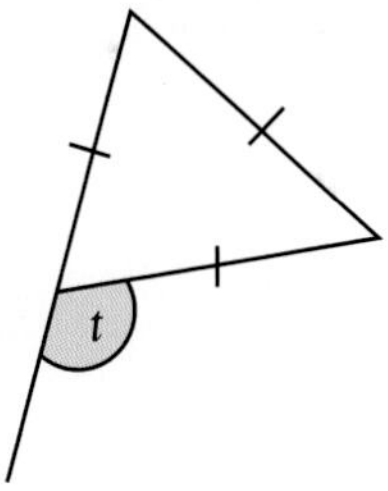

13. 118°, u, w, v

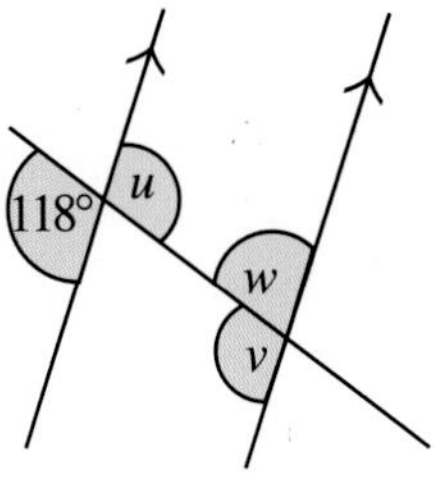

14. y, z, x, 143°

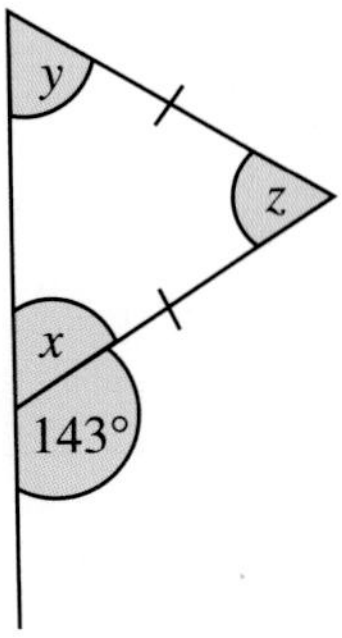

15. 83°, 97°, a, 30°, b

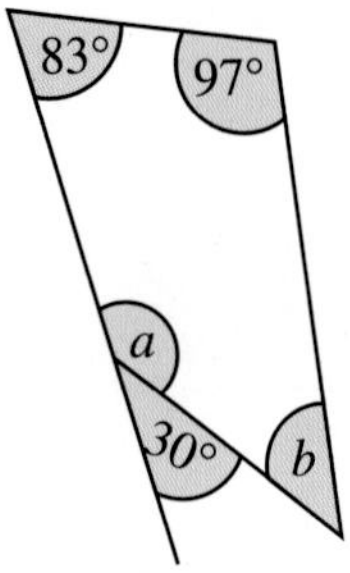

16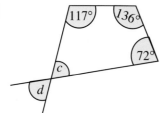

17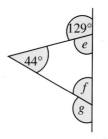

18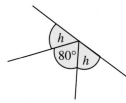

19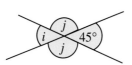

20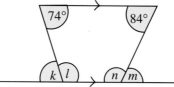

21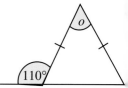

22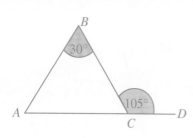

23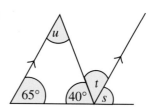

24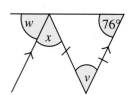

Angle proof

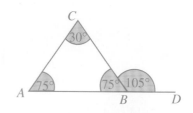

Prove that triangle *ABC* is isosceles.

Give all your reasons clearly.

$A\hat{C}B = 180° - 105° = 75°$ (angles on a straight line)

$B\hat{A}C = 180° - 30° - 75° = 75°$ (angles in a triangle add up to 180°)

$A\hat{C}B = B\hat{A}C$ so triangle *ABC* is isosceles.

84

1

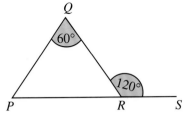

Prove that triangle *PQR* is equilateral.

2

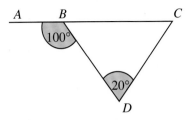

Prove that triangle *BCD* is isosceles.

3 Copy and complete this proof for the sum of the angles in a triangle.

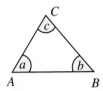

Here is triangle *ABC*.

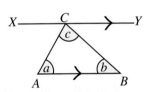

Draw line *XCY* parallel to *AB*.

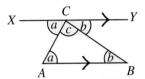

$A\hat{B}C = Y\hat{C}B$ (alternate angles)

$B\hat{A}C = \boxed{}$ (alternate angles)

$a + b + c = \boxed{}$ (angles on a straight line). Angles in a triangle $a + b + c = 180°$

4

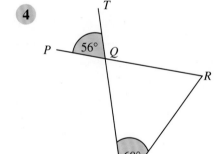

Prove that triangle *QRS* is isosceles.

Give all your reasons clearly.

5 Copy and complete this proof for the sum of the angles in a quadrilateral.

Draw any quadrilateral *ABCD* with diagonal *BD*.

Now $a + b + c = \boxed{}$ (angles in a triangle add up to 180°)

and $d + e + f = \boxed{}$ (angles in a triangle add up to 180°)

so $a + b + c + d + e + f = \boxed{}$

This proves the result.

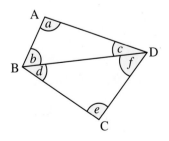

Key Facts

A polygon is a shape with straight sides.

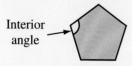

Interior angle

A polygon with 5 sides
is called a pentagon

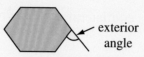

exterior angle

A polygon with 6 sides
is called a hexagon

A **regular** polygon has equal sides and equal angles.

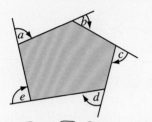

Put all the exterior angles together.
We can see that the sum of the
angles is 360°. This is true for
any polygon.

Exterior angles of a polygon add up to 360°

Note – in a regular polygon, all exterior angles are equal.

Find the value of angle x.

Sum of exterior angles = 360°

There are 8 sides so 8 equal exterior angles.

One exterior angle = 360° ÷ 8 = 45°

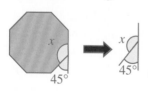

interior and exterior angles add up to 180°

so $x + 45° = 180°$

so $x = 135°$

1 Each shape below is a *regular* polygon.

Find the angles marked with letters.

(10 sides)

2 Find the angles marked with letters.

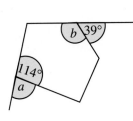 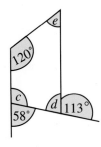 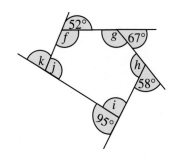

3 A dodecagon has 12 sides.

(a) Find the size of each exterior angle of a *regular* dodecagon.

(b) Write down the size of the interior angle for the same shape.

4 (a) Find the size of each exterior angle of a *regular* nonagon (9 sides)

(b) Write down the size of the interior angle for the same shape.

5 Find the exterior angles of *regular* polygons with

(a) 15 sides　　(b) 20 sides　　(c) 60 sides　　(d) 90 sides

6 Find the interior angle of each polygon in Question **5** .

7 Each exterior angle of a *regular* polygon is 8°. How many sides has the polygon?

8 Each exterior angle of a *regular* polygon is 20°. How many sides has the polygon?

9 This diagram shows the interior and exterior angles of a *regular* polygon. How many sides has the polygon?

interior angle

exterior angle

168°　12°

10 Find the size of the interior angle of a *regular* polygon with 24 sides.

87

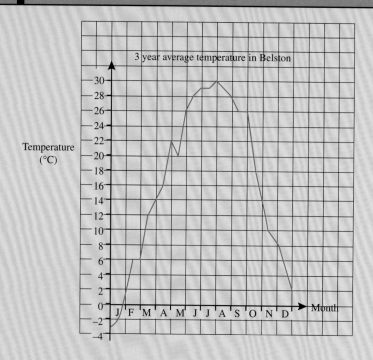

3 year average temperature in Belston

Alisha and her 3 friends are all seventeen years old. They want to camp for 8 nights around Belston.

They want to go camping when the temperature is likely to be between 26°C and 28°C but the amount of rainfall should be less than 4 cm.

They can choose from 4 campsites but want showers to be available.

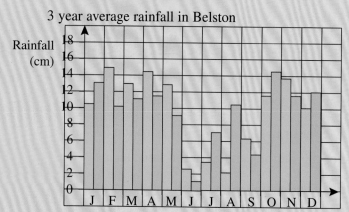

3 year average rainfall in Belston

Task A

Use the charts and tables 1 and 2 to find out when and where Alisha and her friends should camp and how much the 8 nights will cost them.

Table 1	Patton Drive	Halby Coombe	Belston Park	Mowley Bush
under 18's allowed with no adults		✓		✓
electric hookup	✓		✓	✓
dogs allowed	✓			✓
showers avaiable	✓	✓	✓	

Table 2

per night		30th March to 10th May	11th May to 20th June	21st June to 19th July	20th July to 31st August	1st September to 10th October	11th October to 15th November
Patton Drive	tent	£9.25	£12.50	£13.75	£14.50	£12.50	£8.50
	electric	£2.60	£2.60	£2.60	£2.60	£2.60	£2.60
	each dog	£0.50	£0.50	£0.50	£0.50	£0.50	£0.50
Halby Coombe	tent	£8.25	£9.75	£11.25	£12.75	£9.75	£8.25
Belston Park	tent	£8.75	£10.50	£12.50	£13.50	£10.50	£8.50
	electric	£2.85	£2.85	£2.85	£2.85	£2.85	£2.85
Mowley Bush	tent	£9.50	£11.50	£13.50	£14.75	£11.50	£9.50
	electric	£2.75	£2.75	£2.75	£2.75	£2.75	£2.75
	each dog	£0.60	£0.60	£0.60	£0.60	£0.60	£0.60

Trains	Monday to Saturday							Sunday			
Chesham	0747	0832	1015	–	1402	1613	–	0859	1154	1308	1712
Fulton	0812	0857	1040	1253	1427	1638	1809	0924	1219	1333	1737
Denby	0827	0912	1055	1308	1442	1653	1824	0939	1234	1348	1752
Derrington	0850	0935	1118	1331	1505	1716	1847	1002	1257	1411	1815
Canton	0910	0955	1138	1351	1525	1736	1907	1022	1317	1431	1835
Towley	0932	1017	1200	1413	1547	1758	1929	1044	1339	1453	1857
Bisham	0948	1033	1216	1429	1603	1814	1945	1100	1355	1509	1913
Witton	1017	1102	1245	1458	1632	1843	2014	1129	1424	1538	1942
Alton	1032	1117	1300	1513	1647	1858	2029	1144	1439	1553	1957

Task B

Alisha and her friends live in Denby. To go camping they must catch a train to Alton then a bus to Belston. Their campsite will not let new people in after 7 p.m.

At Alton it takes 9 minutes to walk from the train to the bus stop. At Belston it takes 12 minutes to walk from the bus stop to the campsite.

What is the latest train Alisha and her friends can catch in Denby on a Friday and how long does it take to get from Denby to the campsite?

Bus timetable

Henlow	0715	0745	0815	at these	15	until	2115
Rowton	0723	0753	0823	minutes	23		2123
Hanvale	0733	0803	0833	past each hour	33		2133
Corston	0740	0810	0840		40		2140
Alton	0743	0813	0843		43		2143
Parry-le-Hole	0748	0818	0848		48		2148
Barrow Tarn	0750	0820	0850		50		2150
Chinnock	0752	0852	0852		52		2152
Catley	0755	0855	0855		55		2155
Belston	0757	0857	0857		57		2157
Harley	0759	0859	0859		59		2159

TEST YOURSELF ON UNIT 3

---

1. Identifying acute, obtuse, reflex and right angles

For each of these angles say whether they are acute, obtuse, reflex or a right angle:

(a) 　　(b) 　　(c) 　　(d)

(e) 　　(f) 　　(g) 　　(h)

---

2. Labelling angles

Name each shaded angle below: (example: *BÂC*)

(a) 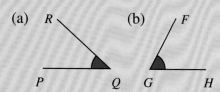　(b)　(c) 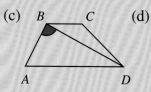　(d)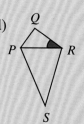

---

3. Finding angles on a straight line and angles at a point

Find the angles marked with the letters.

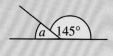　　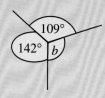　　

---

4. Finding vertically opposite angles and angles in a triangle

Find the angles marked with the letters.

　　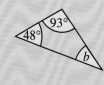　　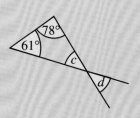

5. Using isosceles and equilateral triangles

Find the angles marked with the letters

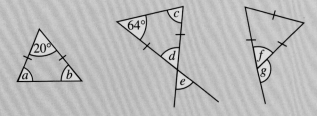

6. Finding alternate and corresponding angles

Find the angles marked with the letters

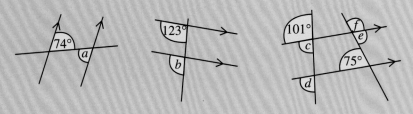

7. Using reflection symmetry and rotational symmetry

For each shape below, write down how many lines of symmetry it has and the order of rotational symmetry.

(a)   (b)   (c)

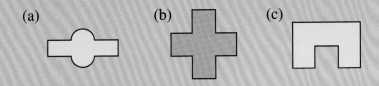

8. Recognising common quadrilaterals

Name the shapes below and for each shape, write down

  (i) how many lines of symmetry it has and

  (ii) its order of rotational symmetry.

(a)   (b)   (c)   (d)

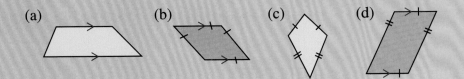

Find the angles marked with the letters

  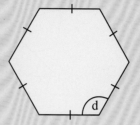 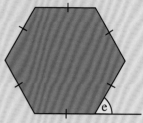

Mixed examination questions

1

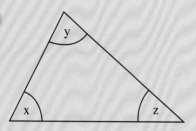

(i) The diagram shows a triangle

Which of the following correctly describes angle x?

acute angle,   obtuse angle,

reflex angle,   right-angle.

(ii) What is the value of $x + y + z$?

(AQA)

2

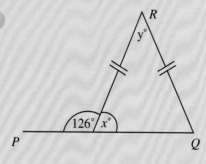

PQ is a straight line.

(a) Work out the size of the angle marked x.

(b) (i) Work out the size of the angle marked y.

   (ii) Give reasons for your answer.

(EDEXCEL)

3 State the order of rotational symmetry for each tile below.

(a) 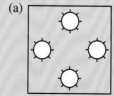   (b)   (c)

4 The diagram shows a rectangle.

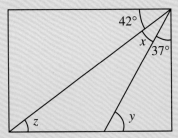

Work out the size of angles x, y and z.   (AQA)

5

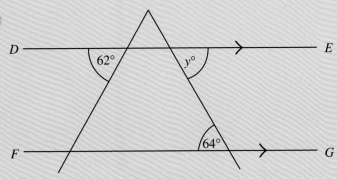

DE is parallel to *FG*.

Find the size of the angle marked $y°$.   (EDEXCEL)

6 Shade two more squares on the diagram so that the final pattern has line symmetry AND rotational symmetry.

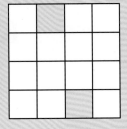

(AQA)

7

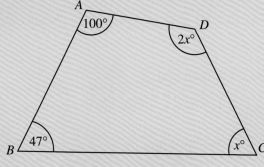

ABCD is a quadrilateral.

Work out the size of the largest angle in the quadrilateral.

(EDEXCEL)

In this unit you will learn how to:

– use letters and symbols in algebra

– substitute numbers for letters

– substitute numbers into formulas

– collect like terms

– simplify terms

– multiply out brackets

– take out common factors

– ⟨USE YOUR MATHS!⟩ – Money for your holiday

Substitution

🔑 Key Facts

Letters can be used in place of numbers to solve problems:

Example – shoes cost £40

        shoes cost £x

$a + b$ is an algebraic *expression*

$3a$ means $3 \times a$ ab means a $\times$ b

a^2 means a $\times$ a $7a + 2$ means '$7 \times a$ then add 2'

$\dfrac{a}{b}$ means $a \div b$ $7(a + 2)$ means '$a + 2$ then multiply by 7'

a^3 means $a \times a \times a$ $4a^2$ means '$a \times a$ then multiply by 4'

$(4a)^2$ means '$4 \times a$ then square the answer'

Find the value of each expression when $a = 3$, $b = 2$ and $c = 5$

$ab = 3 \times 2 = 6$

$c^2 = 5 \times 5 = 25$

$5a - 1 = 5 \times 5 - 1 = 24$

$4(b + 3) = 4 \times (2 + 3) = 4 \times 5 = 20$

$\dfrac{c}{b} = 5 \div 2 = 2.5$

$(3b)^2 = (3 \times 2)^2 = 6^2 = 6 \times 6 = 36$

$3b^2 = 3 \times b \times b = 3 \times 2 \times 2 = 12$

Key Facts

Remember: BODMAS. The order of operations is Brackets then $\div \times + -$

M4. 1

In Questions **1** to **20** find the value of each expression when $a = 6$, $b = 2$, $c = 4$

1 $4a$	**2** $a + b + c$	**3** $2a - b$	**4** $a + b - c$
5 bc	**6** $3c - 5$	**7** ab	**8** $7b + 2c$
9 c^2	**10** a^2	**11** $a^2 + b^2$	**12** $4(b + c)$
13 $3(a - c)$	**14** $b(a + c)$	**15** $\dfrac{a - c}{b}$	**16** $a(c - b)$
17 $a(b + c)$	**18** $b(2a - c)$	**19** $\dfrac{3b + a}{c}$	**20** $\dfrac{6c}{a}$

In Questions **21** to **40** find the value of each expression when $x = 3$
$y = 0$
$z = 8$

21 $6x$

22 $2z$

23 $3x - z$

24 $4z + x$

25 $3z + 7$

26 $x + z$

27 $x + z - y$

28 $z - 2x$

29 $14 + 2z$

30 $3x - 2y$

31 x^2

32 $y^2 + x^2$

33 xy

34 yz

35 xyz

36 $x^2 + y^2 + z^2$

37 $3(2x + z)$

38 $x(z - y)$

39 $4(x^2 + z^2)$

40 $\dfrac{10x}{5x}$

In Questions **41** to **49** find the value of each expression

41 $3x + 2$ if $x = 4$

42 $5x - 7$ if $x = 6$

43 $2a + 9$ if $a = 5$

44 $b^2 + 4$ if $b = 6$

45 $6(a - 3)$ if $a = 5$

46 $x^2 - 6$ if $x = 5$

47 $8 + 2b$ if $b = 4$

48 $9(x^2 - 3)$ if $x = 2$

49 $a(5a - 9)$ if $a = 3$

E4. 1

In Questions **1** to **20** find the value of each expression when $x = 5$
$y = 4$
$z = 7$

1 $y^2 + z^2$

2 x^2

3 $4x^2$

4 $(4x)^2$

5 $(2y)^2$

6 $2z^2$

7 $3y^2$

8 xyz

9 $2(x^2 + y^2)$

10 $2y + 3x$

11 $x^2 + y^2 + z^2$

12 $2x^2 - y^2$

13 $y(3z - 2x)$

14 $z(4x + 2y)$

15 $\dfrac{21(x - y)}{z}$

16 $6(x^2 - y^2)$

17 $y(2z + 3y)$

18 $(2x)^2 - 2x^2$

19 $6(3x + y^2)$

20 $\dfrac{5z + x}{y}$

In Questions **21** to **29** find the value of each expression

21 $x^2 - 3$, if $x = 7$ **22** $2b^2$, if $b = 3$ **23** $3a^2$, if $a = 1$

24 $7(p - 2)$, if $p = 2$ **25** $(4a)^2$, if $a = 1$ **26** $3x$, if $x = -2$

27 $20 + b$, if $b = -6$ **28** $3 - 6x$, if $x = 2$ **29** $5(a - 6)$, if $a = 2$

In Questions **30** to **45** find the value of each expression when $a = 4$
$b = -2$
$c = -3$

30 bc **31** $5a + 3b$ **32** $3c - 2$ **33** $2b + 4c$

34 b^2 **35** $a^2 + b^2$ **36** $2c^2$ **37** $3(4b - 2)$

38 $b(a + c)$ **39** abc **40** $9c$ **41** $(3b)^2$

42 $8(a - b)$ **43** $24 - c$ **44** $5c + 10$ **45** $3a + 2b - c$

Using formulas

If base = 9 cm and height = 6 cm

then $b = 9$ and $h = 6$

Area A= $\dfrac{bh}{2}$

so A = $\dfrac{9 \times 6}{2} = 27$

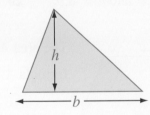

M4. 2

In Questions **1** to **12** you are given a formula. Find the value of the letter required in each case.

1 $a = 5b + 2$

Find a when $b = 3$

2 $x = 7y - 6$

Find x when $y = 3$

3 $a = \dfrac{b}{4} + 5$

Find a when $b = 20$

4 $c = \dfrac{d}{3} - 2$

Find c when $d = 15$

5 $g = 4h + 9$

Find g when $h = 6$

6 $p = 2(q + 8)$

Find p when $q = 3$

7 $m = n + 3p$

Find m when $n = 8$ and $p = 6$

8 $p = 6q + 2r$

Find p when $q = 4$ and $r = 5$

9 $v = 2(3w + 2y)$

Find v when $w = 4$ and $y = 5$

10 $a = \dfrac{4b + 7c}{5}$

Find a when $b = 4$ and $c = 2$

11 $x = 3y + 6z - 8$

Find x when $y = 4$ and $z = 2$

12 $e = \dfrac{f}{3} + \dfrac{d}{4}$

Find e when $f = 15$ and $d = 28$

In Questions **13** to **16** use the formula $s = ut$ to find the value of s (s means distance, u means speed and t means time taken).

13 $u = 7, t = 8$

14 $u = 47, t = 16$

15 $u = 23, t = 41$

16 $u = 4.1, t = 3.6$

In Questions **17** to **20** use the formula $v = at + u$ to find the value of v.

17 $a = 7, t = 6$ and $u = 43$

18 $a = 17, t = 32$ and $u = 217$

19 $a = 3.6, t = 7$ and $u = 8.9$

20 $a = 5.2, t = 3.6$ and $u = 7.17$

21 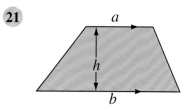 The area A of a trapezium can be found using the formula $A = \dfrac{1}{2} h(a+b)$

$\left(\dfrac{1}{2}h \text{ means } \dfrac{1}{2} \text{ of } h\right)$

Find the area of a trapezium when $h = 8$, $a = 8.9$ and $b = 6.1$

22 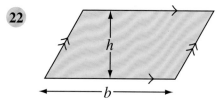 The area A of a parallelogram can be found using the formula

$$A = bh$$

Find the area of a parallelogram when $b = 6.2$ and $h = 4.9$

23 $a = \dfrac{v - u}{t}$ Use the formula to find the value of a when $v = 11$, $u = 4$ and

$t = 0.5$

24 x and y are connected by the formula $x = 5(2y - 3)$. Find x when $y = 5.6$

25 c, d and e are connected by the formula

$$c = \sqrt{(d^2 + e^2)}$$

Find c when $d = 3$ and $e = 4$

E4. 2

1 Below are several different formulas for z in terms of x. Find the value of z in each case.

(a) $z = 10x - 6$ when $x = 3.5$

(b) $z = \dfrac{5x + 3}{2}$ when $x = 3$

(c) $z = 4(3x + 7)$ when $x = 2$

2 Using the formula $a = 100 + 2b$, find the value of a when

(a) $b = 6$ (b) $b = 100$ (c) $b = \dfrac{1}{2}$

3 In the formulas below v is given in terms of a and t. Find the value of v in each case.

(a) $v = 7t + 3a$ when $t = 4$ and $a = 5$

(b) $v = 8t + 5a - 12$ when $t = 3$ and $a = 4$

(c) $v = at + 6$ when $a = 4$ and $t = 8$

4 Here are some polygons.

Number of sides :   3   4   5
Sum of angles :   180°   360°   540°

The sum of the angles in a polygon with n sides is given by the formula

$$\text{sum of angles} = (n - 2) \times 180°$$

(a) Find the sum of the angles in a hexagon (6 sides)

(b) Find the sum of the angles in a polygon with 102 sides

(c) Show that the formula gives the correct answer for the sum of the angles in a pentagon (5 sides)

5 Here is a formula $h = t^2 - 7$. Find the value of h when

   (a) $t = 6$ (b) $t = 1$ (c) $t = -3$

6 Using the formula $C = N^2 - P^2$

   find the value of C when

     (a) $N = 8$ and $P = 5$ (b) $N = 4$ and $P = 7$

     (c) $N = -3$ and $P = -6$

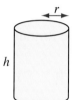

7 Using the formula $V = 3B^2$ find the value of V when

     (a) $B = 5$ (b) $B = 10$ (c) $B = -2$ (d) $B = -8$

8 An estimate for the volume of a cylinder of radius r and height h is given by the formula $V = 3r^2h$

     (a) Find the value of V when $r = 10$ and $h = 2$

     (b) Find the value of V when $r = 5$ and $h = 4$

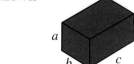

9 Find the value of c using formulas and values given.

     (a) $c = mx + 7$; $m = 5$ $x = -1$

     (b) $c = 2t + t^2$; $t = 3$

     (c) $c = 2pq + p^2$; $p = 3$ $q = 2$

     (d) $c = (a + b^2)$; $a = 5$ $b = -2$

10 If $T = a^2 + 3a - 5$, find the values of T when

     (a) $a = 3$ (b) $a = 10$ (c) $a = 1$

11 The total surface area A of the solid cuboid shown is given by the formula

$$A = 2bc + 2ab + 2ac$$

Find the value of A when $a = 2, b = 3, c = 4$

12 Using the formula $P = QR + S$, find the value of P when

     (a) $Q = -2, R = -4, S = -5$ (b) $Q = -3, R = 5, S = 10$

In the Questions below round off the answers to the **nearest whole number**.

13 Using the formula $x = \dfrac{y + z}{z - y}$ find the value of x when

    (a) $y = 6, z = 11$ (b) $y = 0.3, z = -2.8$

14 Using the formula $A = \dfrac{2B + C}{B + 3C}$ find the value of A when

    (a) $B = -7, C = 4$ (b) $B = -24, C = -2$

15 Here is a formula $M = \sqrt{(4N - 1)}$. Find the value of M when

    (a) $N = 6$ (b) $N = 20$ (c) $N = 5.8$

16

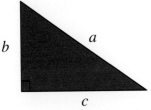

For any right-angled triangle:
$$a = \sqrt{(b^2 + c^2)}$$

Find the value of a when

    (a) $b = 7, c = 2$ (b) $b = 12, c = 5$ (c) $b = 8, c = 15$

17 Using the formula $R = 8 - \sqrt{S}$, find the value of R when

    (a) $S = 3$ (b) $S = 38$ (c) $S = 300$

18

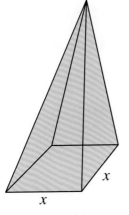

The volume V of this pyramid is given by the formula
$$V = \dfrac{x^2 h}{3}$$
where h is the height of the pyramid.

Find the value of V when

    (a) $x = 4, h = 10$ (b) $x = 5, h = 7$ (c) $x = 20, h = 15$

19 Using the formula $f = \dfrac{uv}{u + v}$, find the value of f when

    (a) $u = 6, v = 4$ (b) $u = 8, v = 20$ (c) $u = 5, v = 32$

Key Facts

$a + b$ cannot be added together because the *term a* is not like the term b

$a + 3a = 4a$ because the term a is like the term $3a$

a and $3a$ are *like terms*

Examples

(a) $6a + 4b + 2a + 3b = 8a + 7b$ (b) $5p + p + 3p = 9p$

(c) $ab + 3b + 2b = ab + 5b$ (d) $4x^2 + 3x + 2x^2 + 6x = 6x^2 + 9x$
     (ab is *not* like $3b$)

(e) $7a + 3 + 2a = 9a + 3$

M4. 3

Collect like terms

1 $3a + 4b + 2a$ **2** $5a + 6a + a$ **3** $3a + 4a + 4b$

4 $4p + 8q + 3p$ **5** $9p + 2p + 5q$ **6** $3p + 4q + 5q + 4p$

7 $8p + 5p + 6q + 2q$ **8** $7x + 5y - 3x$ **9** $7x + 3y - 7x$

10 $5x + 7y - 4y$ **11** $5a + 6a - 2a$ **12** $6x + 9x + 4y$

13 $8x - 3x + 4x$ **14** $9x - 5x + 2y$ **15** $6a + 3 + 5a - 2$

16 $9x - 3 + 3x - 5x$ **17** $8p + 4q + 4q - 3p$ **18** $6c + 3c - 2 + 5c$

19 $8a + 3a + 7a + 4$ **20** $6x + 4y + 5y - 2x$ **21** $6c + 3 + 6 - 3c$

Find the perimeter of each shape in Questions **22** to **25**. Simplify each answer.

22
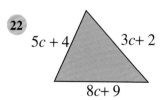
$5c + 4$ $3c + 2$
$8c + 9$

23
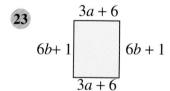
$3a + 6$
$6b + 1$ $6b + 1$
$3a + 6$

24
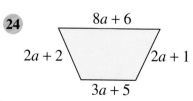
$8a + 6$
$2a + 2$ $2a + 1$
$3a + 5$

25
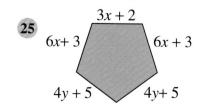
$3x + 2$
$6x + 3$ $6x + 3$
$4y + 5$ $4y + 5$

102

Simplify Questions 26 to 35 .

26 $8m - 3m + 2n$

27 $8a - 3a + 6b + 2b$

28 $a + 6b - a - 3b$

29 $8x + 7y + 3x + 6x$

30 $9a + 3a + 10 - 4a$

31 $5x - 2x + 8x + 6 - 2$

32 $4p + 6q + 3q - 8q - 2p$

33 $5a + 8 - 3 + 2 + 3a$

34 $6a + 9a - 10a + 3b - 2$

35 $8x - 6x + 2y + 3x - y$

E4. 3

Simplify

1 $8a + a$

2 $-5c + 7c$

3 $-7a + a$

4 $-b + 6b$

5 $-a + a$

6 $8a - 3b + 2a + 6b$

7 $8p + 3q - p + 4q$

8 $4m - 2n + 6m$

9 $3a + 2b - 5a - b$

10 $a + 4b - a - 3b$

11 $4a + b - 3b - 2a$

12 $6x + 2x - 8x - 3x$

13 $6p - 2 + 8 - 2p$

14 $5p - 3p - 6p - 2$

15 $5a - 1 - 1 - a$

16 $6x - 3y + 2y - x$

17 $3a + 6a + 8 - 10$

18 $5c - 2c - c - 7$

19 $8p - 3p + 2q - 8p$

20 $9a - 3 - 6 - 4a$

21 $6x - 3x - 8 + 3$

22

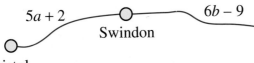

5a + 2   Swindon   6b − 9   8a + 1   London

Bristol   Reading

Use algebra to show how far it is between:

(a) Bristol and London

(b) Bristol and Reading

(c) Swindon and London

23

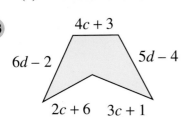

4c + 3

6d − 2   5d − 4

2c + 6   3c + 1

Find the perimeter of this shape.

Simplify your answer.

Simplify Questions **24** to **41**.

24 $3x + x^2 + 5x$

25 $4x^2 + 3x^2 + 5x^2$

26 $3x^2 + 6x + 2x + 4x^2$

27 $8a^2 + 3a + 4a^2 + 6a$

28 $3ab + a + 2ab$

29 $6ab + 3a + 2a + 2ab$

30 $4xy + 2xy - 3xy$

31 $5xy - 2 - 3 - 2xy$

32 $9ab + 3ab + 6 + 5ab$

33 $6xy - 3xy + 5xy - 2xy$

34 $7ab + 3ab - 2a + 4b$

35 $5xy - 2xy + 3x - 6x$

36 $4a^2 + a^2 + 9 - 2$

37 $7a^2 - 3a + 5a^2 - 2a$

38 $3ab + 2a^2 + 4ab + 5a^2$

39 $6x^2 + 3x + 3x^2 - x + y^2 - y$

40 $8a + 3a^2 - 2a + 4ab - a^2$

41 $5pq + 3pq - p + 6p - 10pq$

Can you still?

Can you still?

4A **Fractions–Decimals (see Unit 2)**

Change the fractions below into decimals:

1. $\dfrac{7}{100}$ **2.** $\dfrac{19}{100}$ **3.** $\dfrac{3}{4}$ **4.** $\dfrac{1}{5}$ **5.** $\dfrac{3}{20}$ **6.** $\dfrac{9}{25}$

Change the decimals below into fractions:

7. 0.3   **8.** 0.67   **9.** 0.25   **10.** 0.4   **11.** 0.08   **12.** 0.32

In Questions **13** to **15** below, write down which number is the larger:

13. $\boxed{0.7}$ or $\dfrac{4}{5}$ **14.** $\boxed{0.28}$ or $\dfrac{6}{25}$ **15.** $\dfrac{7}{20}$ or $\boxed{0.34}$

Simplifying terms

(a) $4a \times 2 = 8a$ $c \times c = c^2$

(b) $3a \times 2a = 6a^2$ *multiply numbers first then the letters*

(c) $3m \times 2n = 6mn$ $5y \times y = 5y^2$

(d) $6a \div 2 = 3a$ $28n \div 7 = 4n$

M4. 4

Do the following multiplications and divisions.

1 $4x \times 2$ **2** $3x \times 5$ **3** $8x \times 2$ **4** $4y \times 2$

5 $5y \times 4$ **6** $7a \times 6$ **7** $8x \times 10$ **8** $4a \times 9$

9 $3d \times 6$ **10** $6 \times 4c$ **11** $9 \times 4p$ **12** $5 \times 9x$

13 $7 \times 2c$ **14** $9 \times 3d$ **15** $6 \times 8x$ **16** $8x \div 4$

17 $24x \div 4$ **18** $4p \div 2$ **19** $20x \div 4$ **20** $21A \div 3$

21 $27Q \div 9$ **22** $42n \div 6$ **23** $9A \div 3$ **24** $36N \div 4$

25 $16r \div 4$ **26** $90t \div 9$ **27** $48T \div 4$ **28** $35a \div 5$

29 $80R \div 10$ **30** $12b \div 3$ **31** $a \times a$ **32** $c \times c$

33 $Q \times Q$ **34** $3c \times c$ **35** $4p \times p$ **36** $5d \times d$

37 $r \times 2r$ **38** $B \times B$ **39** $c \times 5c$ **40** $a \times 6a$

41 $2a \times 4b$ **42** $3y \times 6y$ **43** $7a \times 2a$ **44** $5t \times 5t$

E4. 4

Do the following multiplications and divisions.

1 $3a \times 2b$ **2** $6x \times 3y$ **3** $5p \times 2q$ **4** $7e \times 3e$

5 $8m \times 3n$ **6** $6c \times 9c$ **7** $3x \times 8x$ **8** $2B \times 8B$

9 $5P \times 9Q$ **10** $3v \times 12u$ **11** $8c \div 2$ **12** $15A \div 3$

13 $64p \div 8$ **14** $72x \div 9$ **15** $a \times b \times c$ **16** $3a \times 2b \times 2c$

17 $4x \times 3y \times 5z$ **18** $2a \times 6b \times 3c \times 2d$

In Questions **19** to **33** answer 'true' or 'false'.

19 $c \times d = cd$ **20** $n \times n = n^2$

21 $2n \times 3n = 5n^2$ **22** $a \times 3a = 3a^2$

23 $p + p = p^2$ **24** $3 \times a = a \times 3$

25 $8n \times 4n = 32n^2$ **26** $10a \div 2 = 5a$

27 $3c \times 12d = 36cd$ **28** $12p \div 3 = 9p$

29 $3a - a = 3$ **30** $4n + 4n = 8n^2$

31 $n \times n \times n = n^3$ **32** $a + a^2 = a^3$

33 $m \times 3 \times n = 3mn$

Simplify

34 $m \times -m$ **35** $2a \times -3b$ **36** $-4c \times 5d$ **37** $-2x \times -4y$

38 $-9y \div 3$ **39** $-6a \div -2$ **40** $-8P \div 4$ **41** $-6c \times -3d$

42 $8x \times -5y$ **43** $28q \div -4$ **44** $-9y \times 6$ **45** $3a \times -7a$

46 $-14x \div -2$ **47** $18a \times -3b$ **48** $-9P \times -6P$

(4B) **Negative numbers (see Unit 1)**

Work out

1. $-3 + 1$ **2.** $-8 - 2$ **3.** $-6 + 7$ **4.** $-9 + 3$ **5.** $2 - 10$

6. $-5 - -1$ **7.** $-10 - 3$ **8.** $-9 - -4$ **9.** $-9 - 4$ **10.** $-5 - -5$

11. -6×4 **12.** -8×-3 **13.** -6×-5 **14.** -6×3 **15.** 8×-2

16. $-8 \div 2$ **17.** $-24 \div -3$ **18.** $-36 \div 9$ **19.** $42 \div -7$ **20.** $-56 \div -8$

Multiplying out brackets

(a) Multiply out $2(3 + 5)$ means 2×3 add $2 \times 5 = 6 + 10 = 16$

(b) Multiply out $2(a + b)$ means $2 \times a$ add $2 \times b = 2a + 2b$

(c) Expand $3(5a - 4)$ means $3 \times 5a$ subtract $3 \times 4 = 15a - 12$

(d) Expand $a(b + c)$ means $a \times b$ add $a \times c = ab + ac$

(e) Multiply out $p(2q - 3)$ means $p \times 2q$ subtract $p \times 3 = 2pq - 3p$

(f) Expand $n(n + 2)$ means $n \times n$ add $n \times 2 = n^2 + 2n$

(g) Expand $5n(2n + 3)$ means $5n \times 2n$ add $5n \times 3 = 10n^2 + 15n$

M4. 5

Multiply out

1 $2(a + 3)$ **2** $8(2y - 1)$ **3** $6(4x - 2)$ **4** $5(3x + 4)$

5 $7(3x - 5)$ **6** $4(7y + 2)$ **7** $5(a - b)$ **8** $2(2a + b)$

9 $7(3x + y)$ **10** $3(x + 2y)$ **11** $6(3x + 2)$ **12** $4(p + q)$

13 $4(p + 2q)$ **14** $6(3a - 5b)$ **15** $9(4c + 8d)$ **16** $x(x + y)$

17 $x(2x + y)$ **18** $a(b - c)$ **19** $a(b + a)$ **20** $p(p - q)$

21 $c(2c + d)$ **22** $p(p + 3)$ **23** $a(a - 7)$ **24** $3a(a + 1)$

25 $5x(y + 2)$ **26** $3b(c + 2d)$ **27** $4a(a + 2b)$ **28** $3m(2m - 5n)$

29 $6a(4b - 8c)$ **30** $3x(2x + 3y)$

(a) Multiply out $-4(x - 2)$ means $-4 \times x$ and $-4 \times -2 = -4x + 8$

(b) Expand $-3(2a + 4)$ means $-3 \times 2a$ and $-3 \times 4 = -6a - 12$

(c) Expand $-a(a + b)$ means $-a \times a$ and $-a \times b = -a^2 - ab$

(d) Multiply out $-b(b - c)$ means $-b \times b$ and $-b \times -c = -b^2 + bc$

107

Expand

1 $-2(x + 6)$ **2** $-5(y - 3)$ **3** $-3(a - 2)$ **4** $-2(x + 4)$

5 $-5(c + 10)$ **6** $-2(3x - y)$ **7** $-4(3p - 5)$ **8** $-5(2a + 1)$

9 $-4(8b - 2)$ **10** $-3(2c + 4)$ **11** $-3(5a + 2)$ **12** $-6(3x - 3)$

13 $-4(5a - 6)$ **14** $3(3b - 7)$ **15** $7(1 - 2x)$ **16** $-a(b + c)$

17 $-e(f - g)$ **18** $-x(x - y)$ **19** $-p(2p + q)$ **20** $-y(3y + z)$

21 $-x(2x - y)$ **22** $-a(a + b)$ **23** $-m(m - n)$ **24** $-(3x - y)$

25 $-(2p + 5q)$ **26** $-3a(a + b)$ **27** $2b(3a - 2b)$ **28** $5x(3x - 2y)$

(a) Simplify $2(3n + 1) + 3n$ multiply out brackets first

$= 6n + 2 + 3n$ now collect like terms

Answer $= 9n + 2$

(b) Simplify $3(2a + 2) + 4(a + 1)$

$= 6a + 6 + 4a + 4$

Answer $= 10a + 10$

Simplify

1 $2(x + 3) + 5$ **2** $5(2x + 1) + 3$

3 $4(3x + 2) + 2x$ **4** $5(3x + 4) + 7x$

5 $9(2x + 3) - 14$ **6** $3(2a + 4) - 2a$

7 $6(4a + 3) - 8a$ **8** $9(3y + 2) - 6$

9 $5(a + 2) + 2(2a + 1)$ **10** $3(x + 4) + 6(x + 2)$

11 $6(x + 1) + 3(2x + 4)$

12 $5(2a + 3) + 4(a - 2)$

13 $3(4a + 8) + 2(a - 3)$

14 $7(2x + 3) + 4(3x + 1)$

15 $4(2d + 2) + 6(3d + 4)$

16 $6x + 9 + 3(4x + 2)$

17 $3a + 2(4a + 7) - 10$

18 $8(2x + 1) + 3(4x - 1)$

19 $6a + 3(2a + 4) + 2(5a + 4)$

20 $3x + 2(3x + 4) + 5(2x - 1)$

(a) Simplify $\underbrace{5(2a + 1) - 3(a - 2)}$

$= 10a + 5 - 3a + 6$

Note

$= 7a + 11$

(b) Simplify $\underbrace{8(x + 3) - 2(2x + 4)}$

$= 8x + 24 - 4x - 8$

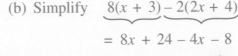

Note

$= 4x + 16$

E4. 6

Expand and simplify

1 $3(4a + 2) - 2(a - 2)$

2 $5(3x + 1) - 3(3x - 2)$

3 $6(2x + 3) - 4(2x + 2)$

4 $5(3a + 2) - 3(2a + 1)$

5 $3(4d + 1) - 2(6d - 5)$

6 $9y - 5(y + 2) - 3$

7 $11x + 2 - 3(2x - 5)$

8 $6a + 2(3a + 1) - 7 + 2a$

9 $9(x + 2) - 4 + 2(2 - 3x)$

10 $6(c + 3) - 2(2c - 4)$

11 $7(3a + 2) - 2(5a - 4)$

12 $8(c + 9) - 3(2c + 6)$

13 $5(2c + 6) - 4(c + 5)$

14 $8x - 4(x - 9) - 10$

15 $3a + 11 - 2(a + 3)$

16 $9(3a + 4) + 2a - 4(2a - 3)$

17 $15(n + m) - 6(2n - m)$

18 $8(2a + b) - 3(3a + 2b)$

19 $5(3x + 6) - 4(2x - 3)$

20 $8x + 6(2 - x) + 2(3x + 5)$

Multiplying out 2 brackets

Each term in one bracket must be multiplied by each term in the other bracket.

Consider $(a+b)(c+d)$

F	$(a+b)(c+d)$ multiply the <u>F</u>irst terms in each bracket	$\Rightarrow$ ac
O	$(a+b)(c+d)$ multiply the <u>O</u>uter terms in each bracket	$\Rightarrow$ $+\,ad$
I	$(a+b)(c+d)$ multiply the <u>I</u>nner terms in each bracket	$\Rightarrow$ $+\,bc$
L	$(a+b)(c+d)$ multiply the <u>L</u>ast terms in each bracket	$\Rightarrow$ $+\,bd$

First ⎫
Outer ⎪ follow this order
Inner ⎬ each time to make $\Rightarrow$ $(a+b)(c+d)\; = \; ac+ad+bc+bd$
Last ⎭ sure you do not
miss any terms

(a) Multiply out $(x+3)(x+5)$

$(x+3)(x+5)$

$\quad$ F $\quad$ O $\quad$ I $\quad$ L
$= (x^2)(+5x)(+3x)(+15)$

these middle 2 terms can be collected together

$= x^2 + 8x + 15$

(b) Expand $(x+4)(x+2)$

$(x+4)(x+2)$

$= x^2 + 2x + 4x + 8$
$= x^2 + 6x + 8$

M4. 7

1 Copy and complete the following

(a) $(x+3)(x+4)$

$= x^2 + 4x + \square + 12$

$= x^2 + \square + 12$

(b) $(x+1)(x+6)$

$= \square + 6x + x + \square$

$= \square + 7x + \square$

(c) $(x+9)(x+4)$

$= x^2 + \square + \square + 36$

$= x^2 + \square + 36$

Expand the following

2 $(x + 2)(x + 6)$ **3** $(p + 1)(p + 5)$ **4** $(a + 3)(a + 7)$

5 $(m + 2)(m + 8)$ **6** $(y + 3)(y + 6)$ **7** $(n + 1)(n + 1)$

Multiply out the following:

8 $(x + 7)(x + 3)$ **9** $(y + 4)(y + 5)$ **10** $(p + 3)(p + 10)$

11 $(a + 9)(a + 7)$ **12** $(f + 4)(f + 8)$ **13** $(y + 6)(y + 8)$

Find the area of each rectangle below

14

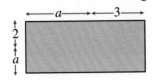

15

Expand   **16** $(x + 3)(x + 3)$ **17** $(x + 3)^2$ **18** $(x + 5)^2$

19 $(x + 8)^2$ **20** $(x + 2)^2$ **21** $(x + 9)^2$

(a) Expand $(x - 4)(x + 2)$

$(x - 4)(x + 2)$

$= x^2 + 2x - 4x - 8 = x^2 - 2x - 8$

(b) Expand $(x - 5)^2$

$(x - 5)(x - 5)$

$= x^2 - 5x - 5x + 25 = x^2 - 10x + 25$

E4. 7

1 Copy and complete the following

(a) $(x + 2)(x - 6)$

$= x^2 - \square + 2x - 12$

$= x^2 - \square - 12$

(b) $(a - 5)(a + 3)$

$= \square + 3a - 5a - \square$

$= \square - 2a - \square$

(c) $(m - 7)^2 = (m - 7)(m - 7)$

$= m^2 - \square - \square + \square$

$= m^2 - \square + \square$

Expand   **2** $(m + 3)(m - 1)$ **3** $(n - 5)(n + 2)$ **4** $(b - 8)(b + 3)$

5 $(x - 6)(x + 8)$ **6** $(c - 8)(c - 3)$ **7** $(q - 2)(q - 7)$

8 $(f - 2)(f - 10)$ **9** $(a + 9)(a - 4)$ **10** $(y - 4)(y - 9)$

11 $(x - 4)(x - 4)$ **12** $(x - 4)^2$ **13** $(x - 6)^2$

14 $(m - 1)^2$ **15** $(y - 10)^2$ **16** $(a - 8)^2$

17 $(2 + n)(n + 3)$ **18** $(x + 5)(6 + x)$ **19** $(y + 4)(3 - y)$

20 $(x + 1)^2 + (x + 3)^2$ **21** $(n + 4)^2 + (n - 2)^2$

111

For each Question below write out the decimals in order of size, starting with the smallest.

1. 0.04, 0.4, 0.35

2. 0.1, 0.09, 0.089

3. 0.04, 0.14, 0.2, 0.53

4. 1.2, 0.12, 0.21, 1.12

5. 2.4, 2.04, 0.85, 0.09

6. 0.73, 0.37, 0.703, 0.4, 0.137

7. 0.091, 0.19, 0.109, 0.901, 0.91

8. 0.86, 0.816, 0.608, 0.68, 0.628, 0.806

Common factors

🔑 Key Facts

We know that $3(a + b)$ is the same as $3a + 3b$ so $3a + 3b = 3(a + b)$

Consider

3 is *a factor* of both $3a$ and $3b$

so 3 is the *common factor* of $3a$ and $3b$

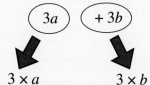

$3 \times a$ $3 \times b$

Common factors can be extracted from algebraic expressions.

Take out common factor 3.

$3a + 3b$ ➡ Write remaining terms in a bracket ➡ $3(a + b)$

Multiply out bracket to check you have the same expression you started with

This is called '*factorising*' $3a + 3b$

Examples

Factorise $7x - 7y$

$7x$ and $7y$ have common factor 7

so $7x - 7y = 7(x - y)$

Factorise $5a + 10b$

5 divides into $5a$ and $10b$

so $5a$ and $10b$ have common factor 5

so $5a + 10b = 5(a + 2b)$

Copy and complete

1 $6a + 15 = 3(2a + \boxed{})$

2 $9c + 6 = 3(3c + \boxed{})$

3 $5x - 15 = 5(x - \boxed{})$

4 $12a + 18 = 6(\boxed{} + 3)$

5 $15m + 20 = 5(\boxed{} + \boxed{})$

6 $7n - 35 = 7(\boxed{} - \boxed{})$

7 $8x + 32 = \boxed{}(x + \boxed{})$

8 $9x + 36 = 9(\boxed{} + \boxed{})$

9 $14a - 35 = 7(2a - \boxed{})$

10 $16n - 24 = 8(2n - \boxed{})$

11 $45x + 36 = \boxed{}(\boxed{} + \boxed{})$

12 $48a - 40 = \boxed{}(\boxed{} - \boxed{})$

Factorise the expressions below:

13 $8a + 10$

14 $6x + 27$

15 $5x - 20$

16 $6m + 42$

17 $25a - 35$

18 $16x - 4$

19 $27p - 18$

20 $18a + 24b$

21 $16x + 40y$

22 $14a - 21b$

23 $24m - 20n$

24 $21x + 28y$

25 $56a + 32b$

26 $20x - 10y$

27 $36x - 27y$

28 $72c + 40d$

29 $10a + 15b + 25c$

30 $6p + 9q + 3r$

31 $7x + 14y - 7z$

32 $9a - 9b - 21c$

33 $24m + 12n + 16p$

34 $42a + 35b - 14$

35 $18a - 27b + 36c$

36 $28x - 36y + 16$

Letters as well as numbers can be the common factors.

(a) Factorise $ab + ac$

ab and ac have common factor a

So $ab + ac = a(b + c)$ **multiply out to check the answer is correct**

(b) Factorise $5ac + 15bc$

$5ac$ and $15bc$ have common factor $5c$

so $5ac + 15bc = 5c(a + 3b)$

Factorise $4x^2 - 6x$

$4x^2$ and $6x$ have common factor $2x$

so $4x^2 - 6x = 2x(2x - 3)$

Copy and complete

1 $xy + xz = x(y + \boxed{})$

2 $ab - ac = a(\boxed{} - \boxed{})$

3 $x^2 + 6x = x(x + \boxed{})$

4 $5a + a^2 = a(5 + \boxed{})$

5 $3b^2 - 12b = 3b(\boxed{} - \boxed{})$

6 $cd + c^2 = c(\boxed{} + \boxed{})$

7 $3xy + 15xz = 3x(y + \boxed{})$

8 $8ab - 24bc = 8b(\boxed{} - \boxed{})$

9 $12x^2 - 8x = \boxed{}(3x - \boxed{})$

10 $6m^2 - m = \boxed{}(6m - \boxed{})$

Factorise the expressions below:

11 $ef + fg$

12 $p^2 + 3p$

13 $7a - a^2$

14 $x^2 - 8x$

15 $a^2 + 5a$

16 $2pq + 4pr$

17 $8ab - 12bc$

18 $6xy - 9yz$

19 $5x^2 - 15x$

20 $5st + 35s$

21 $8pr - 40pq$

22 $6ab + 4b$

23 $3a^2 + 8a$

24 $12x - 16x^2$

25 $x^2 + xy$

26 $3x^2 + 21xy$

27 $20ab - 50b$

28 $a^2b - a^2c$

29 $a^2 + abc$

30 $5x^2 - 6xy$

31 $20p^2 - 30pq$

32 $36abc - 16b^2$

33 $49x^2 + 42xy$

34 $63a^2 - 35ab$

USE YOUR MATHS! – Money for your holiday

Exchange rate

This is the amount of foreign money you will get in exchange for £1.

At the time of writing:

£1 = 1.45 euros (Europe)	£1 = 51.18 rubles (Russia)
£1 = 1.82 dollars (USA)	£1 = 19.84 pesos (Mexico)
£1 = 196 yen (Japan)	£1 = 6.84 riyals (Saudi Arabia)
£1 = 11.98 rand (South Africa)	£1 = 2.39 dollars (Australia)

Converting pounds into foreign money

> Multiply the number of pounds by the chosen exchange rate

Examples

£1 = 1.82 dollars (USA)

so £10 = 10 × 1.82 = 18.2 dollars

£1 = 51.18 rubles (Russia)

so £300 = 300 × 51.18 = 15354 rubles.

Converting foreign money into pounds

> Divide the foreign money by the chosen exchange rate

Examples

£1 = 196 yen (Japan)

4508 yen = 4508 ÷ 196 = £23

£1 = 1.45 euros

150 euros = 150 ÷ 1.45 = £103.448276

= £103.45 (to the nearest penny)

Beware!

When converting your money, the bank (or whatever organization you use) will charge you a fee. This is called the 'commission'.

Different organizations charge different amounts of commission. Always look around for the best deal.

TASK

Using the exchange rate at the start of this section, convert the following amount of money.

1   £200 into euros

2   £350 into pesos

3   £150 into Australian dollars

4   £900 into rand

5   300.3 American dollars into pounds

6   11904 pesos into pounds

7   13328 yen into pounds

8   £454 into riyals

9   1015 euros into pounds

10   17970 rand into pounds

11 A digital radio costs £164 in the UK. Sarah sees a
    similar digital radio for 31360 yen in Japan. In
    which country is the digital radio cheaper?

12 Jonathan was lucky enough to have two holidays last
    year, one in France and one in Australia. A can of
    cola was 1.16 euros in France and 1.68 dollars in
    Australia. In which country was the can of cola
    cheaper?

13 Candice comes back from holiday in Mexico with
    992 pesos. Shabina returns from holiday in the USA
    with 98.28 dollars. Who has more money left?

14 Stephen takes 547.2 riyals to a Bureau de Change to convert them into pounds.
    The Bureau de Change charges 4% commission. How much money does
    Stephen get back?

15 Maggie takes 2047.2 rubles to a bank to change them into pounds. The bank
    charges 3% commission. How much money does Maggie get back?

TEST YOURSELF ON UNIT 4

1. Substituting numbers for letters

Find the value of each expression below:

(a) $5a$ if $a = 3$ (b) $3x - 4$ if $x = 7$

(c) p^2 if $p = 9$ (d) $2(c + d)$ if $c = 3, d = 8$

(e) $a(3b + 4)$ if $a = 5, b = 3$ (f) $5 + 7a$ if $a = -2$

(g) $3b^2$ if $b = 2$

2. Using formulas

(a) $y = 6x - 1$ Find the value of y when $x = 3$

(b) $a = \dfrac{b}{4} + 6$ Find the value of a when $b = 20$

(c) $V = IR$ Find the value of V when $I = 6.2, R = 20.1$

(d) $v = u + at$ Find the value of v when $u = 10, a = 5, t = 7$

(e) $f = \dfrac{u + v}{u}$ Find the value of f when $u = 0.6, v = 3.6$

3. Collecting like terms

Simplify

(a) $3x + 7y + 3x$ (b) $9a + 6b - 4a$ (c) $4p + 2 + 3p$

(d) $8m - 2m + 3n + n$ (e) $5 + 2x - 2 + 3x$ (f) $6x - 5x$

(g) $3p + 2q - q$ (h) $x^2 + x^2 + x^2$ (i) $4a + 2ab + 3ab$

4. Multiplying and dividing terms

Simplify

(a) $5a \times 3$ (b) $7 \times 2c$ (c) $A \times A$ (d) $3b \times 2b$

(e) $6p \div 2$ (f) $45b \div 5$ (g) $6m \times 4n$ (h) $12F \div 3$

5. Multiplying out brackets

Expand (this means 'multiply out')

(a) $3(x + 7)$ (b) $6(2a - b)$ (c) $5(x + 5y)$ (d) $p(q + 6)$

(e) $a(2a - 5)$ (f) $b(2b + 3c)$ (g) $3x(y - 2x)$ (h) $-4(2a - b)$

(i) $(x + 3)(x + 7)$ (j) $(y + 2)(y - 6)$ (k) $(p - 2)^2$

6. Multiplying out brackets and collecting like terms

(a) $5(a + 2) + 3$ (b) $5(2x + 4) - 3x$

(c) $3(x + 2) + 5(x + 6)$ (d) $4(2m + 3) + 5(3m + 1)$

(e) $3(6a + 3) - 2(2a - 5)$ (f) $4x - 3(x - 2)$

7. Extracting common factors

(a) $5x + 15$ (b) $8a - 24$ (c) $35p - 21$ (d) $4a + 10b - 8c$

(e) $cd + ce$ (f) $x^2 - 4xy$ (g) $6pq - 10qr$ (h) $5a^2 + 30ab$

Mixed examination questions

1 Use the formula $v = u + at$

to calculate v when $u = 5$, $a = 3$ and $t = 10$.

2 (a) Simplify (i) $5c + 2c - 3c$ (ii) $5p - 8r + 12r - 6p$

(b) Find the value of

(i) $5x + 2y$ when $x = 3$ and $y = 6$.

(ii) $4g - 2h$ when $g = 2$ and $h = -4$. (EDEXCEL)

3 (a) Simplify $3a - 2a + a$.

(b) What is the value of $x^2 + 5$ when x is -3? (AQA)

4 Tom spilt some coffee on his Maths work.

It had already been marked correct.

Part of the work could no longer be seen.

$3x + 2y - 4z + \qquad\qquad = 5x + y$

Work out the expression that has been covered by the spill. (OCR)

5 (a) Simplify $2x - x + 1$.

(b) Find the value of $3x + y^2$ when $x = -2$ and $y = 3$. (AQA)

6 (a) In this question $a = 5$, $b = -4$ and $c = 3$.

Work out (i) $a^2 + b$ (ii) $\dfrac{ab}{2c - b}$

(b) Multiply out the brackets $7(2x + 3y)$. (OCR)

7 Simplify

(a) $x + x + x$

(b) $2a + 4b + a - 2b$

(c) Expand $3(a + 2)$

(d) Expand and simplify $2(x - 1) + 3(2x + 1)$ (EDEXCEL)

8 (a) Simplify   (i) $5p + 3q - 4q$ (ii) $3x \times 4y$

(b) Multiply out   (i) $5(3h - 2)$ (ii) $-(3r - 4)$ (EDEXCEL)

9 This is an approximate rule to change a temperature in degree Celsius (C), into one in degrees Fahrenheit (F):

Double the Celsius temperature then add 30

(a) Write this approximate rule as a formula for F in terms of C.

(b) Use your formula, or otherwise, to find

(i) F when $C = 54$ (ii) C when $F = 54$ (CCEA)

10 Multiply out the brackets and simplify this expression.

$3(2x + 3) + 2(4x - 1)$ (OCR)

11 Factorise   (i) $10x + 15$ (ii) $x^2 - 3x$ (OCR)

12 Factorise $a^2 + 3a$.   (AQA)

13

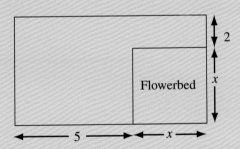

The diagram represents a garden in the shape of a rectangle.

All measurements are given in metres.

The garden has a flowerbed in one corner.

The flowerbed is a square of side x.

(a) Write down an expression, in terms of x, for the shortest side of the garden.

(b) Find an expression, in terms of x, for the perimeter of the garden. Give your answer in its simplest form.   (EDEXCEL)

In this unit you will learn how to:

– write one number as a fraction of another number

– find a fraction of a number

– convert improper fractions and mixed numbers

– add and subtract fractions

– multiply fractions

– divide fractions

– ⟨USE YOUR MATHS!⟩ – Mobile phones

One number as a fraction of another number

M5. 1

1 Which of these squares are split into quarters?

(a) (b) (c) (d)

2 What fraction of each of these shapes is red?

(a) (b) (c) (d)

(e) (f) (g) (h)

3 In a class of 33 students, 18 are girls.

    (a) What fraction of the class are girls?

    (b) What fraction of the class are boys?

4 What fraction of these people have spiky hair?

5 In a class of 30 students, 25 are right-handed. What fraction are left-handed? (Try and cancel your answer)

6 What fraction of these shapes are squares?

7 2, 3 and 5 are prime numbers.

What fraction of these numbers are prime?

8	2	5	6	4	5	2
6	8	4	4	2	9	3
9	8	9	3	6	4	8

8 What fraction of £1 is:

    (a) 10p   (b) 25p   (c) 40p   (d) 3p   (e) 65p   (f) 48p   *Try to cancel your answers*

9 What fraction of the numbers from zero to ninety-nine contain the number 8?

10 Find $\frac{1}{4}$ of: (a) 12   (b) 28   (c) 52   (d) 100

11 Find $\frac{1}{3}$ of: (a) 15   (b) 27   (c) 24   (d) 60

12 Find $\frac{1}{5}$ of: (a) 15   (b) 40   (c) 60   (d) 100

Work out

13 $\frac{1}{10}$ of £70   **14** $\frac{1}{7}$ of £49   **15** $\frac{1}{8}$ of 48 g   **16** $\frac{2}{3}$ of 12

17 $\frac{3}{4}$ of 16   **18** $\frac{3}{5}$ of 40   **19** $\frac{4}{7}$ of 21   **20** $\frac{7}{10}$ of 50

21 $\frac{2}{3}$ of these sheep are sold.

How many sheep are sold?

22 The petrol tank of a car holds 60 litres. How much petrol is in the tank when it is $\frac{3}{5}$ full?

23 $\frac{9}{10}$ of your body is made up of water.

Terri weighs 70 kg. How much of her body is water?

Work these out. You may **use a calculator** if you need to:

24 $\frac{3}{4}$ of 24   **25** $\frac{3}{4}$ of £64   **26** $\frac{2}{9}$ of £378   **27** $\frac{2}{3}$ of 1275 m

28 $\frac{3}{5}$ of 270   **29** $\frac{2}{3}$ of £144   **30** $\frac{3}{8}$ of £4976   **31** $\frac{1}{8}$ of 12 litres

32 $\frac{2}{5}$ of 40   **33** $\frac{5}{8}$ of 112 cm   **34** $\frac{5}{7}$ of 175 kg   **35** $\frac{1}{10}$ of £75

A TV costs £440. In a sale $\frac{3}{8}$ of the price is knocked off.

How much does the TV cost now?

$\frac{3}{8}$ of 440 = (440 ÷ 8) × 3 = 55 × 3 = £165. 'Knockoff' £165.

TV costs 440 − 165 = £275

M5. 1

Work out

1 $\frac{3}{4}$ of 44   **2** $\frac{3}{7}$ of 63   **3** $\frac{5}{6}$ of 18   **4** $\frac{4}{5}$ of 125

5 Jenny earns £36 for her Saturday job. Jenny got $\frac{1}{3}$ extra as a Christmas bonus.

How much money does Jenny get in total?

6 A packet of jelly tots has $\frac{3}{5}$ extra.

If a packet normally has 45 g in it, how much does it weigh now?

122

7   Sofa normal price £320
        Sale
        $\frac{3}{8}$ off!

How much does the sofa cost in the sale?

8   Jesse's new jeans are 96 cm long when she buys them. After washing they shrink to $\frac{7}{8}$ of their previous length. What is the new length of the jeans?

9   Dom has £28. He spends $\frac{3}{4}$ of his money on a Christmas present. How much money does he have left?

10 Here are calculations with letters. Put the answers in order of size, smallest first. Write down the letters to make a word.

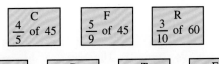

C
$\frac{4}{5}$ of 45

F
$\frac{5}{9}$ of 45

R
$\frac{3}{10}$ of 60

E
$\frac{3}{4}$ of 36

P
$\frac{2}{7}$ of 21

T
$\frac{7}{8}$ of 48

E
$\frac{5}{6}$ of 18

11 Ollie gets £96 for Christmas. He spends $\frac{1}{2}$ of it on clothes and $\frac{3}{8}$ of it on music.

How much money does Ollie have left?

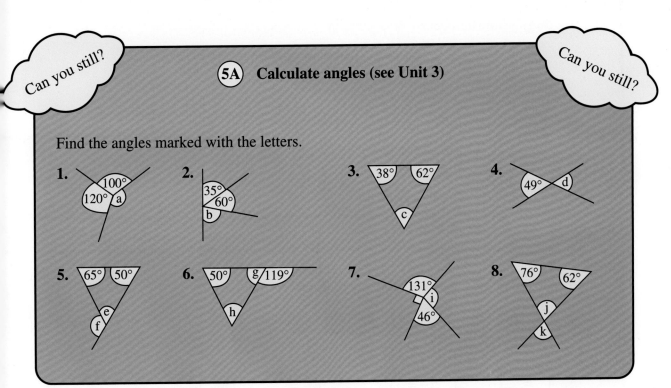

Can you still?   **5A**   **Calculate angles (see Unit 3)**   Can you still?

Find the angles marked with the letters.

1. 100° 120° a

2. 35° 60° b

3. 38° 62° c

4. 49° d

5. 65° 50° e f

6. 50° g 119° h

7. 131° i 46°

8. 76° 62° j k

Improper fractions and mixed numbers

Change the following improper fractions to mixed numbers.

1 ⊘ ⊘ ⊘ ⊘ $\dfrac{7}{2}$ **2** ⊛ ⊛ ⊛ $\dfrac{13}{6}$

3 ⊕ ⊕ ⊕ $\dfrac{11}{4}$ **4** ⊘ ⊘ ⊘ ⊘ $\dfrac{11}{3}$

5 $\dfrac{9}{4} = 2\dfrac{\square}{4}$ **6** $\dfrac{15}{7} = \square\dfrac{\square}{7}$ **7** $\dfrac{25}{8} = \square\dfrac{\square}{8}$ **8** $\dfrac{7}{4} = \square\dfrac{\square}{4}$

9 $\dfrac{20}{7}$ **10** $\dfrac{19}{9}$ **11** $\dfrac{5}{2}$ **12** $\dfrac{35}{6}$ **13** $\dfrac{23}{3}$ **14** $\dfrac{17}{2}$

15 $\dfrac{41}{8}$ **16** $\dfrac{29}{5}$ **17** $\dfrac{17}{6}$ **18** $\dfrac{29}{9}$ **19** $\dfrac{44}{5}$ **20** $\dfrac{27}{4}$

Change $2\dfrac{3}{8}$ to an improper fraction.

Multiply whole number by denominator $2 \times 8 = 16$

Add the numerator. $16 + 3 = 19$

Put sum over denominator. $\dfrac{19}{8}$

$2\left(= \dfrac{16}{8}\right) + \dfrac{3}{8}$ $2\dfrac{3}{8} = \dfrac{19}{8}$

Change the following mixed numbers to improper fractions.

1 ⊘ ⊘ ⊘ $2\dfrac{1}{3}$ **2** ⊘ ⊘ ⊘ ⊘ $3\dfrac{1}{2}$

3 $4\dfrac{3}{4} = \dfrac{19}{\square}$ **4** $5\dfrac{2}{3} = \dfrac{17}{\square}$ **5** $4\dfrac{1}{2} = \dfrac{\square}{2}$ **6** $5\dfrac{3}{4} = \dfrac{\square}{4}$

124

7 $6\frac{1}{3}$ **8** $3\frac{7}{8}$ **9** $4\frac{2}{3}$ **10** $5\frac{3}{5}$ **11** $3\frac{2}{9}$ **12** $4\frac{3}{7}$

13 $8\frac{3}{4}$ **14** $7\frac{4}{9}$ **15** $9\frac{5}{7}$ **16** $6\frac{2}{5}$ **17** $8\frac{6}{7}$ **18** $5\frac{3}{8}$

Can you still?

Can you still?

5B **Find angles in isosceles and equilateral triangles (see Unit 3)**

Find the angles marked with the letters.

1.

2.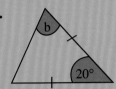

3.

4.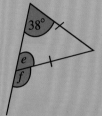

5.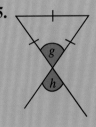

6.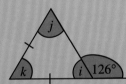

7.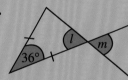

8.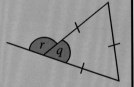

Adding and subtracting fractions

(a) $\frac{1}{7} + \frac{2}{7} = \frac{3}{7}$ ⟶ add the numerators (top numbers)
⟶ denominator (bottom number) stays same.

(b) $\frac{3}{5} - \frac{2}{5} = \frac{1}{5}$ ⟶ subtract the numerators
⟶ denominator says same

(c) $\frac{1}{5} + \frac{1}{10} = \frac{2}{10} + \frac{1}{10} = \frac{3}{10}$ The denominators must be the same before adding.

(d) $\frac{3}{4} - \frac{1}{6} = \frac{9}{12} - \frac{2}{12} = \frac{7}{12}$ $\overset{\times 3}{\frac{3}{4}} = \frac{9}{12}$ and $\overset{\times 2}{\frac{1}{6}} = \frac{2}{12}$
   $\underset{\times 3}{}$ $\underset{\times 2}{}$

125

Work out

1. $\dfrac{2}{5} + \dfrac{1}{5}$ 2. $\dfrac{2}{7} + \dfrac{3}{7}$ 3. $\dfrac{5}{7} + \dfrac{1}{7}$ 4. $\dfrac{2}{9} + \dfrac{5}{9}$

5. $\dfrac{3}{8} + \dfrac{3}{8}$ 6. $\dfrac{3}{10} + \dfrac{2}{10}$ 7. $\dfrac{5}{7} - \dfrac{3}{7}$ 8. $\dfrac{10}{11} - \dfrac{7}{11}$

9. $\dfrac{11}{20} - \dfrac{3}{20}$ 10. $\dfrac{9}{10} - \dfrac{2}{10}$ 11. $\dfrac{8}{9} - \dfrac{5}{9}$ 12. $\dfrac{5}{8} - \dfrac{3}{8}$

13. Add $\dfrac{2}{11}$ onto: (a) $\dfrac{1}{11}$ (b) $\dfrac{3}{11}$ (c) $\dfrac{6}{11}$ (d) $\dfrac{7}{11}$ (e) $\dfrac{8}{11}$

14. Subtract $\dfrac{2}{9}$ from: (a) $\dfrac{7}{9}$ (b) $\dfrac{4}{9}$ (c) $\dfrac{8}{9}$ (d) $\dfrac{3}{9}$ (e) $\dfrac{5}{9}$

In Questions 15 to 17, which answer is the odd one out?

15. (a) $\dfrac{3}{7} + \dfrac{1}{7}$ (b) $\dfrac{6}{7} - \dfrac{2}{7}$ (c) $\dfrac{2}{7} + \dfrac{1}{7}$

16. (a) $\dfrac{9}{10} - \dfrac{2}{10}$ (b) $\dfrac{3}{10} + \dfrac{6}{10}$ (c) $\dfrac{3}{10} + \dfrac{4}{10}$

17. (a) $\dfrac{3}{5} + \dfrac{1}{5}$ (b) $\dfrac{4}{5} - \dfrac{1}{5}$ (c) $\dfrac{2}{5} + \dfrac{2}{5}$

Copy and complete Questions 18 to 20

18. $\dfrac{1}{5} + \dfrac{2}{3}$

$= \dfrac{3}{15} + \dfrac{\square}{15}$

$= \dfrac{\square}{15}$

19. $\dfrac{3}{4} - \dfrac{2}{7}$

$= \dfrac{\square}{28} - \dfrac{\square}{28}$

$= \dfrac{\square}{28}$

20. $\dfrac{3}{8} + \dfrac{3}{10}$

$= \dfrac{\square}{40} + \dfrac{\square}{40}$

$= \dfrac{\square}{\square}$

Work out

21. $\dfrac{1}{3} + \dfrac{2}{15}$ 22. $\dfrac{5}{8} - \dfrac{1}{4}$ 23. $\dfrac{4}{5} + \dfrac{1}{10}$ 24. $\dfrac{1}{6} + \dfrac{2}{3}$

25. $\dfrac{2}{5} + \dfrac{3}{10}$ 26. $\dfrac{5}{8} - \dfrac{1}{2}$ 27. $\dfrac{1}{10} - \dfrac{1}{20}$ 28. $\dfrac{7}{8} - \dfrac{1}{2}$

29. $\dfrac{1}{3} - \dfrac{1}{4}$ 30. $\dfrac{1}{2} + \dfrac{1}{3}$ 31. $\dfrac{2}{3} + \dfrac{1}{4}$ 32. $\dfrac{3}{4} - \dfrac{1}{3}$

Copy and complete Questions 33 to 35 by changing to improper fractions

33 $1\dfrac{1}{2} + \dfrac{1}{4}$

$= \dfrac{\boxed{}}{2} + \dfrac{1}{4}$

$= \dfrac{\boxed{}}{4} + \dfrac{1}{4}$

$= \dfrac{\boxed{}}{4} = \boxed{}\dfrac{\boxed{}}{4}$

34 $2\dfrac{1}{4} + \dfrac{2}{3}$

$= \dfrac{\boxed{}}{4} + \dfrac{2}{3}$

$= \dfrac{\boxed{}}{12} + \dfrac{\boxed{}}{12}$

$= \dfrac{\boxed{}}{12} = \boxed{}\dfrac{\boxed{}}{12}$

35 $2\dfrac{1}{5} + 1\dfrac{3}{4}$

$= \dfrac{\boxed{}}{5} + \dfrac{\boxed{}}{4}$

$= \dfrac{\boxed{}}{20} + \dfrac{\boxed{}}{20}$

$= \dfrac{\boxed{}}{20} = \boxed{}\dfrac{\boxed{}}{20}$

Work out

36 $2\dfrac{1}{3} + \dfrac{5}{8}$

37 $1\dfrac{7}{8} + \dfrac{5}{6}$

38 $5\dfrac{1}{2} + \dfrac{3}{5}$

39 $2\dfrac{1}{3} + 1\dfrac{1}{2}$

40 Match each Question to the correct answer:

A $\dfrac{3}{5} + 1\dfrac{1}{10}$

B $1\dfrac{7}{8} + \dfrac{3}{4}$

C $1\dfrac{7}{10} + \dfrac{1}{4}$

P $2\dfrac{5}{8}$

Q $1\dfrac{19}{20}$

R $1\dfrac{7}{10}$

S $1\dfrac{4}{15}$

41 Work out

(a) $1\dfrac{1}{2} - \dfrac{3}{8}$

(b) $1\dfrac{9}{10} - \dfrac{2}{5}$

(c) $2\dfrac{1}{10} - \dfrac{2}{3}$

(d) $3\dfrac{1}{4} - 1\dfrac{1}{2}$

42

A

? km   B   C

$3\dfrac{2}{3}$ km

The total distance along the road from A to C is $8\dfrac{1}{4}$ km.

What is the distance between A and B along the road?

43 Work out

(a) $2\dfrac{3}{4} - \dfrac{2}{5}$

(b) $3\dfrac{1}{4} - 1\dfrac{1}{10}$

(c) $3\dfrac{3}{5} - 1\dfrac{1}{2}$

127

A The diagram shows that $\dfrac{1}{2}$ of $\dfrac{1}{3}$ = $\dfrac{1}{6}$.

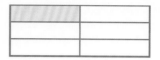

We say $\dfrac{1}{2} \times \dfrac{1}{3} = \dfrac{1}{6}$

To multiply fractions, multiply the numerators and multiply the denominators

(a) $\dfrac{1}{3} \times \dfrac{2}{5} = \dfrac{2}{15}$ (b) $\dfrac{1}{2} \times \dfrac{1}{5} = \dfrac{1}{10}$ (c) $\dfrac{1}{2} \times \dfrac{2}{3} = \dfrac{2}{6} = \dfrac{1}{3}$ by cancelling

(d) $1\dfrac{1}{5} \times \dfrac{2}{3}$ (e) $\dfrac{2}{15} \times 20$ (f) $2\dfrac{1}{2} \times 3\dfrac{2}{5}$

$= \dfrac{2\;\cancel{6}}{5} \times \dfrac{2}{\cancel{3}_1}$ (cancel) $= \dfrac{2}{\underset{3}{\cancel{15}}} \times \dfrac{\overset{4}{\cancel{20}}}{1}$ $= \dfrac{1\,\cancel{5}}{2} \times \dfrac{17}{\cancel{5}_1}$

$= \dfrac{4}{5}$ $= \dfrac{8}{3} = 2\dfrac{2}{3}$ $= \dfrac{17}{2} = 8\dfrac{1}{2}$

B How many halves are there in 3?

Answer: 6

So: $3 \div \dfrac{1}{2} = 6$

Notice that $3 \times \dfrac{2}{1} = \dfrac{6}{1} = 6$

To divide two fractions, turn the second fraction upside-down and then multiply

(a) $\dfrac{1}{2} \div \dfrac{3}{4} = \dfrac{1}{2} \times \dfrac{4}{3} = \dfrac{4}{6} = \dfrac{2}{3}$

(b) $\dfrac{2}{9} \div \dfrac{3}{5} = \dfrac{2}{9} \times \dfrac{5}{3} = \dfrac{10}{27}$

(c) $2\dfrac{1}{2} \div \dfrac{2}{3} = \dfrac{5}{2} \times \dfrac{3}{2} = \dfrac{15}{4} = 3\dfrac{3}{4}$

Work out

1 (a) $\frac{1}{2}$ of $\frac{1}{4}$ (b) $\frac{1}{3}$ of $\frac{1}{3}$ (c) $\frac{1}{4}$ of $\frac{1}{3}$ (d) $\frac{1}{2}$ of $\frac{1}{6}$

2  Draw this rectangle and put in more lines to show that $\frac{1}{4}$ of $\frac{1}{3} = \frac{1}{12}$

3 (a) $\frac{1}{5}$ of $\frac{1}{6}$ (b) $\frac{1}{3}$ of $\frac{1}{5}$ (c) $\frac{1}{6}$ of $\frac{1}{4}$ (d) $\frac{1}{4}$ of $\frac{1}{5}$

4 (a) $\frac{1}{2}$ of $\frac{3}{4}$ (b) $\frac{2}{3}$ of $\frac{3}{4}$ (c) $\frac{1}{4}$ of $\frac{2}{3}$ (d) $\frac{1}{2}$ of $\frac{2}{5}$

(cancel your answers where possible)

5 (a) $\frac{4}{5}$ of $\frac{2}{7}$ (b) $\frac{1}{5}$ of $\frac{5}{6}$ (c) $\frac{1}{3}$ of $\frac{3}{4}$ (d) $\frac{2}{3}$ of $\frac{3}{5}$

Work out the following Questions (you must cancel your answers where possible):

6 $\frac{2}{3} \times \frac{1}{7}$ **7** $\frac{1}{9} \times \frac{1}{10}$ **8** $\frac{3}{4} \times \frac{1}{5}$ **9** $\frac{5}{7} \times \frac{14}{15}$

10 $\frac{1}{3} \times \frac{1}{8}$ **11** $\frac{2}{3} \times \frac{1}{8}$ **12** $\frac{3}{4} \times \frac{2}{3}$ **13** $\frac{2}{9} \times \frac{3}{8}$

14 $\frac{1}{9} \times \frac{1}{4}$ **15** $\frac{3}{4} \times \frac{1}{9}$ **16** $\frac{3}{5} \times \frac{5}{9}$ **17** $\frac{7}{9} \times \frac{3}{14}$

18 A house contains 40 pieces of furniture. A family take $\frac{7}{10}$ of the furniture to their new house.
Work out $\frac{7}{10}$ of 40.

19 Copy and complete the Questions below:

(a) $\frac{3}{8} \times 16 = \frac{3}{\underset{1}{\cancel{8}}} \times \frac{\overset{2}{\cancel{16}}}{1} = \frac{\square}{\square} = \square$

(b) $\frac{2}{3} \times 6 = \frac{2}{3} \times \frac{6}{\square} = \frac{\square}{\square} = \square$

Work out

20 $\frac{2}{5} \times 20$ **21** $\frac{3}{4} \times 20$ **22** $\frac{1}{8} \times 6$

Copy and complete Questions ㉓ to ㉕.

㉓ $\dfrac{3}{4} \times 1\dfrac{2}{5}$

$= \dfrac{3}{4} \times \dfrac{\square}{5}$

$= \dfrac{\square}{20}$

$= \square\dfrac{\square}{20}$

㉔ $3\dfrac{1}{3} \times 2\dfrac{1}{2}$

$= \dfrac{\square}{3} \times \dfrac{\square}{2}$

$= \dfrac{\square}{3} \times \dfrac{5}{1}$ (cancel)

$= \dfrac{\square}{3} = \square\dfrac{\square}{3}$

㉕ $\dfrac{1}{20} \times 15$

$= \dfrac{1}{20} \times \dfrac{15}{1}$

$= \dfrac{1}{4} \times \dfrac{\square}{1}$ (cancel)

$= \dfrac{\square}{4}$

Work out

㉖ $3\dfrac{1}{2} \times \dfrac{8}{21}$

㉗ $1\dfrac{1}{4} \times \dfrac{3}{5}$

㉘ $1\dfrac{2}{3} \times 1\dfrac{1}{5}$

㉙ $3\dfrac{1}{2} \times 1\dfrac{1}{21}$

㉚ $2\dfrac{1}{4} \times 3\dfrac{1}{5}$

㉛ $4\dfrac{1}{2} \times 2\dfrac{2}{3}$

㉜ $\dfrac{2}{5} \times 1\dfrac{1}{3}$

㉝ $1\dfrac{1}{9} \times 5\dfrac{2}{5}$

㉞ Match each Question to the correct answer:

A $\boxed{2\dfrac{1}{2} \times \dfrac{2}{5}}$

B $\boxed{1\dfrac{1}{2} \times 1\dfrac{1}{3}}$

C $\boxed{1\dfrac{3}{4} \times 1\dfrac{1}{2}}$

P $\boxed{2}$

Q $\boxed{2\dfrac{5}{8}}$

R $\boxed{1}$

Copy and complete Questions ㉟ to ㊲:

㉟ $\dfrac{1}{4} \div \dfrac{1}{3}$

$= \dfrac{1}{4} \times \dfrac{\square}{1}$

$= \dfrac{\square}{4}$

㊱ $\dfrac{2}{7} \div \dfrac{5}{9}$

$= \dfrac{2}{7} \times \dfrac{\square}{5}$

$= \dfrac{\square}{\square}$

㊲ $\dfrac{1}{8} \div \dfrac{5}{7}$

$= \dfrac{1}{8} \times \dfrac{\square}{5}$

$= \dfrac{\square}{\square}$

Work out

㊳ $9 \div \dfrac{1}{3}$

㊴ $2 \div \dfrac{1}{2}$

㊵ $8 \div \dfrac{1}{4}$

㊶ $6 \div \dfrac{1}{5}$

㊷ $1 \div \dfrac{1}{10}$

㊸ $12 \div \dfrac{1}{3}$

㊹ $3 \div \dfrac{1}{2}$

㊺ $7 \div \dfrac{1}{9}$

46 Match each Question to the correct answer:

A $\dfrac{1}{6} \div \dfrac{3}{4}$

B $\dfrac{3}{8} \div \dfrac{5}{7}$

C $\dfrac{1}{6} \div \dfrac{3}{8}$

?

P $\dfrac{21}{40}$ S $\dfrac{21}{13}$

Q $\dfrac{4}{9}$

R $\dfrac{2}{9}$

Work out

47 $1\dfrac{1}{5} \div \dfrac{3}{10}$ **48** $4\dfrac{1}{2} \div \dfrac{7}{10}$ **49** $2\dfrac{1}{10} \div 3\dfrac{1}{5}$ **50** $5\dfrac{3}{8} \div 2\dfrac{1}{2}$

51 $2\dfrac{5}{8} \div \dfrac{1}{2}$ **52** $1\dfrac{2}{5} \div 1\dfrac{3}{20}$ **53** $1\dfrac{1}{5} \div 2\dfrac{1}{10}$ **54** $2\dfrac{9}{20} \div 5\dfrac{3}{10}$

55 $3\dfrac{1}{2} \div \dfrac{5}{16}$ **56** $3\dfrac{3}{5} \div 1\dfrac{7}{10}$ **57** $1\dfrac{1}{3} \div \dfrac{5}{6}$ **58** $6\dfrac{5}{6} \div 2\dfrac{1}{3}$

59 A recipe for a cake uses $\dfrac{2}{3}$ of a pound of sugar. How many cakes can be made from 6 pounds of sugar?

60 A farmer has $37\dfrac{1}{2}$ kg of potatoes. He packs them into $2\dfrac{1}{2}$ kg bags. How many bags of potatoes will the farmer have?

USE YOUR MATHS! – Mobile phones

1 Do you have a mobile phone?

2 If yes, which one?

3 Why did you choose this phone?

4 When do you use your phone most often?

| Monday to Friday (during the day) | or | Monday to Friday (during the evening) | or | At the weekend |

5 How many minutes do you spend on the phone per day?

| 0 | or | 1–5 | or | 6–15 | or | 16–30 | or | 31–60 | or | more than 60 |

6 How many texts do you send per day?

 0 or 1–5 or 6–10 or 11–15 or more than 15

7 What are the advantages and disadvantages of having a mobile phone?

8 Collect the above class data together with your teacher. Discuss the main findings.

Mobile phone bills

Contracts

You often pay a fixed monthly amount which allows you a certain number of minutes of phone calls and a certain number of text messages. You may have to pay extra if you exceed your limit.

Pay As You Go

You pay money in advance (sometimes by buying cards which allow you a certain amount of money on your phone). As soon as you have used up all your money, you have to buy more phone credit in advance.

Remember

Text messages are usually cheaper to send than making phone calls.

The best deal?

A tariff is a way of paying to use a mobile phone. The best tariff depends on how many minutes you use your phone for and what time of the day you use the phone.

Task

Compare these two tariffs.

| TARIFF P |
| 4p per minute |
| anytime |

| TARIFF Q |
| £9 per month |
| plus 1p per minute anytime |

The best choice depends on how many minutes are used.

1 20 minutes on tariff P would cost 20 × 4p = 80p. Copy and complete this table for tariff P.

minutes	0	20	40	100	200	300	400
cost (£)	0	0.80	1.60				

132

2 (a) Copy the axes opposite onto squared paper.

   (b) Plot points from the tariff P table and join them up to make a straight line.

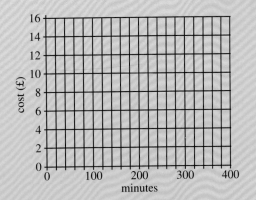

3 20 minutes on tariff Q would cost £9, then add on (20 × 1p) which is £0.20. 20 minutes cost £9.20.

   Copy and complete this table for tariff Q.

minutes	0	50	100	200	300	400
cost (£)	9					

4 Plot points from the tariff Q table using the *same axes* as before. Join them up to make a straight line.

   Your graph should look like this.

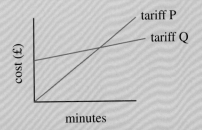

5 After how many minutes do the 2 lines cross?

6 What is the cost on both tariffs when the 2 lines cross?

7 If the number of minutes you use your mobile phone is less than your answer to Question **5**, which tariff is cheaper for you?

8 If the number of minutes you use your mobile phone is more than your answer to Question **5**, which tariff is cheaper for you?

9 Compare these two tariffs.

   | TARIFF Y £5 per month plus 2p per minute | | TARIFF Z 4.5p per minute anytime |

   (a) Repeat Questions **1** to **4** for these new tariffs.

   (b) After how many minutes is the cost the same for both tariffs?

   (c) Which tariff would you advise if you use your mobile phone for 150 minutes?

   (d) Which tariff would you advise if you use your mobile phone for 320 minutes?

133

TEST YOURSELF ON UNIT 5

---

1. Writing one number as a fraction of another number

(a) There are 29 people on a bus. 17 are women. What fraction of people on the bus are women?

(b) There are 11 animals waiting to be seen by a vet. 5 of the animals are dogs, the rest are cats. What fraction of the animals are cats?

(c) 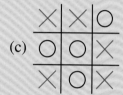 What fraction of these noughts and crosses are the crosses?

(d) What fraction of the days of the week begin with the letter T?

---

2. Finding a fraction of a number

Find

(a) $\frac{1}{3}$ of £18   (b) $\frac{1}{8}$ of £24   (c) $\frac{2}{3}$ of £21   (d) $\frac{5}{6}$ of 42 kg

(e)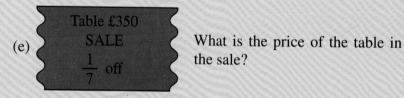

Table £350
SALE
$\frac{1}{7}$ off

What is the price of the table in the sale?

(f) Geena earns £300 each week. One week she gets paid $\frac{3}{10}$ extra for overtime. How much money does she get paid that week?

---

3. Converting improper fractions and mixed numbers

Change the following improper fractions to mixed numbers.

(a) $\frac{23}{4}$ (b) $\frac{9}{2}$ (c) $\frac{17}{5}$ (d) $\frac{32}{5}$

Change the following mixed numbers to improper fractions.

(e) $2\frac{1}{4}$ (f) $5\frac{2}{3}$ (g) $3\frac{2}{7}$ (h) $4\frac{3}{8}$

4. Adding and subtracting fractions

Work out

(a) $\dfrac{3}{7} + \dfrac{2}{7}$ (b) $\dfrac{4}{7} - \dfrac{1}{5}$ (c) $\dfrac{1}{4} + \dfrac{1}{3}$ (d) $\dfrac{3}{7} + \dfrac{2}{5}$

(e) $2\dfrac{1}{2} + \dfrac{3}{5}$ (f) $1\dfrac{7}{8} - \dfrac{3}{4}$ (g) $\dfrac{5}{6} + 2\dfrac{1}{4}$ (h) $2\dfrac{1}{3} + 1\dfrac{3}{4}$

5. Multiplying fractions

Work out

(a) $\dfrac{1}{3}$ of $\dfrac{1}{8}$ (b) $\dfrac{2}{5} \times \dfrac{1}{3}$ (c) $\dfrac{2}{7} \times \dfrac{3}{4}$ (d) $\dfrac{3}{8} \times \dfrac{4}{5}$

(e) $\dfrac{10}{11} \times \dfrac{22}{30}$ (f) $3\dfrac{2}{3} \times 1\dfrac{4}{5}$ (g) $\dfrac{8}{9} \times 12$ (h) $4\dfrac{3}{4} \times 3\dfrac{1}{5}$

6. Dividing fractions

Work out

(a) $\dfrac{1}{9} \div \dfrac{1}{8}$ (b) $\dfrac{2}{7} \div \dfrac{5}{9}$ (c) $\dfrac{3}{8} \div 6$ (d) $5\dfrac{1}{2} \div 3$

(e) $1\dfrac{1}{6} \div \dfrac{4}{9}$ (f) $3\dfrac{2}{5} \div 2\dfrac{1}{2}$ (g) $8\dfrac{1}{2} \div 5\dfrac{1}{4}$ (h) $4\dfrac{5}{6} \div 4\dfrac{2}{3}$

Mixed examination questions

1 (a) Shade $\frac{2}{3}$ of the shape below.

(b) (i) What fraction of the shape below is shaded?

(ii) What fraction of this shape is not shaded?   (WJEC)

2 Work out, giving your answer as a fraction in its simplest form.

(a) $\frac{2}{5} \times \frac{1}{4}$ (b) $\frac{2}{5} - \frac{1}{4}$ (OCR)

3 Work out   (i) $\frac{3}{4} - \frac{1}{3}$ (ii) $\frac{3}{8} \div 6$

4 This is a drawing of a bolt. It is not drawn to scale.

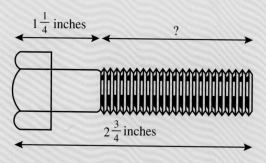

Calculate the length marked '?'.   (OCR)

5 I planted $\frac{1}{4}$ of my garden with vegetables, $\frac{3}{8}$ of my garden with roses and the rest as lawn. What fraction of the garden have I left for lawn?   (AQA)

6 Calculate $2\frac{3}{8} + 1\frac{1}{2}$.   (CCEA)

In this unit you will learn how to:
- convert between fractions and percentages
- express one number as a percentage of another number
- find a percentage of a number
- find percentage increases and decreases
- convert between percentages and decimals
- find percentage changes
- do compound interest-type problems
- use percentage multipliers
- find ratios
- deal with direct proportion
- share in a given ratio
- USE YOUR MATHS! – trim it

Fractions and percentages

 Key Facts

Per cent means 'out of 100'.

Percentages are fractions with denominator (bottom number) equal to 100.

63% means $\dfrac{63}{100}$ 7% means $\dfrac{7}{100}$

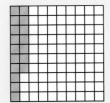

17 out of 100 small squares are shaded.

Fraction shaded $= \dfrac{17}{100}$

Percentage shaded $= 17\%$

Example

In a survey about favourite drinks, 37 out of 100 people said they preferred wine. Write this as a percentage.

$\dfrac{37}{100} = 37\%$ so 37% of the people said they preferred wine.

1

(a) What fraction of the large rectangle is pink?

(b) What percentage of the large rectangle is pink?

2 5 out of every 100 Britons donate blood at least once a year. Write down the percentage of Britons who donate blood at least once a year.

3 70% of people in Great Britain drive to work. What percentage of people do *not* drive to work?

4 If 35% of a rectangle is shaded, what percentage of the rectangle is *not* shaded?

5 57 out of every 100 workers in the UK would choose a different job if they could have their time again. Write this as a percentage.

6 Approximately 67% of the earth's surface is covered with water. What percentage of the earth's surface is land?

7 75% of women make their bed every day but only 45% of men do.

(a) What percentage of women do *not* make their bed every day?
(b) What percentage of men do *not* make their bed every day?

8 12 out of every 100 British people are left-handed. Write down the percentage of British people who are left-handed.

9 Cleator Moor, near Whitehaven in Cumbria, has the highest percentage of Christians in the country (89%). What percentage of the people in Cleator Moor are *not* Christians?

10 In 2001, 40% of 16 to 74-year-olds in Fairlight, near Hastings, were retired, the highest percentage of retired people in England and Wales. What percentage of 16 to 74-year-olds in Fairlight were *not* retired?

Changing percentages into fractions

$41\% = \dfrac{41}{100}$

$18\% = \dfrac{18}{100} = \dfrac{9}{50}$ ÷2 (top and bottom)

cancel when you can

$35\% = \dfrac{35}{100} = \dfrac{7}{20}$ ÷5 (top and bottom)

cancel when you can

Changing fractions into percentages

(a)

$50\% = \dfrac{50}{100} = \dfrac{1}{2}$ ÷50 (top and bottom)   so $\dfrac{1}{2}$ means 50%

To change a fraction into a percentage, multiply the fraction by 100

(b) Change $\dfrac{7}{24}$ into a percentage

$\dfrac{7}{24} \times 100$ Use calculator

$\dfrac{7}{24} \times 100 = 29.16666...$

$= 29\%$ (to the nearest whole number)

E6. 1

1 Change these percentages into fractions. Cancel the answers when possible.

(a) 10%   (b) 3%   (c) 11%   (d) 40%   (e) 75%   (f) 15%

(g) 80%   (h) 22%   (i) 32%   (j) 95%   (k) 48%   (l) 5%

2 Carl gave Michelle 30% of his CD's. What *fraction* of his CD's did Carl give to Michelle?

3 Nina used 55% of the petrol in her car when travelling from Manchester to Newcastle. What *fraction* of her petrol did she use?

4 Zak spent 64% of his money in town on Saturday. What *fraction* of his money did he spend?

5 Change these fractions into percentages (remember: multiply by 100 unless you can see a quicker way).

(a) $\dfrac{1}{4}$ (b) $\dfrac{7}{100}$ (c) $\dfrac{4}{5}$ (d) $\dfrac{7}{20}$ (e) $\dfrac{3}{4}$ (f) $\dfrac{3}{25}$ (g) $\dfrac{9}{25}$

(h) $\dfrac{9}{100}$ (i) $\dfrac{2}{5}$ (j) $\dfrac{7}{10}$ (k) $\dfrac{14}{25}$ (l) $\dfrac{9}{10}$ (m) $\dfrac{17}{20}$ (n) $\dfrac{21}{50}$

6 Ivan ran $\frac{39}{50}$ of a marathon race before he had to drop out. What percentage of the race did he manage to run?

7 Silvio scored 13 out of 25 in a test. What percentage was this?

8 Jane has to use $\frac{11}{20}$ of her money to pay her rent. What percentage of her money does she use to pay her rent?

9 Use a calculator to change these fractions into percentages (give your answers to the nearest whole number).

(a) $\frac{12}{17}$ (b) $\frac{8}{29}$ (c) $\frac{5}{16}$ (d) $\frac{11}{40}$ (e) $\frac{13}{16}$ (f) $\frac{12}{41}$

(g) $\frac{6}{37}$ (h) $\frac{29}{39}$ (i) $\frac{58}{73}$ (j) $\frac{9}{32}$ (k) $\frac{26}{27}$ (l) $\frac{88}{143}$

10 In a cricket match, Michael Vaughan scored $\frac{29}{49}$ of his team's runs. What percentage of his team's runs did he score? (Give your answer to the nearest whole number)

Expressing one number as a percentage of another number

🔑 Key Facts

Write the two numbers as a fraction of each other then multiply by 100 to change into a percentage.

Suppose there are 25 cars in the staff car park. 9 of the cars were made in Japan. What percentage of the cars were made in Japan?

$$\frac{9}{25} \times 100 = \frac{9}{\underset{1}{25}} \times \frac{\overset{4}{100}}{1} = \frac{36}{1} = 36\%$$

1 (a) Write down 6 as a percentage of 25   (b) Write down 9 as a percentage of 50

   (c) Write down 8 as a percentage of 20   (d) Write down 40 as a percentage of 200

2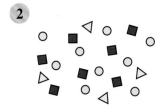

What percentage of these shapes are:

(a) squares

(b) circles

(c) triangles

3 13 people in a class of 25 have blonde hair. What percentage of the class have blonde hair?

4 Mehur scored 13 out of 20 in his maths exam and 18 out of 50 in his science exam.

   (a) What percentage did Mehur score in his maths exam?

   (b) What percentage did Mehur score in his science exam?

   (c) Which exam did Mehur do better in?

5 In a box of 20 chocolates, 14 of them are milk chocolates. What percentage are milk chocolates?

6 In a school of 800 students, there are 472 girls.

   (a) What is the percentage of *girls* in the school?

   (b) What is the percentage of *boys* in the school?

7 250 people go to a rock concert. 145 of the people are male.

   (a) What is the percentage of *males* at the rock concert?

   (b) What is the percentage of *females* at the rock concert?

8 This table shows the number of cars of each colour in a car park.

What percentage of the total number of cars were:

(a) red   (b) blue   (c) white

(d) gold   (e) yellow   (f) green

colour	number of cars
red	18
blue	12
white	6
gold	3
yellow	15
green	6
total	60

141

9 In a survey, 150 people were asked about smoking. 45 people said they smoke. The rest of the people said they do *not* smoke. What percentage of the people said they do *not* smoke?

10 2 twins, Meg and Charlie, sat 5 exams. The results are opposite.

Find the percentage that Meg scored in *each* subject.

Write down who got the higher marks in most subjects.

subject	Meg	Charlie
english	$\dfrac{17}{20}$	79%
maths	$\dfrac{14}{25}$	50%
science	$\dfrac{23}{50}$	52%
art	$\dfrac{26}{40}$	62%
geography	$\dfrac{42}{60}$	75%

E6. 2

Use a calculator for the Questions in this exercise. Give your answers to the nearest whole number.

1 Change these test scores into percentages:

(a) $\dfrac{13}{40}$ (b) $\dfrac{36}{42}$ (c) $\dfrac{5}{16}$ (d) $\dfrac{54}{72}$ (e) $\dfrac{45}{63}$ (f) $\dfrac{23}{30}$

2 Brenda saves £5 each week out of her Saturday job. If she gets paid £17.50, work out the percentage of her wage that she saves.

3 A chocolate bar weighs 68 g. If 47 g of the bar is nougat, work out what percentage of the bar is nougat.

4 A house costs £115, 000. Sam must pay a deposit of £10, 000. What is the deposit as a percentage of the total cost of the house?

5

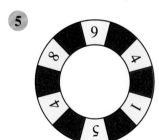

$$1^2 = 1 \times 1 = 1$$
$$2^2 = 2 \times 2 = 4$$
$$3^3 = 3 \times 3 = 9$$
$$4^4 = 4 \times 4 = 16$$

These are the first 4 square numbers.

Look at the picture opposite. What percentage of the numbers are square numbers?

6 Orange squash is to be made with 24 ml of juice and 126 ml water. What is the percentage of juice in the *whole* drink?

142

7

S	M	O	K	I
N	G	I	S	B
A	D	F	O	R
Y	O	U	R	H
E	A	L	T	H

What percentage of the letters in the square are

(a) the letter H

(b) vowels (A, E, I, O, U)

8 In the 'horror' of the First World War, the numbers of people killed from the main countries are shown.

Work out the percentage of people killed who came from (a) Britain (b) France (c) Germany. What a tragic waste of life!

Germany	1,800,000
Russia	1,700,000
France	1,384,000
Austria–Hungary	1,290,000
Britain	743,000
Italy	615,000
Roumania	335,000
Turkey	325,000
Others	454,000
Total	8,646,000

9 Peter asks people what their favourite drink was. The results are shown in this table.

Write down the percentage of people who like *each* type of *drink*.

drink	number of people
juice	21
wine	18
cola	32
lemonade	21
beer	34
cider	12
total	138

10

BARCLAYS PREMIERSHIP

		HOME					AWAY						
	P	W	D	L	F	A	W	D	L	F	A	GD	Pts
1 CHELSEA	16	6	2	0	15	3	6	1	1	14	3	+25	39
2 EVERTON	17	6	1	2	11	9	5	2	1	10	5	+7	36
3 ARSENAL	16	5	3	0	23	9	5	1	2	19	11	+22	34
4 MAN UTD	16	6	3	0	12	3	3	2	10	7	+12	30	
5 MIDDLESBRO	17	4	3	1	13	9	4	2	3	16	13	+7	29
6 ASTON VILLA	16	5	3	0	14	4	1	4	3	7	13	+4	25
7 LIVERPOOL	16	6	0	1	15	5	1	3	5	9	13	+6	24
8 CHARLTON	17	4	2	2	12	8	3	1	5	7	19	-8	24
9 BOLTON	17	4	2	2	12	8	2	3	4	14	17	+1	23
10 PORTSMOUTH	16	5	1	2	15	11	1	3	4	7	12	-1	22
11 TOTTENHAM	17	2	2	4	11	12	4	2	3	6	6	-1	22
12 NEWCASTLE	17	3	3	3	16	16	2	3	3	12	16	-4	21
13 MAN CITY	17	3	3	3	10	6	2	2	4	11	12	+3	20
14 FULHAM	16	3	0	5	8	15	2	2	4	10	12	-9	17
15 NORWICH	17	2	4	3	12	15	0	5	3	5	12	-11	15
16 BIRMINGHAM	16	1	4	3	5	7	1	4	3	7	11	-4	14
17 C PALACE	17	2	2	5	8	11	1	3	4	9	13	-7	14
18 BLACKBURN	17	1	5	2	10	14	1	3	5	6	16	-14	14
19 SOUTHAMPTON	17	2	5	2	13	13	0	2	6	4	13	-9	13
20 WEST BROM	17	1	4	4	7	14	0	3	5	8	18	-17	10

This table shows the Barclays Premiership in December 2004.

(a) What percentage of the teams begin with the letter 'B'?

(b) What percentage of the teams have played 17 games (look down the 'P' column)?

(c) What percentage of the teams have *more than* 25 points (look down the 'Pts' column)?

143

(6A) **Convert between fractions and decimals (see Unit 2)**

1 Change these decimals into fractions. (cancel answers where possible)

(a) 0.3   (b) 0.2   (c) 0.29   (d) 0.36   (e) 0.72

2 Change these fractions into decimals.

(a) $\dfrac{31}{100}$ (b) $\dfrac{9}{10}$ (c) $\dfrac{7}{20}$ (d) $\dfrac{1}{4}$ (e) $\dfrac{16}{25}$

3 Match up each decimal with its equivalent fraction
(Warning: one of the fractions is not needed).

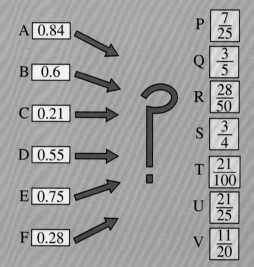

A 0.84   P $\dfrac{7}{25}$

B 0.6   Q $\dfrac{3}{5}$

C 0.21   R $\dfrac{28}{50}$

D 0.55   S $\dfrac{3}{4}$

E 0.75   T $\dfrac{21}{100}$

F 0.28   U $\dfrac{21}{25}$

     V $\dfrac{11}{20}$

Percentage of a number

Common percentages

$50\% = \dfrac{1}{2}$ $25\% = \dfrac{1}{4}$ $75\% = \dfrac{3}{4}$ $33\frac{1}{3}\% = \dfrac{1}{3}$ $66\frac{2}{3}\% = \dfrac{2}{3}$

(a) 25% of 60   (b) 75% of 36   (c) $66\frac{2}{3}\%$ of 24

$= \dfrac{1}{4} \times 60$ $= \dfrac{3}{4} \times 36$ $= \dfrac{2}{3} \times 24$

$= 60 \div 4 = 15$ $= (36 \div 4) \times 3 = 27$ $= (24 \div 3) \times 2 = 16$

Multiples of 10% $10\% = \dfrac{1}{10}$

To work out 20%, find 10% then multiply by 2

To work out 30%, find 10% then multiply by 3 and so on

1 Find 50% of:

(a) 80   (b) 42   (c) 28   (d) 120   (e) 9   (f) 25

2 Find 25% of:

(a) 80   (b) 28   (c) 48   (d) 100   (e) 200   (f) 30

3 Find 75% of:

(a) 20   (b) 32   (c) 80   (d) 12   (e) 400   (f) 52

4 There are 280 children in a school. 75% of the children play sport for a school team. How many children play for a school team?

5 Find $33\frac{1}{3}\%$ of:

(a) 12   (b) 30   (c) 60   (d) 18

6 Find $66\frac{2}{3}\%$ of:

(a) 15   (b) 21   (c) 45   (d) 60   (e) 300   (f) 72

7 Find 10% of:

(a) 80   (b) 90   (c) 20   (d) 200   (e) 50   (f) 600

8 Find 30% of:

(a) 80   (b) 90   (c) 20   (d) 200   (e) 50   (f) 600

9 Find 70% of:

(a) 40   (b) 10   (c) 80   (d) 40   (e) 300   (f) 140

10 Find 5% of:

(a) 80   (b) 20   (c) 60   (d) 140   (e) 30   (f) 90

11 Find 15% of: (hint: work out 10% and 5% then add together)

(a) 80   (b) 60   (c) 120   (d) 200   (e) 50   (f) 30

12 25% of a chocolate bar is caramel. If the chocolate bar weighs 60 g, how much is caramel?

13 An egg is made up of 60% egg white, 30% yolk and the rest is shell.

    (a) What percentage of the egg is shell?

    (b) If the egg weighs 50 g, what is the weight of the yolk?

14 Find the odd one out
    (a) 50% of £30   (b) 20% of £80   (c) 25% of £60

15 Find the odd one out

    (a) 5% of £160   (b) 25% of £36   (c) 10% of £80

16 $66\frac{2}{3}\%$ of adults like a cup of tea first thing in the morning. If 150 adults were asked, how many said they liked a cup of tea first thing in the morning?

17 160 people walked through a shop. 5% of these people had their noses pierced. How many of these people had their noses pierced?

18 360 people were asked if they had flown at any point in their life. 70% said they had flown. How many people was that?

19 Copy the 2 grids below:

60	38	3		63	90	38	11		66	15

40	12	63	50	9		9	50	90	9	50

There is a hidden message.

Answer the Questions listed below then write the letter under the answer number in your grids.

Example. Letter U is 15% of 20   Answer: 3. Write the letter 'U' under all the 3's in the grid.

letter A is 40% of 30	letter O is 10% of 380
letter E is 20% of 250	letter S is $33\frac{1}{3}\%$ of 27
letter I is 75% of 88	letter T is 30% of 50
letter K is 90% of 70	letter U is 15% of 20
letter M is 80% of 50	letter W is 5% of 220
letter N is 25% of 360	letter Y is $66\frac{2}{3}\%$ of 90

Key Facts

Harder percentages

$1\% = \dfrac{1}{100}$ To find 1% of a number, divide the number by 100

Find 23% of a number.

Divide the number by 100 to find 1% then multiply by 23 to find 23% of the number.

(a) Find 12% of 2300

    1% of 2300 = 2300 ÷ 100

    12% of 2300 = (2300 ÷ 100) × 12

               = 276

(b) Work out, to the nearest penny:

    6% of £12.99

    $\overbrace{(12.99 \div 100)}^{1\%} \times 6$

    = 0.7794

    = £0.78, to the nearest penny.

Note 4.5 on a calculator display means £4.50 if the number is showing £'s.

E6. 3

Use a calculator when needed.

1 Find 1% of:

   (a) 600   (b) 400   (c) 350   (d) 850   (e) 65   (f) 9

2 Find 3% of:

   (a) 600   (b) 400   (c) 350   (d) 850   (e) 65   (f) 9

3 Find 9% of:

   (a) 200   (b) 700   (c) 300   (d) 650   (e) 320   (f) 8

4 Find 24% of:

   (a) 500   (b) 800   (c) 450   (d) 240   (e) 68   (f) 3

5 Find 81% of:

   (a) 300   (b) 400   (c) 150   (d) 750   (e) 49   (f) 7

6 Find 17.5% of:

  (a) 200   (b) 120   (c) 380   (d) 685   (e) 72   (f) 4

Work out

7 9% of £450   **8** 4% of £770   **9** 47% of £185

10 7% of £550   **11** 85% of £600   **12** 8% of £350

13 48000 people watch Liverpool play Everton.
62% of the people are Liverpool supporters.
How many Liverpool supporters watch the match?

14 53% of the students in a school are girls. If there are
1300 students in the school, how many are girls?

15 Find the odd one out

  (a) 3% of 68   (b) 8% of £32   (c) 12% of £17

16 Match each Question to the correct answer:
(the answers have been rounded off to the nearest penny)

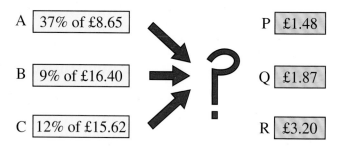

A | 37% of £8.65 | P | £1.48 |

B | 9% of £16.40 | Q | £1.87 |

C | 12% of £15.62 | R | £3.20 |

17 Work out, correct to the nearest penny:

  (a) 12% of £17.60   (b) 26% of £91   (c) 14% of £8.50

  (d) 29% of £6.87   (e) 67% of £11.27   (f) 18% of £28.53

  (g) 6.5% of £174   (h) 9.2% of £9.25   (i) 12.5% of £38.17

18 9% of a cereal is sugar. How much sugar is there in a 750 g box of cereal?

19 Sean has £850. He uses 37.2% of his money to buy a new music centre.
How much did he spend on the music centre?

20 Which is larger?

  (a) 7.3% of £8.99   or   (b) 9.4% of £6.81

148

6B **Substitute numbers for letters (see Unit 4)**

In Questions **1** to **8** find the value of each expression when

$$a = 3$$
$$b = 1$$
$$c = 5$$

1. $2a$ **2.** $c - a$ **3.** bc **4.** $3a + 2c$

5. c^2 **6.** $a^2 + b^2$ **7.** $a(b + c)$ **8.** $6c - 4b$

In Questions **9** to **16** find the value of each expression when

$$x = 6$$
$$y = 2$$
$$z = 4$$

9. $7y$ **10.** x^2 **11.** yz **12.** $3x + 2z$

13. $5(x - z)$ **14.** $\dfrac{x}{y}$ **15.** $y(x + z)$ **16.** xyz

17. $a = b + 9c$ Find a when $b = 4$ and $c = 3$

18. $f = \dfrac{m}{4} - 6$ Find f when $m = 32$

Percentage increase and decrease

Find the given percentage then '*add on*' for '*increase*' or '*subtract*' for '*decrease*'.

(a) Increase £70 by 10%   (b) Decrease £90 by 20%

$$10\% \text{ of } 70 = 70 \div 10 = 7 \qquad\qquad 20\% \text{ of } 90 = \overbrace{(90 \div 10)}^{10\%} \times 2 = 18$$

$$70 + 7 = £77 \qquad\qquad\qquad\qquad 90 - 18 = £72$$

                  ↑

increase   decrease

Do *not* use a calculator.

1. (a) Increase £60 by 10%
   (b) Increase £90 by 30%
   (c) Increase £30 by 60%
   (d) Decrease £50 by 40%
   (e) Decrease £300 by 25%
   (f) Increase £800 by 7%
   (g) Reduce (decrease) £30 by $33\frac{1}{3}$%
   (h) Reduce £200 by 4%
   (i) Decrease £60 by 5%
   (j) Increase £20 by 30%

2. A music store is having a sale, with 25% *off* all prices. A guitar normally costs £360. What will it cost in the sale?

3. After one year, a car *loses* 20% of its value. If the car cost £7000 when it was bought, how much will it cost after one year?

4. A shop increases all its prices by 5%. If the price of a computer was £840, what is the new price?

5. A 750 g Cornflake packet has 10% extra free. How much does it weigh now?

In Questions 6 to 14 below:

(a) How much is the price reduced by?   (b) What is the sale price?

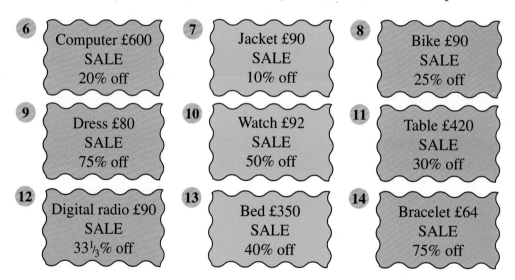

6. Computer £600 SALE 20% off

7. Jacket £90 SALE 10% off

8. Bike £90 SALE 25% off

9. Dress £80 SALE 75% off

10. Watch £92 SALE 50% off

11. Table £420 SALE 30% off

12. Digital radio £90 SALE $33\frac{1}{3}$% off

13. Bed £350 SALE 40% off

14. Bracelet £64 SALE 75% off

15. A restaurant adds a 10% service charge to its bills. If a meal costs £50, how much will it cost with the service added?

16. The price of a house was £160 000. During one year, the price increases by 3%. What is the new price of the house?

17. Hilary weighs 70 kg. She goes on a diet and loses 10% of her weight. How much does she now weigh?

18 Rosie earns £22 000 each year. She gets a pay rise of 4%. How much does she now earn each year?

19 Increase £400 by 17.5% (hint: find 10% then 5% then 2.5% and add them all together)

20 Increase £560 by 17.5%

VAT is Value Added Tax. It is extra money that must be paid when buying many goods. The money is used by the Government to help run the country. It is usually 17.5%.

A printer costs £250 + VAT.

If VAT is 17.5%, work out how much the printer costs altogether.

$$\overset{1\%}{17.5\% \text{ of } 250 = (250 \div 100)} \times 17.5 = 43.75$$

add the tax

printer costs 250 + 43.75 = £293.75

E6. 4

Use a calculator when needed. Give answers to the nearest penny when needed.

1 (a) Increase a price of £90 by 5%   (b) Increase a price of £270 by 3%

(c) Decrease a price of £75 by 7%   (d) Increase a price of £48 by 26%

(e) Decrease a price of £320 by 8.5% (f) Reduce a price of £9 by 83%

(g) Increase a price of £7.40 by 11%   (h) Reduce a price of £463 by 62%

(i) Decrease a price of £21 by 6.3%   (j) Decrease a price of £9.85 by 3.2%

2 A restaurant gives a 10% discount for take-away meals ('discount' means money is 'knocked off'). A meal costs £47.50. How much will the meal cost with the discount?

3 A railcard gives a 20% discount. How much would a £9.65 train journey cost if the railcard was used?

4 The population of Hatton is 11500. If the population decreases by 2%, what is the new population?

5 A computer costs £1099. Tom gets a 14% discount. How much will Tom pay for the computer?

6 A bike costs £412 + VAT.

If VAT is 17.5%, work out how much the bike costs altogether.

7 Copy and complete the table below:

item	price (£)	VAT (17.5%)	price + VAT
TV	325	56.88	381.88
fridge	217		
mobile phone	185		
cd player	133		
sofa	899		
camera	326		
car	12121		
bed	582		
computer game	47		
guitar	332		

8 A car is worth £4650. After an accident its value falls by 38%. How much is it worth now?

9 A holiday is priced at £2118. World oil prices rise which means that the price of the holiday increases by 7.5%. What is the new price of the holiday?

10 A bank pays 4% interest each year (this means if you put money in the bank for one year, you will get 4% of the money extra from the bank). If you put in £70, how much would you have after 1 year?

11 A bank pays 5.2% interest each year.

If you put in £390, how much would you have after 1 year?

12 Copy and complete the table below:

money put into the bank (£)	interest each year	extra money (£)	total money after 1 year (£)
80	3%	2.40	82.40
500	5.5%		
360	2.9%		
25	5%		
2100	4.7%		
5350	3.85%		
473	5.05%		
204	4.79%		
8	5.8%		
791	6.7%		

13 A new car costs £2320 + VAT (17.5%).

(a) What is the total price of the new car?

Its value decreases by 27% after one year.

(b) How much does the car cost after 1 year?

14 A new watch costs £275 + VAT (17.5%).

(a) What is the total price of the new watch?

After a year-and-a-half the shop puts the watch in a sale when the price is reduced by 15%.

(b) How much does the watch cost in the sale?

15 A new TV costs £550 + VAT (17.5%).

(a) What is the total price of the new TV?

In the New Year sales, the price of the TV is reduced by 18%.

(b) How much does the TV cost in the New Year sales?

Can you still?

6C **Collect like terms (see Unit 4)**

Can you still?

Simplify

1. $3a + 2a$

2. $5a - a$

3. $2a + 3b + 5a$

4. $9x + 2y + 5x + 2y$

5. $3x + 7y - 3y$

6. $6p + 3q + 2q - p$

7. $9m - 2m + 3n - 2n$

8. $8a + 4 + a$

9. $3m + 2n + 6m + 3$

Find the perimeter of each shape in Questions **10** and **11**. Simplify each answer.

10.

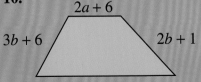

$2a + 6$

$3b + 6$

$2b + 1$

$5a + 17$

11.

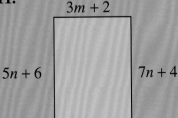

$3m + 2$

$5n + 6$

$7n + 4$

$3m + 2$

Percentages and decimals

$$71\% = \frac{71}{100} = 0.71 \qquad 23\% = \frac{23}{100} = 0.23$$

Note

$$80\% = \frac{80}{100} = 0.80 = 0.8 \quad \text{but} \quad 8\% = \frac{8}{100} = 0.08$$

To change decimals into percentages, the first two numbers after the point give the percent:

$$0.73 = \frac{73}{100} = 73\% \qquad 0.59 = \frac{59}{100} = 59\%$$

Note

$$0.07 = \frac{7}{100} = 7\% \quad \text{but} \quad 0.7 = 0.70 = \frac{70}{100} = 70\%$$

M6. 5

1 Change these percentages into decimals:

(a) 69%　(b) 31%　(c) 93%　(d) 21%　(e) 15%　(f) 60%

2 Change these decimals into percentages:

(a) 0.29　(b) 0.84　(c) 0.14　(d) 0.67　(e) 0.90　(f) 0.02

3 Change these percentages into decimals:

(a) 53%　(b) 28%　(c) 18%　(d) 40%　(e) 3%　(f) 92%

4 Change these decimals into percentages:

(a) 0.08　(b) 0.8　(c) 0.9　(d) 0.09　(e) 0.05　(f) 0.5

5 Which of the following are true?

(a) 3% = 0.03　(b) 3% = 0.3　(c) 70% = 0.07　(d) 70% = 0.7

(e) 2% = 0.2　(f) 2% = 0.02　(g) 4% = 0.4　(h) 40% = 0.4

6 Match up each percentage with its equivalent decimal (warning: one of the decimals is not needed).

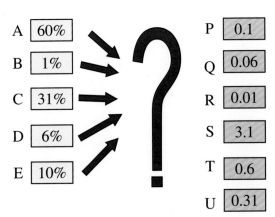

A	60%		P	0.1
B	1%		Q	0.06
C	31%		R	0.01
D	6%		S	3.1
E	10%		T	0.6
			U	0.31

7 Change these percentage into decimals:

(a) 3.5%   (b) 6.7%   (c) 100%   (d) 120%   (e) 248%   (f) 192%

8 In exercise E6.1, we changed fractions and percentages. Look back to remind yourself if you need to.

Copy and complete:

Percentage	Decimal	Fraction
21%		
	0.07	
		$\frac{19}{100}$
25%		
	0.3	
		$\frac{7}{10}$

9 Copy and complete:

Decimal	Percentage	Fraction
0.32		
	43%	
0.06		
		$\frac{7}{50}$
	80%	
		$\frac{3}{20}$

Percentage change

(a) A holiday firm reduces its prices of a holiday from £1740 to £1479.

Find the percentage decrease.

actual decrease = 1740 − 1479

$$= 261$$

percentage decrease $= \left(\dfrac{261}{1740}\right) \times 100$

$$= 15\%$$

(b) Roger buys a box of shirts for £180 and sells them for £232.20.

Find the percentage profit.

actual profit = 232.20 − 180

$$= 52.20$$

percentage profit $= \left(\dfrac{52.20}{180}\right) \times 100$

$$= 29\%$$

Notice that in both calculations we divide by the *original value*.

E6. 5

Use a calculator when needed. Give answers to the nearest whole number when needed.

1 Eddie's wages were increased from £120 to £129.60 per week. What was the percentage increase?

2 A CD player is bought for £60 and sold for £69. What is the percentage profit?

3 Sandra's weekly wage goes up from £240 to £252. What is the percentage increase?

4 Copy and complete the table below:

original price (£)	final price (£)	actual increase or decrease(£)	percentage increase or decrease
280	336		
300	324		
524	550.20		
780	897		
310	170.50		
96	62.40		

5 The value of a bike drops from £240 to £160 in one year. What is the percentage decrease in that year?

6 The population of a country increases from 2,374,000 to 2,445,220. What is the percentage increase?

7 'Dobbs Autos' has to reduce its workforce from 120 people to 93 people. What is the percentage decrease?

8 Kevin bought a car for £7350 and sold it quickly for £8100. Calculate the percentage profit.

9 Copy and complete the table below:

old price (£)	new price (£)	actual profit or loss (£)	percentage profit or loss
80	100		
130	91		
520	400		
63	50		
119	200		
48	75		

10 Carla buys a house for £221,000. She sells it 3 years later for £247,520. What percentage profit does Carla make?

11 Simon buys 300 cans of drink at 30p for each can. The cans are sold at a school disco for 36p a can. What is the percentage profit if all the cans are sold?

12 The cost of a first-class stamp is increased from 28p to 29p. What is the percentage increase?

13 The 'King's Arms' pub buys some of its items at the costs shown below and sells them at the prices shown below. Find the percentage profit on each item.

Item	cost price	selling price
pint of lager	£1.20	£2.70
packet of crisps	25p	60p
pint of bitter	£1.15	£2.50
packet of nuts	27p	75p

14 Arnie the grocer bought 100 cabbages at 30p each. He sold 80 of the cabbages at 65p each. The other 20 cabbages went rotten and had to be thrown away. Find the percentage profit Arnie made on the 100 cabbages.

Compound interest-type problems

(a) Suppose £2000 is invested at 10% per annum (year) compound interest. How much money will there be after 2 years?

'**compound**' interest here means that the interest must be worked out separately for each year.

After 1 year: interest = 10% of 2000 = 200
                total money = 2000 + 200 = £2200

money at start of year   interest

Do a new calculation for the interest in the second year.

After 2 years: interest = 10% of 2200 = 220

money at start of year

total money = 2200 + 220 = £2420

money at start of 2nd year   interest

(b) A car is bought for £12000. Each year, its value depreciates (goes down) by 5% of its value at the start of the year.

How much is the car worth after 2 years?

After 1 year: loss = 5% of 12000 = 600

value of car = 12000 − 600 = 11400

After 2 years: loss = 5% of 11400 = 570

value of car = 11400 − 570 = £10830

Simple interest

This means work out the interest for one year then multiply by the number of years.

£2000 is invested at 10% per annum (year) simple interest. How much money will there be after 2 years?

interest = 10% of 2000 = 200
total interest for 2 years = 200 × 2 = 400
total money after 2 years = 2000 + 400 = £2400

money at start   total interest

Use a calculator when needed. Give answers to the nearest penny when needed.

1 £5000 is invested at 10% per annum (year) compound interest. How much money will there be after 2 years?

2 Ben invests £6000 in a bank at 5% per annum compound interest. How much money will be have in the bank after 2 years?

3 A bank pays 6% per annum compound interest. How much will the following people have in the bank after the number of years stated?

(a) Kim: £9000 after 2 years.   (b) Freddie: £4000 after 3 years.

(c) Les: £2500 after 2 years.   (d) Olive: £600 after 2 years.

4 A stereo loses 30% of its value every year. Tim bought it for £800. How much would it be worth after:

(a) 2 years?   (b) 3 years?

5 The number of fish in a lake is decreasing by 5% each year. There are 10000 fish in the lake at the start of 2005. How many fish are there in the lake

(a) at the end of 2005?   (b) at the end of 2006?

6 Inflation is how much more expensive things in the shop get each year. Inflation is about 3%.

If a pair of shoes costs £50, how much will the pair of shoes cost after:

(a) 2 years?   (b) 3 years?

7 A new car is bought for £23000. Each year, its value depreciates (goes down) by 15% of its value at the start of the year. How much is the car worth after 3 years?

8 The population of a country decreases by 4% of its value at the start of every year. If the population is 8 million, what will it be after 3 years?

9 A bacteria culture starts with 4000 bacteria. Each hour the number of bacteria increases by 20%. How many bacteria will there be after 3 hours?

10 Mohammed puts £200 in a bank at 6% p.a. (per annum) compound interest. Geena puts £210 in a bank at 4% p.a. compound interest.

(a) Who will have more money in the bank after 2 years?

(b) How much more?

£500 is invested in a bank at 14% per annum compound interest. How much money is in the bank after 5 years?

Use a *percentage multiplier* 1.14 (100% + 14% = 114%)

Now multiply by 1.14 every year to get the new amount.

Start with £500:

after 1 year: $500 \times 1.14 = 570$

after 2 years: $\times 1.14 = 649.80$ and so on

after 5 years: total money = $500 \times \underbrace{1.14 \times 1.14 \times 1.14 \times 1.14 \times 1.14}_{5 \text{ years}}$

$$= 962.70|729 \ldots$$
$$= £962.71 \text{ (to the nearest penny)}$$

E6. 6

Use a calculator. Give answers to the nearest penny when needed.

1 £800 is put in a bank with 10% p.a. (per annum) compound interest.

    (a) Work out the total money in the bank after 3 years (use *percentage multiplier* 1.1).

    (b) How much money is in the bank after 5 years?

    (c) How much money is in the bank after 10 years? (just multiply £800 by 1.1 ten times)

2 Another bank pays 7% p.a. compound interest. If you put in £400, how much money would be in the bank after:

    (a) 2 years?   (b) 3 years?   (c) 5 years?

3 A building society offers 4.7% p.a. compound interest. If you put £1200 into the building society, how much would you have 3 years later?

4 (a) What is the percentage multiplier to find a 15% decrease? (Hint: what percentage would you have left after you have taken off 15%?)

    (b) The value of a car depreciates (goes down) by 15% of its value each year. Sally buys the new car for £16000.
    How much will the car be worth after 7 years?

5 The value of a washing machine depreciates by 25% of its value each year. If a new washing machine costs £480, how much will it be worth after 6 years?

6 A bank account gives 5% compound interest each year. Jack puts £600 into the bank. Copy and complete the table below:

after	money in bank
1 year	
3 years	
5 years	
10 years	

7 A car loses 22% of its value each year. A car costs £19500 brand new. Copy and complete the table below:

after	value of car
2 years	
4 years	
5 years	
10 years	

8 The mould on some bread has an area of $20\,\text{cm}^2$. It grows by 8% each week. Copy and complete the table below, giving your answers to the nearest whole number.

after	area of mould
1 week	
2 weeks	
3 weeks	
4 weeks	

9 A population decreases by 11% each year. At the end of year 2000, the population was 3,000,000. Copy and complete the table below, giving your answers to the nearest whole number.

end of year	population
2001	
2002	
2003	
2004	

10 If a 15-year old person put £500 in a bank at 9% p.a. compound interest and left it in the bank for 50 years until retirement, how much money would be in the bank?

Can you still?

6D **Multiply out brackets (see Unit 4)**

Can you still?

Expand (multiply out)

1. $3(a + 3)$ **2.** $5(x - 3)$ **3.** $4(2x + 6)$ **4.** $5(7m - 2)$

5. $7(4a + 2b)$ **6.** $3(6y - 3z)$ **7.** $7(2x - 9y)$ **8.** $a(b + c)$

9. $m(m - 6)$ **10.** $-3(a + 4)$ **11.** $-5(x - 5)$ **12.** $-2(2b - 6)$

Key Facts

We use ratio to compare parts of a whole.

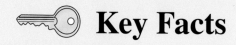

In this diagram, there are 6 black squares and 2 white squares.

We say the *ratio* of black squares to white squares is 6 to 2.

This is written as 6:2

Both numbers in the ratio 6:2 can be divided by 2 so we can reduce the ratio 6:2 to its simplest form of 3:1

(a) In a class of 24 children, 14 are girls. Find the ratio of boys to girls. Give the answer in its simplest form.

There are 10 boys.
Ratio of boys to girls = 10:14
(10 and 14 can both be divided by 2)
Ratio of boys to girls = 5:7

(b) Are the ratios 15:25:30 the same as 3:5:6?
15, 25 and 30 can all be divided by 5

$15 \div 5 = 3$
$25 \div 5 = 5$
$30 \div 5 = 6$

so 15:25:30 = 3:5:6

M6. 7

Copy and fill in the boxes below:

1  The ratio of black to white is ☐ : ☐

2 The ratio of black to white is ☐ : ☐

3 ● ● ● The ratio of black to white is ☐ : ☐
  ○ ●

In Questions 4 to 7, copy the circles and colour them in to match the given ratio.

4 ○○○○○ The ratio of black to white is 3:2.

5 The ratio of black to white is 1:4. ○○○○○

6 ○○○○○○ The ratio of *white* to *black* is 3:3.

162

7 The ratio of *white* to *black* is 2:4.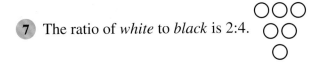

8 For the human body, write down the following ratios. Write the answers in their simplest form (example: thumbs to fingers is 2:8 = 1:4)

    (a) feet to toes   (b) ears to nose   (c) eyes to fingers

9 On a bus, there are 35 people. 25 of the people are female. Find the ratio of males to females. Give the ratio in its simplest form.

10 One evening, a vet sees 16 dogs and 10 cats. Find the ratio of dogs to cats. Give the ratio in its simplest form.

11 For each diagram below, write down the ratio of red to yellow in its simplest form.

    (a)    (b)

    (c)    (d)

12 Maaike makes some models using cubes of different colours.

    (a) Model 1 must have red to blue in the ratio 1:2. She uses 4 red cubes. How many blue does she use?

    (b) Model 2 must have yellow to green in the ratio 2:3. She uses 6 yellow cubes. How many green does she use?

    (c) Model 3 must have green to blue in the ratio 3:5. She uses 10 blue cubes. How many green does she use?

    (d) Model 4 must have white to yellow in the ratio 3:2. She uses 8 yellow cubes. How many white does she use?

    (e) Model 5 must have white to black to red in the ratio 2:1:3. She uses 3 black cubes. How many white does she use?
    How many red does she use?

13 In a hall there are 45 chairs and 9 tables. Find the ratio of chairs to tables in its simplest form.

14 In a class of 30 children, 18 are boys. Find the ratio of boys to girls in its simplest form.

15 Change the following ratios to their simplest form.

    (a) 15:10   (b) 8:12   (c) 9:15   (d) 10:22

    (e) 30:20   (f) 42:49   (g) 12:16   (h) 35:20

(i) 18:24   (j) 18:30   (k) 40:25   (l) 24:60

(m) 8:4:2   (n) 6:9:12   (o) 40:15:25   (p) 8:18:14

16 Frank spends £3 on Monday and 50p on Tuesday. Find the ratio of the money spent on Monday to the money spent on Tuesday (remember to change all the money to pence then give the answer in its simplest form)

17 Tanya is 1.6 m tall and Sid is 2 m tall. Find the ratio of Tanya's height to Sid's height (remember: 1 m = 100 cm so 2 m = 200 cm and 1.6 m = 160 cm). Give the answer in its simplest form.

18 Write the ratios below in their simplest form. Remember to get the units the same first.

(a) 50 cm:1 m   (b) 1 m:20 cm   (c) 2 m:20 cm   (d) 3 m:50 cm

(e) 25 cm:2 m   (f) 75 cm:3 m   (g) 5 m:40 cm   (h) 5 cm:2 m

(i) 50p:£2   (j) 50p:£5   (k) 5p:£2   (l) 80p:£8

Direct proportion

5 doughnuts cost 80p.

How much will 12 doughnuts cost?

Find the cost of 1 doughnut and then find the cost of 12.
5 doughnuts cost 80p
1 doughnut costs 80 ÷ 5 = 16p
12 doughnuts cost 16p × 12 = 192p = £1.92

E6. 7

Do not use a calculator.

1 6 pencils cost 54p. What do 5 pencils cost? (Do not use a calculator)

2 5 rulers cost £1.50. What do 2 rulers cost?

3 5 oranges cost 75p. What do 6 oranges cost?

4 8 bananas cost 64p. What do 5 bananas cost?

5 Magazines cost £21 for 7. Find the cost of 3 magazines.

6 9 pizzas cost £45. How much will 7 pizzas cost?

7 8 rubbers cost 88p. How much will 5 rubbers cost?

8 7 shirts cost £84. Find the cost of 4 shirts.

9 The total weight of 6 CDs is 72 grams. How much do 9 CDs weigh?

10 2 televisions cost £900. How much will 3 televisions cost?

11 A car takes 20 minutes to travel 32 km. How far will the car travel in 40 minutes?

12 4 cups cost £2.80. How much will 5 cups cost?

For the rest of the exercise you may use a calculator if needed.

13 Find the cost of 3 cakes if 9 cakes cost £15.30.

14 3 boxes weigh 14.1 kg. Find the weight of 13 boxes.

In Questions **15** to **18**, copy and complete the tables.

15

number of grapefruit	cost
8	£2.80
1	
7	
10	
50	

16

weight of potatoes	cost
2.5 kg	£2.40
1 kg	
5 kg	
15 kg	
17.5 kg	

17

pounds	dollars
42	79.80
1	
8	
32.50	
75	

18

pounds	euros
9.20	15.18
1	
5	
15	
125	
63.40	

19 Toni used 450 g of mince to make chilli con carne for 4 people. How much mince would have to be used to make chilli con carne for 10 people?

20 5 bottles of beer cost £13.30. Find the cost of 7 bottles of beer.

21 17 adults can go to the cinema for £116.45. How much would 12 adults pay?

22 This recipe for macaroni cheese serves 6 people.

150 g	cheese
300 g	plain flour
250 g	margarine
1	onion
3	eggs
30 g	butter
3	tablespoons of cold water

How much of each ingredient is needed to serve 18 people?

23 This recipe for chocolate sponge serves 8 people.

220 g	butter
220 g	sugar
2	tablespoons of boiling water
4	eggs
220 g	self-raising flour
2	tablespoons of cocoa

How much of each ingredient is needed for 12 people?

24 This recipe for pancakes serves 4 people.

120 g	plain flour
280 ml	milk
2	eggs

How much of each ingredient is needed for 6 people?

25 This recipe for pizza serves 5 people.

250 g	cheese
180 g	dough
150 ml	tomato sauce
25 g	pepperoni

How much of each ingredient is needed for 9 people?

Sharing in a given ratio

Share 40 oranges between Al and Jordan in the ratio 5:3.

Al : Jordan
= 5 : 3
Total of 8 shares

40 oranges
so each share = 40 ÷ 8
= 5 oranges

Al gets 5 shares
= 5 × 5 = 25 oranges
Jordan gets 3 shares
= 3 × 5 = 15 oranges

166

1 (a) Divide £160 in the ratio 1:3
    (b) Divide £90 in the ratio 5:4
    (c) Divide £240 in the ratio 7:5
    (d) Divide 80 g in the ratio 2:3
    (e) Divide 300 g in the ratio 3:7
    (f) Divide 450 g in the ratio 7:2
    (g) Divide 60 minutes in the ratio 3:1
    (h) Divide £800 in the ratio 5:1:2
    (i) Divide £360 in the ratio 2:3:4
    (j) Divide 5000 g in the ratio 8:5:7

2 In a class the ratio of boys to girls is 4:3. If there are 28 children in a class, how many boys are there and how many girls?

3 A woman divides £800 between Cath and Ben in the ratio 5:3. How much money do Cath and Ben each get?

4 Colin and Lily share a bag of 35 sweets in the ratio 2:3. How many sweets does each person get?

5 A metal bar is 27 cm long. If it is cut into 2 parts in the ratio 2:7, how long is each part?

6 The ratio of men to women to children visiting the Eiffel Tower one day was 4:5:6. If 975 people visited the Eiffel Tower, find out how many were:

(a) men   (b) women   (c) children

7 £320 is shared between Omar, Molly and Sachin in the ratio 3:1:4. How much will each person get?

8 Mr Hope has a BMW and a Mini. He puts 75 litres of petrol into the 2 cars so that the ratio of the petrol in the BMW to the Mini is 16:9. How much petrol is put into each car?

9 A green paint is mixed from blue and yellow in the ratio 2:5. How much of each colour is needed to make 56 litres of paint?

10 900 g of alloy is made up of copper, tin and nickel in the ratio 7:3:5. How many grams of each metal are there?

11

The angles x, y and z in a triangle are in the ratio 5:1:3.

Find the sizes of angles x, y and z.

167

12 The angles p, q, r and s in a quadrilateral are in the ratio 3:1:2:4

Find the sizes of angles p, q, r and s

Further questions on ratio

Lola and Dan are given some money in the ratio 6:5. If Lola gets £42, how much does Dan get?

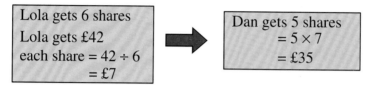

Lola gets 6 shares
Lola gets £42
each share = 42 ÷ 6
= £7

Dan gets 5 shares
= 5 × 7
= £35

E6. 8

1 Ribena is diluted with water in the ratio 1:6.

 (a) If 9 ml of ribena is used, how much water should be added?

 (b) If 60 ml of water is used, how much ribena should be added?

2 Some money is shared between Hamish and Rory in the ratio 11:4. If Rory gets £60, how much will Hamish get?

3 Gravel and cement are mixed in the ratio 5:3 to make mortar.

 (a) If 30 shovels of gravel are used, how many shovels of cement are needed?

 (b) If 12 shovels of cement are used, how many shovels of gravel are needed?

4 For a school trip there needs to be a ratio of adults to young people of 2:17. How many adults are needed for a trip with 85 young people?

5 A father's and son's ages are in the ratio 9:4. If the father is 45 years old, how old is the son?

6 An orange paint is made by mixing red and yellow in the ratio 2:3.

 (a) How much yellow must be used if 16 litres of red are used?

 (b) How much red must be used if 36 litres of yellow are used?

 (c) How much red and how much yellow must be used to make 80 litres of orange?

7 Bread is made from flour and yeast in the ratio 30:1

   (a) How much yeast is mixed with 870 g of flour?

   (b) How much flour is needed to mix with 350 g of yeast?

8 A 'Pink Lady' cocktail is made in the ratio 1 measure gin to 2 dashes Grenadine.

   (a) If 6 measures of gin are used, how many dashes of Grenadine should be added?

   (b) How many measures of gin should be used for 28 dashes of Grenadine?

9 At a college, the ratio of boys to girls is 5:8

   (a) If there are 10 boys in a class, how many girls would there be?

   (b) If there are 264 girls in the college, how many boys are there in the college?

10 Sheila, Gill and Ron are given some money in the ratio 7:3:4. If Gill was given £72, what was the *total* amount of money given to all 3 people?

11 In a factory the ratio of men to women is 5:2. If there are 235 men, how many women are there?

12 A recipe is made from flour, butter and sugar in the ratio 6:3:2 How much flour and sugar is needed if 270 g of butter is used?

13 Purple paint is made from red and blue paint in the ratio 2:5. If 35 litres of blue are used, how much purple paint would be mixed *in total*?

14 Gunpowder is made up of potassium nitrate, sulphur and charcoal in the ratio 17:3:4.

   (a) If 9 kg of sulphur is used, how much potassium nitrate should be added?

   (b) If 20 kg of charcoal is used, how much sulphur should be added?

   (c) How much sulphur should be used to make 216 kg of gunpowder?

15 The seven dwarves are given some money. It is shared between Dopey, Doc, Happy, Bashful, Grumpy, Sneezy and Sleepy in the ratio 8:9:4:3:10:7:12. If Grumpy gets £150, how much money do each of the seven dwarves get? What is the total amount of money?

Body mass index (BMI) is used to consider what a healthy weight is for a given height.

$$BMI = \frac{\text{Weight (in kg)}}{(\text{Height in m})^2}$$

Example: if a person's weight is 74kg and height is 1.73m, the person's

$$BMI = \frac{74}{1.73^2} = 24.7$$

This Body mass index graph is used to examine whether a person has a healthy weight.

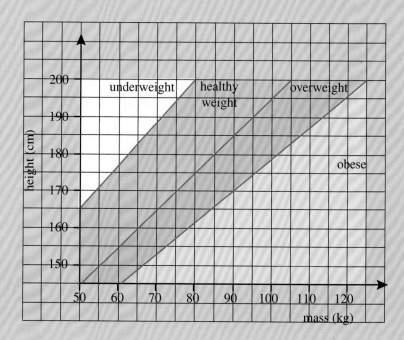

Task A

Jasmine is 1.64m tall and weighs 71 kg

Rory is 1.82m tall and weighs 62 kg

Mark is 1.75m tall and weighs 100 kg

1. Work out the BMI for each person.

2. Use the chart above to decide if each person is underweight, healthy weight, overweight or obese.

A person will lose 400g of fat from exercise if the person burns 3000 extra calories.

Jasmine would burn the number of calories shown below for each hour of the activity

Swimming	446
Mowing lawn	419
Aerobics	532
Cycling	630
House cleaning	274
Walking the dog	386
Badminton	608
Yoga	196
Rowing machine	827
Gardening	248

Mark would burn the number of calories shown below for each hour of the activity

Football	724
Circuit training	735
Aerobics	592
Rowing machine	836
Gardening	272
Golf	397
Cycling	680
House cleaning	314
Swimming	462
Fishing	273

Jasmine does the following extra activities each week

Sat	House cleaning (2 hours)
Sun	Gardening ($1\frac{1}{2}$ hours), Yoga ($\frac{1}{2}$ hour)
Mon	Walking the dog ($\frac{1}{2}$ hour)
Tue	Swimming (1 hour)
Wed	Aerobics ($\frac{1}{2}$ hour)
Thu	Swimming ($\frac{1}{2}$ hour), Cycling ($\frac{1}{2}$ hour)
Fri	Badminton (1 hour)

Mark does the following extra activities each week

Sat	Football (1 hour), Cycling ($\frac{1}{2}$ hour)
Sun	Golf (3 hours), Gardening (1 hour)
Mon	Swimming ($\frac{1}{2}$ hour)
Tue	House cleaning (1 hour)
Wed	Swimming ($\frac{3}{4}$ hour)
Thu	Gardening ($\frac{1}{2}$ hour)
Fri	Fishing ($3\frac{1}{2}$ hours)

Task B

1. Who will burn off more extra calories during one week? Show all your working out.

2. How much fat will Mark lose in one week?

3. Jasmine will be a healthy weight if she loses 1.2 kg. How many weeks will it take her to lose this amount?

TEST YOURSELF ON UNIT 6

1. Converting between fractions and percentages

Change these percentages into fractions. Cancel the answers when possible.

(a) 29%   (b) 20%   (c) 4%   (d) 71%   (e) 85%   (f) 12%

Change these fractions into percentages

(g) $\dfrac{3}{100}$ (h) $\dfrac{1}{2}$ (i) $\dfrac{51}{100}$ (j) $\dfrac{3}{10}$ (k) $\dfrac{7}{25}$ (l) $\dfrac{11}{20}$

2. Expressing one number as a percentage of another

(a) What percentage of these
shapes are stars?

(b) Ned scored 9 out of 25 in his English test. Faye scored 8 out of 29 in her
English test. Who got the higher percentage and by how much was it higher?
(*You may use a calculator*)

(c) Mr. Seymour wants to buy a car for £12000. He pays a deposit of £1000. What
is the deposit as a percentage of the total cost of the car? (*You may use a
calculator*. Give your answer to the nearest whole number)

(d) What percentage of letters in the alphabet are vowels (a, e, i, o, u)? (*You may
use a calculator*. Give your answer to the nearest whole number)

3. Finding a percentage of a number

(a) Find 25% of £36   (b) Find $33\frac{1}{3}$% of £36   (c) Find 10% of £90
(d) Find 30% of £90   (e) Find 5% of £40   (f) Find 15% of £40

You may use a calculator for the Questions below:

(g) Find 3% of £650   (h) Find 23% of £92   (i) Find 17% of £312

4. Finding percentage increases and decreases

(a) Increase £40 by 10%   (b) Decrease £70 by 20%
(c) Reduce £600 by 5%   (d) Decrease £120 by $66\frac{2}{3}$%

(e)

TV £560
SALE
30% off

What is the sale price of
this TV?

(f) A music system costs £628 + VAT.

If VAT is 17.5%, work out how much the music system costs in total?

(g) Increase £610 by 4%   (h) Decrease £385 by 12%

5. Converting between percentages and decimals

Change these percentages into decimals.

    (a) 29%   (b) 79%   (c) 34%   (d) 25%   (e) 70%   (f) 22%

Change these decimals into percentages:

    (g) 0.61   (h) 0.8   (i) 0.08   (j) 0.64   (k) 0.3   (l) 1.27

6. Finding percentage changes

You may use a calculator.

(a) A bike is bought for £310 and sold one year later for £250.

What was the percentage loss? (Give your answer to the nearest whole number)

(b) A necklace is brought for £60 and sold for £75. What is the percentage profit?

(c) Callum earns £260 each week.

His wage is increased to £275.60 each week. What is the percentage increase?

(d) A fairground drops its standard price of £2.50 a ride to £2 a ride. What is the percentage decrease?

7. Doing compound interest-type problems

(a) £4000 is invested at 5% per annum (year) compound interest. How much money will there be after 2 years?

(b) £32000 is invested at 10% per annum (year) compound interest. How much money will there be after 3 years?

(c) A car is bought for £16000. Each year, its value depreciates (goes down) by 4% of its value of the start of the year. How much is the car worth after 2 years?

8. Using percentage multipliers

You may use a calculator.

(a) What is the *percentage multiplier* to find a 12% increase? (Hint: what percentage would you have when you add on 12%)

(b) £700 is put in a bank at 12% p.a. (per annum) compound interest. How much money will be in the bank after 5 years? (Give your answer to the nearest penny)

(c) What is the *percentage multiplier* to find a 21% decrease?

(d) The value of a fridge depreciates by 21% of its value each year.

If a new fridge costs £270, how much will it be worth after 7 years? (Give your answer to the nearest penny)

9. Finding ratios

(a)  What is the ratio of blue to pink?

(b) There are 29 children in a class. 17 are boys. Find the ratio of boys to girls.

(c) Write down the ratio of blue to pink in its simplest form.

Change the following ratios to their simplest form:

(d) 9:24   (e) 60:15   (f) 50 cm:2 m   (g) 25p:£3

10. Dealing with direct proportion

(a) 9 apples cost 54p. What do 7 apples cost?

(b) 3 calculators cost £15. How much will 5 calculators cost?

(c) 7 bags of sugar weigh 5495 g. How much do 3 bags of sugar weigh?

11. Sharing in a given ratio

(a) The ratio of boys to girls in a class is 5:4. If there are 36 children in a class, how many boys are there and how many girls?

(b) £3000 is shared between Ally, Jane and Rob in the ratio 11:4:5.
How much money does each person get?

(c) Lemon squash is diluted using squash and water in the ratio 1:8. If 72 ml of water is used, how much squash must be added?

(d) Green paint is made from blue and yellow paint in the ratio 3:7. If 42 litres of yellow are used, how much blue paint must be used?

Mixed examination questions

1 (a) A dealer bought a mobile phone for £75 and sold it to make a 30% profit. For how much did he sell the phone?

(b) Bushra has a mobile phone. She pays a charge of £12.50 per month and the phone calls cost 3 pence per minute. VAT of 17.5% is added to the total of charge and the calls. How much is Bushra's phone bill in a month when she has made calls for 170 minutes? (OCR)

2 David's salary in 1998 was £17550. He was promoted in January 1999 and given an 18% increase in his salary. What is his new salary? (WJEC)

3 (a) (i) Write 25% as a fraction.

(ii) Write 0.2 as a fraction.

(iii) Write $\frac{3}{10}$ as a percentage.

(b) Write 25%, 0.2 and $\frac{3}{10}$ in order of size, smallest first.

(c) Write 9% as (i) a fraction (ii) a decimal (OCR)

4 Kelly bought 4 identical computer disks for £3.60.

Work out the cost of 9 of these computer disks.

(EDEXCEL)

5 A bar of Fruit & Nut chocolate normally weighs 200 g. The ratio by weight of a special offer bar to a normal bar is 5:4. What is the weight of a special offer bar? (AQA)

6 This is a list of ingredients for making a pear & almond crumble for 4 people.

> Ingredients for 4 people.
>
> 80 g plain flour
> 60 g ground almonds
> 90 g soft brown sugar
> 60 g butter
> 4 ripe pears

Work out the amount of each ingredient needed to make a pear & almond crumble for 10 people. (EDEXCEL)

7 Alan, Brendan and Chloe shared £768 in the ratio 5:4:3.

How much did each receive? (OCR)

8 There are 800 students at Prestfield School.

144 of these students were absent from school on Wednesday.

(a) Work out how many students were **not** absent on Wednesday.

Trudy says that more than 25% of the 800 students were absent on Wednesday.

(b) Is Trudy correct? Explain your answer.

45% of these 800 students are girls.

(c) Work out 45% of 800.

There are 176 students in year 10.

(d) Write 176 out of 800 as a percentage.   (EDEXCEL)

9 (a) This year Jo's class has 160 maths lessons.

Next year they will have 20% fewer lessons.

How many maths lessons will they have next year?

(b) This year each lesson lasts 50 minutes.

Next year each lesson will be 20% longer.

How long will each lesson be next year?

(c) Jo thinks this means they will have exactly the same total amount of maths lesson time. She is wrong. By what percentage will it change?   (OCR)

10 At the end of any year the value of a car is 20% lower than at the beginning of that year.

At the beginning of the year I bought a car for £5000.

Work out how much my car is worth 2 years later.   (OCR)

11 Josie invests £800 in an account that pays her 3% **simple** interest every year.

How much interest will she have been paid in total after 6 years?   (OCR)

12 Each year the value of a cooker falls by 8% of its value at the beginning of that year. Sally bought a new cooker on 1st January 2001.

By 1st January 2002 its value had fallen by 8% to £598.

(a) Work out the value of the new cooker on 1st January 2001.

(b) Work out the value of the cooker by 1st January 2005.
Give your answer to the nearest penny.   (EDEXCEL)

In this unit we will explore bank accounts and buying on credit.

WATCH YOUR MONEY! – Bank accounts 1

Most people have an account with a bank or a building society. Money is kept safely in the bank. Bills can be paid directly from the bank or with a debit card. Cash can be withdrawn or cheques can be used.

Writing a cheque

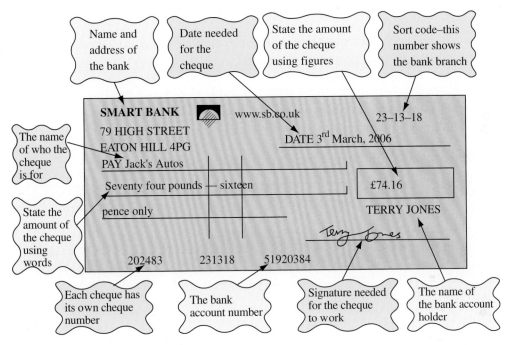

Note

- the amount in words must match the amount in figures.

- the cheque must be used within six months of the date.

- if you make a mistake when filling out a cheque, you may correct it so long as you write your signature by the mistake.

- the bank will not pay the money for your cheque if you do not have enough money in your bank account.

Cheque guarantee card

Once you are over 18, your bank may allow you a cheque guarantee card. If the cheque guarantee card number is written on the back of the cheque, the bank will definitely pay the money (the maximum amount is usually £100).

Being overdrawn

If you spend more money than is in your bank account without arranging with the bank beforehand, you will go overdrawn. The bank will charge you extra money and you will *owe* them *even more money*. You will then have to sort it out quickly or you could run into even greater difficulties.

WYM 7.1

1 Pat has £56 in her account. Her bank will charge her £30 if she goes overdrawn. She pays out two cheques, one of £39.19 and another of £27. How much will she now owe the bank?

2 Zak's bank has agreed that he may go up to £50 overdrawn without paying a penalty. If he breaks the agreement, he will have to pay a £35 charge.

Zak has £32 in his account. He makes payments of £28, £16.29 and £34.96. How much will Zak now owe the bank?

3 Chloe has the same agreement with her bank as Zak in Question **2**. Chloe has £93 in her account. She makes payments of £61.14, £73.06 and £25.32. How much will Chloe now owe the bank?

4 Colin sends the following cheque to his phone company.

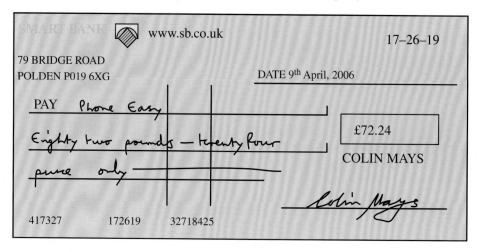

By looking at the cheque earlier in this section, write down:

(a) the sort code   (b) the bank account number

(c) the website address for the bank   (d) the cheque number

(e) The bank will not cash this cheque. Explain why.

5 Lara has £128.16 in her bank account. She makes payments of £17.11, £32.68 and £41.23. What is the biggest cheque she could now pay out without going overdrawn?

178

6. Investigate different banks. Find out if they pay interest on bank accounts. How much can you go overdrawn before you are charged? How much would the bank charge you if you went too much overdrawn? Discuss as a class.

WATCH YOUR MONEY! – Bank accounts 2

To keep track of your money, the bank or building society will send you a regular **'statement'**.

ATM (Automated Teller Machine) – this shows cash taken out of a cash machine with a cash card

Balance brought forward – the amount of money in the account at the start of this period

D (overdrawn) – this shows the account is overdrawn and money is owed to the bank

CHQ – this shows any cheques paid out (202485 is the cheque number)

DD (Direct Debit) – this is money taken out of the account by an organisation to pay bills when permission has been given

CR (Credit) – this is any money paid into the account

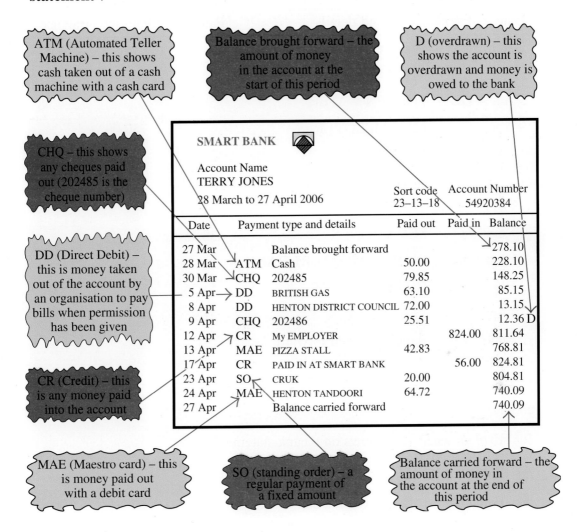

SMART BANK

Account Name
TERRY JONES
28 March to 27 April 2006

Sort code 23–13–18

Account Number 54920384

Date	Payment type and details		Paid out	Paid in	Balance
27 Mar		Balance brought forward			278.10
28 Mar	ATM	Cash	50.00		228.10
30 Mar	CHQ	202485	79.85		148.25
5 Apr	DD	BRITISH GAS	63.10		85.15
8 Apr	DD	HENTON DISTRICT COUNCIL	72.00		13.15
9 Apr	CHQ	202486	25.51		12.36 D
12 Apr	CR	My EMPLOYER		824.00	811.64
13 Apr	MAE	PIZZA STALL	42.83		768.81
17 Apr	CR	PAID IN AT SMART BANK		56.00	824.81
23 Apr	SO	CRUK	20.00		804.81
24 Apr	MAE	HENTON TANDOORI	64.72		740.09
27 Apr		Balance carried forward			740.09

MAE (Maestro card) – this is money paid out with a debit card

SO (standing order) – a regular payment of a fixed amount

Balance carried forward – the amount of money in the account at the end of this period

179

SMART BANK

Account Name
COLIN MAYS

3 April to 2 May 2006

					Sort code 172619	Account Number 32718425

Date	Payment type and details		Paid out	Paid in	Balance
2 Apr		Balance brought forward			416.25
3 Apr	CHQ	419330	63.10		**1**
5 Apr	DD	POLDEN WATER	58.17		294.98
9 Apr	CR	MY EMPLOYER		750.00	**2**
14 Apr	MAE	PETROLGO	28.64		**3**
16 Apr	DD	MID ELECTRICITY	67.00		949.34
18 Apr	CHQ	419331	**4**		823.74
19 Apr	SO	MR. S. JONES	38.45		**5**
22 Apr	CR	PAID IN AT SMART BANK		**6**	850.29
23 Apr	MAE	HORTON STORE	43.26		**7**
28 Apr	MAE	AQUAPLAY	21.95		**8**
2 May		Balance carried forward			**9**

For questions **1** to **9** , write down the correct amount of money for each box above.

10 Explain what 'DD' shows on a bank statement.

11 Explain what 'ATM' shows on a bank statement.

12 Explain what 'D' shows on a bank statement.

If you do not have enough money to buy an item, you might buy *on credit*. There are different ways of doing this such as hire purchase, credit cards, store cards, bank overdrafts and personal loans.

Make sure you know the true cost of buying on credit.

This section deals with hire purchase.

> Hire purchase allows you to buy items straight away but you pay for them in instalments (usually monthly).
>
> You probably will not own the items until all the instalments have been paid. If you stop paying the instalments, the items could be taken back.

Music Centre £650
(or a 20% deposit plus 24 monthly payments of £27.50 each month)

If you buy the music centre on credit:

$$\text{deposit} = 20\% \text{ of } £650 = £130$$

$$24 \text{ monthly payments} = 24 \times £27.50 = £660$$

$$\text{total credit price} = £130 + £660 = £790$$

How much extra does the hire purchase cost you?

extra cost = £790 – £650 = £140

       ↑   ↑

    Credit Cash
    Price   price

You would have to decide if you do not mind paying this *extra money* to be able to get this music centre.

GET WISE

If shops and other places offer interest-free periods, find out exactly what you have to pay in the end. It may *cost* you a lot of *extra money*.

1 A washing machine costs £420. You can buy it for a 10% deposit plus 36 equal monthly payments at £14.

(a) How much is the deposit?

(b) How much are the 36 monthly payments?

(c) What is the total credit price?

(d) How much extra does the hire purchase cost?

2 A TV costs £560. You can buy it for a 15% deposit plus 36 equal monthly payments of £15.50.

(a) How much is the deposit?

(b) How much are the 36 monthly payments?

(c) What is the total credit price?

(d) How much extra does the hire purchase cost?

3 Copy and complete the table below:

Item	cash price (£)	deposit (£)	number of monthly instalments	each monthly instalment (£)	total credit price (£)	extra cost of hire purchase (£)
(a) cooker	735	100	24	30		
(b) bike	390	80	24	15		
(c) car	12400	3000	48	224		
(d) phone	230	40	12	17.50		
(e) dishwasher	465	55	36	14.99		

4

New windows £3250	Pay a 20% deposit then *nothing for 2 years.* Followed by 12 equal monthly payments of £299.

How much extra does the hire purchase cost?

5

Boiler   £4100

Pay a £1000 deposit then *nothing for 1 year.*
Finally 48 equal monthly payments of £85.

How much is saved by paying the cash price?

If you do not have enough money to buy an item, you might buy *on credit*. There are different ways of doing this such as hire purchase, credit cards, store cards, bank overdrafts and personal loans.

Make sure you know the true cost of buying on credit.

This section deals with credit cards and store cards.

Credit cards

- A credit card can be used to buy items now and pay for them at a later date. They can be used to get cash but this can be expensive to do.

- Credit cards are good if the person pays off the bill within a certain number of days. If the bill is not paid off, interest is charged which means the person will *owe even more money.*

- Prople usually have to be 18 or over to get a credit card (not everyone is able to get a credit card).

- Each person has a credit limit. If the person tries to spend more than this, the card will not work or the person will get a penalty charge.

Monthly payment

If a person cannot pay off the bill in full, at least £5 or 5% of the total bill (whichever is the greater) has to be paid. The percentage may be different for some credit cards. If the person does not pay this, there will be a penalty charge and the person will *owe even more money.*

APR (annual percentage rate)

Look at the APR to compare the cost of borrowing for different credit cards. The APR is given as a yearly percentage. It takes into account all the costs involved and the method of repayment.

In general, the lower the APR, the better the deal.

Store cards

Credit cards can be an expensive way to borrow money over a long period of time. A store card often has a higher APR than a standard credit card so is even more expensive. The advantage of a store card is that you can spread out the cost of buying items and many stores give special offers with their cards at times.

Richard's tale

Richard has a credit card with a credit limit of £3000. Each month the interest rate is 1.32%. During the first year of his credit card he spends up to his limit and at the end of January he owes £2998.

1. The credit card company want a payment of 5% of £2998. How much is this?

2. Richard cannot afford this payment so ignores it. The monthly interest of 1.32% of £2998 is added onto his debt. How much does he now owe? (give your answer to the nearest penny)

3. Richard did not make his monthly payment so has a penalty charge of £20. How much does he now owe?

4. The credit card company notice that Richard has gone over his credit limit and decide to increase his limit to £5000. How much money is Richard now allowed to spend before reaching this limit?

5. Over the next 4 months Richard spends happily and his credit card debt increases by another £1879. How much does he now owe?

6. The monthly payment is due. This is 5% of what Richard now owes. How much is the monthly payment? (give you answer to the nearest penny)

7. Richard can afford no more than £200. How much more would he need to make the monthly payment?

8. He fails to make this payment. The monthly interest of 1.32% of his debt is added onto his debt. How much does he now owe? (give your answer to the nearest penny)

9. Richard gets a penalty charge of £20 for not making his monthly payment. How much does he now owe?

10. Richard is now over his £5000 credit limit. He is getting more and more into debt. Maybe the credit card company will raise his credit limit again? What would be your advice to Richard? **Discuss with your teacher** the advantages and disadvantages of credit cards.

GEOMETRY 2

8

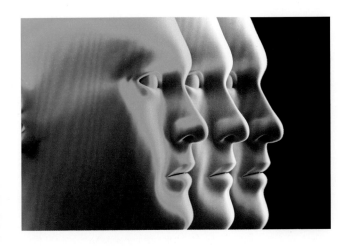

In this unit you will learn how to:

– recognise congruent shapes

– use co-ordinates

– translate shapes

– reflect shapes in mirror lines

– rotate shapes

– enlarge shapes

USE YOUR MATHS! –
 who's working now?

Congruent shapes

 Key Facts

Shapes A, B, C and D are exactly the same (even though C is upside down and D is on its side).

We say shapes A, B, C and D are congruent.

'congruent' means 'exactly the same size and shape'.

Note

If you are not sure if 2 shapes are congruent, use tracing paper. The shapes must fit on top of each other exactly (you may 'flip' the tracing paper upside down if you need to).

185

Use tracing paper if needed.

1 Which shapes are *congruent* to shape A?

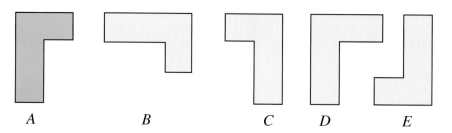

| A | B | C | D | E |

2 Which shapes are congruent to shape P?

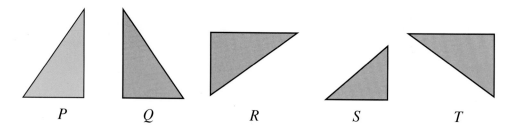

| P | Q | R | S | T |

3 Which shapes are congruent to shape P?

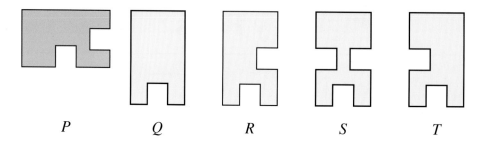

| P | Q | R | S | T |

4 Which 2 shapes are congruent?

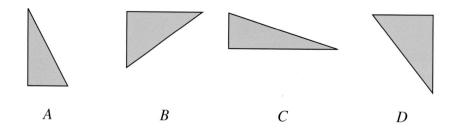

| A | B | C | D |

5 Each shape below is congruent to 2 other shapes. Write down the letters of each group of congruent shapes.

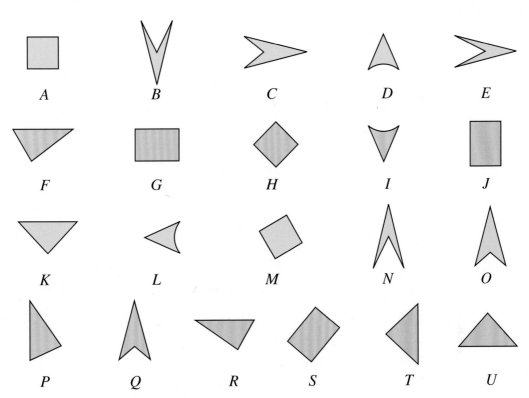

Show how each of these shapes can be split into two congruent shapes.

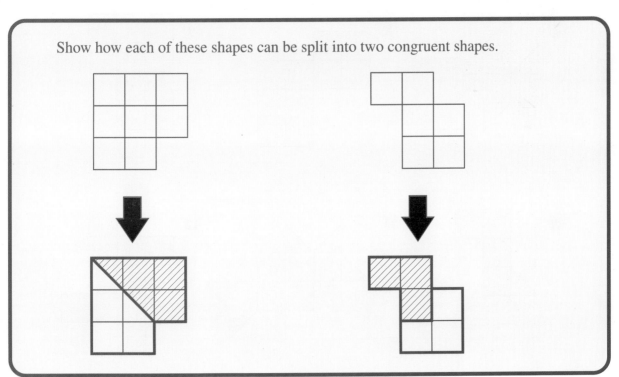

Copy each shape below.

Show how each shape can be split into two congruent shapes.

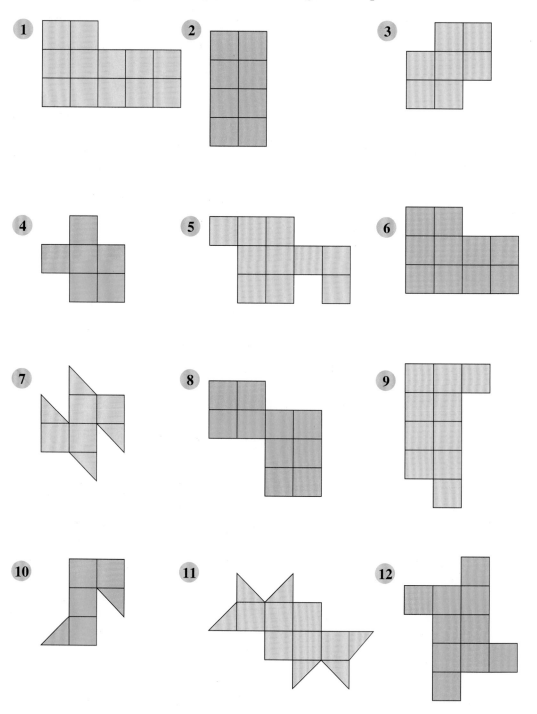

Key Facts

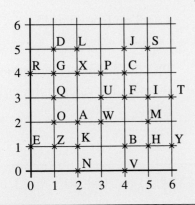

The position of a point on a grid is given by its co-ordinates. The *across* co-ordinate always comes first.

Point W is (3, 2)   Point N is (2, 0)

Point H is (5, 1)   Point R is (0, 4)

M8. 2

1 Use the grid above to spell out this message.

(5, 3)   (2, 5) (1, 2) (4, 0) (0, 1)   (4, 1) (2, 5) (5, 3) (2, 0) (1, 4)

2 Use co-ordinates to write the word MATHEMATICS.

3 Use the grid above to spell out this joke. Read across.

(3, 2) (5, 1) (2, 2) (6, 3)   (2, 5) (5, 3) (0, 1) (5, 5)   (2, 2) (6, 3)

(6, 3) (5, 1) (0, 1) (4, 1) (1, 2) (6, 3) (6, 3) (1, 2) (5, 2) (1, 2) (4, 3) (6, 3) (5, 1) (0,1)

(5, 5) (0, 1) (2, 2) (2, 2) (2, 0) (1, 5) (5, 5) (5, 1) (5, 3) (4, 0) (0, 1) (0, 4) (5, 5)?

(2, 2) (2, 0) (0, 1) (0, 4) (4, 0) (1, 2) (3, 3) (5, 5) (3, 2) (0, 4) (0, 1) (4, 4) (2, 1).

4 Write a message or joke of your own using co-ordinates. Ask a friend to work out your message.

5

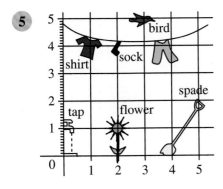

What are the co-ordinates of:

(a) the sock   (b) the top of the spade

(c) the flower

What is at:

(d) (3, 5)   (e) (1, 4)   (f) (0, 1)

189

6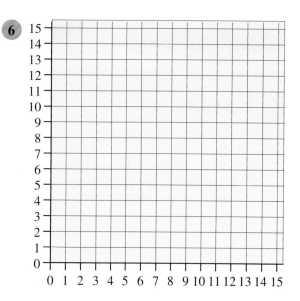

Draw a grid on squared paper as shown.

Label across from 0 to 15 (horizontal axis).

Label up from 0 to 15 (vertical axis).

Plot the points below and join them with a ruler in the order given.

$\left(5, 5\frac{1}{2}\right)$	$\left(4, 5\frac{1}{2}\right)$	$(3, 6)$	$\left(2\frac{1}{2}, 7\right)$	$\left(2\frac{1}{2}, 8\right)$	$\left(3, 9\frac{1}{2}\right)$
$(4, 10)$	$(5, 10)$	$\left(7\frac{1}{2}, 9\frac{1}{2}\right)$	$(8, 10)$	$(9, 10)$	$\left(9\frac{1}{2}, 9\frac{1}{2}\right)$
$\left(13\frac{1}{2}, 10\right)$	$\left(14\frac{1}{2}, 9\frac{1}{2}\right)$				

On the same picture plot the points below and join them up with a ruler in the order given. Do not join the last point in the box above with the first point in the new box.

$(5, 10)$	$\left(5, 10\frac{1}{2}\right)$	$\left(4\frac{1}{2}, 11\right)$	$(4, 11)$	$\left(4\frac{1}{2}, 12\right)$
$\left(7, 12\frac{1}{2}\right)$	$\left(11\frac{1}{2}, 12\right)$	$(11, 11)$	$(10, 10)$	$(10, 8)$
$\left(12, 7\frac{1}{2}\right)$	$(12, 8)$	$\left(13\frac{1}{2}, 9\right)$		

$(11, 0)$	$(10, 2)$	$(6, 2)$	$(4, 0)$	$(6, 2)$	$(6, 3)$	$(4, 4)$

$(13, 7)$ $(13, 8)$ $\left(8, 4\frac{1}{2}\right)$ $\left(8, 5\frac{1}{2}\right)$

$(4, 11)$ $\left(3\frac{1}{2}, 11\right)$ $\left(3, 10\frac{1}{2}\right)$ $\left(3, 9\frac{1}{2}\right)$ $(8, 5)$ $(7, 4)$ $(4, 4)$ $\left(3, 4\frac{1}{2}\right)$ $\left(4, 5\frac{1}{2}\right)$

$(10, 2)$	$(12, 6)$	$(13, 6)$	$(14, 7)$	$(14, 8)$	$\left(13\frac{1}{2}, 9\right)$
$\left(13\frac{1}{2}, 13\right)$	$\left(11, 14\frac{1}{2}\right)$	$\left(7, 14\frac{1}{2}\right)$	$(3, 13)$	$(1, 11)$	$\left(4\frac{1}{2}, 12\right)$

$\left(7\frac{1}{2}, 9\frac{1}{2}\right)$ $\left(7\frac{1}{2}, 8\frac{1}{2}\right)$ $(8, 8)$ $(9, 8)$ $\left(9\frac{1}{2}, 8\frac{1}{2}\right)$ $\left(9\frac{1}{2}, 9\frac{1}{2}\right)$

Draw a • at $(9, 9)$ and a • at $(4, 10)$ Colour me in?

190

1

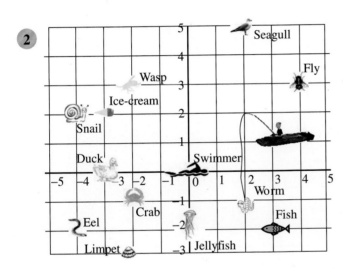

Remember: the 'across' co-ordinate always comes first.

Use the grid to spell out this message.

$(-2, 1)(1, 3)(1, -1)(-3, -2)$

$(1, -1)(-3, -2)$

$(1, -2)(-3, 3)(-3, -2)(0, -1)$

2

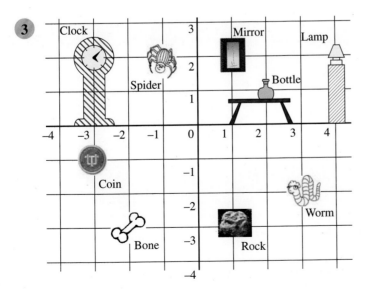

What are the co-ordinates of

(a) the fish   (b) the ice-cream

(c) the seagull (d) the limpet

(e) the eel   (f) the jellyfish

What is at:

(g) $(2, -1)$ (h) $(-2, -1)$

(i) $(0, 0)$ (j) $(4, 3)$

(k) $(-3, 0)$ (l) $(-2, 3)$

3

What are the co-ordinates of:

(a) the coin   (b) the spider

(c) the bottle (d) the rock

What is at:

(e) $(2, 1)$ (f) $(-2, -3)$

(g) $(-3, 2)$ (h) $(1, 2)$

(i) $(3, -2)$

4 Draw a horizontal axis from −4 to 8 and a vertical axis from −8 to 11.

Plot the points below and join them up with a ruler in the order given.

$(0, 1)$ $(−2, 1)$ $\left(−2\frac{1}{2}, \frac{1}{2}\right)$ $\left(−2\frac{1}{2}, −\frac{1}{2}\right)$ $\left(2, −\frac{1}{2}\right)$ $\left(4, −1\frac{1}{2}\right)$ $(5, −1)$ $\left(4, −1\frac{1}{2}\right)$

$(4, −3)$ $\left(3, −2\frac{1}{2}\right)$ $\left(−1\frac{1}{2}, −2\frac{1}{2}\right)$ $(0, −5)$ $\left(\frac{1}{2}, −5\frac{1}{2}\right)$ $(1, −7)$ $(6, −5)$ $\left(5\frac{1}{2}, −4\right)$

$\left(4, −4\frac{1}{2}\right)$ $(2, −5)$ $\left(\frac{1}{2}, −5\frac{1}{2}\right)$ $(−1, −7)$ $(0, −5)$

On the same picture plot the points below and join them up with a ruler in the order given. Do not join the last point in the box above with the first point in the new box.

$(6, −1)$ $(6, 1)$ $\left(6\frac{1}{2}, 3\right)$ $\left(6, 3\frac{1}{2}\right)$ $\left(5\frac{1}{2}, 3\right)$ $\left(5\frac{1}{2}, 2\right)$ $(5, 2)$

$(5, 7)$ $(4, 8)$ $(0, 8)$ $\left(−2, 6\frac{1}{2}\right)$ $(−2, 4)$ $\left(−2\frac{1}{2}, 3\right)$

$(6, 2)$ $(6, 3)$

$(4, 3)$ $(4, 2)$ $(3, 1)$ $(2, 1)$ $(1, 2)$ $(1, 3)$ $(2, 4)$ $(3, 4)$ $(4, 3)$ $\left(5\frac{1}{2}, 3\right)$

$\left(−2, 6\frac{1}{2}\right)$ $(−3, 7)$ $(−3, 8)$ $(−1, 10)$ $\left(1, 10\frac{1}{2}\right)$ $\left(5, 10\frac{1}{2}\right)$ $(7, 9)$

$(7, 0)$ $\left(6\frac{1}{2}, −1\right)$ $(6, −1)$ $\left(5\frac{1}{2}, −4\right)$

$\left(−2\frac{1}{2}, −\frac{1}{2}\right)$ $(−3, −1)$ $\left(−3, −2\frac{1}{2}\right)$ $\left(−1\frac{1}{2}, −2\frac{1}{2}\right)$

$(1, 3)$ $\left(\frac{1}{2}, 3\right)$ $\left(\frac{1}{2}, 2\right)$ $\left(−\frac{1}{2}, 1\right)$ $\left(−1\frac{1}{2}, 1\right)$ $\left(−2\frac{1}{2}, 2\right)$ $\left(−2\frac{1}{2}, 3\right)$

$\left(−1\frac{1}{2}, 4\right)$ $\left(−\frac{1}{2}, 4\right)$ $\left(\frac{1}{2}, 3\right)$

$(−2, −1)$ $\left(−2\frac{1}{2}, −2\right)$

$(−1, −1)$ $\left(−1\frac{1}{2}, −2\right)$

$(0, −1)$ $\left(−\frac{1}{2}, −2\right)$

$(1, −1)$ $\left(\frac{1}{2}, −2\right)$

$(2, −1)$ $\left(1\frac{1}{2}, −2\right)$

$(3, −1)$ $\left(2\frac{1}{2}, −2\right)$

Draw a • at $(2, 2)$ and a • at $(−2, 2)$

Colour me in?

192

Key Facts

A **translation** means movement in a straight line (no turning).

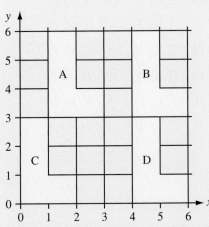

Describe the following *translations*. In each case, write down how many units left or right and how many units up or down.

(a) *A* to *B*

(b) *A* to *D*

(c) *B* to *C*

(d) *C* to *A*

Pick one corner (vertex) of the shape and follow where it moves to.

(a) 3 right, 0 up   (3R 0U)

(b) 3 right, 3 down   (3R 3D)

(c) 4 left, 3 down   (4L 3D)

(d) 1 right, 3 up   (1R 3U)

M8. 3

1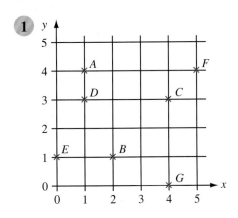

Describe the following *translations*. In each case, write down how many units left or right and how many units up or down:

(a) *A* to *B*   (b) *A* to *C*

(c) *A* to *E*   (d) *A* to *G*

(e) *A* to *F*   (f) *B* to *C*

(g) *B* to *D*   (h) *B* to *G*

(i) *G* to *C*   (j) *C* to *F*

2

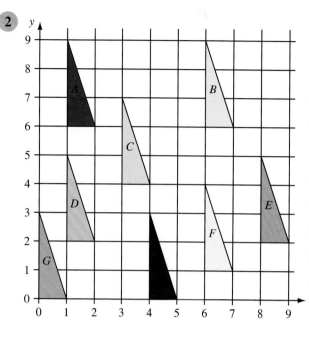

Describe the following *translations*. In each case, write down how many units left or right and how many units up or down:

(a) *A* to *C* (b) *A* to *D*

(c) *A* to *F* (d) *C* to *G*

(e) *E* to *B* (f) *C* to *D*

(g) *B* to *A* (h) *H* to *C*

(i) *F* to *D* (j) *E* to *F*

(k) *G* to *B* (l) *H* to *A*

3

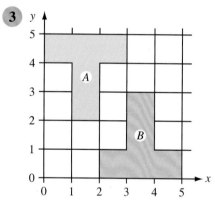

Shape *A* has moved to shape *B*.
Explain why this is *not* a translation.

4

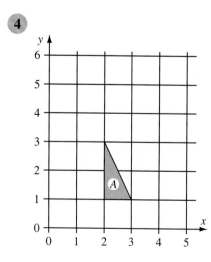

Copy the grid opposite and draw the triangle *A* as shown.

(a) Translate triangle *A* 1 unit to the right and 3 units up. Label the new triangle *B*.

(b) Translate triangle *A* 2 units to the left and 1 unit down. Label the new triangle *C*.

(c) Translate triangle *A* 1 unit to the left and 1 unit up. Label the new triangle *D*.

(d) Translate triangle *A* 0 units to the right and 2 units up. Label the new triangle *E*.

Translation vector

To describe a translation, we do not have to use the words 'left', 'right', 'up' and 'down'. We use a vertical bracket like this:

$$\begin{pmatrix} 2 \\ 3 \end{pmatrix}$$

The number at the *top* shows 2 units to the *right*.
(If the number at the top was −2 it would be 2 units to the *left*)

The number at the *bottom* shows 3 units *up*.
(If the number at the bottom was −3 it would be 3 units *down*)

Note

The vertical axis is often called the *y*-axis.
The horizontal axis is often called the *x*-axis.

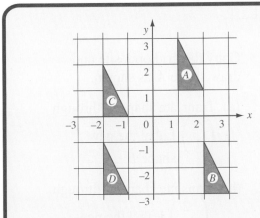

Use translation vectors to describe the following translations.

(a) *A* to *B*   (b) *A* to *C*

(c) *A* to *D*   (d) *B* to *C*

(a) $\begin{pmatrix} 1 \\ -4 \end{pmatrix}$ (b) $\begin{pmatrix} -3 \\ -1 \end{pmatrix}$ (c) $\begin{pmatrix} -3 \\ -4 \end{pmatrix}$ (d) $\begin{pmatrix} -4 \\ 3 \end{pmatrix}$

E8. 3

1

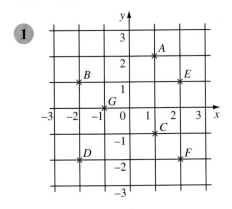

Use translation vectors to describe the following translations.

(a) *A* to *B*   (b) *A* to *F*

(c) *A* to *G*   (d) *B* to *C*

(e) *F* to *G*   (f) *D* to *G*

(g) *E* to *B*   (h) *B* to *F*

2

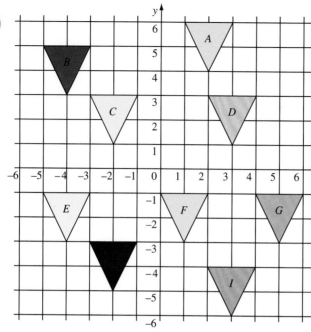

Use translation vectors to describe the following translations.

(a) A to D (b) A to G

(c) A to H (d) A to I

(e) B to E (f) B to H

(g) C to D (h) C to A

(i) C to E (j) D to B

(k) D to H (l) E to G

(m) E to D (n) F to C

(o) G to I (p) G to B

(q) H to D (r) I to C

3

Copy the grid opposite and draw shape A as shown.

(a) Translate shape A through $\begin{pmatrix} 5 \\ 1 \end{pmatrix}$ Label the new shape B

(b) Translate shape B through $\begin{pmatrix} 2 \\ -3 \end{pmatrix}$ Label the new shape C

(c) Translate shape C through $\begin{pmatrix} -2 \\ -5 \end{pmatrix}$ Label the new shape D

(d) Translate shape D through $\begin{pmatrix} -4 \\ 4 \end{pmatrix}$ Label the new shape E

(e) Translate shape E through $\begin{pmatrix} -3 \\ -5 \end{pmatrix}$ Label the new shape F

(f) Use a translation vector to describe the translation that moves shape E to shape B

(g) Use a translation vector to describe the translation that moves shape A to shape F

(h) Use a translation vector to describe the translation that moves shape D to shape B

Reflect this shape in the mirror line.

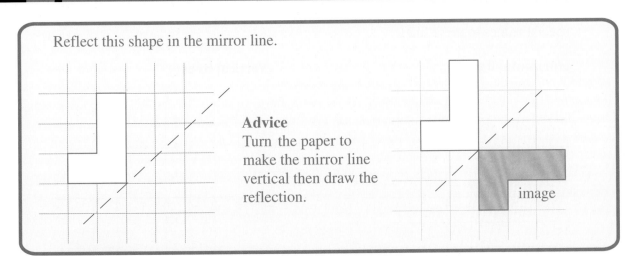

Advice
Turn the paper to make the mirror line vertical then draw the reflection.

image

M8. 4

Draw each shape below and reflect in the mirror line.

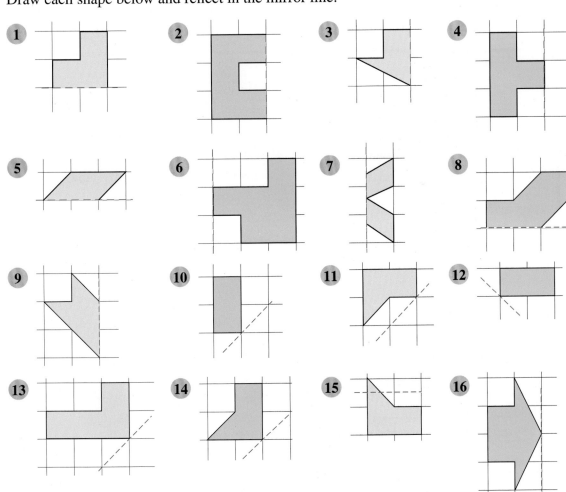

197

Mirror line

The mirror line is sometimes called the *line of reflection*. We can sometimes give special names to these lines.

Horizontal lines

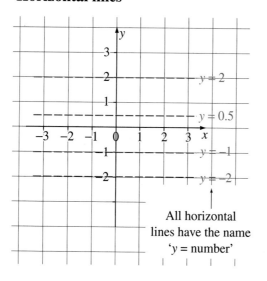

All horizontal lines have the name 'y = number'

Vertical lines

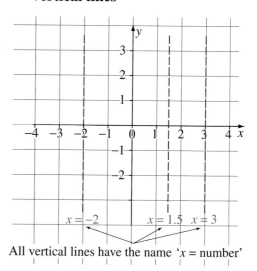

All vertical lines have the name 'x = number'

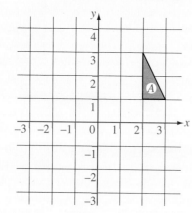

(a) Reflect triangle *A* in the *x*-axis.
Label the image (new triangle) *B*.

(b) Reflect triangle *A* in the line $x = 1$.
Label the image (new triangle) *C*.

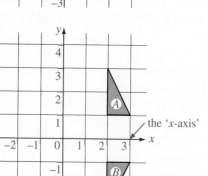

the 'x-axis'

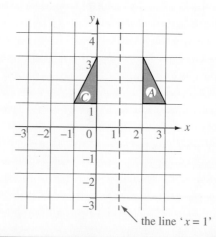

the line 'x = 1'

1

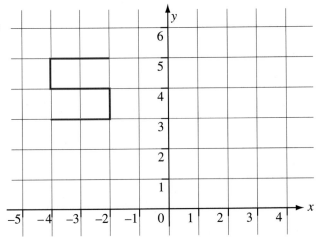

Copy this grid.
Copy the letter then
reflect it in the
y-axis.

2 Copy this grid.
Copy the shape then
reflect it in the
x-axis.

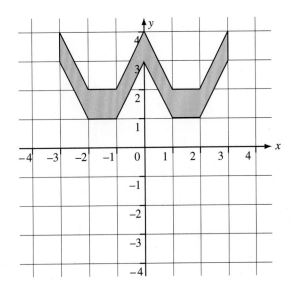

3

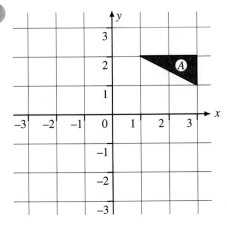

Copy the grid and shape opposite.

(a) Reflect triangle A in the y-axis.
Label the image (new triangle) B.

(b) Reflect triangle A in the x-axis.
Label the image C.

(c) Reflect triangle C in the y-axis.
Label the image D.

(d) Describe how you could *transform*
(change) triangle D into triangle B.

199

4

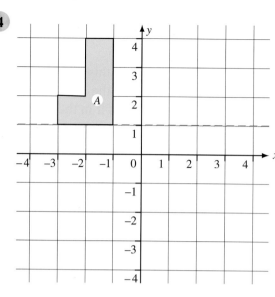

Copy the grid and shape opposite.

(a) Reflect shape A in the y-axis. Label the image B.

(b) Reflect shape A in the line $y = 1$ (the dotted line). Label the image C.

(c) Reflect shape B in the line $y = 1$. Label the image D.

(d) Describe how you could *transform* (change) shape C into shape D.

5

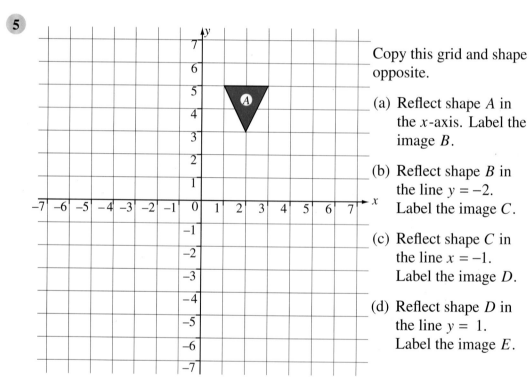

Copy this grid and shape opposite.

(a) Reflect shape A in the x-axis. Label the image B.

(b) Reflect shape B in the line $y = -2$. Label the image C.

(c) Reflect shape C in the line $x = -1$. Label the image D.

(d) Reflect shape D in the line $y = 1$. Label the image E.

(e) Reflect shape E in the y-axis. Label the image F.

(f) Reflect shape F in the line $y = 3$. Label the image G.

6

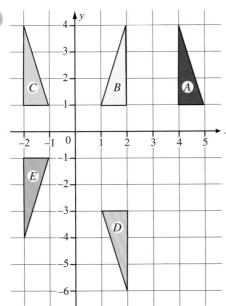

For each pair of triangles below, write down the name (equation) of the *line of reflection*.

(a) *A* to *B*

(b) *B* to *C*

(c) *B* to *D*

(d) *C* to *E*

Can you still?

8A **Find a fraction of a number (see Unit 5)**

Can you still?

Work out

1. $\frac{1}{4}$ of 24

2. $\frac{3}{4}$ of 24

3. $\frac{1}{6}$ of 30

4. $\frac{5}{6}$ of 30

5. $\frac{3}{8}$ of 56

6. $\frac{2}{7}$ of 21

7. $\frac{5}{9}$ of 36

8. $\frac{7}{8}$ of 72

9. | Computer £720 |
   | SALE |
   | $\frac{1}{5}$ off |

   How much does the computer cost?

10. Hal has £42. He spends $\frac{5}{7}$ of his money on a pair of trousers. How much money does he have left?

11. A tin of beans contains 360 g. If the tin of beans contains $\frac{2}{9}$ extra in a special offer, how much does the tin now contain?

12. Ginny scores 64% in an English exam. There is a mistake in the marking so that Ginny should have $\frac{3}{8}$ extra. What is her total mark now?

201

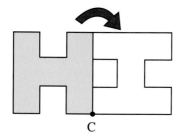

This shape has turned clockwise through a right angle (90° turn).

Remember:  clockwise

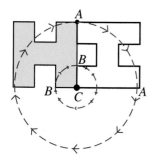

Each point in the shape rotates around a circle with its centre at the dot (C).

The dot (C) is called the **centre of rotation**.

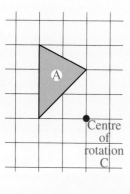

Rotate triangle *A* 90° anticlockwise about *C*.

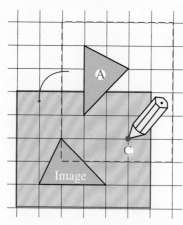

Trace the triangle. Hold your pencil on point *C*. Turn the tracing paper 90° anticlockwise to see the new position of the triangle.

Note

For 90° rotations, horizontal lines become vertical and vice versa.

Use tracing paper.

For each Question, draw the shape and the centre of rotation (C). Rotate the shape as indicated and draw the image.

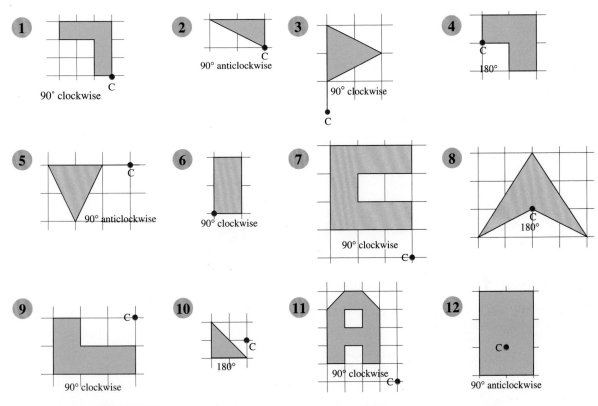

In Questions 13 to 16 copy each diagram. Draw the shaded shape on tracing paper. Place the tip of a pencil on different points until the shape can be rotated onto the other shape. Mark the centre of rotation with a dot.

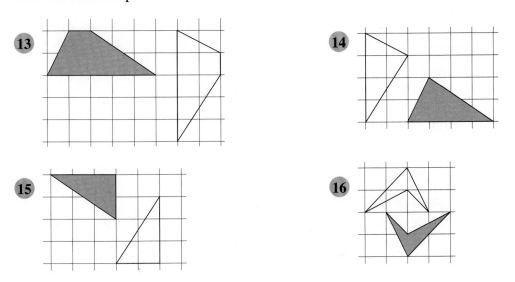

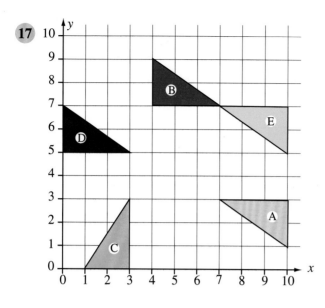

17 Find the co-ordinates of the centres of the following rotations:

(a) triangle A onto triangle B

(b) triangle A onto triangle C

(c) triangle A onto triangle D

(d) triangle C onto triangle E

🔑 Key Facts

Note   The point $(0, 0)$ is called the '**origin**.'

We need 3 things to *describe fully* a rotation:

1. the angle

2. the direction (clockwise or anticlockwise)

3. the centre of rotation

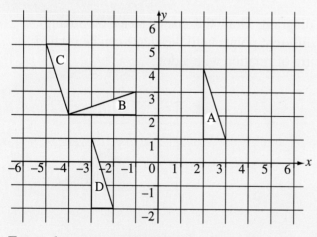

Describe fully the rotation which transforms:

(a) triangle A onto triangle B

(b) triangle B onto triangle C

(c) triangle B onto triangle D

For each answer, we must write down the angle, direction and centre of rotation.

(a) rotates 90° anticlockwise about $(0, 0)$

(b) rotates 90° anticlockwise about $(-4, 2)$

(c) rotates 90° clockwise about $(-4, 1)$

Use tracing paper

1

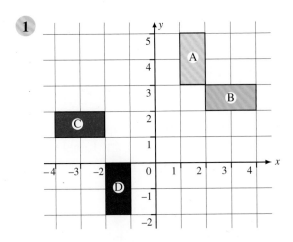

Describe *fully* the rotation which transforms:

(a) shape A onto shape B

(b) B onto C

(c) C onto D

2

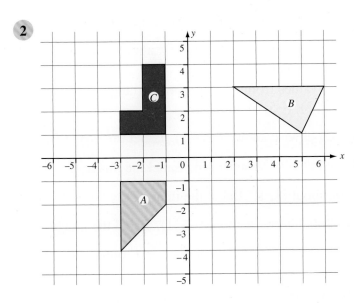

Copy the grid and shapes opposite.

(a) Rotate shape A $90°$ anticlockwise about $(-3, -4)$. Label the image P.

(b) Rotate shape B $90°$ clockwise about $(1, 0)$. Label the image Q.

(c) Rotate shape C $90°$ clockwise about $(2, 1)$. Label the image R.

3 (a) Draw x and y axes with values from -5 to 5.

Draw rectangle A with vertices (corners) at $(0, 2)$, $(0, 5)$, $(-2, 5)$, $(-2, 2)$.

(b) Rotate rectangle A $180°$ about $(-2, 2)$. Label the image B.

(c) Rotate rectangle B $90°$ clockwise about $(0, -1)$. Label the image C.

(d) Rotate rectangle C $180°$ about $(2, 0)$. Label the image D.

(e) Rotate rectangle D $90°$ clockwise about $(3, -2)$. Label the image E.

4

Copy the grid opposite. The x-axis goes from −5 to 5. The y-axis goes from −4 to 4. Shape A has vertices (corners) at (−1, 2), (−1, 3), (−3, 3), (−3, 0), (−2, 0) and (−2, 2).

(a) Rotate shape A 180° about (0, 2). Label the image B.

(b) Rotate shape B 90° clockwise about (1, 0). Label the image C.

(c) Rotate shape C 90° anticlockwise about (2, −2). Label the image D.

(d) Rotate shape D 90° anticlockwise about (0, −3). Label the image E.

(e) Rotate shape E 90° anticlockwise about (−5, 0). Label the image F.

5 (a) Draw x and y axes with values from −6 to 6. Draw triangle A with vertices (corners) at (−5, 2), (−5, 6) and (−3, 5).

(b) Rotate triangle A 90° clockwise about (−4, −2). Label the image B.

(c) Rotate triangle B 90° clockwise about (6, 0). Label the image C.

(d) Rotate triangle C 180° about (1, 1). Label the image D.

(e) Rotate triangle D 90° anticlockwise about (−5, 1). Label the image E.

(f) Describe *fully* the rotation which transforms triangle E onto triangle A.

6 (a) Draw the x axis from −4 to 4.

Draw the y axis from −3 to 3.

Draw triangle A with vertices at (−1, −2), (−2, −2), (−2, 0).

(b) Rotate triangle A 90° clockwise about (0, −1). Label the image B.

(c) Rotate triangle B 180° about (1, 1). Label the image C.

(d) Reflect triangle C in the x-axis. Label the image D.

(e) Reflect triangle D in the line y = −2. Label the image E.

(f) Translate triangle E through $\begin{pmatrix} -5 \\ 1 \end{pmatrix}$. Label the image F.

(g) Describe *fully* the rotation which transforms triangle F onto triangle A.

An **enlargement** makes the shape larger (or smaller). The original and the enlargement must be exactly the same shape. All angles in both shapes stay the same.

Note

Enlarge this shape by a scale factor $\frac{1}{2}$

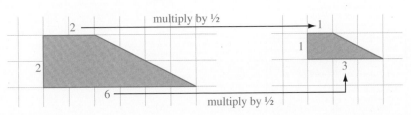

The shape gets smaller when the scale factor is a fraction between 0 and 1.

M8. 6

Enlarge these shapes by the scale factor given. Make sure you leave room on your page for the enlargement!

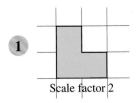

1   Scale factor 2

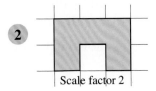

2   Scale factor 2

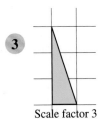

3   Scale factor 3

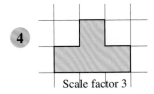

4   Scale factor 3

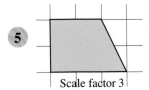

5   Scale factor 3

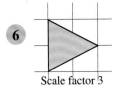

6   Scale factor 3

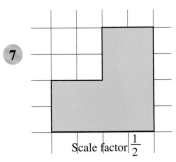

7   Scale factor $\frac{1}{2}$

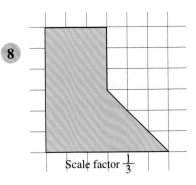

8   Scale factor $\frac{1}{3}$

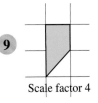

9   Scale factor 4

207

Look at each of the following pairs of diagrams and decide whether or not one diagram is an enlargement of the other. For each Question write the scale factor of the enlargement or write 'not an enlargement'.

10

11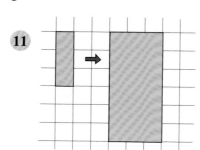

12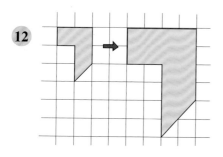

Centre of enlargement

A *mathematical enlargement* always has a centre of enlargement as well as a scale factor.

The centre of enlargement is formed by drawing a broken line through a corner of the new shape and the same corner of the old shape.

Do this for each pair of points as shown in the diagram.

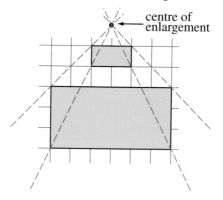

centre of enlargement

The centre of enlargement is the point where all the broken lines meet (intersect).

We need 2 things to describe fully an enlargement:
1. the **scale factor**
2. the **centre of enlargement**

208

Drawing an enlargement

Draw an enlargement of triangle *A* with scale factor 3 about the centre of enlargement *C*.

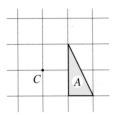

Join the centre *C* to one vertex (corner) with a dotted line

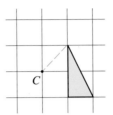

Multiply the length of the dotted line by the scale factor (do this by measuring or by counting squares) then draw the longer dotted line from *C*

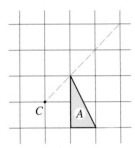

This shows where the top vertex will move to

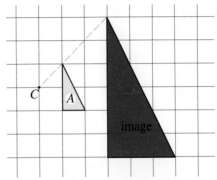

The rest of the enlarged shape can be drawn from this new vertex.

Describe fully the enlargement which transforms shape *A* onto shape *B*.

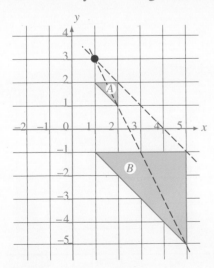

Draw broken lines through each corner of the new shape and the same corner of the old shape.

The centre of enlargement is where the broken lines meet (intersect).

Answer: enlargement by scale factor 4 about (1,3).

For Questions **1** to **5** , draw the grid and the 2 shapes then draw broken lines through pairs of points in the new shape and the old shape. Describe *fully* the enlargement which transforms shape *A* onto shape *B*.

1

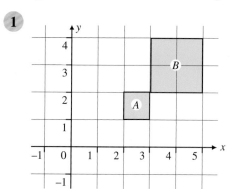

2

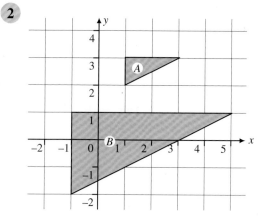

3

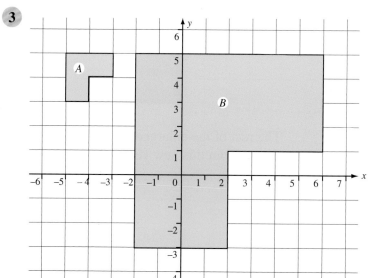

4

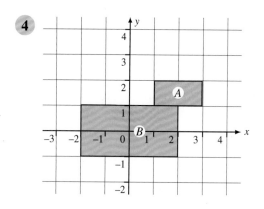

5

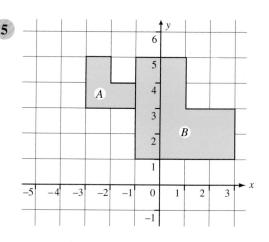

For Questions ⑥ to ⑪, copy the diagram and then draw an enlargement using the scale factor and centre of enlargement (C) given.
Leave room for the enlargement!

6

C

Scale factor 2

7

C

Scale factor 2

8

C

Scale factor 3

9

C

Scale factor $\frac{1}{2}$

10

C

Scale factor 2

11

C   Scale factor $\frac{1}{3}$

12 Look at your diagram for Question ⑧

(a) Write down the area of the original shape.

(b) Write down the area of the enlarged shape.

(c) How many times bigger is the area of the enlarged shape? Compare this to the scale factor.

13

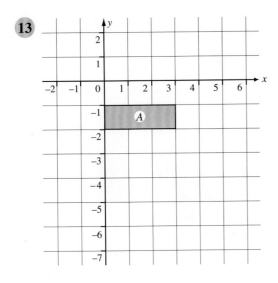

(a) Copy the grid and rectangle A. Enlarge rectangle A by scale factor 2 about $(0, 0)$. Label the image B.

(b) Write down the area of A.

(c) Write down the area of B.

(d) How many times bigger is the area of B? Compare this to the scale factor.

211

14

Copy the grid and square A

Enlarge square A by scale factor $\frac{1}{2}$ about $(0, 0)$

Label the image B

15 (a) Draw the x-axis from -4 to 8. Draw the y-axis from -4 to 6.
Draw the triangle A with vertices (corners) at $(1, 3)$, $(1, 4)$, $(3, 4)$.
(b) Enlarge triangle A by scale factor 2 about $(1, 5)$. Label the image B.
(c) Enlarge triangle B by scale factor $\frac{1}{2}$ about $(-3, 1)$. Label the image C.
(d) Enlarge triangle C by scale factor 3 about $(-2, 3)$. Label the image D.

16 (a) Draw the x-axis from -6 to 6. Draw the y-axis from -7 to 7.
Draw the triangle A with vertices at $(2, 2)$, $(2, 6)$, $(4, 6)$.
(b) Enlarge triangle A by scale factor $\frac{1}{2}$ about $(0, 0)$. Label the image B.
(c) Reflect triangle B in the y-axis. Label the image C.
(d) Enlarge triangle C by scale factor 3 about $(-1, 4)$. Label the image D.
(e) Rotate triangle D $90°$ clockwise about $(-1, -5)$. Label the image E.
(f) Enlarge triangle E by scale factor $\frac{1}{3}$ about $(5, 1)$. Label the image F.

Can you still?

8B **Multiply and divide fractions (see Unit 5)**

Can you still?

Work out (cancel the answers if possible):

1. $\frac{1}{5}$ of $\frac{1}{4}$ **2.** $\frac{2}{3}$ of $\frac{6}{7}$ **3.** $\frac{2}{5} \times \frac{1}{8}$ **4.** $\frac{3}{4} \times \frac{5}{9}$

5. $\frac{1}{4} \times \frac{8}{9}$ **6.** $\frac{4}{5} \times \frac{10}{11}$ **7.** $\frac{3}{4} \times 28$ **8.** $\frac{2}{7} \times 21$

9. $\frac{1}{9} \div \frac{1}{5}$ **10.** $\frac{1}{3} \div \frac{4}{5}$ **11.** $\frac{3}{8} \div \frac{3}{10}$ **12.** $\frac{7}{9} \div \frac{5}{6}$

13. $\frac{3}{4} \div \frac{7}{8}$ **14.** $\frac{5}{9} \div 3$ **15.** $\frac{3}{5} \div 2$ **16.** $\frac{2}{11} \div \frac{4}{5}$

M8. 7

You may use tracing paper.

1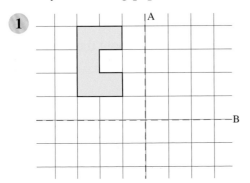

Copy the shape and the mirror lines.

(a) Reflect the shape in mirror line A.

(b) Reflect the image (new shape) in mirror line B.

2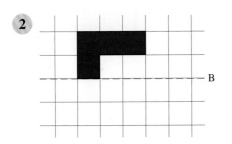

Copy the shape and the mirror line.

(a) Reflect the shape in the mirror line.

(b) Translate the image (new shape) 3 units to the right and 1 unit up.

3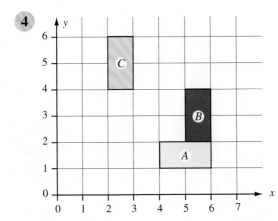

Copy the shape and the mirror line.

(a) Reflect the shape in the mirror line.

(b) Rotate the image $90°$ clockwise about the point C.

4

(a) Describe *fully* the rotation which moves shape A onto shape B.

(b) Describe *fully* the translation which moves shape B onto shape C.

213

5

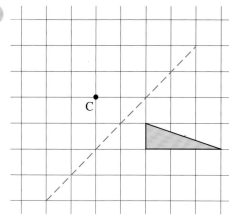

Copy the shape and the mirror line.

(a) Reflect the shape in the mirror line.

(b) Rotate the image $90°$ anticlockwise about the point C.

6 Copy the shape.

(a) Rotate the shape $180°$ about the point C.

(b) Translate the image 4 units to the left and 2 units down.

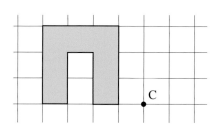

7

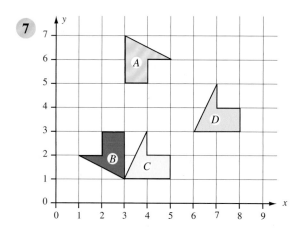

(a) Describe *fully* the rotation which moves shape A onto shape B.

(b) Describe *fully* the rotation which moves shape B onto shape C.

(c) Describe *fully* the translation which moves shape C onto shape D.

Can you still?   *Can you still?*

8C **Multiply out brackets and collect like terms (see Unit 4)**

Simplify

1. $3(x + 4)$

2. $5(2x - 3)$

3. $4(3x + 6) + 2$

4. $4(2x + 1) + 7$

5. $3(x + 2) + 2(x + 3)$

6. $4(3x + 4) + 3(2x + 3)$

7. $8x + 5 + 4(3x - 1)$

8. $2(5x + 2) - 3(2x - 4)$

9. $5(x + 4) + 2(3x - 5)$

You may use tracing paper.

1

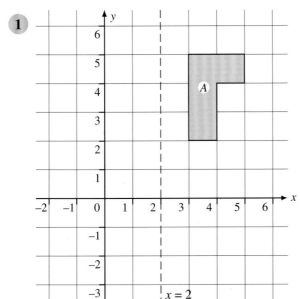

Copy the grid and shape opposite.

(a) Reflect shape A in the line $x = 2$. Label the image B.

(b) Reflect shape B in the line $y = 1$. Label the image C.

(c) Rotate shape C $90°$ clockwise about $(1, -3)$. Label the image D.

2

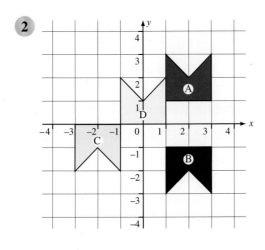

(a) Describe *fully* the transformation which transforms shape A onto shape B.

(b) Describe *fully* the transformation which transforms shape B onto shape C.

(c) Describe *fully* the transformation which transforms shape C onto shape D.

(d) Describe *fully* the transformation which transforms shape D onto shape A.

3 (a) Draw the x-axis from -4 to 8.

Draw the y-axis from -5 to 5.

Draw triangle A with vertices of $(1, 1)$, $(1, 2)$, $(3, 2)$.

(b) Enlarge triangle A by scale factor 2 about $(0, 0)$. Label the image B.

(c) Rotate triangle B $90°$ anticlockwise abut $(6, 4)$. Label the image C.

(d) Translate triangle C through $\begin{pmatrix} -1 \\ -4 \end{pmatrix}$ Label the image D

(e) Reflect triangle D in the line $x = 3$. Label the image E.

(f) Rotate triangle E $90°$ clockwise about $(1, 0)$. Label the image F.

4

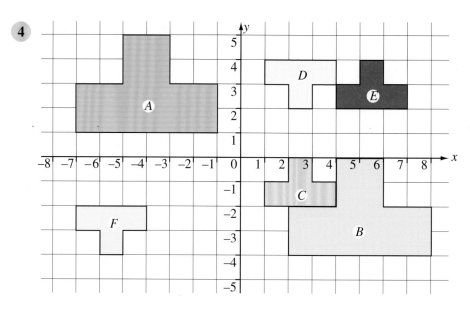

Describe *fully* the transformation which moves:

(a) shape A onto shape B (b) shape B onto shape C

(c) shape C onto shape D (d) shape D onto shape E

(e) shape E onto shape F

5 (a) Draw the x-axis from -5 to 10.

    Draw the y-axis from -8 to 5.

    Draw shape A with vertices at $(2, 2)$, $(2, 4)$, $(3, 3)$, $(5, 3)$, $(5, 2)$.

(b) Rotate shape A $180°$ about $(3, 1)$. Label the image B.

(c) Enlarge shape B by scale factor 3 about $(1, 1)$. Label the image C.

(d) Reflect shape B in the y-axis. Label the image D.

(e) Reflect shape D in the line $y = 1$. Label the image E.

(f) Describe *fully* the translation which moves shape E onto shape A.

6 (a) Draw the x-axis from -8 to 4.

    Draw the y-axis from -5 to 5.

    Draw shape A with vertices $(-1, 2)$, $(-1, 5)$, $(-2, 5)$, $(-2, 3)$, $(-3, 3)$, $(-3, 5)$, $(-4, 5)$, $(-4, 2)$.

(b) Rotate shape A $90°$ anticlockwise about $(-4, 1)$. Label the image B.

(c) Reflect shape B in the line $x = -2$. Label the image C.

(d) Reflect shape C in the x-axis. Label the image D.

(e) Rotate shape D $90°$ clockwise about $(0, 0)$. Label the image E.

(f) Describe *fully* the transformation that would move shape E onto shape A.

A manager has six people willing to work one weekend at the 'Dog and Elephant' pub.

At any one time he needs two people behind the bar, one person serving food and one person in the kitchen. This is not the case towards the end of the evening when food is no longer served.

This table shows what the six people can do which depends on their age and experience.

Name	Bar	Serving food	Kitchen
Joe	✓	✓	
Kate	✓	✓	✓
Ben		✓	✓
Penny		✓	✓
Nazrul	✓	✓	
Milly	✓	✓	✓

On Saturday the six people can work the hours shown below.

Name	Joe	Kate	Ben	Penny	Nazrul	Milly
Hours	8	9	5	3½	9	8

Task A

No person can work more than 3 hours without taking a break of at least ½ hour.

Make a copy of the Saturday schedule below then fill in who works where and when. It may be better to use a pencil and have a rubber handy.

Saturday schedule

	12pm	1pm	2pm	3pm	4pm	5pm	6pm	7pm	8pm	9pm	10pm	11pm	12am
Bar													
Bar													
Serving food													
Kitchen													

217

On Sunday five people can work the hours shown below.

Name	Joe	Kate	Ben	Penny	Milly
Hours	6	5	2	6	6

Task B

On Sunday the pub is shut between 3 pm and 7 pm. Make a copy of the Sunday schedule below then fill in who works where and when. *Remember no person can work more than 3 hours without taking a break of at least $\frac{1}{2}$ hour.*

Sunday schedule

	12pm	1pm	2pm	3pm	4pm	5pm	6pm	7pm	8pm	9pm	10pm	11pm	12am
Bar													
Bar													
Serving food													
Kitchen													

Rate of pay per hour	
Bar	£6.70
Serving food	£5.90
Kitchen	£5.90

Task C

Using your schedules, work out how much each of the six people earn during this weekend.

Their total pay should add up to £428.65

Task D

Get a partner to check through your two schedules to make sure you have not broken any rules.

TEST YOURSELF ON UNIT 8

1. Recognising congruent shapes

Which shapes are congruent to shape A?

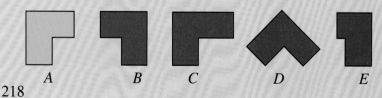

A *B* *C* *D* *E*

2. Using co-ordinates

(a)

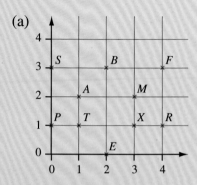

Write down the co-ordinates of each letter that spells the word A X E S

3. Translating shapes

(a)

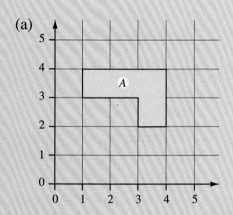

Copy the grid opposite and draw the shape shown.

(i) Translate shape A 1 unit to the left and 2 units down. Label the new shape B.

(ii) Translate shape B 2 units to the right and 3 units up. Label the new shape C.

(b)

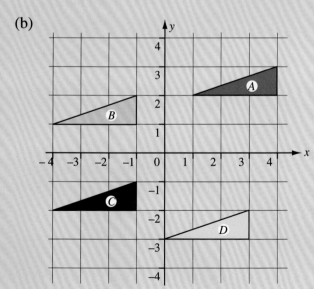

Describe the following translations.

(i) A to C

(ii) A to D

(iii) D to B

(iv) B to A

4. Reflecting shapes in mirror lines

Draw each shape below and reflect in the broken mirror line.

(a)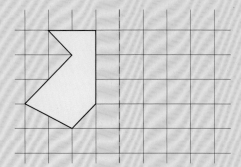

(b)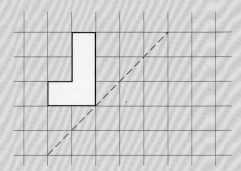

5. Rotating shapes

(a)

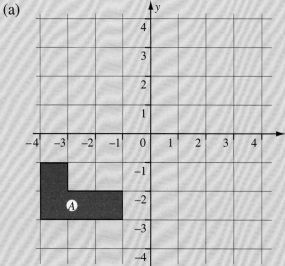

Copy the grid and shape A opposite.

(i) Rotate shape A $90°$ anticlockwise about (0, 0). Label the image B.

(ii) Rotate shape A $180°$ about (−1, −2). Label the image C.

(b)

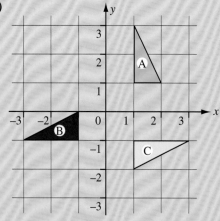

Describe *fully* the rotation which transforms:

(i) shape A onto B

(ii) shape A onto C

6. Enlarging shapes

Copy the diagrams below and then draw an enlargement using the scale factor and centre of enlargement (C) given.

(a)

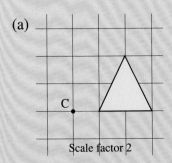

Scale factor 2

(b)

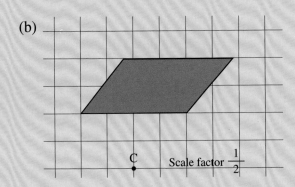

C   Scale factor $\frac{1}{2}$

(c)

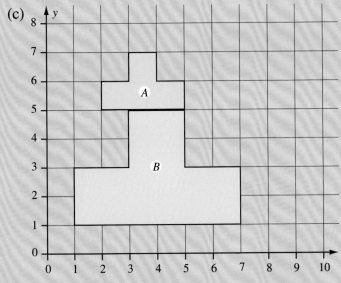

Describe *fully* the enlargement which transforms shape *A* onto shape *B* (draw the grid and 2 shapes if you need to)

Mixed examination questions

1 Which **two** of the following shapes are congruent to each other?

(a) (b) (c) (d)

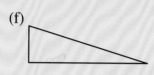

(e) (f) (g)

(WJEC)

2

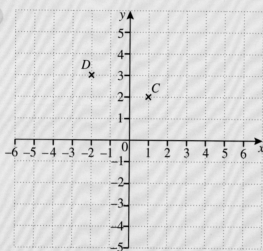

(a) Write down the co-ordinates of the points and C and D.

(b) Copy the grid and plot the points $E(-5, -1)$ and $F(2, -4)$.

Label each point clearly.

(OCR)

3 (a) Describe fully the single transformation which takes A onto B.

(b) Describe fully the single transformation which takes B onto A.

(c) A is mapped onto D by transformation $\begin{pmatrix} -2 \\ 3 \end{pmatrix}$.

Copy the grid and draw the position of D on the diagram.

(AQA)

4

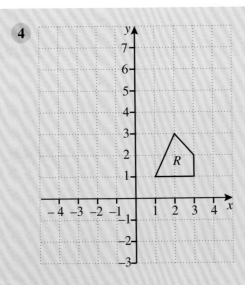

(a) Copy the grid opposite. R is mapped onto S by a reflection in the y-axis. Draw and label S.

(b) S is mapped onto T by reflection in the line $y = 4$. Draw and Label T.

(c) Describe fully the single transformation which maps T onto R.

(AQA)

5 (a) Copy the grid opposite. Reflect the triangle A in the line $x = 4$. Label the image P.

(b) Translate triangle A by 4 squares to the left and 3 squares down.

Label the image Q.

(c) Triangle B is an enlargement of triangle A. Write down the scale factor of the enlargement.

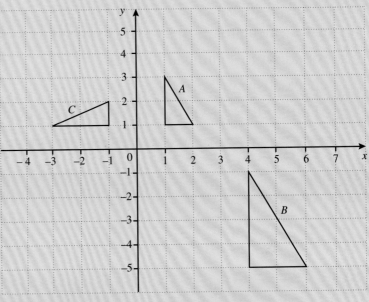

(d) Describe fully the single transformation that maps triangle A onto triangle C.

(OCR)

In this unit you will learn how to:

– add and subtract decimals

– multiply decimals

– divide decimals by whole numbers

– divide by decimals

– round off numbers to the nearest 10, 100, 1000 or whole number

– round off to decimal places

– estimate answers

– use a calculator

– round off to significant figures

– check answers

– USE YOUR MATHS! – save it in the home

Adding and subtracting decimals

(a) 3.2 + 4.31

put a zero

$$\begin{array}{r} 3.20 \\ + 4.31 \\ \hline 7.51 \\ \uparrow \end{array}$$

(line up the points)

(b) 0.27 + 5 + 14.2

$$\begin{array}{r} 0.27 \\ 5.00 \\ + 14.20 \\ \hline 19.47 \end{array}$$

(write 5 as 5.00)

(c) 8 – 3.7

$$\begin{array}{r} {}^{7}\cancel{8}{}^{1}0 \\ - 3.7 \\ \hline 4.3 \end{array}$$

(write 8 as 8.0)

M 9.1

1 Work out

(a) $\begin{array}{r} 13.6 \\ + 22.3 \end{array}$

(b) $\begin{array}{r} 361.8 \\ + \ 32.7 \end{array}$

(c) $\begin{array}{r} 7.34 \\ + 8.4 \end{array}$

(d)	18.6	(e)	30.75	(f)	13.0
	+ 13.4		+ 7.8		+ 0.39

(g)	17.5	(h)	8.36	(i)	14.0
	− 6.2		− 2.8		− 2.6

2

0.71	0.54	0.96	0.37
0.22	0.8	0.63	0.41
0.46	0.29	0.04	0.61
0.39	0.2	0.78	0.59

This grid is full of pairs of numbers which add up to 1. Write down every pair (there are 8 pairs of numbers).

3 Copy and complete the following:

(a)	73.16	(b)	3816.3	(c)	2628.32
	+ 0.52		+ 507.2		− 316.21

(d)	68.17	(e)	213.72	(f)	362.7
	− 26.32		− 61.36		+ 257.8

4 Work out the following (Remember to line up the decimal point):

(a) $1.7 + 3.27$ (b) $5.16 + 4.99$ (c) $0.082 + 3.07$

(d) $6 + 0.31$ (e) $8.28 + 4.19$ (f) $38.64 + 13.8$

(g) $47.3 − 21.8$ (h) $63.7 − 28.8$ (i) $38.4 − 16$

(j) $7 − 4.4$ (k) $12 − 6.3$ (l) $7.7 − 5.39$

E 9.1

1

0.281	0.049	0.213	0.12
0.251	0.18	0.17	0.28
0.13	0.06	0.087	0.019
0.202	0.02	0.098	0.24

This grid is full of pairs of numbers which add up to 0.3. Write down every pair (there are 8 pairs of numbers).

2 Work out

(a) $712.6 + 32.8 + 163.9$ (b) $807.3 + 216.8 + 36.7$ (c) $68.3 + 121.62 + 31.94$

(d) $61.87 - 13.9$ (e) $107.2 - 68.14$ (f) $2.174 - 1.38$

3

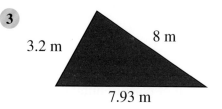

3.2 m   8 m   7.93 m

Find the perimeter of this triangle.

4 How much change from a £20 note do you get if you spend:

(a) £3.72   (b) £14.53   (c) £11.06   (d) £6.85

(e) £4.48   (f) £3.99   (g) £8.63   (h) £17.57

5 David has £50. He buys a book for £6.95 and a CD for £14.95. How much money does he have left?

6 Geri has £40. She spends £13.87 on food and £15.50 on travel. How much money does she have left?

7

TV	£487.50
computer	£874.99
CD player	£88.45
printer	£124.75

Dan has £1600 to spend. Can he afford to buy all the items opposite? If so, how much money will he have left?

In Questions **8** to **10**, find the odd answer out.

8 (a) $12.63 + 11.85 + 1.28$ (b) $20.3 + 4.19 + 1.37$ (c) $18.38 + 4.9 + 2.58$

9 (a) $11.6 - 5.18$ (b) $14.4 - 7.88$ (c) $16 - 9.58$

10 (a) $5.66 - 2.3$ (b) $16.96 - 13.7$ (c) $11.16 - 7.9$

11 Which is larger?

A   sum of 7.22 and 8   or   B   difference between 23 and 7.68

12 Find the missing digits

(a) $\quad \square . 5 \square$
$\quad \underline{- 4 . \square 3}$
$\qquad 3 . 73$

(b) $\quad 4 . \square 7$
$\quad \underline{+ \square . 9 \square}$
$\qquad 9 . 03$

(c) $\quad 3 . 17 \square$
$\quad \underline{- \square . 4 \square 8}$
$\qquad 0 . \square 48$

226

9A **Convert improper fractions and mixed numbers (see Unit 5)**

Change the following improper fractions to mixed numbers.

1. $\dfrac{9}{4}$ 2. $\dfrac{13}{5}$ 3. $\dfrac{27}{10}$ 4. $\dfrac{17}{6}$ 5. $\dfrac{38}{7}$

Change the following mixed numbers to improper fractions.

6. $3\dfrac{2}{3}$ 7. $5\dfrac{1}{2}$ 8. $7\dfrac{2}{5}$ 9. $3\dfrac{6}{7}$ 10. $8\dfrac{3}{4}$

Multiplying decimals

(a) $4.23 \times 10 = 42.3$

(b) $0.0063 \times 100 = 0.63$

(c) $10.9 \times 1000 = 10900$

(d) 6×0.1

$= 6 \times \dfrac{1}{10}$

$= 6 \div 10$

$= 0.6$

(e) 0.7×0.1

$= 0.7 \times \dfrac{1}{10}$

$= 0.7 \div 10$

$= 0.07$

(f) 20.3×0.01

$= 20.3 \times \dfrac{1}{100}$

$= 20.3 \div 100$

$= 0.203$

M 9.2

Work out

1. 6.12×10
2. 3.97×10
3. 0.618×100
4. 5.81×100

5. 0.093×10
6. 0.0081×100
7. 3.226×1000
8. 13.6×1000

9. 7.36×100
10. 0.0612×1000
11. 5.73×100
12. 3.298×10

13. 0.38×1000
14. 6.1×1000
15. 0.3×100
16. 0.5×1000

17. 0.1×10
18. 0.79×1000
19. 2.14×10
20. 0.824×100

Work out

21. 4×0.1
22. 0.2×0.1
23. 18×0.01
24. 7.4×0.01

25. 9×0.1
26. 0.8×0.1
27. 2×0.01
28. 15×0.1

227

29 19×0.1 **30** 0.36×0.1 **31** 64×0.01 **32** 5×0.1

33 25×0.1 **34** 1×0.01 **35** 87×0.01 **36** 0.4×0.1

37 Here are 4 rules:

| $\times 10$ | $\times 0.1$ | $\times 100$ | $\times 0.01$ |

Copy each chain of numbers below and fill in the empty boxes with the correct rule (Remember: $\times 0.1$ means $\div 10$ and $\times 0.01$ means $\div 100$).

(a) $3.9 \rightarrow \square \rightarrow 39 \rightarrow \square \rightarrow 390 \rightarrow \square \rightarrow 3.9 \rightarrow \square \rightarrow 0.39$

(b) $670 \rightarrow \square \rightarrow 67 \rightarrow \square \rightarrow 6.7 \rightarrow \square \rightarrow 670 \rightarrow \square \rightarrow 6.7$

(c) $83.2 \rightarrow \square \rightarrow 8320 \rightarrow \square \rightarrow 832 \rightarrow \square \rightarrow 8.32 \rightarrow \square \rightarrow 0.832$

(d) $0.24 \rightarrow \square \rightarrow 24 \rightarrow \square \rightarrow 2.4 \rightarrow \square \rightarrow 240 \rightarrow \square \rightarrow 0.24$

When we multiply two decimal numbers together, the answer has the same number of figures after the decimal point as the total number of figures after the decimal point in the Question.

(a) 0.7×0.4

($7 \times 4 = 28$)

so $0.\underline{7} \times 0.\underline{4} = 0.\underline{2}\,\underline{8}$

(b) 0.8×0.009

($8 \times 9 = 72$)

so $0.8 \times 0.\underline{0}\,\underline{0}\,\underline{9} = 0.\underline{0}\,\underline{0}\,\underline{7}\,\underline{2}$

Note:

When a number is multiplied by a decimal between 0 and 1, the answer will be smaller than the starting number.

E 9.2

1 Copy the Questions below and put the decimal point in the correct place in each answer.

(a) $3.8 \times 0.7 = 266$

(b) $0.3 \times 0.78 = 234$

(c) $8.6 \times 6 = 516$

(d) $0.17 \times 0.29 = 493$

(e) $3.1 \times 0.94 = 2914$

(f) $3.28 \times 2.8 = 9184$

(g) $0.619 \times 3.6 = 22284$

(h) $27 \times 0.19 = 513$

(i) $0.05 \times 1.67 = 835$

(j) $8 \times 1.084 = 8672$

2 Work out

(a) 0.9×0.4 (b) 0.2×0.8 (c) 0.03×0.7

(d) 0.4×0.04 (e) 0.03×0.6 (f) 0.5×0.007

(g) 0.03×0.4 (h) 0.8×0.7 (i) 0.04×0.003

(j) 0.8^2 (k) 0.3^2 (l) 0.9^2

3 Work out

(a) 3×0.72 (b) 6.9×4 (c) 12.3×5

(d) 14.6×6 (e) 7×13.2 (f) 0.027×8

4 Find the total cost of 3 kg of meat at £4.74 per kg.

5 Find the total cost of 5 cereal packets at £1.89 for each packet.

6 Find the total cost of 7 bottles of tomato ketchup at £1.63 for each bottle *and* 4 large packets of crisps at £1.28 for each packet.

7 If 1 kg of cheese costs £5.29, find the cost of 4 kg.

8 A new car tyre costs £41.49.
What is the total cost of 4 new tyres?

9 Find the total cost of 6 batteries at £1.47 each.

10 £1 = $1.52. Change the money below to dollars by multiplying by 1.52.

(a) £3   (b) £7   (c) £8   (d) £20

11 Work out

(a) 27×0.02 (b) 14×0.05 (c) 18×0.03 (d) 0.5×0.05

(e) 44×0.02 (f) 1.6×0.4 (g) 4.1×0.5 (h) 2.63×0.3

(i) 3.4×0.6 (j) 0.49×0.7 (k) 0.38×0.02 (l) 0.22×0.03

(m) 6.22×0.07 (n) 18.4×0.8 (o) 40.9×0.3

12 Copy below and fill in the empty boxes.

(a) $0.4 \times 3 = \boxed{}$ (b) $0.7 \times \boxed{} = 4.2$

(c) $\boxed{} \times 0.6 = 0.18$ (d) $0.02 \times \boxed{} = 0.014$

(e) $0.8 \times \boxed{} = 0.048$ (f) $\boxed{} \times 0.06 = 0.0054$

229

Dividing decimals by whole numbers

(a) $11 \div 8$

$$
\begin{array}{r}
1.\ 3\ 7\ 5 \\
8\overline{)\ 11.^30\ ^60\ ^40}
\end{array}
$$
↑ ↑ ↑
Note the extra zeros

(b) $7.3 \div 4$

$$
\begin{array}{r}
1.\ 8\ 2\ 5 \\
4\overline{)\ 7.^33\ ^10\ ^20}
\end{array}
$$
↑ ↑
Note the extra zeros

M 9.3

Work out

1 $3\overline{)\ 18.6}$ **2** $4\overline{)\ 36.48}$ **3** $6\overline{)\ 20.46}$

4 $6\overline{)\ 15.36}$ **5** $7\overline{)\ 34.3}$ **6** $9\overline{)\ 39.15}$

7 Divide the numbers below by 4.

     (a) 13.2   (b) 18.94   (c) 13   (d) 27

8 Divide the numbers below by 8.

     (a) 21.12   (b) 3.6   (c) 17   (d) 31

Work out

9 $18.52 \div 4$ **10** $14.82 \div 6$ **11** $205.2 \div 6$ **12** $18.93 \div 6$

13 $1.085 \div 5$ **14** $26.67 \div 7$ **15** $1.96 \div 4$ **16** $70.28 \div 7$

17 $8.7 \div 5$ **18** $0.58 \div 8$ **19** $0.02352 \div 6$ **20** $0.3724 \div 7$

21 A prize of £259.50 is shared by six winners. How much should each person receive?

22 Hannah and three of her friends go to the cinema. The tickets cost £23. What is the cost of 1 ticket?

23 Five people share the fuel cost of a car journey. The total fuel cost is £32.35. How much does each person pay?

24 Tom, Sally and Cherie club together to buy some flowers for their dear old Gran. The flowers cost £37.35. How much does each person pay?

25 Christmas crackers cost £11.94 for six. How much does each cracker cost?

26 Four identical boxes weigh 193 kg in total. How much does each box weigh?

27 A multipack containing 4 soap bars costs £2.52. Single soap bars can be bought for 67p each. How much do you save on each bar by buying the multi-pack?

28 A piece of wood is 4.23 m long. It is cut into 9 equal parts. How long is each part?

Dividing by decimals

To divide by a decimal, multiply both numbers by 10, 100, 1000, … so that the decimal you are dividing by becomes a whole number. Now divide the 2 numbers to get the answer.

(a) $3.2 \div 0.\underline{4}$

multiply both numbers by 10

$= 32 \div 4$

$= 8$

(b) $5.517 \div 0.\underline{9}$

multiply both numbers by 10

$= 55.17 \div 9$

$$\begin{array}{r} 6.\,1\;3 \\ 9\overline{)55.^1 1^2 7} \end{array}$$

(c) $3.5882 \div 0.\underline{0}\,\underline{0}\,\underline{7}$

multiply both numbers by 1000

$= 3588.2 \div 7$

$$\begin{array}{r} 51\,2.\,6 \\ 7\overline{)358^18.^42} \end{array}$$

Note:

When a number is divided by a decimal between 0 and 1, the answer will be larger than the starting number.

E 9.3

1 Copy the Questions below and fill in the empty boxes

(a) $4.6 \div 0.2 = \boxed{} \div 2 = \boxed{}$

(b) $3.2 \div 0.04 = \boxed{} \div 4 = \boxed{}$

(c) $1.65 \div 0.5 = \boxed{} \div 5 = \boxed{}$

(d) $2.64 \div 0.002 = \boxed{} \div 2 = \boxed{}$

2 Divide the numbers below by 0.5.

(a) 3.5   (b) 4   (c) 6.5   (d) 8

3 Divide the numbers below by 0.3.

(a) 6   (b) 2.4   (c) 3.6   (d) 0.18

4 Divide the numbers below by 0.7.

(a) 2.8   (b) 6.3   (c) 21   (d) 0.42

Work out

5 7.2 ÷ 0.4   **6** 3.8 ÷ 0.2   **7** 1.84 ÷ 0.8

8 14.98 ÷ 0.7   **9** 0.084 ÷ 0.03   **10** 0.496 ÷ 0.08

11 0.444 ÷ 0.06   **12** 3.25 ÷ 0.05   **13** 26.6 ÷ 0.7

14 0.075 ÷ 0.003   **15** 0.144 ÷ 0.04   **16** 0.065 ÷ 0.002

17 A bottle of lemonade holds 1 litre. How many glasses can be filled from this bottle if each glass holds 0.2 litres?

18 A box of sweets contains 2.4 kg. How many packets can be filled from this box if each packet holds 0.15 kg?

In Questions **19** to **21**, find the odd answer out.

19 (a) 0.63 ÷ 0.7   (b) 0.57 ÷ 0.6   (c) 0.72 ÷ 0.8

20 (a) 7.02 ÷ 0.09   (b) 5.18 ÷ 0.07   (c) 2.96 ÷ 0.04

21 (a) 8.82 ÷ 0.6   (b) 7.4 ÷ 0.5   (c) 11.84 ÷ 0.8

22 Each empty square below contains either a number or an operation
(+ , − , × , ÷). Copy each square and fill in the missing details. The arrows
are equal signs.

(a)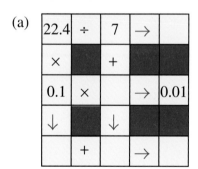

(b)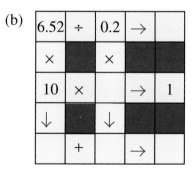

23 147 × 382 = 56154

use this to work out:

(a) 1470 × 382

(b) 147 × 38200

(c) 14.7 × 38.2

(d) 1.47 × 3820

24 64.848 ÷ 28 = 2.316

use this to work out:

(a) 64848 ÷ 28

(b) 6484.8 ÷ 280

(c) 0.64848 ÷ 0.028

(d) 2316 × 28

(9B) Calculate angles (see Unit 3)

Find the angles marked with letters.

1.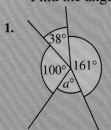

2.

3.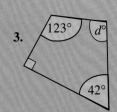

4.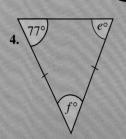

5.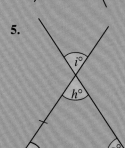

6.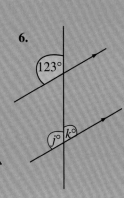

7.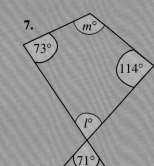

8.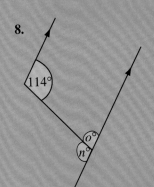

Rounding off numbers

1. *Rounding to the nearest whole number.*

   If the first digit after the decimal point is *5 or more* round *up*. Otherwise round down.

	rounds to	
68.3	$\longrightarrow$	68
49.8	$\longrightarrow$	50
3.5	$\longrightarrow$	4

2. *Rounding to the nearest 100.*

   If the digit in the tens column is 5 or more round up. Otherwise round down.

387	$\longrightarrow$	400
138	$\longrightarrow$	100
3712	$\longrightarrow$	3700

M 9.4

1 Which of the numbers below will round to 70 when rounded to the nearest 10?

63 64 65 66 67 68 69 70 71 72 73 74 75 76 77

2 Which of the numbers below will round to 140 when rounded to the nearest 10?

133 134 135 136 137 138 139 140 141 142 143 144 145

146 147 148

3 Which of the numbers below will round to 400 when rounded to the nearest 100?

330 340 349 350 351 375 399 400 401 408

420 437 440 445 449 450 451 460

4 Round each of these numbers to the nearest 100.

(a) 684   (b) 393   (c) 807   (d) 814   (e) 485

(f) 755   (g) 1586   (h) 2111   (i) 6394   (j) 3423

5 Which of the numbers below will round to 3000 when rounded to the nearest 1000?

2400 2499 2500 2506 2700 2900 3000 3100 3300 3400

3450 3499 3500 3550 3600

6 The population of some Scottish towns in the year 1800 are shown on the map.

Write down each town and round its population to the nearest 1000.

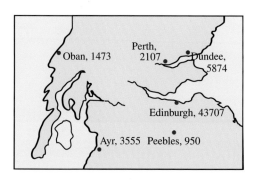

7 Round each of these numbers to the nearest whole number:

(a) 5.2   (b) 8.7   (c) 2.5   (d) 3.4   (e) 8.5

(f) 0.7   (g) 12.2   (h) 25.8   (i) 41.1   (j) 69.2

(k) 249.9   (l) 174.6   (m) 3.17   (n) 8.32   (o) 7.64

8 Which of the numbers below are correctly rounded off?

(a) 67 $\longrightarrow$ 70   (to nearest 10)   (b) 4729 $\longrightarrow$ 4700   (to nearest 100)

(c) 3186 $\longrightarrow$ 3100 (to nearest 100)   (d) 38194 $\longrightarrow$ 38000 (to nearest 1000)

(e) 2743 $\longrightarrow$ 2750 (to nearest 10)   (f) 791 $\longrightarrow$ 800   (to nearest 10)

(g) 2.38 $\longrightarrow$ 3 (to nearest whole number)

(h) 5.16 $\longrightarrow$ 5 (to nearest whole number)

(i) 35 $\longrightarrow$ 30 (to nearest 10)

(j) 13.82 $\longrightarrow$ 13 (to nearest whole number)

9 What is the smallest number that will round to 820 when rounded to the nearest 10?

10 What is the largest whole number that will round to 2700 when rounded to the nearest 100?

11 A newspaper reports that 42000 people went to a football match. If this number had been rounded to the nearest 1000, write down the lowest number of people that could have been at the football match.

12 12400 people live in the town of Tadcaster (to the nearest 100). Write down the greatest number of people that might live in Tadcaster.

E 9.4

1 Round each of these numbers to the nearest £1:
(a) £3.87 (b) £7.63 (c) £1.26 (d) £4.50 (e) £8.53

2 Round each of these numbers to the nearest 1m:
(a) 6.7 m (b) 3.12 m (c) 11.4 m (d) 7.89 m (e) 0.84 m

3 3.$\underline{5}$178924 is 4 to the nearest whole number because the first digit after the decimal point is 5 or more so round up.

Round each of these numbers to the nearest whole number:

(a) 7.14862 (b) 3.471894 (c) 8.721893 (d) 5.07213

(e) 3.631089 (f) 12.941628 (g) 17.718253 (h) 11.31874

(i) 34.278914 (j) 0.825164

4 Work out these answers on a calculator and then round off the answer to the nearest whole number.

(a) $321 \div 19$ (b) $898 \div 19$ (c) 78.1×4.7 (d) $302 \div 0.13$

(e) 7.16×3.28 (f) 28.2×3.47 (g) 83.7×5.9 (h) 13.2×0.39

(i) $382.7 \div 9.4$ (j) $507 \div 0.23$ (k) $85.6 \div 13$ (l) $2.33 \div 0.13$

5 Work out a rough answer to each Question below by rounding each number to the nearest 10:

(a) 38×11 (b) 63×29 (c) 72×41

(d) $372 - 159$ (e) $249 - 82$ (f) 61×49

(g) $418 + 213$ (h) $1337 + 2181$ (i) 59×89

Decimal places

Rounding off to 1 decimal place

If the figure in the 2nd decimal place is 5 or more, round up. Otherwise do not.

$3.8\underline{7}2 = 3.9$ $14.4\underline{5} = 14.5$ $2.4\underline{3}7 = 2.4$

   ↑   ↑   ↑

5 or more   5 or more   less than 5

round up   round up   round down

Rounding off to 2 decimal places

If the figure in the 3rd decimal place is 5 or more, round up. Otherwise do not.

$3.87\underline{2} = 3.87$ $15.52\underline{5} = 15.53$ $2.43\underline{7} = 2.44$

   ↑   ↑   ↑

less than 5   5 or more   5 or more

round down   round up   round up

Note

5.96 rounded to the nearest whole number is 6

5.96 rounded to 1 decimal place is 6.0 (the zero is needed)

M 9.5

1  Round 3.3812 to 1 decimal place.

2 Round these numbers to 1 decimal place.

    (a) 6.31   (b) 5.83   (c) 8.37   (d) 6.75

    (e) 0.352   (f) 9.841   (g) 12.618   (h) 15.747

3 Which numbers below round to 7.3 (to 1 decimal place)?

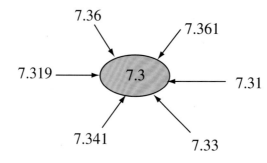

4 Round these numbers to 2 decimal places.

    (a) 2.346   (b) 7.053   (c) 13.333   (d) 2.074

    (e) 0.2365   (f) 23.676   (g) 0.9393   (h) 7.086

5 Which numbers below round to 8.16 (to 2 decimal places)?

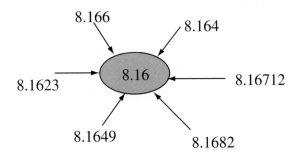

6 Round these numbers to 3 decimal places.

    (a) 2.1683   (b) 5.6414   (c) 8.3257   (d) 4.2318

    (e) 7.2515   (f) 13.7109   (g) 17.3298   (h) 41.61352

7 Work out these answers on a calculator and then round the answers correct to 2 decimal places.

    (a) $9.76 \div 7$ (b) 0.38×0.81 (c) 2.57^2 (d) $3186 \div 416$

    (e) 0.89×0.37 (f) $19.32 \div 17$ (g) 3.9×0.518 (h) 0.87^2

    (i) $0.38 \div 51$ (j) $\sqrt{7.6}$ (k) $\sqrt{17}$ (l) $5.9 \div 37$

8 (a) Measure the sides of each triangle below. Write down each length, in cm, correct to 1 decimal place.

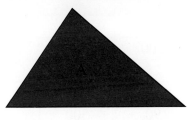
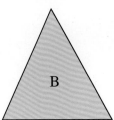

    (b) For each triangle, add together the lengths of the 3 sides to find the perimeter.

Key Facts

Jack worked out 7.02 × 8.9 equals 624.78. He can check his answer by rounding off numbers in the question.

7.02 is roughly 7   8.9 is roughly 9

so   7.02 × 8.9 is roughly 7 × 9 = 63

Clearly Jack's answer is wrong. He put the decimal point in the wrong place. His answer should have been 62.478.

Examples

Find rough answers to the questions below:

(a) 29.7 × 3.1   (b) 38.8 ÷ 1.981   (c) 12% of £68.99

is roughly 30 × 3   is roughly 40 ÷ 2   is roughly 10% of £70

= 90   = 20 $= \dfrac{1}{10}$ of £70 = £7

E 9.5

Do *not* use a calculator.

From the table below, choose the most sensible **rough** answer from A, B or C.

	Calculation	A	B	C
1	7.78 × 8.95	32	72	720
2	3.1 × 97	300	90	30
3	4.16 × 6.99	28	15	280
4	603 ÷ 4.93	12	60	120
5	88.7 ÷ 0.97	90	300	900
6	604 × 10.46	4000	6000	600
7	68.6 × 39 + 271	400	100	4000
8	2.12 × 70.4	700	140	7
9	7.13^2	14	50	200
10	728 ÷ 9.88	70	700	350
11	48% of £28300	£28	£280	£14000
12	9% of £394.60	£20	£40	£200

13 A quick way of adding lots of figures on a shopping bill is to round every number to the nearest pound (eg. £2.37 becomes £2, £0.94 becomes £1, £0.36 becomes £0 and so on).

Use this method to estimate the total for each bill below:

(a)
APPLE GRNNY SMTH	
0.540 kg @£1.08/kg	£0.58
CLEMENTINES	£1.69
GRAPEFRUIT RED	£0.38
CONFERENCE PEARS	£1.49
CHICORY 160G	£1.08
ORGANIC CARROTS	£0.84
ORGNC/WATERCRESS	£1.39
BANANAS	
0.710 kg @£0.74/kg	£0.53
MANGE TOUT 200G	£1.39
ORGNC/WATERCRESS	£1.39
CELERY	£0.53
ORGANIC CARROTS	£0.84
SALAD CRESS	£0.23
SALAD CRESS	£0.23
TTD CHC GNG BISC	£1.09
GRAPES RD SEEDLS	
0.425 kg @£2.99/kg	£1.27

(b)
RTB BAGUETTE	£0.95
RTB BAGUETTE	£0.95
APPLES COX	
1.495 kg @£1.49/kg	£2.23
SATSUMAS	
0.985 kg @£1.49/kg	£1.47
JS CEYLON TEA	£0.82
JS CEYLON TEA	£0.82
JS SLC HVST FHSE	£0.69
JS SLC HVST FHSE	£0.69
ONIONS LARGE	
0.225 kg @£0.64/kg	£0.14
*240W BULBS	£0.45
*LDT CORNET BOX	£3.29
*COMP C/TKY/VEG	£1.46
JS U/S BRT BUTTR	£1.09
*2 100W BULBS	£0.49
GOUDA WHEEL	£3.66
JS CHICKEN BURGR	£1.09

(c) Use a calculator to work out the exact total bill above.
Was the estimate larger or smaller than the exact total bill?

14 Do not use a calculator.

Use sensible **rough** answers to match each Question below to the correct answer:

A 7.1 × 4.9   P 101.7375

B 41 × 4.95   Q 34.79

C 8139 ÷ 80   R 70.9

D 0.99 × 61   S 202.95

E 29.6 + 41.3   T 60.39

15 Keira earns £97 each week. *Estimate* how much Keira earns in one year (52 weeks) by rounding off to sensible rough numbers.

16 Josh burns off 590 kcals each time he visits the Gym. *Estimate* how many kcals he burns off during 21 trips to the Gym?

17

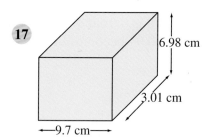

6.98 cm

3.01 cm

←—9.7 cm—→

The volume of this box is $6.98 \times 3.01 \times 9.7$

Estimate the volume of this box.

18 Do not use a calculator.

Use sensible **rough** answers to match each Question below to the correct answer:

A	$203.1 \div 5$		P	54.994
B	6.2×8.87		Q	9.4
C	9.08^2		R	82.4464
D	$202.1 \div 21.5$		S	200.6467
E	39.89×5.03		T	40.62

Can you still?

Can you still?

9C **Convert between fractions, decimals and percentages**
(see Unit 6)

Put all the numbers below into groups of 3 so that the numbers in each group are equal to each other. $\left(\text{Example: } 6\% = 0.06 = \dfrac{3}{50}\right)$

7% $\qquad \dfrac{3}{50} \qquad\qquad \dfrac{7}{10}$

$0.6 \qquad\qquad 0.35 \qquad\qquad 0.06$

$\qquad\qquad 0.04 \quad \dfrac{7}{100} \quad \dfrac{1}{4}$

$\dfrac{7}{20} \qquad\qquad\qquad 6\% \qquad 60\%$

$\qquad\qquad\qquad 70\% \qquad\qquad 4\%$

$0.07 \quad \dfrac{1}{25} \qquad\qquad 25\%$

$0.25 \qquad\qquad 0.7 \quad 35\% \quad \dfrac{3}{5}$

240

Money

To work out £16.80 ÷ 6, key in 16.8 ÷ 6 =

The answer is 2.8   Remember this means £2.80

Order of operations   Make sure you always follow the rule BODMAS
Brackets first then *Divide*, *Multiply*, *Add* and *Subtract*
in that order.

(a) Work out $3.9 + \dfrac{2.4}{12}$

$\dfrac{2.4}{12}$ means 2.4 ÷ 12 and Division must be done before Adding.

Key in 2.4 ÷ 12 = then + 3.9 =

Answer is 4.1

(b) Does $\dfrac{3.6}{1.8 + 5.4}$ equal 7.4 or 0.5?

1.8 + 5.4 = 7.2 so the denominator (bottom number) is larger than the
numerator (top number) which means the answer must be smaller than 1.

3.6 ÷ 1.8 + 5.4 = gives 7.4

This is wrong. All the denominator must be divided, not just 1.8

M 9.6

1 Work out the following. Give answers to the *nearest whole number*.

(a) $3.6 + 6.3 \times 1.8$ (b) $17 - 3.6 \times 2.1$ (c) $31 + 16 \div 0.8$

(d) $6.1 + \dfrac{3.8}{1.65}$ (e) $9.7 - \dfrac{6.1}{4.82}$ (f) $\dfrac{1.8 + 4.81}{3.7}$

(g) $(8.1 - 3.06) \times (4.7 + 2.93)$ (h) $\dfrac{11.3 - 6.28}{4.6}$

(i) $\dfrac{(8.91 + 3.6)}{0.69}$ (j) $\dfrac{(5.3 - 1.21)}{0.07}$ (k) $\dfrac{19.2 + 13.71}{1.08}$

(l) $\dfrac{(28.01 + 17.6)}{(32 - 29.7)}$ (m) $\dfrac{82.1 - 13.7}{31 + 1.6}$ (n) $\dfrac{47.28}{3.8 - 0.19}$

2 Match each Question below to the correct answer:

A $(4.1 \times 2.6) - 1.9$ → ? P 15.6

B $4.1 \times (2.6 - 1.9)$ → Q 8.76

C $2.6 \times (4.1 + 1.9)$ → R 2.85

D $(2.6 \times 4.1) + 1.9$ → S 2.87

E $1.9 \times (4.1 - 2.6)$ → T 12.56

3 Copy the grid below.

Use a calculator to fill in the grid using the clues (*ignore any decimal points*).

Clues across

1. $3.8 + 1.7 + 1.42$

3. $7 \times (3.6 - 1.9)$

5. $\dfrac{17.6}{0.4} - 3.88$

7. 4.9×150

9. $(0.62 + 0.08) \times 70$

10. $-24.1 - 2.3 + 61.2$

11. $-900 \times (-0.09)$

12. $4.9 \times \left(\dfrac{40}{0.8}\right)$

Clues down

1. $\dfrac{5.1 - 1.7}{0.5}$

2. $3.9 \times 4.8 \times 13.4$

3. $(3.1 + 1.8) \times (6.1 - 3.8)$

4. $121 - (31.2 - 4.85)$

6. $\dfrac{13.8 + 9.12}{0.25}$

8. $(15.1 - 7.6) \times 3.5 + 5.2$

10. $\dfrac{18.1 - 1.1}{0.38 + 0.12}$

Squares, square roots, powers, fractions

Squaring numbers

$4^2 = 4 \times 4 = 16$

Calculator button

 gives 16

Fractions

Key in 3 $a\dfrac{b}{c}$ 4 . This is $\dfrac{3}{4}$

Use the fraction button to work out $\dfrac{5}{6} - \dfrac{3}{4}$

The display should show $1 \lrcorner 12$ because the answer is $\dfrac{1}{12}$.

E 9.6

1 Use a calculator to work out the following:

(a) 14^2 (b) 7.3^2 (c) 4.2^2 (d) 8.9^2

(e) 23^2 (f) $\sqrt{225}$ (g) $\sqrt{361}$ (h) $\sqrt{10.24}$

(i) $\sqrt{28.09}$ (j) $\sqrt{0.49}$ (k) $(3+12)^2$ (l) $(38-16)^2$

(m) $\sqrt{(169-25)}$ (n) $\sqrt{(625-49)}$ (o) $3.4^2 + 6.7^2$ (p) $(5.9^2 - 2.1) \times 8$

2 Use a calculator to match each Question below to the correct answer:

A 3^5 P 256

B 2^8 Q 4096

C 5^5 R 243

D 7^4 S 3125

E 4^6 T 7776

F 6^5 U 2401

3 Write down the fractions shown on the calculator displays below:

(a) $2 \rfloor 7$ (b) $5 \rfloor 9$ (c) $3 \rfloor 2 \rfloor 5$

(d) $6 \rfloor 4 \rfloor 9$ (e) $8 \rfloor 11$ (f) $7 \rfloor 2 \rfloor 7$

4 Use a calculator to work out

(a) $\dfrac{3}{7} + \dfrac{2}{5}$ (b) $\dfrac{5}{8} + \dfrac{3}{4}$ (c) $\dfrac{4}{9} - \dfrac{2}{11}$ (d) $1\dfrac{3}{4} \times 2\dfrac{1}{2}$

(e) $3\dfrac{1}{5} \times 4\dfrac{1}{2}$ (f) $8\dfrac{1}{4} \div \dfrac{3}{5}$ (g) $32 \div \dfrac{4}{7}$ (h) $\left(4\dfrac{1}{5}\right)^2$

5 Copy and complete.

$+$	$\dfrac{3}{8}$		$2\dfrac{1}{2}$	$1\dfrac{2}{3}$
$\dfrac{1}{4}$				
$\dfrac{3}{5}$		$\dfrac{19}{20}$		
			$4\dfrac{5}{6}$	
		$2\dfrac{13}{20}$		

6 Work out and give the answer correct to 2 decimal places.

(a) $3.1^3 \times (5.9 - 1.312)$ (b) $\dfrac{5.12}{(7.8 + 0.314)}$

(c) $3.8^2 - 2.17$ (d) $18.8 \div (2.8^2 - 2.95)$

(e) $\dfrac{(17.2 + 11.25)}{(3.89 + 1.63)}$ (f) $\dfrac{17.2 + 11.25}{3.89 + 1.63}$

(g) $\dfrac{16.18 - 3.892}{12.62 + 19.31}$ (h) $\dfrac{8.312}{(5.6^2 - 4.218)}$

(i) $\dfrac{5.1^2 + 6.34}{17.162 - 2.8^2}$ (j) $\dfrac{3.81^2 + 2.6^3}{1.41^2 - 1.317}$

7 Copy this crossword puzzle and complete it using the clues below.
[The answers are calculator words]

Across

2: $(3.08 + 0.701637) \times 10^6$ readable

5: $2 \times 71 \times 5$ greasy

6: $3 \div 500$ sticky

7: $555 - 44 + 3$ belongs to him

9: $0.6 - 0.22$ good when you're tired

11: $8 \times 4 \times (27 - 8)$ get out your wellies

13: $3^3 \div 30$ green light

14: $2000^2 - 68462$ surround

Down

1: $60 \text{ million} + 436000 + 34$ hibernates in winter

3: $8 \times 9 \times 10 + 4^2 + 3$ for hair

4: $21 \times (40^2 + 67)$ not tight

6: $2^4 \times 5^3 \times 0.41 - 1$ part of a boat

8: $33333 - 1325$ not a good idea

10: $24 \times 25 + (1 + 2 + 3 + 4)$ you might need a spade

12: $10^3 - 65.5 \times 10$ female

9D **Percentage increase and decrease (see Unit 6)**

Do *not* use a calculator.

1. Increase £80 by 5%

2. Decrease £70 by 30%

3. Jamie gets a 4% pay rise. If he now earns £15000 each year, how much will he earn after the pay rise?

4.

Shoes £60
SALE
15% off

What is the sale price of these shoes?

You may *use a calculator* for the Questions below.

5. Decrease £75 by 6%.

6. Increase £58 by 37%.

7. A computer costs £899 + VAT.
If VAT is 17.5%, work out how much the computer costs altogether.

Significant figures

For significant figures we approach from the left and start counting as soon as we come to the first figure which is not zero. Once we have started counting, we count any figure, zeros included.

(a) Round 63.8251 to 3 significant figures (3 s.f.)

63.8251
↑

(Count 3 figures. The 'next' figure is 2 which is less than 5 so do not round up.)
63.8251 = 63.8 (to 3 s.f.)

(b) Round 8.0374 to 3 s.f.   8.0374
↑

(Count 3 figures. The 'next' figure is 7 which is more than 5 so round up.)
8.0374 = 8.04 (to 3 s.f.)

(c) 0.0654516 = 0.0655 (to 3 s.f.)

(d) 6382.7 = 6400 (to 2 s.f.)
↑

Notice that we need the two noughts after the '4' as the original number 6382.7 is approximately 6400 not just 64.

1 Write true or false for each statement below:

(a) $3.174 = 3.17$ (to 3 s.f.) (b) $5.082 = 5.08$ (to 3 s.f.)

(c) $92.29 = 92.2$ (to 3 s.f.) (d) $83.79 = 83.8$ (to 3 s.f.)

(e) $0.0818 = 0.082$ (to 2 s.f.) (f) $0.0734 = 0.074$ (to 2 s.f.)

(g) $0.0605 = 0.061$ (to 2 s.f.) (h) $32751 = 32000$ (to 2 s.f.)

(i) $81768 = 80000$ (to 1 s.f.) (j) $472.23 = 480$ (to 2 s.f.)

2 Which numbers below round to 3.96 (to 3 s.f.)?

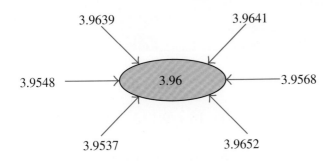

3 Write the numbers below correct to 3 significant figures.

(a) 2.1875 (b) 32.896 (c) 0.8547 (d) 183.21

(e) 18.394 (f) 0.08756 (g) 48873 (h) 0.6555

(i) 3284.3 (j) 6278 (k) 0.02138 (l) 375899

4 Write the following to the number of significant figures shown.

(a) 13.82 (2 s.f.) (b) 7.891 (1 s.f.) (c) 6.412 (2 s.f.)

(d) 0.83554 (3 s.f.) (e) 1736.8 (3 s.f.) (f) 51.382 (3 s.f.)

(g) 31777 (2 s.f.) (h) 0.05483 (2 s.f.) (i) 28639 (1 s.f.)

5 Copy the grid below.

Use a calculator to fill in the grid using the clues (**ignore any decimal points**). You **must** round answers to the number of significant figures shown.

Clues across

1 1.9×9.46 (4 s.f.)

3 $3 \div 0.27$ (2 s.f.)

6 2754.4×0.3 (2 s.f.)

8 3.81^2 (4 s.f.)

9 $\dfrac{38 + 69.4}{0.48}$ (3 s.f.)

11 2.2^3 (2 s.f.)

12 $(3.6 + 5.12) \times 1.01$ (2 s.f.)

13 $5.6^2 + 0.417$ (3 s.f.)

14 $\dfrac{3.1}{(2.83 - 1.9)}$ (2 s.f.)

Clues down

1 $18 \div 9.1$ (3 s.f.)

2 30.8^2 (1 s.f.)

4 $1797.4853 \div 13$ (6 s.f.)

5 0.24×0.17 (2 s.f.)

7 $0.36^2 + 1.7^2$ (3 s.f.)

9 $29 \div 13$ (3 s.f.)

10 $\dfrac{33}{0.12} + 142.9$ (3 s.f.)

12 $99 - 16.182$ (2 s.f.)

Checking answers

- Here are five calculations followed by sensible checks. Some checks involve 'undoing' the calculation.

  (a) $22.2 \div 6 = 3.7$ check $3.7 \times 6 = 22.2$

  (b) $31.7 - 4.83 = 26.87$ check $26.87 + 4.83 = 31.7$

  (c) $42.8 \times 30 = 1284$ check $1284 \div 30 = 42.8$

  (d) $\sqrt{17} = 4.1231$ check 4.1231^2

  (e) $3.7 + 17.6 + 13.9 + 6.2$ check $6.2 + 13.9 + 17.6 + 3.7$
                                                    (add in reverse order)

- Calculations can also be checked by rounding numbers to a given number of significant figures. This gives an estimate which helps to check if the answer is correct.

  (f) $\dfrac{6.1 \times 32.6}{19.3} = 10.3$ (to 3 s.f.)

  Check this answer by rounding each number to 1 significant figure and estimating.

  $$\frac{6.1 \times 32.6}{19.3} \approx \frac{6 \times 30}{20} \approx \frac{180}{20} \approx 9$$

  '$\approx$' means 'approximately equal to'.   This is close to 10.3 so the
                                                        actual answer probably is 10.3

E9.7

1 Use a calculator to work out the following then check the answers as indicated.

(a) $92.5 \times 20 = \square$ check $\square \div 20 = \square$

(b) $14 \times 328 = \square$ check $\square \div 328 = \square$

(c) $63 - 12.6 = \square$ check $\square + 12.6 = \square$

(d) $221.2 \div 7 = \square$ check $\square \times 7 = \square$

(e) $384.93 \div 9.1 = \square$ check $\square \times 9.1 = \square$

(f) $13.71 + 25.8 = \square$ check $\square - 25.8 = \square$

(g) $95.4 \div 4.5 = \square$ check $\square \times 4.5 = \square$

(h) $8.2 + 3.1 + 19.6 + 11.5$ check $11.5 + 19.6 + 3.1 + 8.2$

(i) $\sqrt{39} = \square$ check $\square^2$

(j) $3.17 + 2.06 + 8.4 + 16$ check $16 + 8.4 + 2.06 + 3.17$

249

2 The numbers below are rounded to 1 significant figure to *estimate* the answer to each calculation. Match each Question below to the correct answer.

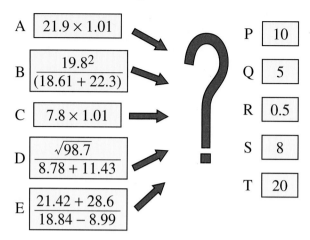

A $\boxed{21.9 \times 1.01}$

B $\boxed{\dfrac{19.8^2}{(18.61 + 22.3)}}$

C $\boxed{7.8 \times 1.01}$

D $\boxed{\dfrac{\sqrt{98.7}}{8.78 + 11.43}}$

E $\boxed{\dfrac{21.42 + 28.6}{18.84 - 8.99}}$

P $\boxed{10}$

Q $\boxed{5}$

R $\boxed{0.5}$

S $\boxed{8}$

T $\boxed{20}$

3 Do *not* use a calculator.

$$281 \times 36 = 10116$$

Work out

(a) $10116 \div 36$ (b) $10116 \div 281$ (c) 28.1×3.6

4 Mavis is paid a salary of £49620 per year. Work out a rough estimate for her weekly pay. (Give your answer correct to one significant figure)

5 In 1996, the population of France was 61 278 514 and the population of Greece was 9 815 972. Roughly how many times bigger is the population of France compared to the population of Greece?
(Hint: round the numbers to 1 significant figure).

6 *Estimate*, correct to 1 significant figure:

(a) $41.56 \div 7.88$

(b) $\dfrac{5.13 \times 18.777}{0.952}$

(c) $\dfrac{1}{5}$ of £14892

(d) $\dfrac{0.0974 \times \sqrt{104}}{1.03}$

(e) 52% of $0.394\,\text{kg}$

(f) $\dfrac{6.84^2 + 0.983}{5.07^2}$

(g) $\dfrac{2848.7 + 1024.8}{51.2 - 9.98}$

(h) $\dfrac{2}{3}$ of £3124

(i) $18.13 \times (3.96^2 + 2.07^2)$

Everyone wants to save money. Most people understand that saving energy will help planet earth by reducing Carbon Dioxide (CO_2) emissions.

More than half the money spent on energy in the home goes on:

heating

The other main uses of energy are for:

kitchen tasks

water heating

washing clothes

lighting

Task A – heating
Loft insulation will cut down the amount of heat escaping from your home. When the savings add up to more than the cost of the insulation, you will be saving money. Look at the table opposite.

	Loft insulation A (0–270 mm)	Left insulation B (50–270 mm)
saving per year	£140	£55
cost of installing	£350	£330
CO_2 savings each year	850 kg	240 kg

1 How long will it be before you start saving money by using loft insulation A?

2 How long before saving money with loft insulation B?

3 How many CO_2 savings will be made in 5 years by using loft insulation A?

4 By the time you start saving money with loft insulation B, how many CO_2 savings will have been made?

5 Put the five types of dwelling opposite in order according to which will have the greatest rate of average heat loss. Give a reason for your answer.

Tip
Turning your central heating down by one degree could save you up to 10% on your heating bill

Types of dwelling
Bungalow
Terrace
Detached
Flat
Semi-detached

Task B – in the kitchen
If you see this energy saving logo when buying electrical goods, the machines will be amongst the most energy efficient you can buy.

1 An energy saving dishwasher costs 20% less to run and saves 24% of CO_2 emissions. Use the table opposite to show how much money is saved in one year and how many CO_2 savings are made in one year.

2 Work out the cost and CO_2 savings if an energy saving fridge costs 25% less to run and saves 20% of CO_2 emissions.

Appliance	Average cost to run each year	CO_2 emissions each year
Fridge	£56	220 kg
Dishwasher	£60	230 kg
Fridge freezer	£175	645 kg

Tip: Washing clothes at 30 °C instead of higher temperatures can save up to 40% of the energy

Energy saving bulbs use between $\frac{1}{5}$ and $\frac{1}{4}$ of the electricity of ordinary lights to produce the same amount of light

Task C – lighting
Which energy saving bulb listed below would produce the same amount of light as an ordinary 60 watt bulb?

8–10 Watt   11–14 Watt
18–20 Watt   23–25 Watt

Explain your answer.

TEST YOURSELF ON UNIT 9

1. Adding and subtracting decimals

Work out

(a)   14.9
     + 12.3

(b)   6.71
      − 3.4

(c)   17.0
     − 6.4

(d)   19
      − 12.3

(e) $4.6 + 9.17$ (f) $6.12 + 3 + 8.7$ (g) $28.4 - 16.8$

(h) How much change from a £20 note do you get if you spend £6.27?

2. Multiplying decimals

Work out

(a) 4.98×10 (b) 0.0342×1000 (c) 67×0.1 (d) 0.3×0.1

(e) 0.6×0.03 (f) 0.08×6 (g) 0.7^2 (h) 21.2×0.3

3. Dividing decimals by whole numbers

Work out

(a) $4\overline{)13.28}$ (b) $8\overline{)18.00}$ (c) $7.035 \div 5$

(d) $15 \div 4$ (e) $0.768 \div 6$ (f) $3.6 \div 5$

(g) 4 friends split the cost of a meal equally. If the meal costs £63, how much does each friend have to pay?

4. Dividing by decimals

Copy the Questions below and fill in the empty boxes.

(a) $7.8 \div 0.2 = \square \div 2 = \square$

(b) $1.71 \div 0.3 = \square \div 3 = \square$

Work out

(c) $6.9 \div 0.3$ (d) $5.2 \div 0.05$ (e) $0.288 \div 0.8$ (f) $0.156 \div 0.01$

5. Rounding off numbers to the nearest 10, 100, 1000 or whole number

(a) Round each of these numbers to the nearest 10.
   (i) 23   (ii) 48   (iii) 75   (iv) 135   (v) 464

(b) Round each of these numbers to the nearest 100.
   (i) 382   (ii) 750   (iii) 1210   (iv) 8390   (v) 1650

(c) Round each of these numbers to the nearest 1000.
   (i) 3217   (ii) 8510   (iii) 17232   (iv) 21500   (v) 24320

(d) Round each of these numbers to the nearest whole number.
   (i) 6.7   (ii) 8.6   (iii) 3.12   (iv) 18.5   (v) 27.38

6. Rounding off to decimal places

(a) Round these numbers to 1 decimal place.

(i) 8.23   (ii) 6.35   (iii) 4.16   (iv) 14.34   (v) 8.162

(b) Round these numbers to 2 decimal places.

(i) 3.387   (ii) 2.186   (iii) 15.384   (iv) 0.895   (v) 28.183

(c) Round these numbers to 3 decimal places.

(i) 8.1932   (ii) 0.7235   (iii) 7.4864   (iv) 27.2087   (v) 14.81327

7. Estimate answers

Do *not* use a calculator.

From the table below, choose the most sensible ROUGH answer from A, B or C.

	Calculation	A	B	C
(a)	5.8×2.03	50	120	1200
(b)	8.12×3.02	240	24	60
(c)	$805 \div 9.96$	800	80	8
(d)	$41.2 \div 8.14$	320	50	5
(e)	$68.6 - 19.14$	50	30	90
(f)	789×10.33	800	8000	80
(g)	8.95^2	80	150	20
(h)	$41.2 + 163 + 0.92$	300	200	50

8. Use a calculator

Work out

(a) 8.3^2

(b) $\dfrac{7}{12} \times \dfrac{3}{5}$

(c) $-12 \times (-0.3)$

(d) $(-7)^2$

(e) $2\dfrac{1}{5} + 3\dfrac{5}{7}$

(f) $\sqrt{14.44}$

(g) 2.7^3

(h) $\dfrac{4+8}{0.5}$

(i) $4 + \left(\dfrac{8}{0.5}\right)$

(j) $\dfrac{13.6 - 5.9}{0.12 + 0.08}$

(k) $\dfrac{6.8^2}{15.8 - 15.79}$

(l) $\dfrac{\sqrt{28 - 12}}{0.5^2}$

Write the following to the number of significant figures (s.f.) shown.

(a) 17.81 (3 s.f.)   (b) 23.69 (2 s.f.)   (c) 31.685 (3 s.f.)

(d) 213182 (3 s.f.)   (e) 384.67 (2 s.f.)   (f) 0.61087 (3 s.f.)

(g) 0.020714 (2 s.f.)   (h) 379418 (1 s.f.)   (i) 2374.23 (2 s.f.)

10. Checking answers

Do *not* use a calculator.

(a) If $38 \times 27 = 1026$,   does $1026 \div 27 = 38$?

(b) If $310 \times 23 = 7130$,   does $7130 \div 310 = 23$?

(c) If $2646 \div 42 = 63$,   does $2646 \div 63 = 42$?

(d) If $2646 \div 42 = 63$,   does $63 \times 42 = 2646$?

(e) If $14.61 + 13.093 = 27.703$,   does $27.703 - 13.093 = 14.61$?

(f) If $4.08^2 = 16.6464$,   does $\sqrt{16.6464} = 4.08$?

Estimate, correct to 1 significant figure:

(g) $59.89 \div 20.2$ (h) 24% of 792 kg

(i) $\dfrac{19.6 - 1.987}{\sqrt{4.01}}$ (j) $\dfrac{7.16^2}{3.912 + 0.99}$

Mixed examination questions

1 In a shop, Alan spends
£ 1.33 on milk
£ 3.14 on coffee
£ 0.74 on sugar

i Calculate the total amount that Alan spends.

ii Alan pays with a £10 note. How much change should be given?

iii Barbara is organising a coach trip for 260 people. Each coach will hold 48 people. How many coaches will be needed?   (OCR)

2 The prices of a bottle of red wine and a kilogram of cheddar cheese are shown.

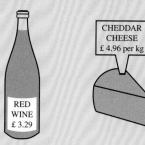

CHEDDAR
CHEESE
£ 4.96 per kg

RED
WINE
£ 3.29

What is the total cost of twelve bottles of red wine and a quarter
of kilogram of cheddar cheese? (AQA)

3 Nick takes 26 boxes out of his van.

The weight of each box is 32.9 kg.

Work out the **total** weight of the 26 boxes. (EDEXCEL)

4 Three friends, Ali, Brenda and Chris, go to the cinema together.
The total cost of their three tickets is £11.55. Each ticket costs
the same. Work out the cost of one ticket. (AQA)

5 Joe can do, on average, 4 calculations on his calculator every minute.

(a) How many calculations, on average, can he do in $7\frac{1}{2}$ minutes?

(b) Use your calculator to work out the value of $\sqrt{(15 + 27.25)}$ (EDEXCEL)

6 The answers to the following calculations have been rounded to the nearest
whole number. In each case the first digit of the answer is missing.
Use estimation to work out the missing first digit in each calculation.
Make clear the estimates you use.

$8.98^2 \times 2.43 = \square 96 \qquad \dfrac{402 \times 87}{47} = \square 44$ (OCR)

7 Use approximations to estimate the value of $\dfrac{9.67^2}{0.398}$.

You **must** show all your working. (AQA)

ALGEBRA 2

10

In this unit you will learn how to:
- draw straight line graphs
- draw curves from equations
- solve simultaneous equations graphically
- find gradients of straight lines
- read graphs
- use travel graphs
- USE YOUR MATHS! – Electricity, gas and water

Drawing straight line graphs

M10. 1

1 Write down the equations of the lines marked A, B and C.

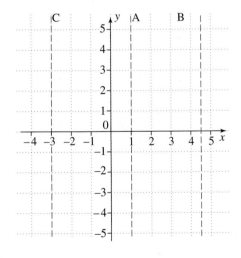

2 Write down the equations of the lines marked P, Q, R and S.

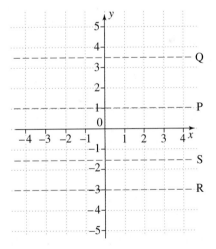

3 (a) Draw axes like those above.

(b) Plot the points $A(4, 3)$, $B(-3, -2)$, $C(4, -1)$, $D(-3, 3)$

(c) Write down the equation of the line passing through

    (i) A and C (ii) B and D (iii) A and D

4

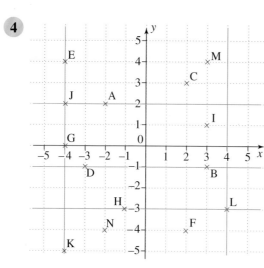

(a) J lies on the line $y = 2$. Which other letter lies on $y = 2$?

(b) Which letter lies on $x = 4$?

(c) Which letters lie on $y = -1$?

(d) Which letters lie on $x = -4$?

(e) How many letters lie on $y = -3$?

(f) Which letter lies on $y = 2$ and $x = -4$?

(g) Which letter lies on $x = 4$ and $y = -3$?

5 The outside edge of Frank's face is made by straight lines.

Write down the equation of each line (2 of the lines will have the same equation).

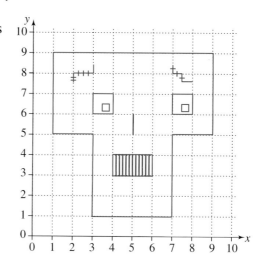

Can you still?

10A **Percentage Change (see Unit 6)**

Can you still?

1. Freddie's salary was increased from £5000 to £5500. What was the percentage increase?

2. In one year, Sandra's height increases from 160 cm to 164 cm. What is the percentage increase?

3. Tom bought a car for £12000. He sold the car for £9000. What was the percentage loss?

4. Carol buys 20 books for £120. She sells each book for £7.50. What percentage profit did Carol make?

5. A box of 50 CDs cost £400. All were sold in a sale for £7.50 each. What was the percentage loss on each CD?

Sloping lines

Draw the straight line $y = x + 3$.

When $x = 1$, $y = x + 3 = 1 + 3 = 4 \rightarrow (1, 4)$

When $x = 2$, $y = x + 3 = 2 + 3 = 5 \rightarrow (2, 5)$

When $x = 3$, $y = x + 3 = 3 + 3 = 6 \rightarrow (3, 6)$

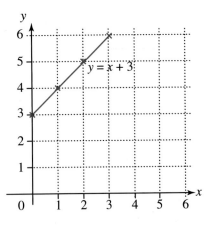

Note

When working out the y-values, we usually write them in a table

x	0	1	2	3
y	3	4	5	6

E10. 1

(Check all your graphs with a computer or graphical calculator if your teacher wants you to!)

For Questions **1** to **5**, you will need to draw axes like those below:

1 Complete the table below then draw the straight line $y = x + 4$

x	0	1	2	3
y				

2 Complete the table below then draw the straight line $y = x + 6$

x	0	1	2	3
y				

3 Complete the table below then draw $y = 2x$

x	0	1	2	3
y				

4 Complete the table below then draw $y = 2x + 2$.

x	0	1	2	3
y				

5 Complete the table below then draw $y = 3x + 1$.

x	0	1	2	3
y				

6 Using x-values from 0 to 4, complete a table then draw the straight line $y = 3x$ (make sure you draw the axes big enough).

7 Using x-values from 0 to 5, complete a table then draw the straight line $y = 6 - x$.

8 Using x-values from 0 to 5, complete a table then draw $y = 8 - x$.

9 Draw $y = 2x + 3$ using x-values from 0 to 4.

10 (a) Using x-values from 0 to 3, draw $y = x$ *and* $y = 6 - 2x$ on the *same graph*.

(b) Write down the co-ordinates where the two lines meet.

11 Find the value of these when $x = -2$:

(a) $x + 3$ (b) $3x$ (c) $x - 2$ (d) $2x$ (e) $2x + 3$

12 Find the value of y when $x = -3$:

(a) $y = x + 1$ (b) $y = 2x$ (c) $y = x - 3$ (d) $y = 3x$ (e) $y = 3x - 2$

Check your answers to questions **11** and **12** before doing question **13**. Discuss any wrong answers with your teacher.

For Questions **13** to **17**, you will need to draw axes like these:

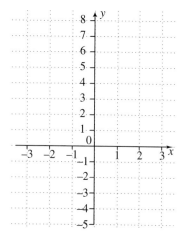

13 Complete the table below then draw the straight line $y = x - 2$.

x	-2	-1	0	1	2
y					

14 Complete the table below then draw the straight line $y = 2x + 4$.

x	-2	-1	0	1	2
y					

260

15 Complete the table below then draw $y = x - 3$.

x	-2	-1	0	1	2
y					

16 Complete the table below then draw $y = 2x - 1$.

x	-2	-1	0	1	2
y					

17 Complete the table below then draw $y = -2x$.

x	-2	-1	0	1	2
y					

18 Complete this table for $y = 3x - 1$.

x	-3	-2	-1	0	1	2	3
y							

Draw an x-axis from -3 to 3 and a y-axis from -10 to 8.

Plot the points and draw the straight line $y = 3x - 1$.

19 Using x-values from -2 to 2, complete a table then draw the straight line $y = 3x - 2$ (make sure you draw the axes big enough).

20 Using x-values from -2 to 2, complete a table then draw $y = -3x$.

21 Draw $y = 3 - 2x$ using x-values from -3 to 3.

22 Draw $y = \frac{1}{2}x$ using x-values from -4 to 4.

23 Draw an x-axis from -3 to 3 and a y-axis from -10 to 8. Using the *same* set of axes, draw

$$y = 4x \qquad\qquad y = 2x - 3$$

$$y = 1 - 2x \qquad\qquad y = 3x - 4$$

Label each line clearly.

10B **Compound Interest (see Unit 6)**

1. £4000 is invested at 5% per annum (year) compound interest. How much money will there be after 2 years?

2. £10,000 is invested at 10% per annum compound interest. How much money will there be after 3 years?

3. £6000 is invested at 4% per annum compound interest. How much money will there be after 2 years?

4. A new car is bought for £14000. Each year, its value depreciates (goes down) by 20% of its value at the start of the year. How much is the car worth after 2 years?

Drawing curves

Draw $y = x^2 + 3$, using x-values from -3 to 3.

x	-3	-2	-1	0	1	2	3
y							

draw a table

⇓

Start with $x = 0$ and positive x-values first

$y = 0^2 + 3 = 0 + 3 = 3$

$y = 1^2 + 3 = 1 + 3 = 4$

$y = 2^2 + 3 = 4 + 3 = 7$

$y = 3^2 + 3 = 9 + 3 = 12$

Now be careful with the negative x-values

$y = (-3)^2 + 3 = 9 + 3 = 12$

$-3 \times -3 = 9$

$y = (-2)^2 + 3 = 4 + 3 = 7$

$-2 \times -2 = 4$

$y = (-1)^2 + 3 = 1 + 3 = 4$

$-1 \times -1 = 1$

x	-3	-2	-1	0	1	2	3
y	12	7	4	3	4	7	12

262

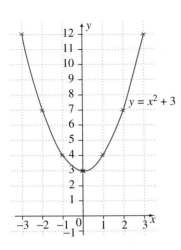

- draw axes so that *all* the points can be plotted

- plot each point

- join up all the points with a smooth curve

- label the curve with its equation

M10. 2

(Check all your graphs with a computer or graphical calculator if your teacher wants you to!)

1 Find the value of these when $x = 3$:

(a) x^2 (b) $x^2 + 1$ (c) $x^2 - 3$ (d) $x^2 + x$ (e) $x^2 + 2x$

2 Find the value of these when $x = -4$:

(a) x^2 (b) $3x$ (c) $x^2 + 2$ (d) $x^2 - 6$ (e) $x^2 + x$

3 Find the value of these when $x = -1$:

(a) $2x$ (b) x^2 (c) $x^2 + 3$ (d) $x^2 - x$ (e) $x^2 + 2x$

Check your answers to Questions **1** to **3**. Discuss with your teacher if the answers are not clear.

For Questions **4** to **8**, you will need to draw axes like these:

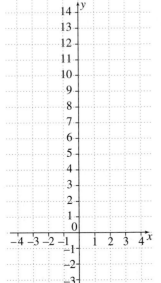

4 Complete the table below then draw the curve $y = x^2$

x	-3	-2	-1	0	1	2	3
y							

5 Complete the table below then draw the curve $y = x^2 + 1$

x	-3	-2	-1	0	1	2	3
y							

6 Complete the table then draw $y = x^2 - 3$

x	-3	-2	-1	0	1	2	3
y							

263

7 Complete the table then draw $y = x^2 - 2$.

x	-3	-2	-1	0	1	2	3
y							

8 Complete the table then draw $y = x^2 + 5$.

x	-3	-2	-1	0	1	2	3
y							

Discuss with your teacher the shape of each curve you have drawn in questions **4** to **8**.

9 (a) Complete the table below for $y = 2x^2$ ($2x^2$ means 'x^2 then multiply by 2').

x	-3	-2	-1	0	1	2	3
y	18				2		

$x = 1$ so $y = 2x^2 = x^2 \times 2 = (1)^2 \times 2 = 1 \times 2 = 2$

(b) Draw an x-axis -3 to 3 (use 2 cm for 1 unit) and a y-axis from 0 to 18 (use 1 cm for 2 units).

Plot the points from the table and draw the curve $y = 2x^2$.

10 (a) Complete the table below for $y = 3x^2$ ($3x^2$ means x^2 then 'multiply by 3').

x	-3	-2	-1	0	1	2	3
y		12					

(b) Draw an x-axis from -3 to 3 (use 2 cm for 1 unit) and a y-axis from 0 to 28 (use 1 cm for 2 units). Draw the curve $y = 3x^2$.

11 Using x-values from -3 to 3, complete a table then draw $y = 2x^2 + 1$ (make sure you draw the axes big enough).

12 (a) Using x-values from 1 to 6, complete a table for $y = \frac{6}{x}$ (you may use a calculator).

$\frac{6}{x}$ means $6 \div x$

x	1	2	3	4	5	6
y						

(b) Draw an x-axis from 0 to 6 and a y-axis from 0 to 6. Draw the curve $y = \frac{6}{x}$.

13 Using x-values from 1 to 6, complete a table then draw $y = \frac{12}{x}$ (make sure you draw the axes big enough).

Curves with several terms

Using x-values from -3 to 3 draw $y = x^2 + 4x - 1$.

Do each part separately in the table then add together at the end to find y.

	−3	−2	−1	0	1	2	3
	9	4	1	0	1	4	9
	−12	−8	−4	0	4	8	12
	−1	−1	−1	−1	−1	−1	−1
	−4	−5	−4	−1	4	11	20

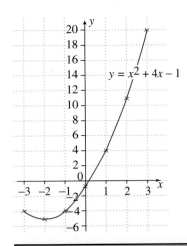

> **Note**
> A curve is called a 'quadratic' graph if the highest power of x is x^2.

E10. 2

1

(a) Complete the table for $y = x^2 + x + 2$.

(b) Draw an x-axis from -4 to 2 and a y-axis from 0 to 14. Draw the curve $y = x^2 + x + 2$ (the bottom of the curve should be curved $\smile$ *not* flat $\diagdown\diagup$)

	−4	−3	−2	−1	0	1	2
	9						
	−3						
2	2	2	2	2	2	2
	8						

For Questions **2** to **5**, you will need to draw axes like these:

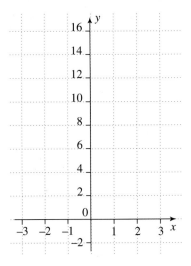

2 Complete the table below then draw the curve $y = x^2 + x$.

	−3	−2	−1	0	1	2	3
		1					9
		−1					3
		0					12

3 Complete the table below then draw the curve $y = x^2 + 2x$.

	−3	−2	−1	0	1	2	3
		4			1		
		−4			2		
		0			3		

265

4 (a) Complete the table then draw the curve $y = x^2 - 2x$.

(b) Read off the value of y from your curve when $x = 1.5$.

	−3	−2	−1	0	1	2	3
	4						
	4						
	8						

5 (a) Complete the table then draw the curve $y = x^2 - x + 2$.

(b) Read off the value of y from your curve when $x = 0.5$.

	−3	−2	−1	0	1	2	3
	9						
	3						
	2						
	14						

6 Using x-values from -4 to 2, complete a table then draw $y = x^2 + 3x - 2$ (make sure you draw the axes big enough).

7 x^3 means $x \times x \times x$ so $2^3 = 2 \times 2 \times 2 = 4 \times 2 = 8$

Complete the table below then draw $y = x^3$.

x	−3	−2	−1	0	1	2	3
y	−27						

8 Using x-values from -3 to 3 draw:

(a) $y = x^3 + 1$ (b) $y = x^3 + x$

(c) $y = x^3 + 3x - 4$ (d) $y = x^3 + x^2 + 1$

[All these curves are called *'cubic'* graphs because the highest power of x is x^3]

9 Using x-values from 1 to 6 draw:

(a) $y = \dfrac{24}{x}$ (b) $y = \dfrac{1}{x}$

[These curves are called *'reciprocal'* graphs because x is in the denominator.]

10 Using x-values from -5 to 5, draw $y = \dfrac{10}{x^2}$ (be very careful when $x = 0$)

Discuss this graph with your teacher.

Cover-up method for drawing straight lines

In this unit we have drawn equations of straight lines where y is on its own
(examples: $y = 2x + 1$, $y = 3x - 2$)

If x and y are on the same side of the '=' sign
(examples: $x + y = 2$, $2x - 3y = 6$), we can find the points to join up on a graph
by using the cover-up method.

🔑 Key Facts

Draw $2x + 3y = 6$.

Use $\boxed{x = 0}$ so $2x = 0$ *Cover up $2x$ in the equation.*

$$2x + 3y = 6 \text{ becomes } \text{▨} + 3y = 6 \text{ so } \boxed{y = 2}$$

Use $\boxed{y = 0}$ so $3y = 0$ *Cover up $3y$ in the equation.*

$$2x + 3y = 0 \text{ becomes } 2x + \text{▨} = 6 \text{ so } \boxed{x = 3}$$

Always use $x = 0$ then $y = 0$.

Plot the points $x = 0, y = 2$ and $x = 3, y = 0$ on the graph and join them up to get your
straight line.

M10. 3

1   (a) Draw these axes.

(b) If $x + 2y = 4$, find the value
of y when $x = 0$.

(c) If $x + 2y = 4$, find the value
of x when $y = 0$.

(d) Plot 2 points from (b) and (c)
and join them up to make the
straight line $x + 2y = 4$.

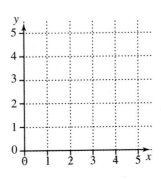

267

2 (a) Draw the same axes as in Question **1**.

(b) Use $x = 0$ then $y = 0$ to find 2 points for $3x + y = 3$.

(c) Draw the straight line $3x + y = 3$.

3 (a) Draw an x-axis from $x = 0$ to 10 and a y-axis from $y = 0$ to 10.

(b) Use the cover-up method with $x = 0$ and $y = 0$ to draw $x + 5y = 10$.

4 (a) Draw the same axes as in Question **3**.

(b) Use the cover-up method to draw $3x + 2y = 18$.

5 Draw each line below with the cover-up method. You need to find the 2 points first then draw the axes big enough.

(a) $5x + 3y = 15$ (b) $2x + 5y = 10$ (c) $9x + y = 18$

(d) $3x + 4y = 12$ (e) $6x + 5y = 30$ (f) $2x + 7y = 28$

Simultaneous equations on a graph

If $x = 2$ and $y = 8$ then $4x + y = 16$

If $x = 3$ and $y = 4$ then $4x + y = 16$

There are many pairs of values of x and y which fit the equation $4x + y = 16$

There are also many pairs of values of x and y which fit the equation $15x - y = 3$

There is only *one pair* of values of x and y which satisfy both equations at the same time (*simultaneously*).

If $x = 1, y = 12$ then $4x + y = 16$ ⎫ the 2 equations are called
If $x = 1, y = 12$ then $15x - y = 3$ ⎭ *simultaneous equations.*

$x = 1$ and $y = 12$ are called the *solutions* of the *simultaneous equations.*

The solutions of simultaneous equations can be found by drawing a graph.

Solve the simultaneous equations

$3x + y = 6 \qquad x + y = 4$

(a) Draw the line $3x + y = 6$

when $x = 0, y = 6$

when $y = 0, 3x = 6$ so $x = 2$

(b) Draw the line $x + y = 4$

when $x = 0, y = 4$

when $y = 0, x = 4$

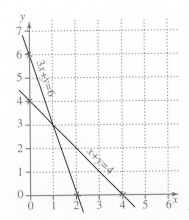

(c) The lines intersect at $(1, 3)$.

The solutions of these simultaneous equations are $x = 1, y = 3$.

E10. 3

1 Use the graph to solve the simultaneous equations

$$x + y = 7$$
$$2x - y = -1$$

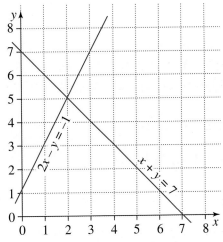

2 Use the graph to solve the simultaneous equations.

(a) $2x + y = 8$

$x + y = 5$

(b) $x - y = -5$

$x + y = 5$

(c) $2x + y = 8$

$x - y = -5$

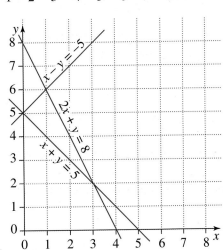

269

3 (a) Draw x and y axes from 0 to 9.

(b) Use the cover-up method to draw the line $3x + 4y = 24$.

(c) Use the cover-up method to draw the line $3x + 2y = 18$.

(d) Write down the solutions of the simultaneous equations $3x + 4y = 24$

$$3x + 2y = 18$$

4 (a) Draw x and y axes from 0 to 6.

(b) Draw the lines $x + y = 6$ and $y = x + 3$.

(c) Solve the simultaneous equations $x + y = 6$

$$y = x + 3$$

5 (a) Draw x and y axes from 0 to 5.

(b) Solve graphically the simultaneous equations $x + y = 5$

$$y = x + 2$$

6 (a) Draw x and y axes from 0 to 13.

(b) Solve graphically the simultaneous equations $x + 2y = 11$

$$2x + y = 13$$

7 Use the graph to solve the simultaneous equations.

(a) $x + y = 11$

$x + 3y = 13$

(b) $2x - y = -2$

$x + y = 11$

(c) $x + 3y = 13$

$2x - y = -2$

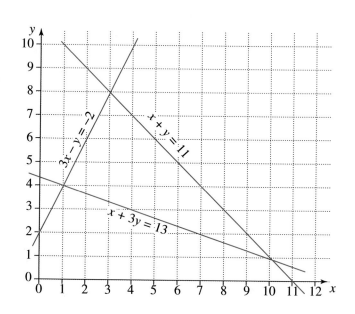

270

Have you ever seen signs like this?

This is the gradient – how steep the hill is.

The '**1 in 10**' means that the hill goes up 1 m for every 10 m across.

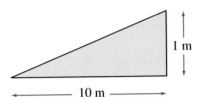

Gradient = 1 in 10 = $\dfrac{1}{10}$

The steeper the hill, the bigger the gradient.

$$\text{Gradient} = \frac{\text{vertical distance}}{\text{horizontal distance}}$$

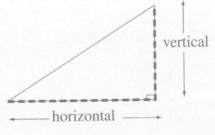

(a) Find the gradient of this line.

(b) Find the gradient of this line.

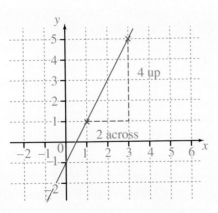

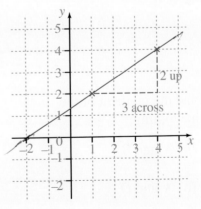

$$\text{Gradient} = \frac{4 \text{ up}}{2 \text{ across}} = \frac{4}{2} = 2$$

$$\text{Gradient} = \frac{2 \text{ up}}{3 \text{ across}} = \frac{2}{3}$$

Find the gradient of each line.

1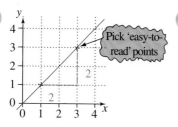

Pick 'easy-to-read' points

2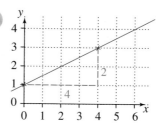

3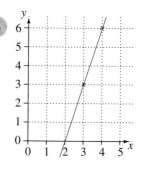

4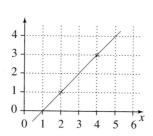

5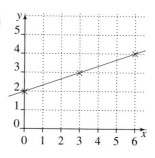

6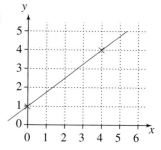

7 Find the gradient of each line below:

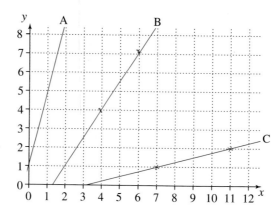

8 Find the gradient of the line joining:

(a) *A* and *B*

(b) *A* and *D*

(c) *C* and *D*

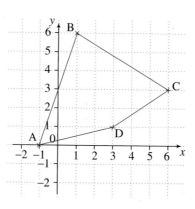

Key Facts

Negative gradient

If a line slopes downwards to the right, it has a *negative gradient*.

sloping downwards to the right ➡

Find the gradient of this line.

$$\text{Gradient} = \frac{4 \text{ down}}{2 \text{ across}}$$

$$= \frac{-4}{2}$$

$$= -2$$
↑

4 down

2 across

negative because line sloping downwards to the right

E10. 4

Find the gradient of each line.

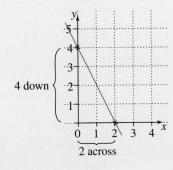

1

2

3

4 Find the gradient of each line below:

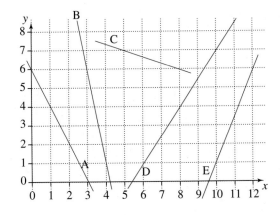

5 You will need to draw axes like these:

(a) Complete the table below then draw the straight line $y = 2x + 3$.

x	1	2	3
y			

(b) Use another table to draw $y = 2x$ on the same grid.

(c) Draw $y = 2x + 1$ on the same grid.

(d) Draw $y = 2x - 1$ on the same grid.

(e) Find the gradient of each line.

(f) What do you notice about the gradient of each line and its equation? *Discuss* with your teacher.

6 The equation of any straight line can be written in the form $y = mx + c$ where m is the gradient and c is where the line crosses the y-axis.

(a) Which lines below have the same gradient?

$y = 3x + 1$ $y = 3x - 2$ $y = 2x + 3$ $y = 3 + 4x$ $y = 7 + 3x$

(b) Which lines below are parallel?

$y = x + 2$ $y = 3 + 4x$ $y = 5 - x$ $y = 4x - 2$ $y = 2x + 4$

7 Write down the gradient of each line below.

(a) $y = 7x - 1$ (b) $y = 9x + 4$ (c) $y = 6 + 2x$ (d) $y = \frac{1}{2}x + 3$
(e) $y = 4 - 2x$

Can you still?

10C   **Sharing in a given ratio (see Unit 6)**

Can you still?

1. Divide £300 in the ratio 1:5

2. Divide 420 g in the ratio 3:7

3. £2500 is shared between Millie, Ken and Simon in the ratio 2:5:3 How much will each person get?

4. Lemon squash is diluted using squash and water in the ratio 2:9 If 40 ml of squash is used, how much water must be added?

5. The angles in a triangle are in the ratio 7:4:9 If the smallest angle is 36°, find the size of each of the other angles.

M10. 5

1 A scientist records the height of a growing plant every day for 20 days.

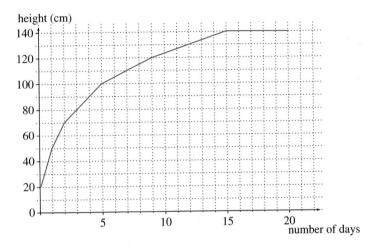

(a) What was the height of the plant after 5 days?

(b) After how many days was the height

(i) 70 cm   (ii) 105 cm?

(c) What was the greatest increase in height in one day?

(d) What was the full-grown height of the plant?

2 The graph below shows how many cars pass through a car wash during one day.

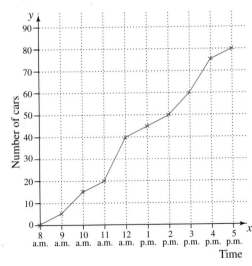

How many cars had passed through the car wash by the following times?

(a) 12 am   (b) 11:30 am

(c) 9:30 am   (d) 2:30 pm

(e) During which one hour period did *most* cars pass through the car wash. How many cars was this?

3 The graph below shows how to convert miles into kilometres.

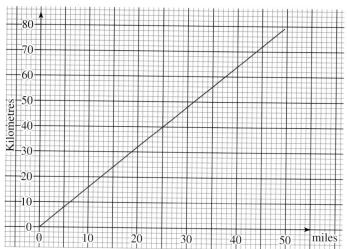

(a) How many kilometres is one small square worth on the vertical axis?

Use the graph to find how many kilometres are the same as:

(b) 25 miles   (c) 15 miles   (d) 45 miles   (e) 5 miles

Use the graph to find how many miles are the same as:

(f) 64 km   (g) 56 km   (h) 16 km   (i) 32 km

4 The graph below shows how to convert pounds into euros.

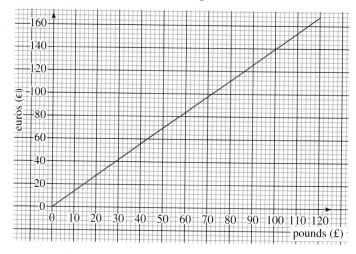

Use the graph to find how many euros are the same as:

(a) £20   (b) £80   (c) £50

Use the graph to find how many pounds are the same as:

(d) €56   (e) €84   (f) €140

(g) Tim spends €154 on clothes in Paris. How many pounds has he spent?

276

5 The number of people sitting down in a cinema was recorded every quarter of an hour. The results are shown below.

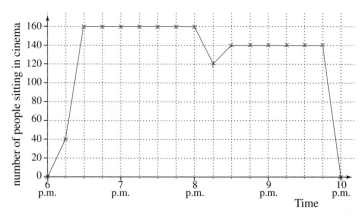

(a) How many people were sitting down at 7 p.m.?

(b) How many people were sitting down at 8:15 p.m.?

(c) When do you think the first film started?

(d) When do you think the second film started?

(e) How long did the first film last for?

(f) Which film was more popular?

Travel graphs

E10. 5

1 Jennifer walked 18 km between 9 a.m. and 2 p.m. The graph below shows how far she had walked at various times.

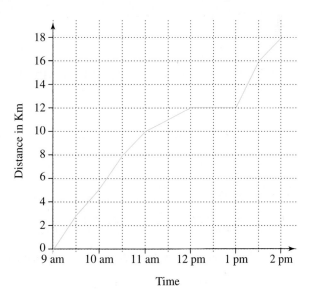

What distance had Jennifer walked by the following times?

(a) 9:30 a.m.   (b) 11:30 a.m.   (c) 1:30 p.m.

(d) 9:45 a.m.   (e) 1:15 p.m.   (f) 1:45 p.m.

(g) Between what times did Jennifer stop for a rest?

(h) During which half-hour interval did Jennifer walk the furthest?

 What distance was this?

2 Colin and Kris run a 400-metre race. The graph below shows how far they had run at different times.

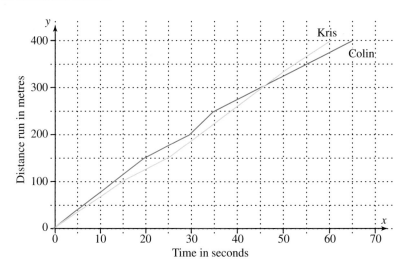

How far has Kris run after:

(a) 15 seconds?   (b) 25 seconds?   (c) 60 seconds?

(d) How long does it take Colin to run the first 150 metres?

(e) How long does it take Colin to run the first 250 metres?

(f) After how many seconds have Colin and Kris run the *same* distance?

(g) Who won the race?

3 (a) Jack travels 40 km in 30 minutes. How far will he travel in 1 hour?

(b) Sonia travels 9 km in 10 minutes. How far will she travel in 1 hour?

(c) Kim travels 150 km in 2 hours. How far did she travel in 1 hour?

(d) Sid travels 25 km in 15 minutes. How far will he travel in 1 hour?

4 For each graph below find the speed of the journey from *A* to *B*
(give the answer in km/h).

(a)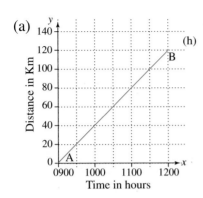

(b)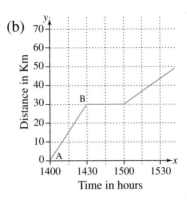

(c)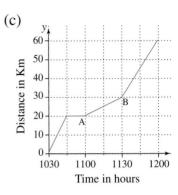

5

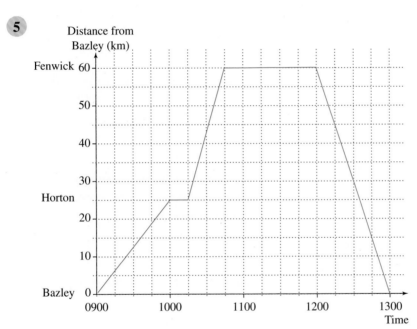

The graph above shows a car journey from Bazley.

(a) When did the car arrive back in Bazley?

(b) How long did the car stop in Horton?

(c) When did the car leave Horton after stopping?

(d) How long did the car stop in Fenwick?

(e) Find the speed (in km/h) of the car between Bazley and Horton.

(f) Find the speed (in km/h) of the car between Horton and Fenwick.

(g) Find the speed (in km/h) of the car from Fenwick back to Bazley.

In Questions **6** and **7** below, copy the axes then draw a travel graph to show each journey.

6 Distance from home (km)

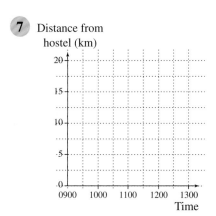

At 1400 Jason leaves home and drives 60 km in 1 hour at a steady speed. He stops at a café for $\frac{1}{2}$ hour. He travels another 40 km in $\frac{1}{2}$ hour. He then stops for 1 hour before returning home in 1 hour at a steady speed.

7 Distance from hostel (km)

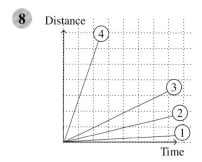

Some friends go for a long walk. They leave their hostel at 0900 and walk 4 km in $\frac{1}{2}$ hour at a steady speed. They walk 7 km during the next hour. They then rest for $\frac{1}{2}$ hour. They walk another 4 km in the next $\frac{1}{2}$ hour then return to the hostel in $1\frac{1}{2}$ hours at a steady speed.

8

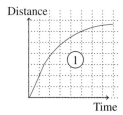

These four lines are the graphs for travel:

(A) in a car   (B) on foot

(C) on a bike   (D) in a rocket

Which graph is which?

9 Which of the graphs below shows:

(A) steady speed   (B) car that speeds up   (C) car that slows down

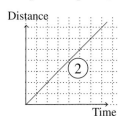

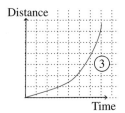

280

10 Water is poured at a constant rate into each of the containers A, B and C. Which of the graphs below fits each container?

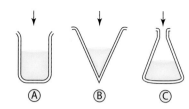

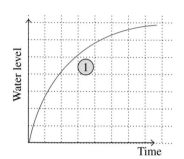

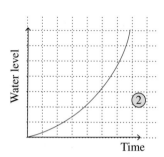

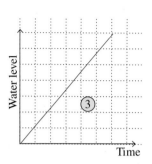

11 Which of the graphs below best fits each of the following statements:

(A) After a poor start, car sales have increased massively this year.

(B) The price of milk has remained the same over the past year.

(C) The world's population continues to rise rapidly.

(D) The price of computers has fallen steadily over the last year.

(E) The number of visitors to a seaside resort rose in the Summer then dropped off towards Winter.

(F) The number of people going to the cinema in the UK has increased steadily this year.

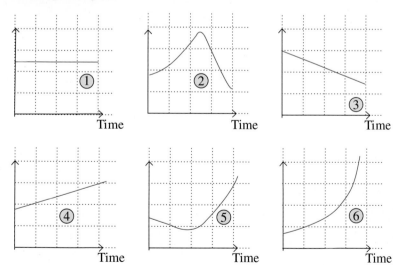

Some people say 'you don't get 'owt for nowt in this life'. Most things have to be paid for and that includes the electricity, gas and water you use in your home.

The amount of electricity, gas (and water in some homes) used is recorded on a *meter*. The meter is read every 3 months and a bill is sent. An electricity bill could look like the one below:

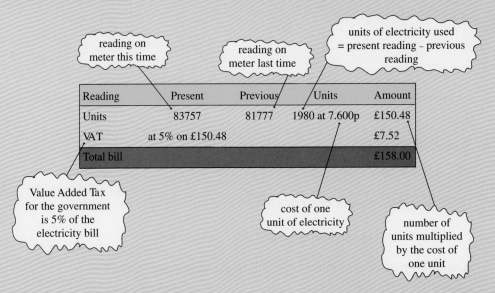

Reading	Present	Previous	Units	Amount
Units	83757	81777	1980 at 7.600p	£150.48
VAT	at 5% on £150.48			£7.52
Total bill				£158.00

- reading on meter this time
- reading on meter last time
- units of electricity used = present reading – previous reading
- Value Added Tax for the government is 5% of the electricity bill
- cost of one unit of electricity
- number of units multiplied by the cost of one unit

Payment

Some people simply pay their bill when it arrives. Other people arrange to pay part of their bill each month. They are often given a small discount if they arrange to pay the bill each month.

Ally has received his electricity bill:

present reading = 61982 previous reading = 60732

cost of one unit of electricity = 7.6 p.

VAT is 5%.

How much does Ally have to pay?

units used = present – previous = 61982 – 60732 = 1250

cost of units = 1250 × 7.6 p = 9500 p = £95.00

VAT = 5% of £95.00 = $\frac{5}{100}$ × 95.00 = £4.75

Total bill = £99.75

1 Nerys has received her electricity bill:

present reading = 53164   previous reading = 51083

cost of one unit of electricity = 9.3 p.

Copy and complete the bill below:

units used = present − previous = 53164 − ☐ = ☐

cost of units = ☐ × 9.3 p = ☐ p = £ ☐

$$VAT = 5\% \text{ of } £\,☐ = \frac{5}{100} \times ☐ = £\,☐$$

Total bill = £ ‾‾‾‾

2 Work out the cost of each electricity bill below.

VAT is payable at 5% each time.

Bill	present reading	previous reading	cost of one unit of electricity
a	81659	80292	8.3 p
b	23748	22095	7.6 p
c	5186	4417	7.6 p
d	63746	62640	9.4 p
e	9187	8089	8.2 p
f	5613	4688	11.4 p
g	71248	69325	7.9 p

> **1. Drawing straight line graphs**

(a)

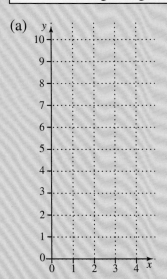

Draw these axes.

Complete the table below then draw $y = 4x + 1$.

x	0	1	2
y			

(b) Using x-values from 0 to 4, complete a table then draw $y = 7 - x$.

(c) Look at points on the straight line. Copy and complete the table below:

x-coordinate	y-coordinate
2	0
3	
4	
5	

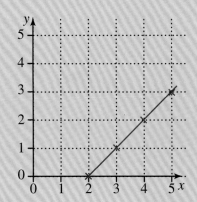

(d) Find a rule connecting the x-coordinate and the y-coordinate. $y = \ldots\ldots$

> **2. Drawing curves from equations**

(a) Complete the table below then draw the curve $y = x^2 + 2$.

x	−3	−2	−1	0	1	2	3
y							

(b) Complete the table below then draw the curve $y = x^2 - 4$.

x	−3	−2	−1	0	1	2	3
y							

(a)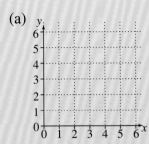

(i) Draw these axes.

(ii) Use $x = 0$ then $y = 0$ to find 2 points for $x + 3y = 6$.

(iii) Draw the straight line $x + 3y = 6$.

(b) Draw x and y axes from 0 to 6.

Draw the straight line $4x + 5y = 20$.

4. Solving simultaneous equations on a graph

(a) Use the graph to solve the simultaneous equations

$$2y - x = 4$$

$$x + y = 5$$

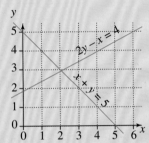

(b) Draw x and y axes from 0 to 6.

Solve graphically the simultaneous equations $3x + y = 6$

$$x + y = 4.$$

(c) Draw x and y axes from 0 to 8.

Solve graphically the simultaneous equations $2x + y = 8$

$$2x + 3y = 12.$$

5. Finding gradients of straight lines

Find the gradient of each line below:

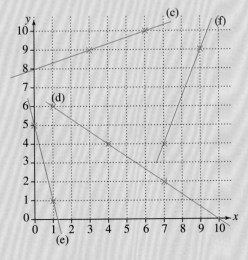

285

The graph below shows the weights of Ed and Serena during one year.

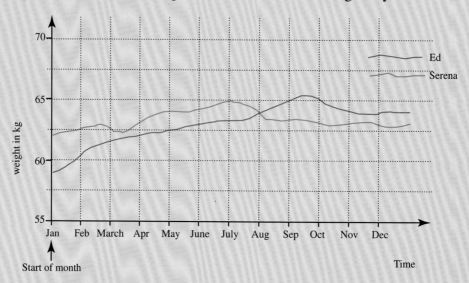

How much did Ed weigh at the start of:

(a) March?   (b) September?   (c) December?

(d) At the start of which month did Serena weigh 65 kg?

(e) How much did Serena weigh at the start of January?

(f) When did Ed and Serena weigh the *same* amount? How much did they weigh
    then?

(g) How much *more* did Serena weigh than Ed at the start of February?

(h) How much *more* did Ed weigh than Serena at the start of November?

Mixed examination questions

1. (a) Copy and complete the table of values for $y = 2x + 3$

x	-2	-1	0	1	2	3
y		1	3			

(b) Draw the graph of $y = 2x + 3$ (EDEXCEL)

2. The distance, by boat, from Poole Quay to Wareham is 12 miles. The diagram shows the distance-time graph of a boat trip from Poole Quay to Wareham and back.

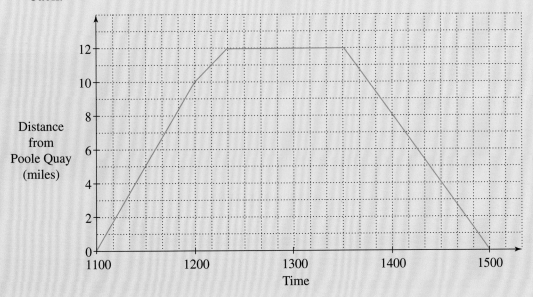

(a) Describe what happened to the speed of the boat at 1200 hours.

(b) How long did the boat stay in Wareham?

(c) What was the average speed of the boat on the return journey from Wareham to Poole Quay? (AQA)

3. (a) Complete the table of values for $y = 5 - x^2$.

x	-3	-2	-1	0	1	2	3
y		1	4	5			-4

(b) Draw the graph of $y = 5 - x^2$ for values of x from -3 to 3. (AQA)

4. The line $y + 4x = 14$ is shown on the right.

(a) On a copy of the diagram draw the line $y = 2x - 1$.

(b) Use your graph to solve the simultaneous equations

$$y + 4x = 14$$
$$y = 2x - 1$$

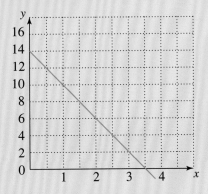

In this unit you will learn how to:

- use the probability scale

- use relative frequency

- find probabilities

- list possible outcomes

- deal with mutually exclusive events

- ⟨ USE YOUR MATHS! ⟩ – the school prom

The probability scale

The probability of something happening is the likelihood or chance that it might happen.

If the probability of something happening is 'impossible', we say the probability is 0 (0% or 'no chance').

If the probability of something happening is 'dead certain', we say the probability is 1 (100% certain).

All the probabilities lie between 0 and 1.

```
0|————————————————+————————————————|1
impossible    unlikely    even chance    likely    certain
```

This is the 'probability scale'.

Think about the probability of these events. Place them on a probability scale.

A You will eat during the next week.

B You will get 'heads' if you toss a coin.

C It will rain on the 10th February.

D You could swim to Australia without stopping.

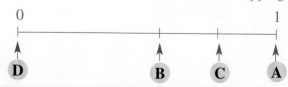

For each of these statements write one of these probabilities:

impossible   unlikely   even chance   likely   certain

1 Your teacher was born on a Monday.

2 You roll a dice and get a 3.

3 A baby will be born somewhere in the UK in the next hour.

4 It will rain on the 4th July.

5 You will brush your teeth sometime tomorrow.

6 You will drive a bus home tomorrow evening.

7 You will have a birthday in the next year.

8 You will choose a king if you pick one card from a pack of playing cards (there are 4 kings in a pack of 52 playing cards).

9 You will fly to the moon during the next year.

10 You will do *all* your maths homework for the rest of the year.

11 Think about the probability of the events below. Place them on a probability scale.

(a) Someone in your family will win the National Lottery Jackpot next week.

(b) You will wash your hair during the next week.

(c) There will be a school holiday during the next year.

(d) You will get 'tails' if you toss a coin.

(e) All pupils in your class will wear correct school uniform every day next term.

12 Think about the probability of the events below. Place them on a probability scale.

(a) It will snow on Christmas Day.

(b) The first person to walk into your next maths lesson will be a girl.

(c) You will go to the toilet during the next 24 hours.

(d) You roll a dice and get an 'odd' number.

(e) You will get married one day.

11A **Use co-ordinates (see Unit 8)**

1.

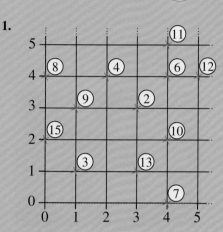

Write down the numbers at each of the co-ordinates given below:

(4, 5)   (1, 1)   (3, 1)   (3, 3)   (4, 0)

These numbers are a special type of number. Write down their name.

2. Draw x and y axes with values from –5 to 5. Plot the points below and join them up in order.

a) (–2, –3)   (–1, –3)   (0, –2)   (–2, 0)   (–2, 1)   (–3, 2)

   (–4, 1)   (–4, 3)   (–3, 4)   (–2, 4)   (0, 2)   (–1, 1)

   (–1, 0)   (1, –1)   (3, –1)   (3, 0)   (1, 2)   (0, 2)

On the same grid, plot the points below and join them up in order.

b) (2, –1)   (4, –3)   (3, –4)   (2, –2)   (0, –2)

On the same grid, plot the points below and join them up in order.

c) (–4, 1)   (–3, 3)   (–3, 4)   (–3, 2)

d) Draw a dot at (–2, 3).

Relative frequency

Sometimes it is useful to *estimate* the probability of something happening.

We collect data (maybe by doing an experiment). Each time the experiment is done is called a 'trial' (e.g. throwing a dice).

We use these results to estimate the chance of something happening. This estimate is called the *relative frequency*.

Relative frequency of 'X' happening $= \dfrac{\text{number of times 'X' happens}}{\text{total number of trials}}$

Maggie thinks her dice is biased (not fair). She throws the dice 600 times. The table below shows her results.

Score	1	2	3	4	5	6
Frequency	96	84	186	72	78	84

(a) How many times should each number come up if the dice is fair?

(b) From Maggie's results, estimate the probability of getting a '3' (this is called the relative frequency).

(c) Do you think the dice is fair?

Answer:

(a) 6 numbers so each number should come up 100 times.

(b) Relative frequency of getting a '3' $= \dfrac{186}{600} = 0.31$ (using a calculator)

(c) The dice is not fair (it landed on '3' nearly twice as often as it should).

E11.1

1 Joe spins a coin 100 times. The coin lands on 'heads' 71 times and 'tails' 29 times.

(a) How many times should 'heads' come up if the coin is fair?

(b) From Joe's results, find the 'relative frequency' of getting 'heads'.

(c) Do you think the coin is fair? Explain the answer you give.

2 Will thinks his dice is biased (not fair). He throws the dice 300 times. The table below shows his results.

Score	1	2	3	4	5	6
Frequency	51	46	47	54	53	49

(a) How many times should each number come up if the dice is fair.

(b) From Will's results, use a calculator to estimate the 'probability' of getting a '4'.

(c) Do you think the dice is fair? Discuss your answer with your teacher.

3 Mary throws a drawing pin 200 times. It lands 'point down' 78 times.

(a) Use a calculator to find the relative frequency that the drawing pin will land 'point down'.

(b) How many times does the drawing pin land 'point up'?

(c) Find the relative frequency that the drawing pin will land 'point up'.

4 Lola is throwing a 10-sided dice. She throws the dice 500 times. The table below shows her results.

Score	1	2	3	4	5	6	7	8	9	10
Frequency	44	48	51	50	47	52	40	82	45	41

(a) How many times should each number come up if the dice is fair?

(b) From Lola's results, use a calculator to estimate the probability of getting each score (1 up to 10).

(c) Do you think the dice is fair? Explain the answer you give.

5 Gavin has to feed 900 people. He asks 60 people to choose their favourite meal from a menu of 3 dishes. The results are shown opposite.

(a) Estimate the probability that the first person to arrive for a meal would choose chicken kurma.

(b) Based on Gavin's survey, how many servings of *each* meal should he prepare to feed all 900 people?

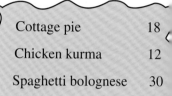

Cottage pie   18

Chicken kurma   12

Spaghetti bolognese   30

Can you still?   Can you still?

11B   **Translate and reflect shapes (see Unit 8)**

1.

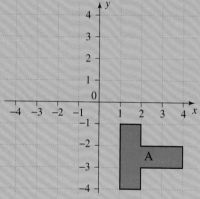

Copy this grid. Copy shape A.

(a) Reflect shape A in the x–axis. Label the image (new shape) B.

(b) Translate shape B through $\begin{pmatrix} -3 \\ -1 \end{pmatrix}$. Label the new shape C.

(c) Describe *fully* the translation which moves shape C onto shape A.

(d) Which shapes are *congruent* to shape A?

2.

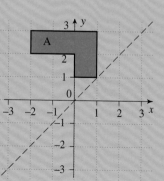

Copy this grid. Copy shape B.

(a) Reflect shape A in the broken mirror line. Label the image (new shape) B.

(b) Translate shape B through $\begin{pmatrix} -4 \\ 1 \end{pmatrix}$. Label the new shape C.

Finding probabilities

Probability = $\dfrac{\text{the number of ways the event can happen}}{\text{the total number of possible outcomes}}$

A bag contains 5 black beads and 4 red beads.
I take out one bead.

(a) The probability of taking out a black bead is $\dfrac{5}{9}$

We may write p (black) = $\dfrac{5}{9}$

(b) The probability of taking out a red bead = $\dfrac{4}{9}$

(c) The probability of taking out a red or black bead = $\dfrac{9}{9}$ = 1 (This is 'dead certain')

(d) The probability of taking out a yellow bead = 0 (This is impossible)

M11.2

1. Mo has a bag of sweets.
   She has 3 chews and 2 mints left.
   She picks out a sweet.
   What is the probability that she picks a mint?

2. Tina rolls a dice.

   What is the probability that she rolls a:

   (a) 1? (b) 3? (c) 4? (d) 3 or 4?

3. Billy has 9 cards as shown below:

   Billy picks a card at random.

   What is the probability that he picks the letter:

   (a) C? (b) F? (c) a vowel?

4 Rowan has a box of chocolates.

There are 5 truffles, 4 toffees and 2 nuts.

Rowan picks a chocolate.

Find the probability that he chooses a:

(a) toffee (b) truffle (c) toffee or nut

5 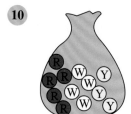 Thelma spins this spinner.

Find the probability that she gets

(a) a 5 (b) an even number (c) an odd number

6 Ten discs numbered 1, 2, 2, 2, 3, 6, 8, 9, 9, 9, are placed in a bag. One disc is selected at random.

Find the probability that it is:

(a) an even number b) 2 c) less than 6

7 Phil has 15 pencils in his pencil case. 7 pencils are red, 5 are blue and the rest are green.

Phil takes out a pencil at random.

What is the probability that he takes out:

(a) blue? (b) green? (c) red or green? (d) yellow?

8 Sarah is taking part in a TV Quiz show. She must choose one box from a choice of 10 to win a prize. 4 boxes are empty, 5 boxes contain prizes for the home and 1 box has the 'star' prize.

What is the probability that Sarah will win:

(a) the 'star' prize? (b) nothing? (c) a prize for the home?

9 One card is picked at random from a pack of 52.

Find the probability that it is:

(a) the Queen of clubs (b) a red card (c) a spade

10 A bag contains 12 balls. There are 5 red, 4 white and 3 yellow.

(a) Find the probability of selecting a red ball.

(b) The 4 white balls are replaced by 4 yellow balls. Find the probability of selecting a yellow ball.

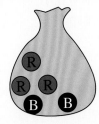

There are 3 red beads and 2 black beads in a bag. A bead is picked from this bag 75 times and replaced each time. How many red beads would you expect to get?

Probability of picking 'red' = $\dfrac{3}{5}$

Expect to get $\dfrac{3}{5}$ of 75

$$= (75 \div 5) \times 3$$
$$= 15 \times 3$$
$$= 45 \text{ reds.}$$

E11.2

1. A bag contains one green bead and 3 yellow beads. A bead is picked from the bag 80 times and replaced each time.

   How many yellow beads would you expect to get?

2. A dice is thrown 180 times.

   How many times would you expect to get

   (a) a 4   (b) a 3   (c) an even number   (d) a 2 or 3

3. A coin is spun 60 times. How many tails would you expect to get?

4. A box has 30 pencils in it. The probability of picking a red pencil is $\frac{1}{6}$. How many red pencils are in the box?

5. A bag has 25 beads in it. The probability of picking a white bead is $\frac{3}{5}$. How many white beads are in the bag?

6. In a game this spinner is spun 60 times. How many wins would you expect?

7. The chance of Jim playing football in a games lesson is $\frac{1}{4}$. There are 16 lessons in a term. How many times will Jim expect to play football?

8. A bag contains 7 red discs, 8 black discs and 5 white discs. Sandra pulls out one at random and then puts it back. If she does this 80 times, how many times would she pick:

   (a) a red disc?   (b) a white disc?   (c) a black disc?

9. The probability that a train will arrive *on time* the next day at Swindon is 0.8. If 60 trains arrive at Swindon the next day, how many will be *on time*?

10 The probability of getting a grade C or better in an English GCSE is 0.6. If 300 young people take their English GCSE, how many would you expect to get a grade C or better?

11 Ann keeps trying her luck in the National Lottery. The probability that the first ball chosen will be hers is $\frac{6}{49}$. During one year, she plays 98 times.

How many times would she expect the first ball chosen to be hers?

12 There are 15 balls in a bag. Sandeep takes a ball from the bag, notes its colour and then returns the ball to the bag. Sandeep does this 20 times.

red	6
yellow	1
black	11
green	2

Here are the results.

(a) What is the smallest number of green balls there could be in the bag?

(b) Sandeep says 'There cannot be any white balls in the bag because there are no whites in my table'.

Explain why Sandeep is wrong.

(c) Sandeep takes one more ball from the bag. What is the most likely colour of the ball?

13 The probability of it raining in November in Aberdeen is $\frac{5}{6}$. How many days would you expect it to rain in November?

14 A bag has only blue and white balls in it. The probability of picking blue is $\frac{3}{4}$.

(a) What is the probability of picking a white ball?

(b) Ken picks a ball at random. He picks a white ball. What is the smallest number of white balls there could be in the bag?

(c) Ken then picks out another white ball. What is the smallest number of blue balls there could be in the bag?

15 I have two bags of beads.

12 red beads
16 blue beads

11 red beads
14 blue beads

Which bag has the greater probability of getting a red counter? (you may *use a calculator* to help explain your answer)

11C **Rotate and enlarge shapes (see Unit 8)**

(You may use tracing paper)

1.

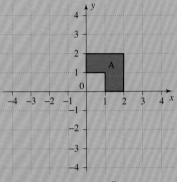

(a) Copy the grid. Copy shape A.

(b) Rotate shape A 180° clockwise about (0, 0). Label the image (new shape) B.

(c) Enlarge shape B by scale factor 2 about (0, 0). Label the image C.

2.

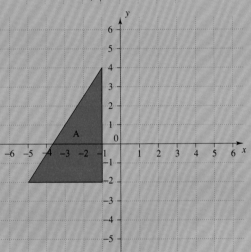

(a) Copy the grid. Copy shape A.

(b) Enlarge shape A by scale factor $\frac{1}{2}$ about (−3, −4). Label the image B.

(c) Rotate shape B 90° clockwise about (−1, −4). Label the image C.

Listing possible outcomes

When more than one event occurs, it is usually helpful to make a list of all the possible outcomes. Use a system when making the list.

If you throw 2 coins, they could land as:

1st. coin	2nd. coin
head	head
head	tail
tail	head
tail	tail

} there are 4 possible outcomes

297

1 For breakfast, Ellie eats cereal or toast. She drinks juice or tea.
Copy and complete the table below to show all the different breakfasts
she might have.

food	drink
cereal	juice
	tea
toast	

2 Ivy throws a coin and a dice. She could get a 'head' and a '5' (H 5). She could get a 'tail' and a '5'. List the 12 possible outcomes.

3 Here are 2 spinners. If I spin both spinners, I could get a 3 and a 9 (3, 9).

a) List *all* the possible outcomes.

b) How many possible outcomes are there?

4 Alfonso sells ice-cream in tubs which contain 2 scoops. He has chocolate chip, vanilla and raspberry ripple. A tub could have one scoop of vanilla and one scoop of raspberry ripple or it could have 2 scoops of raspberry ripple. List all the different kinds of tubs which can be made.

5 At a restaurant, each person has a starter, main course and dessert.

One evening the menu is:

    starter: melon or soup

    main course: lamb, turkey or pork

    dessert: apple pie, creme brulé or rhubarb crumble

List all the different meals that could be ordered.

6 Four people, Tom, Sasha, Becky and Ronnie, work at a garage. Two people work at any one time. List all the possible pairs of people that could be working together at any one time.

7 Three coins are thrown together. List all the possible outcomes for the three coins.

8 You can choose from 4 possible drinks in a drinks machine.

| coke | | fanta | | sprite | | diet coke |

Zak buys one drink for himself and one for his friend. Write down all the possible pairs of drink Zak and his friend could have.

9 Jack has 2 spinners. He spins both spinners and adds up the numbers to get a total. For example a '4' and a '3' give a total of 7.

(a) Copy and complete this grid to show all the possible outcomes and totals.

(b) Find the probability of getting a total of 7.

+	1	3	5
2	3		
4		7	
6			

10

+	1	2	3	4	5	6
1						
2						
3		5				
4						
5		7				
6						

2 dice are thrown. The numbers are then added together to get a total.

(a) Copy and complete this grid to show all the possible outcomes and totals.

(b) Find the probability of getting a total of 6.

(c) Find the probability of getting a total which is an even number.

(d) Find the probability of getting a score which is *more* than 9.

Mutually exclusive events

Events are mutually exclusive if they cannot occur at the same time.

For example:

- selecting a queen
  selecting a '3' } from the same pack of cards
- tossing a 'head'
  tossing a 'tail'
- selecting a red ball from a bag
  selecting a white ball from the same bag

The sum of the probabilities of mutually exclusive events is 1.

A bag contains balls which are either red, blue or yellow.

The probability of selecting a red is 0.3.

The probability of selecting a blue is 0.4.

What is the probability of selecting a yellow?

The probability of selecting a red *or* blue = 0.3 + 0.4 = 0.7 ('or' often suggests you *add* the probabilities)

Sum of probabilities = 1

Probability of selecting a yellow = 1 – p (red or blue)

$$= 1 - 0.7$$

$$= 0.3$$

E11.3

1 Which of the following pairs of events are mutually exclusive?

(a) choose a club or an ace from a pack of cards.

(b) win or lose a football match.

(c) get a red light or green light on traffic lights.

(d) the sun shines or it rains.

(e) wear a blue tie or brown shoes.

(f) get a '3' or a '4' on a dice.

2 Kerry has a drawer full of blue, black or red socks. The probability of choosing blue socks is 0.5. The probability of choosing black socks is 0.3.

(a) What is the probability of selecting blue *or* black socks?

(b) What is the probability of selecting red socks?

3 In a Games lesson, students play football, basketball or hockey.

The probability of playing football is 0.4.

The probability of playing basketball is 0.5.

(a) What is the probability of playing football or basketball?

(b) What is the probability of playing hockey?

4 In a football match the probability of Everton winning is 0.5. The probability of losing is 0.3. What is the probability of Everton drawing?

5 A bag contains balls which are either yellow, blue or green.

The probability of selecting a yellow ball is 0.15.

The probability of selecting a blue ball is 0.55.

(a) Find the probability of selecting a green ball.

(b) Find the probability of selecting a ball which is *not* yellow.

6 Emma has one drink for her breakfast. The table shows the probability of her choosing each drink.

tea	coffee	orange juice	grape fruit juice
0.4	x	0.3	0.1

(a) What is the probability of Emma choosing orange juice or grapefruit juice?

(b) What is the probability of Emma choosing coffee?

(c) During the month of April, how many days would you expect Emma to choose tea?

7 Terry has a selection of shirts. The table shows the probability of Terry choosing a particular shirt colour.

blue	white	yellow	red	green
0.3	0.3	0.15	x	0.05

(a) What is the probability of Terry choosing a yellow or green shirt?

(b) What is the probability of Terry choosing a red shirt?

(c) For every 50 times that Terry chooses a shirt, how many times would you expect him to choose a white shirt?

8 The probability of pulling out a Queen from a pack of cards is $\frac{1}{13}$. What is the probability of *not* pulling out a Queen?

9 4 people play a game of poker. The probability of each person winning the game is shown below in the table.

Darryl	Simon	Dan	Mark
0.35	0.25	0.25	x

(a) What is the probability of Darryl or Simon winning?

(b) What is the probability of Mark winning.

(c) If they play 60 times, how many times would you expect Dan to win?

10 Each time Cassie visits her grandfather he gives her some money. The table shows the probability of her getting a particular amount of money.

£2	£5	£10	£20
x	$\dfrac{1}{4}$	$\dfrac{1}{8}$	$\dfrac{1}{16}$

(a) Find the probability of getting £5 or £10.

(b) Find the probability of not getting £20.

(c) Find the probability of getting £2.

(d) For every 16 visits to her grandfather, how many times would Cassie expect to get £10?

11 The probability of getting a square number when you throw a dice is $\frac{1}{3}$. What is the probability of *not* getting a square number?

12 Every Friday night Jodie goes to a cinema, pub or restaurant. The probability of going to the cinema is $\frac{1}{2}$. The probability of going to the pub is $\frac{1}{4}$. What is the probability that Jodie goes to a restaurant?

Most schools now have a prom for students towards the end of year 11. People usually dress up smartly and glamorously.

The prom often takes place at hired places but sometimes at the school. Some students choose to arrive at the prom in style – for example by limousine or horse-drawn carriage.

Do task A or task B then do task C.

Task A

Terry has £80 to spend on the school prom. He has plenty of friends with similar amounts of money. Use all the prices on this page and the next page to decide on what Terry should spend. Show all your calculations clearly.

Task B

Repeat task A for Annie who has £350 to spend on the school prom.

Task C

Now price up what **you** would do for a school prom. Show all your calculations clearly.

Hire of limos – rate per hour

- White American Stretched Lincoln (8 people) – £138

- White Hummer (16 people) – £360

- Pink Ford Expedition Limo (14 people) – £315

- Black Hummer H2 Leer Jet Door (16 people) – £380

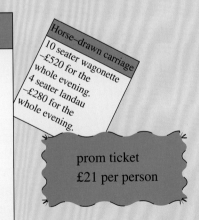

Horse-drawn carriage
10 seater wagonette –£520 for the whole evening.
4 seater landau –£280 for the whole evening.

prom ticket
£21 per person

303

Hire Cost of dinner suits	Suit	Outfit (includes shirt and bow tie)	Outfit plus shoes or waistcoat	Outfit plus shoes and waistcoat
Single Breasted Black	£41	£46	£52	£57
Single Breasted White	£58	£63	£69	£74
Student Deal (Black Only)	£63 for two	£69.50 for two	£79 for two	£86.50 for two
Accidental Damage Waiver £4.75 per suit or outfit				

If you pay the Accidental Damage Waiver, you will not have to pay anything if your suit or outfit is accidently damaged.

Prom dresses (all shown dress prices reduced by 15%)	
Short Taffeta Dress (red, orange, pink turquoise)	£71.60
50s Style Strapless Short Dress (peacock blue)	£122.40
Polka Dot Silver Cocktail Dress	£135.40
Long 2-tone Taffeta Sheath Dress (emerald, lime)	£205
Long Organza Strapless Dress (gold)	£290.20
Long Black Ball Gown with Tulle Skirt and Embroidered Bodice	£332.80

Shoes
Diamante Stiletto Sandals (silver, gold) – £40
Satin pumps (red, pink, pale blue, black, grey, silver, gold) – £29.36
Black Stiletto Court Shoes – £55

3 cm height Diamante Tiara £29.35
Viscose Shimmer Shawl £12.50
(grey, blue, red, orange, emerald)
Black Velvet Evening Wrap £40.95

Evening Bags
Red Beaded Evening Bag – £12.67
Gold Leather and Chainmail Bag – £40
Sequinned and Embroidered Black Clutch Bag – £29.95

Hair Salon
Cut (girls) £28
Cut (boys) £22
Highlighting £80
Home Hair Extensions
23 inch clip in £37.99
10 inch clip in £32.75

Beauty Treatment (10% off shown prices)	
• 40 minute teen facial	£20
• special occasion make-up	£30
• one hour pedicure	£22
• eyebrow shape	£5.40
• spray tan	£27
• manicure-file and polish	£7.50
(French polish £2 extra)	
• self tanning lotion	£13
• nail art – £1.50 per nail	

TEST YOURSELF ON UNIT 11

1. Using the probability scale

Think about the probability of the events below. Place them on a probability scale.

0 ————————————————————————————— 1

(a) You will have a drink in the next 24 hours.

(b) You will get a '2' when you throw a dice.

(c) A car will drive on a motorway today in the UK.

(d) If I put a stone in one of my hands, you will guess correctly which hand has the stone.

(e) Your school will be 'transported' to the planet Mars today.

2. Using relative frequency

Sabrina throws a shoe into the air. The shoe lands on its left side, right side or on its bottom.

She does this 50 times. The table below shows her results.

left side	right side	bottom
16	21	13

Use a calculator to find the relative frequency that the shoe lands on its:

(a) left side

(b) right side

(c) bottom

(d) If Sabrina threw the shoe 200 times, how many times would she expect it to land on its right side?

3. Finding probabilities

(a) Fiona has 8 cards as shown below?

Fiona picks a card at random.

What is the probability that she picks the letter:

(i) B?   (ii) E?   (iii) R?   (iv) a vowel?

305

(b) 12 discs numbered 1, 2, 3, 3, 5, 6, 6, 8, 9, 9, 10, 15 are placed in a bag. One disc is selected at random. Find the probability that it is:

    (i) a prime number   (ii) a 6   (iii) a multiple of 3

(c) This pointer is spun 60 times. How many times would you expect it to point to:

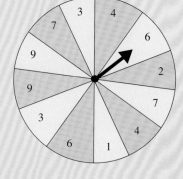

    (i) 2?

    (ii) an even number?

    (iii) a square number?

4. Listing possible outcomes

(a) Kyron throws a dice and spins the spinner shown opposite.

He could get a '4' and a '3' (4, 3). List *all* the possible outcomes. How many possible outcomes are there?

(b) Cath has to choose some of her school subjects from the option blocks below:

A	B	C
french	history	art
german	geography	dt
spanish		

She must choose one subject from column A, one from column B and one from column C. List *all* the different groups of choices she could make (combinations).

(c) How many combinations are there?

5. Dealing with mutually exclusive events

(a) The probability that Ivan is late in the morning is 0.01. What is the probability that Ivan is *not* late in the morning?

(b) A bag contains balls which are either white, green or blue.
The probability of selecting a white ball is 1/3.
The probability of selecting a green ball is 1/2.

    (i) What is the probability of selecting a white *or* green ball?

    (ii) What is the probability of selecting a blue ball?

(c) Gwen likes a wide range of music. The table below shows the probability of Gwen listening to a particular type of music.

rock	opera	jazz	classical
0.5	0.15	x	0.05

(i) What is the probability of Gwen listening to opera or classical music?

(ii) What is the probability of Gwen listening to jazz?

(iii) For the next 50 times that Gwen listens to music, how many times would you expect her to listen to rock music?

Mixed examination questions

1 (a) Marco is recycling his glass bottles.
He has one green (G), one brown (B) and one clear (C) bottle.

List the different orders he could recycle the three bottles. The first one is done for you.

G	B	C

(b) (i) Jane has 11 green, 7 brown and 2 clear bottles to recycle. She picks the first bottle at random.

What is the probability that it is brown?

(ii) The probability that the first bottle she picks is a juice bottle is 0.4.

What is the probability that the first bottle she picks is not a juice bottle?   (OCR)

2 A sack contains a number of gold and silver discs.
An experiment consists of taking a disc from the sack at random, recording its colour and then replacing it.
The experiment is repeated 10, 50, 100, 150 and 200 times.
The table shows the results.

Number of experiments	10	50	100	150	200
Number of gold discs	3	8	23	30	38

(a) Draw a graph to show how the relative frequency of a gold disc changes as the number of experiments increases.

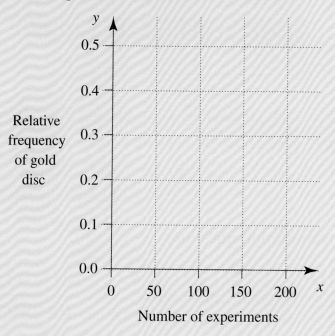

Number of experiments

(b) The sack contains 1000 discs.
Estimate the number of gold discs in the sack.

(AQA)

3 The table shows information about a group of adults.

	Can drive	Cannot drive
Male	32	8
Female	38	12

(a) One of these adults is chosen at random.
What is the probability that the adult can drive?

(b) A man in the group is chosen at random.
What is the probability that he can drive?

(c) A woman in the group is chosen at random.
The probability that she can drive is 0.76.
What is the probability that she cannot drive?

(d) Does the information given support the statement

"More women can drive than men"?

Explain your answer.

(AQA)

4 (a) A bag contains 3 orange sweets and 2 yellow sweets.
One sweet is chosen from the bag at random.
Find the probability that it will be orange.

(b) There are only red, green and blue counters in a box.
The probability of a red or a green counter being chosen is given in the table below.

Colour	Red	Green	Blue
Probability	0.4	0.2	

    (i) Work out the probability of choosing a blue counter.   (OCR)

5 Rovers play Wanderers at football.
The probability that Rovers win the match is 0.55.
The probability that Wanderers win the match is 0.2.

Find the probability that the result is a draw.   (OCR)

6 The table shows the probability for the delivery time of letters posted first class.

Delivery time (days)	1	2	3 or more
Probability	0.7	0.2	0.1

100 letters are posted first class.

How many will be delivered in 1 or 2 days?   (AQA)

ALGEBRA 3

In this unit you will learn how to:

– find numbers in sequences

– find rules for sequences

– solve equations

– solve equations with brackets

– solve equations with the unknown on both sides

– set up equations and solve them

– solve equations by trial and improvement

– USE YOUR MATHS! – hidden car costs

Sequences

- A number sequence is a list of numbers in special order.

- Each number in a sequence is called a *term*.

- The terms are connected by a rule.

  3, 8, 13, 18, 23... the rule is +5 each time.

- To find the rule that links the numbers, study the gaps.

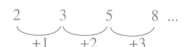

You can now see the pattern so the next number will be 8 + *4* = 12

1 The numbers in boxes make a sequence. Find the next term.

(a) | 2 | | 5 | | 8 | | 11 | | |

(b) | 15 | | 13 | | 11 | | 9 | | |

(c) | 4 | | 9 | | 14 | | 19 | | |

(d) | 3 | | 4 | | 6 | | 9 | | |

In Questions **2** to **15** copy the sequences and write the *next 2 numbers*. What is the rule for each sequence?

2 2, 6, 10, 14…

3 7, 9, 11, 13…

4 7, 15, 23, 31…

5 16, 13, 10, 7…

6 23, 19, 15, 11…

7 5, 14, 23, 32…

8 4, 10, 16, 22...

9 10, 19, 28, 37...

10 5, 7, 10, 14...

11 1, 2, 4, 7...

12 18, 17, 15, 12...

13 80, 75, 65, 50...

14 5, 3, 1, -1...

15 2, 0, -2, -4...

In Questions **16** to **25** write down the missing numbers.

16 7, 11, ☐, 19, ☐

17 8, 11, ☐, 17, ☐

18 21, 16, ☐, 6, ☐

19 32, 26, 20, ☐, ☐

20 5, 12, ☐, 26, ☐

21 –10, –8, ☐, –4, ☐

22 3, 0, ☐, –6, ☐

23 61, 57, 53, ☐, ☐

24 ☐, 2, 0, –2, ☐

25 4, 5, 7, 10, ☐, ☐

26 Do you remember the triangular numbers below?

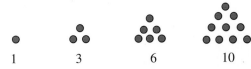

1   3   6   10

Write down the next 3 triangular numbers?

27 shape 1   shape 2   shape 3

How many lines are needed for

(a) shape 4,

(b) shape 5?

311

28 shape 1   shape 2   shape 3

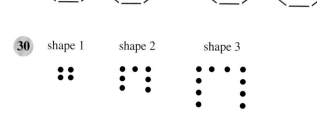

How many dots are needed for

(a) shape 4,

(b) shape 5?

29 shape 1   shape 2   shape 3

How many lines are needed for

(a) shape 4,

(b) shape 5?

30 shape 1   shape 2   shape 3

How many dots are needed for

(a) shape 4,

(b) shape 5?

🔑 # Key Facts

- If the sequence is not a clear adding or subtracting pattern, try multiplying or dividing.

  64, 16, 4, 1… the rule is ÷ 4 each time. The next number will be $1 \div 4$ which is $\frac{1}{4}$.

- If you study the gaps between numbers (we call these *differences*), the *differences* can make a sequence.

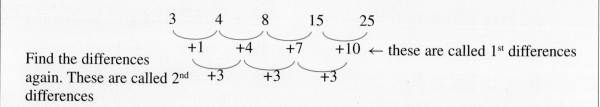

3   4   8   15   25

     +1   +4   +7   +10 ← these are called 1st differences

Find the differences again. These are called 2nd differences +3   +3   +3

So add 3 onto the 1st differences to give +13. Now +13 onto the term 25 to get 38 which is the next term in the sequence.

E12.1

In Questions **1** to **12** copy the sequences and write the next *2 numbers*. What is the rule for each sequence?

1 1, 2, 4, 8...

2 1, 3, 9, 27...

3 5, 10, 20, 40...

4 800, 400, 200, 100...

5 $\frac{1}{2}$, 1, $1\frac{1}{2}$, 2...

6 2, 6, 18, 54...

7 1, 5, 25, 125...

8 243, 81, 27, 9...

9 2, 20, 200, 2000...

10 150, 140, 120, 90...

11 1.3, 1.7, 2.1, 2.5...

12 300, 30, 3, 0.3...

13 shape 1   shape 2   shape 3   shape 4

How many small squares are needed for (a) shape 5?

(b) shape 6?

In Questions **14** to **23** find the next 2 numbers in each sequence (it may help you to work out the 2nd differences).

14 1, 4, 9, 16, 25...

15 6, 7, 10, 15, 22...

16 4, 5, 7, 10, 14...

17 3, 5, 12, 24, 41...

18 1, 4, 10, 19, 31...

19 5, 6, 11, 20, 33...

20 2, 3, 7, 14, 24...

21 1, 9, 25, 49, 81...

22 4, 9, 19, 34, 54...

23 7, 8, 11, 16, 23...

24 Find the next 2 numbers in the sequence below. Try to explain the pattern.

1, 1, 2, 3, 5, 8, 13...

25 Find the next 2 numbers in the sequence 0, 0, 1, 1, 2, 4, 7, 13...

26 This is Pascal's triangle.

```
            1
          1   1
        1   2   1
      1   3   3   1
    1   4   6   4   1
  1   5   10  10  5   1
1   6   15  20  15  6   1
```

(a) Look carefully at how the triangle is made. Write down the next row. It starts: 1 7...

(b) Work out the *sum* of the numbers in each row of Pascal's triangle. What do you notice?

Sequence rules

The *term-to-term* rule explains how one term in a sequence is connected to the next term.

28, 23, 18, 13... the term-to-term rule is 'subtract 5'.

3, 5, 9, 17... the term-to-term rule is 'double then subtract 1'.

The *position-to-term* rule explains how a term in a sequence is connected to its position in the sequence.

Find the position-to-term rule for the sequence below:

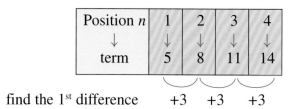

Position n	1	2	3	4
$\downarrow$	$\downarrow$	$\downarrow$	$\downarrow$	$\downarrow$
term	5	8	11	14

find the 1st difference   +3   +3   +3

If the 1st difference is the same, the rule will involve the '1st difference' *multiplied* by the 'position n'

i.e. $3 \times n$ (we write $3n$)

Work out the '$3n$' numbers and write them beneath the terms.

Position n	1	2	3	4
term	5	8	11	14
$3n$	3	6	9	12

We can see that we need to add 2 onto each '$3n$' value to get the term

so each term = $3n + 2$

we call this the formula for the 'n^{th} *term*'

$$n^{th} \text{ term} = 3n + 2$$

We can check this formula by choosing a value of n, for example $n = 2$.
n^{th} term = $3n + 2 = 3 \times 2 + 2 = 8$ so the 2nd term = 8 which we can see is correct.

Find the nth term for the sequence 2, 6, 10, 14.

Draw a table showing positions and terms.

Position n	1	2	3	4
term	2	6	10	14
$4n$	4	8	12	16

1st difference = 4
so work out '$4n$' values.

We need to subtract 2 from each '$4n$' value to get each term.

So the nth term = $4n - 2$ (check with n values of your choice)

M12.2

1. The first term of a sequence is 6 and the term-to-term rule is 'add 5'. Write down the first 5 terms of the sequence.

2 Write down the term-to-term rule for the sequence 28, 21, 14, 7…

3 You are given the first term and the rule of several sequences. Write down the first 5 terms of each sequence.

	First term	Rule
(a)	4	add 7
(b)	26	subtract 3
(c)	3	double
(d)	8000	divide by 10

4 Write down the term-to-term rule for each sequence below:

(a) 70, 64, 58, 52…

(b) 144, 72, 36, 18…

(c) 3.5, 5, 6.5, 8…

(d) 2, 6, 18, 54…

5 The rule for the number sequences below is 'multiply by 3 then add 1'

Find the missing numbers.

(a) 3 $\rightarrow$ 10 $\rightarrow$ 31 $\rightarrow$ 94 $\rightarrow$ ☐

(b) ☐ $\rightarrow$ 7 $\rightarrow$ 22 $\rightarrow$ 67 $\rightarrow$ 202

6 The rule for the number sequences below is 'multiply by 2 and take away 1'

Find the missing numbers.

(a) 2 $\rightarrow$ 3 $\rightarrow$ 5 $\rightarrow$ 9 $\rightarrow$ ☐

(b) ☐ $\rightarrow$ 7 $\rightarrow$ 13 $\rightarrow$ 25 $\rightarrow$ 49

7 Here is a sequence:

3, 8, 13, 18…

The 1st difference is +5.

Copy the table which has a row for '5n'.

Position n	1	2	3	4
term	3	8	13	18
$5n$	5	10	15	20

Copy and complete: 'The nth term of the sequence is $5n -$ ☐'

8 Use the tables below to help you find the nth term of each sequence.

(a) Sequence 8, 10, 12, 14…

(b) Sequence 3, 7, 11, 15…

Position n	1	2	3	4
term	8	10	12	14
$2n$	2	4	6	8

n^{th} term = ☐

Position n	1	2	3	4
term	3	7	11	15
$4n$	4	8	12	16

n^{th} term = ☐

315

(c) Sequence 5, 9, 13, 17

Position n	1	2	3	4
term	5	9	13	17
$4n$				

n^{th} term = [   ]

(d) Sequence 2, 5, 8, 11

Position n	1	2	3	4
term	2	5	8	11
$3n$				

n^{th} term = [   ]

9 For each sequence below find the first difference to help you to make a table like the one in question **7** and use it to find the nth term.

(a) 3, 9, 15, 21...   (b) 4, 11, 18, 25...   (c) 13, 23, 33, 43...

(d) 8, 13, 18, 23...   (e) 1, 9, 17, 25...   (f) 7, 16, 25, 34...

10 Make a table for each sequence below and write the nth term.

(a) 12, 10, 8, 6...   (b) 17, 13, 9, 5...

(c) 2.5, 3, 3.5, 4...   (d) 40, 31, 22, 13...

Here is a sequence of shapes made from sticks.

Let n = shape number and s = number of sticks

    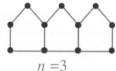

$n = 1$ $n = 2$ $n = 3$
$s = 5$ $s = 9$ $s = 13$

The next shape in the sequence is

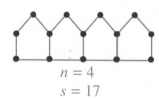

$n = 4$
$s = 17$

Make a table of values.

n	1	2	3	4
s	5	9	13	17
$4n$	4	8	12	16

The 1st difference is +4.

Write the '$4n$' values under the table.

So the nth term = $4n + 1 \Rightarrow$ this means $s = 4n + 1$

If we want to know how many sticks are needed for shape number 50 ($n = 50$), we can use the formula:

$s = 4n + 1 = 4 \times 50 + 1 = 201$ sticks   (much quicker than drawing pictures!)

1 Here is a sequence of shapes made from squares. Let n = shape number and w = number of white squares.

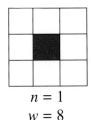

$n = 1$
$w = 8$

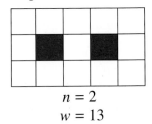

$n = 2$
$w = 13$

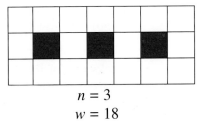

$n = 3$
$w = 18$

(a) Draw the next shape in the sequence.

(b) How many white squares are in shape number 4?

(c) Complete the table of values. The 1ˢᵗ difference is +5. Write out the '5n' values. Use these to find a formula for the number of white squares (w) for the shape number n. Use values of n to *check* if your formula is correct.

n	1	2	3	4
w	8	13	18	

(d) Use your formula to find out how many white squares are in shape number 20.

2 Here is a sequence of shapes made from hexagons.

$n = 1$

$n = 2$

$n = 3$

Let n = shape number and w = number of white hexagons.

(a) How many white hexagons are in each shape?

(b) How many white hexagons would be in the next shape in the sequence?

(c) Complete a table of values.

n	1	2	3	4
w	6			

Find the 1ˢᵗ difference.
Find a formula for the number of white hexagons (w) for the shape number n.
Use values of n to *check* if your formula is correct.

(d) Use your formula to find out how many white hexagons are in shape number 20.

For each of the sequences in Questions ③ and ⑦,

(a) Draw the next shape in the sequence.

(b) Let n = shape number and s = number of sticks.
Complete a table of values for n and s.

(c) Use the table and 1ˢᵗ difference to find a formula for the number of sticks (s) for the shape number n.
Use values of n to *check* if each formula is correct.

(d) Use the formula to find out how many sticks are in shape number 50.

③

$n = 1$ $s = 4$ $n = 2$ $s = 10$ $n = 3$ $s =$

④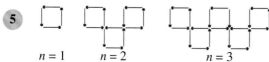

$n = 1$ $n = 2$ $n = 3$

⑤

$n = 1$ $n = 2$ $n = 3$

⑥

$n = 1$ $n = 2$ $n = 3$

⑦

$n = 1$ $n = 2$ $n = 3$

⑧ This table can seat 5 people

The diagrams below show how many people can be seated when tables are joined together.

$n = 1$ $n = 2$ $n = 3$

(a) Draw the diagram for 4 tables.

(b) Let p = number of people and n = number of tables. Make a table of values and use it to find a formula for the number of people according to how many tables.

(c) How many people could be seated with 20 tables?

9 Ponds are surrounded by paving slabs as shown below:

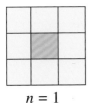 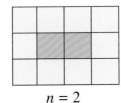 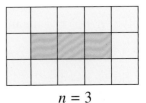

$n = 1$ $n = 2$ $n = 3$

(a) Draw the next shape in the sequence.

(b) How many yellow paving slabs surround each pond?

(c) Find a formula for the number of yellow slabs (y) surrounding each pond n (use a table of values to help you).

(d) How many yellow slabs surround pond number 50?

12A   **Collect like terms (see Unit 4)**

Simplify

1. $6a + 3a$
2. $8a - 2a$
3. $3a + a$
4. $7x + 2y + 2x$
5. $2a + 5b - 3b$
6. $4x + 9y - 2y + 2x$
7. $3p + 5q + 2p - q$
8. $7x + 2 - 3x$
9. $4a + 3b + 2b + 5$

10. Eddie has £ $(5a + 2)$. He spends £ $(3a)$. How much money does he have left?

11. Linda is $(2m + 5n)$ cm tall. During the next year she grows $(3m + 2)$ cm. How tall is she now?

12. Milly is building a table. She will cut one piece of wood into 4 pieces each $(2x + 1)$ cm long. How long is the piece of wood she starts with?

Solving equations

Key Facts

An '*equation*' contains an ' = ' sign.

$n + 3 = 7$ is an equation.

'Solve' $n + 3 = 7$ means 'Find the value of n which fits the *equation*'.

$n = 4$ because $\boxed{4} + 3 = 7$

(a) Solve $n - 4 = 2$
$n = 6$ because $\boxed{6} - 4 = 2$

(b) Solve $3n = 18$
$3n$ means '$3 \times n$'
$n = 6$ because $3 \times \boxed{6} = 18$

(c) Solve $\dfrac{n}{3} = 2$

$\dfrac{n}{3}$ means '$n \div 3$'

$n = 6$ because $\dfrac{\boxed{6}}{3} = 2$

M12.3

1 Work out the missing numbers:

(a) $n + 6 = 10$ (b) $n + 2 = 5$ (c) $n + 6 = 9$ (d) $n - 4 = 1$ (e) $n - 8 = 3$
(f) $n - 20 = 7$ (g) $n - 5 = 12$ (h) $n + 10 = 32$ (i) $n - 1 = 9$ (j) $n + 7 = 14$
(k) $n + 9 = 12$ (l) $n - 7 = 9$

2 Solve these equations:

(a) $x - 15 = 8$ (b) $x - 17 = 12$ (c) $x + 28 = 40$ (d) $x + 16 = 30$
(e) $x + 31 = 52$ (f) $x + 43 = 75$ (g) $x - 24 = 20$ (h) $x - 30 = 27$

3 Solve these equations:

(a) $3 \times n = 21$ (b) $5 \times n = 30$ (c) $3 \times n = 12$ (d) $2 \times n = 32$ (e) $4n = 24$
(f) $10n = 70$ (g) $8n = 48$ (h) $3n = 27$ (i) $6n = 42$ (j) $7n = 56$
(k) $6n = 24$ (l) $8n = 40$

4 Solve:

(a) $n \div 2 = 3$ (b) $n \div 4 = 3$ (c) $n \div 5 = 4$ (d) $n \div 2 = 5$

(e) $\dfrac{n}{5} = 6$ (f) $\dfrac{n}{4} = 8$ (g) $\dfrac{n}{10} = 7$ (h) $\dfrac{n}{6} = 6$

5 Jim thinks of a number and then adds 7. If the answer is 15, what number did Jim think of?

6 Teresa thinks of a number and then subtracts 8. If the answer is 9, what number did Teresa think of?

7 Ed thinks of a number and then subtracts 14. If the answer is 13, what number did Ed think of?

8 Candice thinks of a number and then multiplies it by 6. If the answer is 54, what number did Candice think of?

9 Gemma thinks of a number and then multiplies it by 8. If the answer is 32, what number did Gemma think of?

10 Solve:

(a) $x + 8 = 20$ (b) $x + 17 = 31$ (c) $3x = 15$ (d) $9x = 63$

(e) $x + 43 = 61$ (f) $x - 16 = 23$ (g) $\dfrac{x}{4} = 7$ (h) $x - 32 = 21$

(i) $\dfrac{x}{7} = 5$ (j) $6x = 30$ (k) $x + 88 = 110$ (l) $\dfrac{x}{3} = 12$

Sometimes the missing number may be a *negative number.*

(a) Solve $n + 6 = 2$

$n = -4$ because $\boxed{-4} + 6 = 2$

(b) Solve $n - 3 = -8$

$n = -5$ because

$\boxed{-5} - 3 = -8$

(c) $3n = -12$

$n = -4$ because

$3 \times \boxed{-4} = -12$

E12.3

1 Solve these equations:

(a) $n + 4 = 3$ (b) $n + 6 = 1$ (c) $n + 9 = 4$ (d) $n + 7 = 2$

(e) $n - 2 = -1$ (f) $n - 8 = -13$ (g) $n - 4 = -8$ (h) $n - 4 = -9$

(i) $n - 6 = -3$ (j) $n + 7 = 0$ (k) $n + 12 = 4$ (l) $n - 12 = -20$

2 Solve:

(a) $4n = -20$ (b) $7n = -21$ (c) $5n = -35$ (d) $9n = -18$

(e) $6n = -36$ (f) $-5n = 30$ (g) $-9n = 27$ (h) $-3n = 24$

(i) $-7n = -28$ (j) $-6n = -42$ (k) $-3n = 18$ (l) $-10n = -60$

321

3 Solve:

(a) $n \div 3 = -6$ (b) $n \div 2 = -8$ (c) $n \div 3 = -2$ (d) $\dfrac{n}{5} = -3$

(e) $\dfrac{n}{2} = -4$ (f) $\dfrac{n}{-3} = 7$ (g) $\dfrac{n}{-2} = 3$ (h) $\dfrac{n}{-1} = -6$

(i) $\dfrac{n}{-5} = 4$ (j) $\dfrac{n}{2} = -9$ (k) $\dfrac{n}{-2} = -2$ (l) $\dfrac{n}{7} = -2$

4 If $2n = 1$ then $n = \frac{1}{2}$ because $2 \times \boxed{\tfrac{1}{2}} = 1$

This answer could also be written as $n = 0.5$
Solve these equations:

(a) $2n = 3$ (b) $2n = 7$ (c) $2n = -1$ (d) $2n = -5$

(e) $3n = 1$ (f) $4n = 6$ (g) $10n = -3$ (h) $2n = -9$

(i) $8n = 2$ (j) $5n = -4$ (k) $7n = -1$ (l) $9n = -2$

Solving longer equations

(a) Solve $5n+2 = 17$ OR   Solve $5n+2=17$

$\boxed{5n} + 2 = 17$
↑
This box $=15$ because $\boxed{15} + 2 = 17$

So $\boxed{5n} = 15$
↓
$5n$ means $5 \times n$

So $5 \times n = 15$

So $n = 3$ because $5 \times \boxed{3} = 15$

Take off 2 from each pan

Each $\boxed{n}$ must equal 3 because 5 $\boxed{n}$ boxes are equal to 15
So $n = 3$

M12.4

In Questions **1** to **6**, copy and fill the empty boxes.

1 $\boxed{2n} + 1 = 17$
     $\boxed{2n} = 16$
       $n = \boxed{}$

2 $\boxed{4n} + 3 = 23$
     $\boxed{4n} = 20$
       $n = \boxed{}$

3 $\boxed{5n} + 7 = 17$
     $\boxed{5n} = \boxed{}$
       $n = \boxed{}$

4 $\boxed{2n} - 4 = 20$

$\boxed{2n} = 24$

$n = \boxed{}$

5 $\boxed{3n} - 7 = 14$

$\boxed{3n} = 21$

$n = \boxed{}$

6 $\boxed{5n} - 4 = 26$

$\boxed{5n} = \boxed{}$

$n = \boxed{}$

Find the value of n in Questions **7** to **10** :

7

8 $\boxed{n}\boxed{n}\quad\boxed{7}\qquad\qquad\boxed{19}$

9

10 $\boxed{n}\boxed{n}\boxed{n}\quad\boxed{6}\qquad\qquad\boxed{30}$

Solve these equations:

11 $5n + 6 = 21$

12 $5n + 7 = 17$

13 $4n + 3 = 23$

14 $4n + 7 = 19$

15 $5n + 4 = 34$

16 $3n - 6 = 9$

17 $3n - 2 = 10$

18 $6n - 1 = 29$

19 $8n - 3 = 21$

20 $7n + 6 = 34$

21 $4n + 10 = 26$

; **22** $5n - 5 = 45$

23 $10n - 2 = 38$

24 $4n - 9 = 23$

25 $7n - 12 = 9$

26 $9n - 5 = 22$

27 $3n - 8 = 22$

28 $6n + 8 = 26$

29 $5n + 12 = 32$

30 $10n + 13 = 73$

31 $8n - 4 = 84$

Equations with 'trickier' numbers

(a) Solve $3n + 1 = 2$
Subtract 1 from each
side of equation $3n = 1$

divide each side of
equation by 3 $\dfrac{3n}{3} = \dfrac{1}{3}$

$n = \dfrac{1}{3}$

(b) Solve $5n + 13 = 3$
Subtract 13 from
each side of equation $5n = -10$

divide each side of
equation by 5 $n = -2$

(d) Solve $18 = 20 + 3n$
Subtract 20 from each
side of equation $-2 = 3n$

divide each side of
equation by 2 $\dfrac{-2}{3} = \dfrac{3n}{3}$

$\dfrac{-2}{3} = n$

so $n = \dfrac{-2}{3}$

(c) Solve $2 - 3n = 14$
Subtract 2 from each
side of equation $-3n = 12$

divide each side of $n = -4$
equation by -3

In Questions **1** to **6** , copy and fill the empty boxes.

1 $\boxed{2n} + 1 = 4$

$\boxed{2n} = 3$

$n = \boxed{}$

2 $\boxed{10n} + 7 = 14$

$\boxed{10n} = \boxed{}$

$n = \boxed{}$

3 $\boxed{4n} + 11 = 8$

$\boxed{4n} = -3$

$n = \boxed{}$

4 $5\ \boxed{-2n} = 11$

$\boxed{-2n} = 6$

$n = \boxed{}$

5 $-4\ \boxed{-3n} = -10$

$\boxed{-3n} = -6$

$n = \boxed{}$

6 $30 = 40\ \boxed{+2n}$

$\boxed{} = 2n$

$\boxed{} = n$

Solve these equations:

7 $3x + 4 = 6$

8 $5x + 8 = 12$

9 $2x + 9 = 8$

10 $4x + 9 = 5$

11 $3x + 8 = 7$

12 $8x + 5 = 2$

13 $6x + 10 = 5$

14 $6x + 19 = 16$

15 $4x + 3 = 17$

In questions **16** to **21** below, I am thinking of a number. Write down an equation then solve it to find the number.

If we multiply the number by 3 and then add 1, the answer is 3.

Let the number be n.   Equation is $3n + 1 = 3$

Solve: $3n = 2$ so $n = \dfrac{2}{3}$

16 If we multiply the number by 4 and then add 2, the answer is 3.

17 If we multiply the number by 7 and then add 5, the answer is 8.

18 If we multiply the number by 5 and then add 11, the answer is 6.

19 If we double the number and add 7, the answer is 1.

20 If we multiply the number by 8 and subtract 4, the answer is –20.

21 If we treble the number and add 8, the answer is –7.

Solve these equations:

22 $7x + 8 = -6$

23 $4x - 6 = -22$

24 $6x - 2 = -20$

25 $9x + 4 = -32$

26 $14 = 20 + 2x$

27 $31 = 39 + 4x$

28 $8 = 33 + 5x$

29 $9 - 2x = 17$

30 $16 - 5x = 31$

31 $13 - 7x = -22$

32 $-6 = 9 + 3x$

33 $20 = 48 - 7x$

(**12B**) **Multiply out brackets (see Unit 4)**

1. Jane says '$3(2a + 1) = 6a + 1$'.

   Meg says '$3(2a + 1) = 6a + 3$'.

   Who is correct?

Expand (multiply out)

2. $5(a + 2)$ 3. $2(3a + 2)$ 4. $6(2x - 1)$ 5. $4(5n + 3)$

6. $3(b + 2c)$ 7. $5(3a - 2b)$ 8. $9(2x - y)$ 9. $b(c - e)$

10. $x(x + 3)$ 11. $-4(x + 2)$ 12. $-6(y - 3)$ 13. $-3(3x - 2)$

Equations with brackets

(a) Solve $3(n+2) = 12$

multiply out
brackets first $3n + 6 = 12$

subtract 6 from each
side of equation $3n = 6$

                 $n = 2$

(b) Solve $5(2n-1) = 45$

multiply out.
brackets first $10n - 5 = 45$

add 5 onto each
side of equation $10n = 50$

                 $n = 5$

M12.5

In Questions **1** to **3**, copy and fill the empty boxes.

1 $3(n + 1) = 12$

     $3n + \boxed{} = 12$

        $3n = \boxed{}$

          $n = \boxed{}$

2 $5(n - 2) = 30$

     $\boxed{} - 10 = 30$

        $\boxed{} = 40$

          $n = \boxed{}$

3 $4(2n + 3) = 28$

     $8n + \boxed{} = 28$

        $8n = \boxed{}$

          $n = \boxed{}$

Solve these equations:

4 $4(n+2) = 20$ **5** $5(n+1) = 50$ **6** $8(n+3) = 40$

7 $3(n-4) = 6$ **8** $3(2n+1) = 27$ **9** $2(4n-4) = 12$

10 $5(2n+3) = 75$ **11** $9(2n+1) = 27$ **12** $3(5n-6) = 42$

13 $2(2n-4) = 20$ **14** $5(4n+5) = 105$ **15** $3(3n-4) = 33$

16 $4(2n+5) = 52$ **17** $2(5n-7) = 76$ **18** $6(n-9) = 12$

19 $3(3n-7) = 24$ **20** $10(2n-6) = 40$ **21** $8(2n-3) = 8$

In Questions **22** to **25**, I am thinking of a number. Write down an equation then solve it to find the number.

Add double the number onto 4 then multiply the answer by 3. This gives 24.

Let the number be n.

Equation is $\qquad (2n + 4) \times 3 = 24$

We write this as $\qquad 3(2n + 4) = 24$

Solve: $\qquad 6n + 12 = 24$

$\qquad\qquad 6n = 12$

$\qquad\qquad n = 2$

---

22 Add the number onto 5 then multiply the answer by 6. This gives 48.

23 Add treble the number onto 2 then multiply the answer by 2. This gives 46.

24 Take away 4 from double the number then multiply the answer by 5. This gives 30.

25 Subtract 7 from treble the number then multiply the answer by 4. This gives 8.

Equations with brackets and 'trickier' numbers

(a) Solve $2(n+3) = 5$

Multiply out brackets first $\qquad 2n + 6 = 5$

Subtract 6 from each side of equation $\qquad 2n = -1$

divide each side of equation by 2 $\qquad \dfrac{2n}{2} = \dfrac{-1}{2}$

$\qquad\qquad n = \dfrac{-1}{2}$

(b) Solve $36 = 4(1-2n)$

Multiply out brackets first $\qquad 36 = 4 - 8n$

Subtract 4 from each side of equation $\qquad 32 = -8n$

divide each side of equation by -8 $\qquad \dfrac{32}{-8} = \dfrac{-8n}{-8}$

$\qquad\qquad -4 = n$

so $n = -4$

In Questions ① to ⑥ , copy and fill the empty boxes.

① $5(x + 3) = 10$

$\boxed{} + 15 = 10$

$\boxed{} = -5$

$x = \boxed{}$

② $2(x + 9) = 14$

$2x + \boxed{} = 14$

$2x = \boxed{}$

$x = \boxed{}$

③ $3(2x + 5) = -3$

$6x + \boxed{} = -3$

$6x = \boxed{}$

$x = \boxed{}$

④ $3(x + 2) = 4$

$3x + \boxed{} = 4$

$3x = \boxed{}$

$x = \boxed{}$

⑤ $2(2x + 3) = 5$

$4x + \boxed{} = 5$

$4x = \boxed{}$

$x = \boxed{}$

⑥ $33 = 3(2 - 3x)$

$33 = 6 - \boxed{}$

$27 = -\boxed{}$

$\boxed{} = x$

Solve these equations:

⑦ $3(x + 2) = 6$

⑧ $5(2x + 4) = 0$

⑨ $4(x + 5) = 17$

⑩ $5(x + 9) = 15$

⑪ $2(4x + 10) = 4$

⑫ $3(2x - 3) = -15$

⑬ $4(2x - 3) = -20$

⑭ $5(2x + 1) = 2$

⑮ $5(4x + 3) = 8$

⑯ $2(1 - 2x) = 14$

⑰ $2(3 - 4x) = 30$

⑱ $20 = 10(5 + x)$

⑲ $85 = 5(5 - 2x)$

⑳ $7 = 2(6 - 3x)$

㉑ $25 = 8(4 + 5x)$

Can you still?

Can you still?

12C **Add, subtract and multiply decimals (see Unit 9)**

Work out

1. $\begin{array}{r} 16.2 \\ + \ 0.31 \\ \hline \end{array}$

2. $\begin{array}{r} 21.6 \\ - \ 3.17 \\ \hline \end{array}$

3. $15.6 + 8 + 0.12$

4. $13.2 - 6$

5. $2.13 - 0.37$

6. 0.9×0.02

7. 0.7×0.4

8. 0.12×7

9. 0.5^2

10. Copy and fill in the empty boxes

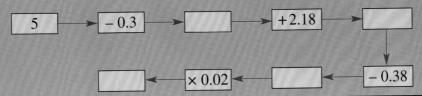

Equations with the unknown on both sides

(a) Solve

$6n - 2 = 2n + 18$

Subtract $2n$ from each
side of equation $\qquad 4n - 2 = 18$

Add 2 onto each
side of equation $\qquad 4n = 20$

$\qquad n = 5$

(b) Solve

$8n + 6 = 3n + 41$

Subtract $3n$ from each
side of equation $\qquad 5n + 6 = 41$

Subtract 6 from each
side of equation $\qquad 5n = 35$

$\qquad n = 7$

M12.6

Find the value of n in Questions **1** to **6** :

1

2

3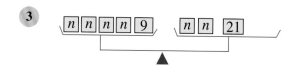

4

5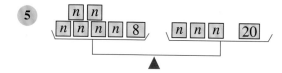

6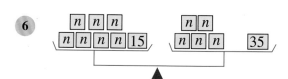

In Questions **7** to **9** , copy and fill the empty boxes.

7 $\quad 8n + 6 = 3n + 26$

$\boxed{5n} + 6 = 26$

$5n = \boxed{}$

$n = \boxed{}$

8 $\quad 9n - 4 = 5n + 20$

$\boxed{} - 4 = 20$

$\boxed{} = 24$

$n = \boxed{}$

9 $\quad 6n - 1 = 4n + 11$

$2n - 1 = 11$

$2n = \boxed{}$

$n = \boxed{}$

328

Solve these equations:

10 $7n + 3 = 3n + 27$

11 $7n + 5 = 5n + 25$

12 $10n + 2 = 7n + 14$

13 $5n + 4 = 2n + 22$

14 $6n + 8 = 2n + 36$

15 $7n - 3 = 4n + 12$

Be careful!

16 $5n - 2 = n + 10$

17 $9n - 7 = 5n + 13$

18 $11n - 9 = 5n + 27$

19 $5n - 10 = 3n + 50$

20 $8n - 3 = 2n + 39$

21 $9n + 14 = 6n + 29$

22 $10n + 17 = 3n + 52$

23 $5n - 16 = n + 20$

24 $8n - 22 = 2n + 8$

25 $9n + 15 = 5n + 47$

'Trickier' equations with the unknown on both sides

(a) Solve $7x - 2 = 3x - 10$
Subtract $3x$ from each
side of equation, $\quad 4x - 2 = -10$
add 2 onto each side
of equation, $\qquad\qquad 4x = -8$
$\qquad\qquad\qquad\qquad x = -2$

(b) Solve $8x + 4 = 34 - 2x$
Add $2x$ onto each
side of equation, $\qquad 10x + 4 = 34$
subtract 4 from each
side of equation, $\qquad\qquad 10x = 30$
$\qquad\qquad\qquad\qquad x = 3$

(c) Solve $5(2x + 3) = 2(3x + 8)$

multiply out brackets first, $\qquad 10x + 15 = 6x + 16$

subtract $6x$ from each side of equation, $\qquad 4x + 15 = 16$

subtract 15 from each side of equation, $\qquad\qquad 4x = 1$

divide each side of equation by 4, $\qquad\qquad \dfrac{4x}{4} = \dfrac{1}{4}$

$\qquad\qquad\qquad\qquad\qquad x = \dfrac{1}{4}$

(d) Solve $3(2x - 1) = 2(5 - x)$
multiply out brackets first, $\qquad 6x - 3 = 10 - 2x$
add $2x$ onto each side of equation, $\qquad 8x - 3 = 10$
add 3 onto each side of equation, $\qquad\qquad 8x = 13$

divide each side of equation by 8, $\qquad\qquad \dfrac{8x}{8} = \dfrac{13}{8}$

$\qquad\qquad\qquad\qquad\qquad x = \dfrac{13}{8}$

we can write $\qquad\qquad\qquad\qquad x = 1\dfrac{5}{8}$

In Questions ① to ③ , copy and fill the empty boxes.

1 $6x - 4 = 3x - 16$

$3x - 4 = -16$

$3x = \boxed{}$

$x = \boxed{}$

2 $7x + 3 = 43 - x$

$\boxed{} + 3 = 43$

$\boxed{} = 40$

$x = \boxed{}$

3 $2(3x + 2) = 4(x + 3)$

$\boxed{} + 4 = \boxed{} + 12$

$\boxed{} + 4 = 12$

$\boxed{} = 8$

$x = \boxed{}$

Solve these equations:

4 $5x + 2 = 3 - 2x$

5 $6x + 4 = 3 - 3x$

6 $5x - 2 = x - 10$

7 $9x + 4 = 3x - 1$

8 $2x - 8 = 12 - 3x$

9 $2 + 9x = 3 - x$

10 $7x - 2 = 1 - 3x$

11 $6x + 5 = 41 - 3x$

12 $5x + 8 = 1 - 4x$

In Questions ⑬ to ⑯ below, I am thinking of a number. Write down an equation then solve it to find the number.

13 If we multiply the number by 7 and add 4, the answer we get is the same as when we multiply the number by 3 and add 12.

14 If we multiply the number by 8 and subtract 5, the answer we get is the same as when we multiply the number by 2 and add 19.

15 If we treble the number and subtract from 9 we get the same answer as when we double the number and add 4.

16 If we double the number, add 5 and then multiply the result by 3, the answer is 27.

Solve these equations:

17 $3(2x + 3) = 2(x + 4)$

18 $2(x + 2) = 5(x - 4)$

19 $4(2x - 2) = 3(3x + 4)$

20 $7(x - 1) = 2(2x + 4)$

21 $8(x - 3) = 4(3 - x)$

22 $6(x - 4) = 2(x - 1)$

23 $3(x + 2) = 4(1 - x)$

24 $3(2x + 1) = 4(7 - x)$

25 $2(3x - 1) = 3(1 - 2x)$

26 $5(2 - x) = 2(4 + 2x)$

27 $2(3 - 2x) = 5(2 - x)$

28 $4(x - 2) = 3(x + 3) - 4$

29 $3(2x + 3) + 4(x - 2) = 8$

30 $6(2x + 5) + 3(2 - 3x) = x$

12D **Dividing decimals** (see Unit 9)

Work out

1. $7\overline{)16.8}$

2. $9\overline{)41.4}$

3. $43.2 \div 6$

4. $3.44 \div 4$

5. $18 \div 0.5$

6. $4 \div 0.1$

7. 3 friends win £ 373.50 in a game. They share the money equally. How much does each friend get?

8. 4 people split a restaurant bill equally. If the bill is £ 78.40, how much does each person have to pay?

9. $3.8 \div 0.2$

10. $0.24 \div 0.3$

11. $17.2 \div 0.04$

12. A bottle of ginger beer holds 2 litres. How many glasses can be filled from this bottle if each glass holds 0.25 litres?

Mixed equations

(a) The perimeter of this rectangle is 44 cm.

Find x then write down the actual length and width of the rectangle.

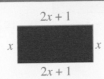

Perimeter $= x + 2x + 1 + x + 2x + 1 = 6x + 2$ (this is equal to 44 cm)

So $6x + 2 = 44$

$\qquad 6x = 42$

$\qquad x = 7$

length $= 2x + 1 = 2 \times 7 + 1 = 15$ cm

width $= x = 7$ cm

(b) Solve $\dfrac{x}{3} + 4 = 6$

subtract 4 from each side of equation $\qquad \dfrac{x}{3} = 2$

$\qquad x = 6$

because $\dfrac{6}{3} = 2$

(c) Solve $\dfrac{x + 4}{3} = 6$

$x + 4 = 18$

because $\dfrac{18}{3} = 6$

so $x = 14$

331

Solve these equations:

1 $2x + 3 = 9$

2 $4x + 2 = 18$

3 $\dfrac{x}{2} + 5 = 10$

4 $\dfrac{x}{2} + 9 = 19$

5 $\dfrac{x}{3} + 4 = 9$

6 $\dfrac{x}{5} + 6 = 8$

7 $\dfrac{x}{3} + 12 = 19$

8 $3x - 2 = 16$

9 $6x - 1 = 23$

10 $5x - 3 = 32$

11 $\dfrac{x}{3} - 2 = 2$

12 $\dfrac{x}{4} - 3 = 2$

13 $\dfrac{x}{5} - 2 = 3$

14 $\dfrac{x}{6} - 3 = 2$

15 $\dfrac{x}{7} - 1 = 3$

16

$x + 3$

$x + 1$ ▮ $x + 1$

$x + 3$

The perimeter of this rectangle is 28 cm.

(a) Write down an equation using the perimeter.

(b) Find x.

(c) Write down the actual length and width of the rectangle.

17

$3x + 2$

$x + 3$ ▨ $x + 3$

$3x + 2$

The perimeter of this rectangle is 58 cm.

(a) Write down an equation using the perimeter.

(b) Find x.

(c) Write down the actual length and width of the rectangle.

18 The perimeter of this rectangle is 34 cm,

(a) Write down an equation using the perimeter.

(b) Find x.

(c) Write down the actual length and width of the rectangle.

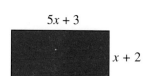

$5x + 3$

$x + 2$

19 The perimeter of this rectangle is 74 cm.

(a) Write down an equation using the perimeter.

(b) Find x.

(c) Write down the actual length and width of the rectangle.

$3x + 1$

$2x + 6$

20

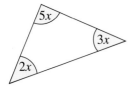

(a) Write down an equation using the angles.

(b) Find x.

(c) Write down the actual value of each angle in this triangle.

21

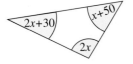

(a) Write down an equation using the angles.

(b) Find x.

(c) Write down the actual value of each angle in this triangle.

Solve these equations:

22 $3x + 5 = 29$

23 $\dfrac{x + 3}{2} = 4$

24 $\dfrac{x + 5}{4} = 5$

25 $\dfrac{x + 9}{3} = 7$

26 $\dfrac{x}{3} + 2 = 7$

27 $6x - 7 = 23$

28 $\dfrac{x - 8}{2} = 5$

29 $\dfrac{x - 3}{4} = 1$

30 $\dfrac{x - 10}{3} = 2$

A rectangle has its length twice its width. If its perimeter is 42 cm, find the width of the rectangle.

Let x = width   so length = $2x$

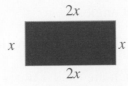

$2x$

x x

$2x$

perimeter $= 2x + x + 2x + x = 6x$

so $6x = 42$ (perimeter $= 42$)

$x = 7$

so width of rectangle = 7 cm.

333

Solve these equations:

1 $7x + 2 = 3x + 5$

2 $9x - 7 = 7x + 6$

3 $6x + 5 = 3x + 24$

4 $5x - 4 = x + 7$

5 $2(x + 9) = 5(x + 1)$

6 $6(x - 1) = 9(x - 3)$

7 $3(x - 1) = 2(x + 8)$

8 $5(2x - 3) = 2(3x + 3)$

9 $4(3x - 2) = 2(5x + 6)$

10 $3(2x - 1) = 4(x - 2)$

11 The area of this rectangle 20 cm².

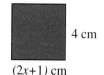

4 cm

$(2x+1)$ cm

Find x then write down the actual width of the rectangle.

12 The area of this rectangle is 46 cm².

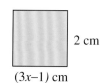

2 cm

$(3x-1)$ cm

Find x then write down the actual width of the rectangle.

13 A rectangle has its length 5 times its width. If the perimeter of the rectangle is 48 cm, find its length and width (remember: let width = x).

14 The length of a rectangle is 3 times its width. If the perimeter of the rectangle is 32 cm, find its length and width.

15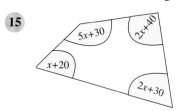

(a) Write down an equation using the angles.

(b) Find x.

(c) Write down the actual value of each angle in this quadrilateral.

16 A triangle has no angle 40° bigger than the smallest angle and the other angle 50° bigger than the smallest angle.

Find the size of each angle (hint : let x = smallest angle).

17 A triangle has 2 angles which are each 4 times the size of the third angle. Find the size of each angle (hint : let x = the third angle).

18 There are 3 children in a family. Each is 3 years older than the next and the sum of the ages is 21. How old is each child? (hint : let x = age of the youngest child)

19 £190 is divided between Jack and Halle so that Jack receives £72 more than Halle. How much does each person get? (hint : let x = Halle's money)

20 A rectangular room is 2 m longer than it is wide. If its perimeter is 32 m, what is its area? (hint : let x = width)

Solve these equations:

21 $\dfrac{x-5}{3} = 4$

22 $\dfrac{x+3}{2} = 7$

23 $\dfrac{2x+1}{4} = 5$

24 $\dfrac{x+6}{8} = -3$

25 $\dfrac{3x-2}{5} = 8$

26 $\dfrac{7x-3}{2} = 9$

27 $\dfrac{9x-5}{7} = 7$

28 $\dfrac{5x+29}{3} = 8$

29 $\dfrac{20}{x} = 5$

30 $8 = \dfrac{56}{x}$

31 $\dfrac{36}{x} = 9$

32 $7 = \dfrac{42}{x}$

Can you still?

Can you still?

12E **Rounding off to decimal places/significant figures**

Round the numbers below to the accuracy shown in brackets:

1. 8.27 (1 decimal place)

2. 0.15 (1 decimal place)

3. 4.894 (2 decimal places)

4. 7.618 (3 significant figures)

5. 21.63 (2 significant figures)

6. 0.08236 (2 significant figures)

7. 8659 (3 significant figures)

8. 24.69 (1 decimal place)

9. 8.61847 (4 significant figures)

10. 481.93 (2 significant figures)

Use a calculator to work out the Questions below. Round each answer to 3 *significant figures.*

11. 6.2×28.3

12. $\sqrt{32}$

13. $418.6 \div 3.71$

14. $\dfrac{4.17 + 3.9}{8.67}$

Trial and improvement

Sometimes it is not easy (or possible) to find the answer to a problem.

We can try out different numbers with a calculator until we get closer and closer to the answer.

The area of the rectangle is 65 cm².

Find x to 1 decimal place.

x cm

9 cm

Area = $9 \times x$

so $9x = 65$

We will use trial and improvement to find x.

| try $x = 8$ | gives $9 \times 8 = 72$ | too large |
| try $x = 7$ | gives $9 \times 7 = 63$ | too small |

We want an answer of 65 so x must be between 7 and 8.

try $x = 7.5$	gives $9 \times 7.5 = 67.5$	too large
try $x = 7.2$	gives $9 \times 7.2 = 64.8$	too small (by 0.2)
try $x = 7.3$	gives $9 \times 7.3 = 65.7$	too large (by 0.7)

We want an answer of 65 so x must be between 7.2 and 7.3. $x = 7.2$ gives an answer which is nearer than the answer given by $x = 7.3$.

$x = 7.2$ to 1 decimal place.

M12.8

The area of this rectangle is 80 cm².

x cm

6 cm

Copy and complete this table to find x to one decimal place.

trial	calculation	too large or too small?
$x = 13$	$6 \times 13 = \ldots$	too small
$x = 14$	$6 \times 14 = \ldots$	too large
$x = 13.5$	$6 \times 13.5 = \ldots$	too ...
$x = 13.4$	$6 \times 13.4 = \ldots$	too ...
$x = 13.3$	$6 \times 13.3 = \ldots$	too ...

so $x = \ldots$ to 1 decimal place.

2

x cm

12 cm

The area of this rectangle is 200 cm².

Copy and complete this table to find x to one decimal place.

trial	calculation	too large or too small?
$x = 17$	$12 \times 17 = $	too ......
$x = 16.8$	$12 \times 16.8 = $	too ......
$x = 16.6$	$12 \times 16.6 = $	too ......
$x = 16.7$	$12 \times 16.7 = $	too ......

so $x = $ ... to 1 decimal place.

3

x cm

x cm

The area of this square is 130 cm².

Use trial and improvement to find x to 1 decimal place.

4 The volume of this cube is 100 cm³.

Volume $= x \times x \times x = x^3$

We want $x^3 = 100$

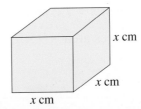

x cm

x cm

x cm

Copy and complete this table to find x to 1 decimal place.

trial	calculation	too large or too small?
$x = 4$	$4 \times 4 \times 4 = 64$	too small
$x = 5$	$5 \times 5 \times 5 = $	too ...
$x = 4.5$	$4.5 \times 4.5 \times 4.5 = $	too ...
$x = 4.7$	$4.7 \times 4.7 \times 4.7 = $	too ...
$x = 4.6$	$4.6 \times 4.6 \times 4.6 = $	too ...

so $x = $ ... to 1 decimal place.

5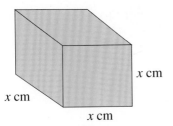

x cm

x cm

x cm

The volume of this cube is 226 cm³.

Use trial and improvement to find x to 1 decimal place.

337

6 Solve these equations by trial and improvement. Give each answer to 1 decimal place.

(a) $x^2 = 60$ (b) $x^2 = 114$ (c) $x^3 = 71$ (d) $x^3 = 460$

7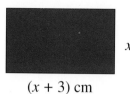

The area of this rectangle is 250 cm².

x cm   area $= x \times (x + 3) = x(x + 3)$

we want $x(x + 3) = 250$

$(x + 3)$ cm

If we try $x = 15$, we get $15 \times 18 = 270$ which is too large.

Use trial and improvement to find x to 1 decimal place.

Greater accuracy

Choosing the correct answer:

Look at the earlier example.

We found $x = 7.2$ gave an area of 64.8 cm²
and $x = 7.3$ gave an area of 65.7 cm²

Area = 65 cm² x cm

9 cm

To choose the correct value of x to 1 decimal place, we should test the value *half way* between $x = 7.2$ and $x = 7.3$, ie. $x = 7.25$.

$x = 7.25$ gives area $= 9 \times 7.25 = 65.25$ cm².

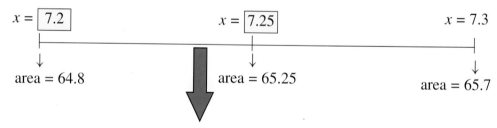

$x = \boxed{7.2}$ $x = \boxed{7.25}$ $x = 7.3$

area = 64.8   area = 65.25   area = 65.7

real area of 65 must be between these
2 values so is nearer to 7.2 than 7.3

so answer = 7.2 to 1 decimal place.

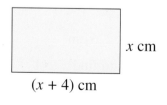

The area of this rectangle is 325 cm².

x cm   Use trial and improvement to find x to *2 decimal places.*

$(x + 4)$ cm   area $= x(x + 4) = 325$

trial	calculation	too large or too small?
$x = 10$	$10 \times 14 = 140$	too small
$x = 20$	$20 \times 24 = 480$	too large
$x = 15$	$15 \times 19 = 285$	too small
$x = 17$	$17 \times 21 = 357$	too large
$x = 16$	$16 \times 20 = 320$	too small
so x is between 16 and 17		
$x = 16.2$	$16.2 \times 20.2 = 327.24$	too large
$x = 16.1$	$16.1 \times 20.1 = 323.61$	too small
so x is between 16.1 and 16.2		
$x = 16.15$	$16.15 \times 20.15 = 325.4225$	too large
$x = 16.14$	$16.14 \times 20.14 = 325.0596$	too large
$x = 16.13$	$16.13 \times 20.13 = 324.4969$	too small
so x is between 16.13 and 16.14		
Test the half way value to choose the correct answer.		
$x = 16.135$	$16.135 \times 20.135 = 324.878225$	too small

So x is between 16.135 and 16.14

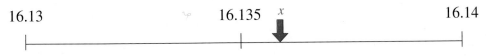

16.13   16.135 x 16.14

So x is closer to 16.14

Answer: $x = 16.14$ to 2 decimal places.

E12.8

1

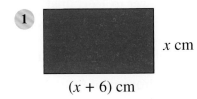

x cm

$(x + 6)$ cm

The area of this rectangle is 270 cm².

area $= x(x + 6) = 270$

Use trial and improvement to find x to 2 decimal places.

2 The area of this rectangle is 500 cm²

Use trial and improvement to find x to 2 decimal places.

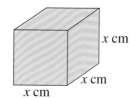

x cm

$(x + 9)$ cm

3 Solve these equations by trial and improvement. Give each answer to *1 decimal place*.

(a) $x^2 + x = 24$ (b) $x^2 - x = 62$ (c) $x^2 + 3x = 100$

(d) $x^3 + x = 200$ (e) $x^3 - x = 85$ (f) $x^3 + 2x = 170$

4

x cm

x cm

x cm

The volume of this cube is 650 cm³.

Use trial and improvement to find x to *2 decimal places*.

5 Solve these equations by trial and improvement. Give each answer to *2 decimal places*.

(a) $x^3 + x = 90$ (b) $x^3 - 2x = 120$ (c) $x^3 + 3x = 374$

6 The volume of this cuboid is 300 cm³

volume $= 7 \times x \times x = 7x^2$

so $7x^2 = 300$

Use trial and improvement to find x to 2 decimal places.

(Remember: $7x^2 = x^2 \times 7$ not $(7x)^2$)

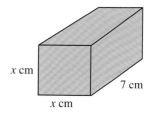

x cm

7 cm

x cm

7 Solve these equations by trial and improvement. Give each answer to 2 decimal places.

(a) $9x^2 = 200$ (b) $4x^2 = 125$ (c) $5x^2 = 179$

8 Solve $5^x = 62$ by trial and improvement. (5^x is '5 to the power x'. On your calculator type 5 y^x your x number $=$)

Give your answer to 1 decimal place.

9 Solve $8^x = 200$ by trial and improvement. Give your answer to 1 decimal place.

10

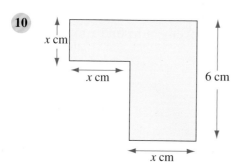

x cm

x cm

6 cm

x cm

The total area of this shape is 74 cm²

Use trial and improvement to find x.
Give your answer to 2 decimal places.

Most people want to learn to drive as soon as possible. How much it costs will depend on how many driving lessons are taken or how much driving practice is done with family members or friends.

> You cannot drive on a road without a provisional driving licence. This costs £50 (at the time of writing).

You must pass a theory test and a practical test.

> theory test £ 31

> practical test £ 62

If you drive with a family member or friend, you must be insured for driving the car. The cost of this will depend on the car and other factors.

A one hour driving lesson will often cost between £20 and £25.

Task A

Brooks Driving School
One hour lesson £23
10 one hour lessons £220

Car insurance for one month
Andrew for Uncle's car £68
Sneha for Mother's car £57

1 Andrew passes his test after 20 Brooks lessons plus two months of extra practice in his Uncle's car. What is the total cost? (remember to include the cost of the tests and provisional licence).

2 Sneha passes her test after 34 Brooks lessons plus one month of extra practice in her Mother's car. What is the total cost?

3 Andrew practises for 4 months using his Uncle's car. He passes his theory test but fails his practical test. He now takes 14 Brooks lessons then does the practical test again. This time he passes. What is the total cost?

4 Sneha passes her theory test and passes her practical test at the third attempt. In total she has 36 Brooks lessons and five months of extra practice in her Mother's car. What is the total cost?

You may want to buy and run a car after passing your driving test. There are many extra costs apart from the price of the car.

An MOT test each year checks the safety level of your car and costs £54 (at the time of writing). The car's carbon dioxide (CO_2) emissions are checked. You must pay car tax each year. Your car is put in a band depending on its CO_2 emissions. You pay a different car tax for each band as shown below.

Band	CO_2 emission (g/km)	12 months rate	6 months rate
A	Up to 100	—	—
B	101–110	£35.00	—
C	111–120	£35.00	—
D	121–130	£120.00	£66.00
E	131–140	£120.00	£66.00
F	141–150	£125.00	£68.75
G	151–165	£150.00	£82.50
H	166–175	£175.00	£96.25
I	176–185	£175.00	£96.25
J	186–200	£215.00	£118.25
K	201–225	£215.00	£118.25
L	226–255	£405.00	£222.75
M	Over 255	£405.00	£222.75

Task B

1 Andrew buys a band J car for £2000. His car insurance is £138 each month. He taxes the car at the 12 months rate, has an MOT plus a car service costing £112.50. In the first year, repairs and petrol amount to £1315.

   (a) How much does Andrew spend in total for this first year?

   (b) Ignoring the cost of the car, how much does Andrew spend on average each week during this first year? (Assume 1 year = 52 weeks)

2 Sneha buys a band F car for £2500. During the first year she taxes the car every six months. Her weekly car insurance is £23.17. She has an MOT which then leads to £196 of repairs. Her car service costs £98.99 and she buys two new tyres for £86.50 in total. Ignoring the cost of the car and petrol, how much does she spend on driving each month during this first year?

TEST YOURSELF ON UNIT 12

1. Finding numbers in sequences

For each sequence below, write down the *next 2 numbers*. What is the rule for each sequence?

(a) 5, 9, 13, 17...

(b) 3, 6, 12, 24...

(c) 25, 22, 19, 16...

(d) 1, 11, 21, 31...

(e)

1   4   9   16   ...

(f) 160, 80, 40, 20...

(g)

1   3   6   10   ...

(h) 3, 6, 11, 18...

2. Finding rules for sequences

(a) The first term of the sequence is 5 and the term-to-term rule is 'add 7'. Write down the first 5 terms of the sequence.

(b) Write down the term-to-term rule for the sequence:

      41, 33, 25, 17...

(c) Sequence 4, 7, 10, 13...

n	1	2	3	4
term	4	7	10	13
$3n$	3	6	9	12

Use this table to find the nth term of the sequence.

(d) Make a table like the one above to find the nth term of the sequence 5, 7, 9, 11...

(e) Find the nth term of the sequence 3, 8, 13, 18...

(f) Here is a sequence of shapes made from sticks. Let n = shape number and s = number of sticks.

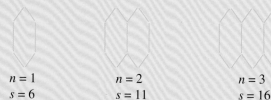

| $n = 1$ | $n = 2$ | $n = 3$ |
| $s = 6$ | $s = 11$ | $s = 16$ |

   (i) Draw the next shape in the sequence.

   (ii) Find a formula for the number of sticks (s) for the shape number n.

   (iii) Use the formula to find out how many sticks are in shape number 100.

---

3. Solving equations

Solve these equations:

(a) $n + 4 = 11$

(b) $n - 3 = 12$

(c) $5n = 40$

(d) $\dfrac{n}{3} = 8$

(e) $6x = -18$

(f) $7x + 2 = 30$

(g) $4x - 9 = 23$

(h) $10n + 8 = 58$

(i) $9x - 7 = 38$

(j) Tom thinks of a number and then subtracts 8. If the answer is 19, what number did Tom think of?

---

4. Solving equations with brackets

Solve these equations:

(a) $3(n + 2) = 24$

(b) $5(n + 3) = 55$

(c) $2(2n - 5) = 30$

(d) $3(2n + 3) = 39$

(e) $4(n - 5) = 16$

(f) $2(3n + 4) = 56$

---

5. Solving equations with the unknown on both sides

Solve these equations:

(a) $9n + 3 = 7n + 13$

(b) $8n + 4 = 3n + 24$

(c) $7n - 4 = 3n + 24$

(d) $10x - 8 = 4x + 16$

(e) $6x + 2 = 4x + 3$

(f) $2x + 6 = 36 - 3x$

6. Setting up equations and solving them

(a) I think of a number. If I multiply the number by 5 and add 3, the answer is 38. What is my number?

(b)

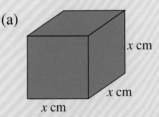

The perimeter of this rectangle is 50 cm.

(i) Write down an equation using the perimeter.

(ii) Find x.

(iii) Write down the actual length and width of the rectangle.

(c) One angle in a triangle is double the smallest angle and one angle is treble the smallest angle.

Find the size of each angle (hint : let x = smallest angle).

7. Solving equations by trial and improvement

(a)

The volume of this cube is 280 cm³.

Use trial and improvement to find x to 1 decimal place.

(b) Solve these equations by trial and improvement. Give each answer to 1 decimal place.

(i) $x^2 + x = 96$ (ii) $x^3 - 2x = 135$

(c) Solve $x^3 - x = 82$ by trial and improvement. Give the answer to *2 decimal places*.

Mixed examination questions

1   The first five terms of a sequence are given.

$$5, 3, 1, -1, -3...$$

(i) What is the next term in the sequence?

(ii) Write down the nth term of the sequence.   (AQA)

2   Solve   (i) $5x - 7 = 23$ (ii) $2(3x + 7) = 38$ (CCEA)

3   Solve these equations.

(a) $5x - 2 = 13$ (b) $3(2x - 1) = 9$ (WJEC)

4 Use a trial and improvement method to find a solution to the equation

$$x^3 + x = 22.$$

Give your answer correct to one decimal place.

You must show all your trials.   (AQA)

5 (a) Here are the first five odd numbers: 1, 3, 5, 7, 9

   (i) Write down the tenth odd number

   (ii) What is the twentieth odd number?

   (b) Here are the first four terms of a sequence: 21, 20, 17, 12...
      Write down the next two terms in the sequence.   (CCEA)

6 Solve these equations.

   (i) $\dfrac{x}{3} = 10$ (ii) $5x - 3 = 7$ (iii) $2(3x + 2) = 7$ (OCR)

7 Solve the following equations.

   (a) $4x - 5 = 7$ (b) $\dfrac{x}{2} = -10$ (c) $3(z - 2) = 27$ (WJEC)

8 Solve $2(5x + 3) = 23$ (OCR)

9 Alistair is 3 years older than Simon. Simon is now x years old.

   (i) Write down Alistair's age in terms of x.
      The total of their ages is 29 years.

   (ii) Write down an equation in x.

   (iii) Solve your equation to find x.   (OCR)

10 Use a trial and improvement method to find the value of x correct to two
   decimal places when

$$x^3 + 4x = 9.$$

You must show all your trials.   (OCR)

In this unit you will learn how to:

– find the mean, median, mode and range for sets of numbers

– use charts and graphs

– use stem and leaf diagrams

– use pie charts

– use two-way tables

– ⟨ USE YOUR MATHS! ⟩ – feed the dogs

Averages and range

The shoe sizes of 6 people were:

6, 2, 8, 5, 8, 7

add up all the numbers

(a) *mean* shoe size $= \dfrac{6 + 2 + 8 + 5 + 8 + 7}{6}$

the total number of people

$\qquad\qquad\quad = \dfrac{36}{6} = 6$

(b) arrange the shoe sizes in order:

$$2\ 5\ 6\ 7\ 8\ 8$$

↑

the median is the $\frac{1}{2}$-way number

$median = \dfrac{6 + 7}{2} = 6.5$

(c) *mode* = 8 because there are more 8s than any other number.

(d) *range* = highest number – lowest number

$\qquad\quad = 8 - 2$

$\qquad\quad = 6$

Key Facts

mean – add up the data then divide by the number of items

median – put numbers in order of size then choose middle item

mode – the item which occurs most often

range – largest value – smallest value

M13. 1

1 Copy and fill the empty boxes.
The marks scored by 7 students in a test are:

$$5 \quad 2 \quad 8 \quad 5 \quad 9 \quad 7 \quad 6$$

(a) The *range* is the highest mark ☐ – the lowest mark ☐ = ☐

(b) The *mode* is the most common value, which is ☐

(c) The *median* is the middle value when the numbers are arranged in size order:

median = ☐

(d) The *mean* is the total marks ☐ ÷ 7 = ☐

2 Find the range of each set of numbers:

(a) 12, 5, 17, 21, 3, 18, 14, 22, 16, 14

(b) 17, 92, 36, 24, 35, 21, 53, 94, 68

(c) 6, 7.5, 4.2, 6.8, 3.3, 7, 7.6, 5.7

3 Find the mode of each set of numbers:

(a) 7, 3, 4, 7, 6, 3, 7, 8, 1, 5, 6, 7, 6

(b) 12, 13, 18, 13, 12, 19, 17, 13, 18, 12, 17, 13

(c) 2.1, 0.8, 3.4, 0.4, 0.7, 2.6, 0.8, 0.7, 2.4, 0.8

4 Find the median of each set of numbers:

(a) 3, 6, 2, 8, 5, 7, 9, 8, 6

(b) 12, 8, 7, 10

(c) 5.6, 2.1, 7.8, 6.3, 4.9

(d) 3, 7, 9, 4, 5, 3, 4, 7, 8, 5, 6, 1, 3, 7

5 Find the mean average of each set of numbers:

(a) 8, 6, 9, 4, 8

(b) 3, 7, 5, 9, 5, 2, 9, 8

(c) 14, 16, 12, 15, 17, 16

(d) 5, 7, 4, 8, 7, 6, 5, 9, 4, 4

6 The heights (in cm) of 8 people are:

  162   183   171   169   153   171   168   170

Find the median height.

7 The parents of 5 children were asked how much money they spent on each child last Christmas. The money is shown below:

  £200   £300   £160   £280   £260

Find the mean average amount of money spent on each child last Christmas.

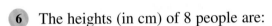

8 The temperature was recorded at midnight in nine towns. The readings were:

  2°, −3°, 0°, 1°, −1°, −2°, 0°, −4°, −2°

What was the range of the temperatures?

9 On a school trip, the ages of the boys were 14, 14, 12, 15, 12, 11 and the ages of the girls were 13, 16, 15, 12.

(a) Find the mean age for the boys.

(b) Find the mean age for the girls.

(c) Find the mean age for all the children.

10

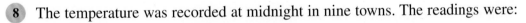

| 2 | 9 | 5 | 3 | 5 | 8 | 9 | 7 |

For the set of numbers above, find

(a) the mean

(b) the median

(c) the mode

(d) the range

Mean, median or mode?

When working out an average, how do I choose which one to use?

Look at the numbers 1, 1, 1, 1, 66

$$\text{mean} = \frac{70}{5} = 14 \qquad\qquad \text{median} = 1$$

Since each number is 1 except the last number, the median gives a more sensible idea of the average.

The mean average is distorted by the one high value 66.

Key Facts

If a set of numbers has extreme values, the mean average can be distorted so it is often better to use the median.

The median and mode are not calculated using all the numbers in the list but the mode is good for finding the most likely value and for data which are not numbers.

The mean average is better for numbers which are spread out in a balanced way.

M13. 1

You may *use a calculator* for this exercise.

1. The shoe sizes of the students in a year 11 class were:

   7, 8, 8, 5, 7, 7, 5, 7, 6, 7

   5, 10, 7, 11, 9, 7, 7, 6, 8, 10

   Find (a) the mode (b) the mean. Which average best describes these shoe sizes, the mode or the mean? Explain why.

2. For the set of numbers below, find (a) the mean and (b) the median.

   (c) Which average best describes this set of numbers? Explain why.

3. The list below shows how many pupils are in each class in Marygate High School.

   31   29   26   27   24   28   30   29   28

   27   27   30   25   28   24   21   28   27

   These numbers are spread out in a balanced way, so find the mean average number of pupils per class.

4 The list below shows the yearly salaries of all the people who work at 'Easiprint'.

£7000	£6900	£6900	£138000
£7500	£5600	£5900	£7100
£7000	£7700	£7900	£7200

(a) Which kind of average would be the most sensible to use? Explain why.

(b) Work out this average.

5 One year the first 12 rounds of golf for Tiger Woods were:

68   69   71   70   73   69   70   66   69   66   70   67

What was his mean average score?

6 Write down 3 numbers with a mean of 7.

7 Write down another 3 *different* numbers with a mean of 7.

8 Write down 7 numbers with a median of 6.

9 Jenny has 5 cards. The 5 cards have a mean of 9 and a range of 6.

	8	9	10	

What are the missing 2 numbers?

10 The mean average pocket money received by 6 children is £5 each week.

(a) What is the total amount of pocket money received by the 6 children each week?

(b) Rowan joins the 6 children. Rowan gets £12 pocket money each week. What is the mean average pocket money for all 7 children?

11 The mean height of 20 people is 160 cm.

(a) What is the total height of all 20 people?

(b) One person of height 179 cm leaves the group. Find the mean height of the remaining 19 people.

12 A theatre needs a mean average of 220 people to attend each show if it is to make enough money to stay open.

The mean average for the first 23 shows is 216. How many people must attend the next show so that the mean average will become 220?

13 In 3 cricket innings, Tariq has a median score of 42 and a mean score of 38. The range of the 3 scores is 14.

What are the three scores?

14 The 6 numbers below have a mean of 9. What is the value of x?

| 12 | 3 | 8 | x | 17 | 6 |

15 In one football game, the mean age of the England team was equal to the mean age of the France team. 21 of the ages are shown below.

England	33	24	26	26	28	31	29	32	35	27	28
France	24	27	x	27	34	29	33	22	33	29	30

Find the value of x.

Can you still?

Can you still?

13A **Number Work (see Unit 1)**

Copy the crossnumber puzzle onto squared paper. Use the clues to complete the crossnumber puzzle.

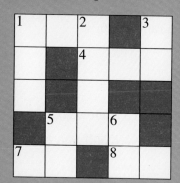

Clues across

1. $157 + 394$

4. $831 - 236$

5. 201×4

7. $-3 + 17$

8. -8×-4

Clues down

1. $712 - 187$

2. 130×12

3. $1575 \div 35$

5. $504 \div 6$

6. $602 \div 14$

Charts and graphs

M13. 2

1 The pictogram below shows how many year 10 students were absent from school during one week.

How many students were absent on:

(a) Friday?

(b) Wednesday?

(c) Thursday?

(d) How many *more* students were absent on Thursday than on Tuesday?

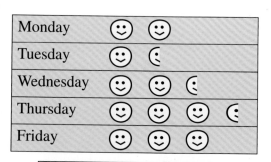

2 In Hart High School, students choose their year 10 options. 60 students choose History, 70 choose Geography, 30 choose Business Studies, 15 choose Spanish and 45 choose Art. Copy and complete the pictogram below:

History	
Geography	⊠ ⊠ ⊠ ▷
Business studies	
Spanish	
Art	

⊠ means 20 students

3 The chart below shows the amount of money spent on different items by the average household in Wales in 2002.

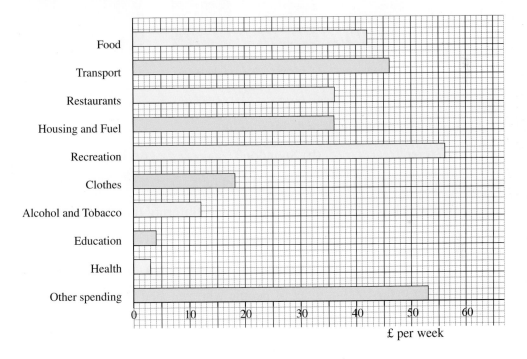

How much money was spent on:

(a) transport   (b) education   (c) clothes

(d) How much *more* money was spent on recreation than on health?

(e) What was the total amount of money spent on food and restaurants?

(f) What was the total amount spent on everything each week?

353

4 Two bands, 'Inferno' and 'Hotplay', tour part of the UK. The bar chart shows how many people watched each concert.

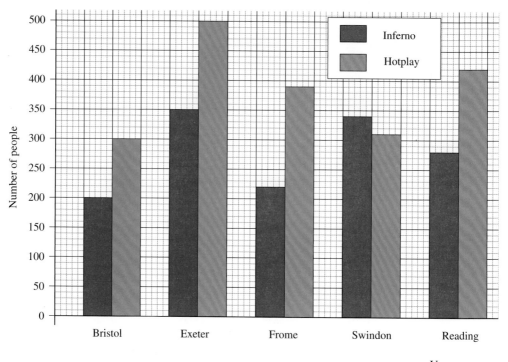

How many people watched 'Inferno' in:

(a) Exeter?   (b) Swindon?   (c) Reading?

(d) Where did 310 people watch 'Hotplay'?

(e) In which place did more people watch 'Inferno' than 'Hotplay'?

(f) How many *more* people watched 'Hotplay' than 'Inferno' in Bristol?

(g) How many *more* people watched 'Hotplay' than 'Inferno' in Reading?

(h) What is the total number of people who watched 'Hotplay' in all 5 venues?

5 A supermarket is looking for new workers. The table shows how many people are interviewed each day during one week.

Draw a bar chart to show the information in the table.

Day	Number of people
Monday	6
Tuesday	8
Wednesday	4
Thursday	9
Friday	3
Saturday	5

6 The graph shows the total number of pupils in Mount Henry High School from 1998 to 2005.

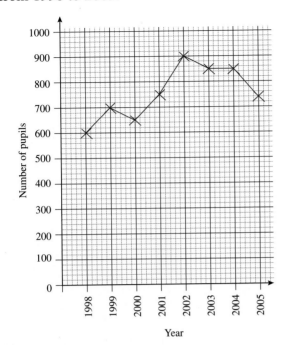

How many pupils were at the school in:

(a) 2000

(b) 2001

(c) 2003

(d) 2005

(e) In which year were the highest number of pupils at the school?

(f) What is the *difference* between the number of pupils at the school in 2004 compared to 1999?

7 The graph opposite shows the percentage of adults who smoked cigarettes in Great Britain.

What percentage of males smoked in:

(a) 1980

(b) 1986

(c) 1998

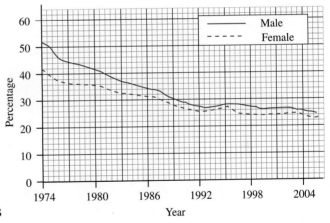

(d) What was the *drop* in the percentage of male smokers between 1974 and 2004?

(e) What was the *drop* in the percentage of female smokers between 1980 and 1998?

(f) What was the *difference* in the percentage of male smokers compared to female smokers in 1980?

8 Some young people were asked how many computer games they have. The results are below:

8	3	13	7	15	5	11	18	23	2	0	1	16	8
26	9	8	24	12	0	28	13	9	15	13	21	19	4
12	8	11	21	17	7	16	22	18	6	0	14	22	12

355

(a) Copy and complete the tally chart below:

(b) Copy and complete this frequency diagram:

Number of games	Tally	Total (Frequency)
0–4	ЍΉ ΙΙ	7
5–9		
10–14		
15–19		
20–24		
25–29		

(c) How many people had 15 or more computer games?

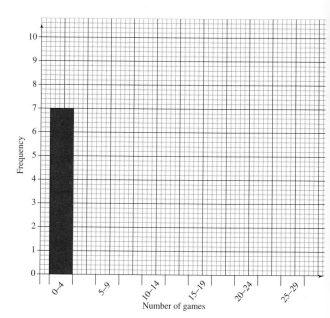

9 The chart below shows the percentage of smokers for different age groups in 2003.

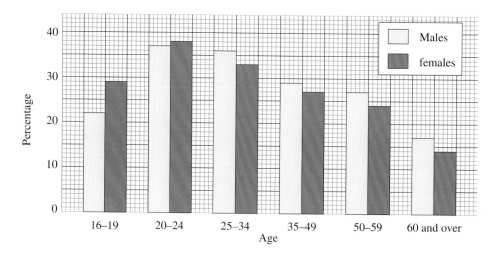

(a) In which age groups were the percentage of female smokers greater than the percentage of male smokers?

(b) What percentage of 25–34 year-old males are smokers?

(c) What percentage of 16–19 year-old females are smokers?

(d) What is the *difference* in the percentage of 16–19 year-old female smokers compared to 16–19 year-old male smokers?

(e) As people get older, what happens to the percentage of people who smoke?

356

Stem and leaf diagrams

Data can be displayed in groups in a stem and leaf diagram.

Here are the marks of 20 girls in a science test.

47	53	71	55	28	40	45	62	57	64
33	48	59	61	73	37	75	26	68	39

We will put the marks into groups 20–29, 30–39..... 70–79.

We will choose the tens digit as the 'stem' and the units as the 'leaf'.

The first four marks are shown [47, 53, 71, 55]

Stem (tens)	Leaf (units)
2	
3	
4	7
5	3 5
6	
7	1

The complete diagram is below ...... and then with the leaves in numerical order:

Stem	Leaf
2	8 6
3	3 7 9
4	7 0 5 8
5	3 5 7 9
6	2 4 1 8
7	1 3 5

Stem	Leaf
2	6 8
3	3 7 9
4	0 5 7 8
5	3 5 7 9
6	1 2 4 8
7	1 3 5

We write a key next to the stem and leaf diagram to explain what the stem digit means and what the leaf digit means.

In this example   Key 4|7 = 47

The diagram shows the shape of the distribution. It is also easy to find the mode, the median and the range.

E13.2

1 Draw a stem and leaf diagram for each set of data below:

(a)
32	29	41	38	52	53	41	28	36	52
44	26	47	43	38	27	36	63	62	28

Stem	Leaf
2	
3	
4	
5	
6	

(b)

29	42	41	35	23	46	23	36
42	53	27	51	29	36	27	43

2 The heights of 26 pupils were recorded to the nearest cm.

162 153 155 146 149 161 155 163 146 155 153 162 148

157 146 148 162 153 151 164 147 149 152 158 149 157

(a) Show this data on a stem and leaf diagram.

(b) Write down the *range* of the data.

Stem	Leaf
14	
15	
16	

3 The number of children in each class in Holland Bank School is recorded below:

28	31	27	28	30	24	23	32	29
29	29	30	26	27	31	27	26	31
25	27	30	28	27	29	30	28	27

(a) Draw a stem and leaf diagram to show this data.

(b) How many classes were there?

(c) What is the median number of children in a class?

(d) Find the range for the number of children in each class.

4 A number of 16/17 year-olds were asked how much money they earned each week from part-time jobs.

The data is recorded below:

32	40	36	51	82	69	38	43	28	51	65
74	63	42	70	65	71	30	25	38	26	70
68	70	32	37	24	42	32	65	48	42	36

(a) Draw a stem and leaf diagram to show this data.

(b) How many people were asked?

(c) What is the median amount of money earned?

(d) Find the range for this data.

5 Dan, Simon, Darryl and Julian try to play golf. The stem and leaf diagram shows the scores for each of their last 5 rounds of golf.

(a) What was their median score?

(b) Find the range of the scores.

Stem	Leaf
7	8 9
8	1 2 2 4 5 5 5 7 9 9
9	0 1 1 3 3 4 6
10	1

Key 8|2 = 82

6

Stem	Leaf
1	1 1 3 3 3 4 5 7 7 8
2	1 1 1 2 3 4 4 5

Key 2|3 = 2.3 litres

This stem and leaf diagram shows the engine sizes of some cars.

(a) What is the median engine size?

(b) What is the range of the engine sizes?

7 The ages of the teachers in Holland Bank School and Grindley High School are shown in the back-to-back stem and leaf diagram.

Holland Bank school		Grindley High school
9 6 6 4	2	2 3 3 5 7 7 7 8
9 8 5 5 4 2	3	0 0 1 3 4 4 6
9 8 8 6 6 6 5 5 0	4	1 2 2 5 7 7 8 8 8
7 7 7 5 5 5 3 2 2	5	0 6 6 7
3 2 2 1	6	0

Key 6|2 = 26   Key 4|5 = 45

(a) Find the median and range for Holland Bank School.

(b) Find the median and range for Grindley High School.

(c) Write a sentence to compare the ages of teachers in each school (use the median and range).

 Can you still?

 Can you still?

13B Add, subtract, multiply and divide fractions (see Unit 5)

Work out

1. $\frac{1}{3}$ of 12

2. $\frac{3}{5}$ of 30

3. $\frac{1}{4} + \frac{1}{5}$

4. $\frac{2}{3} - \frac{3}{7}$

5. $\frac{3}{4} \times 24$

6. $\frac{3}{8} \times \frac{6}{9}$

7. $\frac{2}{9} \div \frac{7}{12}$

8. $\frac{8}{15} \div \frac{2}{3}$

9. $1\frac{1}{2} + 2\frac{1}{3}$

10. $3\frac{3}{4} - \frac{9}{10}$

11. $2\frac{3}{4} \times 1\frac{1}{5}$

12. $2\frac{1}{2} \div 3\frac{1}{3}$

Pie charts

Drawing pie charts

Some people were asked what they had for breakfast. The data is recorded below:

Breakfast	Frequency (number of people)
cereal	18
toast	8
egg	4
nothing	15

To draw a pie chart:

(a) Add up the number of people.
Total frequency = 18 + 8 + 4 + 15 = 45

(b) Whole angle in a pie chart = 360°
This must be split between 45 people.
Angle for each person = 360° ÷ 45 = 8°

(c) Angle for 'cereal' = 18 × 8° = 144°
Angle for 'toast' = 8 × 8° = 64°
Angle for 'egg' = 4 × 8° = 32°
Angle for 'nothing' = 15 × 8° = 120°

Remember

Always find the total frequency then divide it into 360° to find out what angle is needed for each item in the pie chart.

M13. 3

1 Some people were asked what their favourite kind of television programme was. The data is recorded below:

Type of programme	Frequency (number of people)
soap	25
drama	11
news	5
comedy	15
other	4

(a) Find the total frequency.

(b) Work out the angle for each person to help draw a pie chart (i.e. 360° ÷ 'total frequency').

(c) Work out the angle for each type of programme and draw a pie chart.

2 Some people were asked where they were going to spend their Summer holiday. The table below shows the information.

Country	Frequency
France	7
Spain	8
USA	4
Greece	6
UK	15

(a) Find the total frequency.

(b) Work out the angle for each person to help draw a pie chart.

(c) Work out the angle for each country and draw a pie chart.

In Questions **3**, **4** and **5**, work out the angle for each item and draw a pie chart.

3 Favourite football team

Team	Frequency
Arsenal	15
Liverpool	15
Chelsea	20
Manchester Utd.	25
Everton	6
Aston Villa	9

4 Most popular Briton

Briton	Frequency
Shakespeare	15
Churchill	18
Newton	7
Elizabeth 1	12
Brunel	8

5 Favourite snack

Snack	Frequency
crisps	60
fruit	35
nuts	10
biscuits	18
chocolate	34
other	23

6 120 children were asked who their favourite 'Simpsons' character was. The information is shown below.

Character	Frequency	Angle
Homer	52	
Bart	32	
Mr. Burns	17	
Lisa	12	
Marge	7	

Copy and complete the table then draw an accurate pie chart to show this information.

7 Hal carries out a survey of 60 year 10 students. He asks them what their favourite cartoon is. He draws this accurate pie chart.

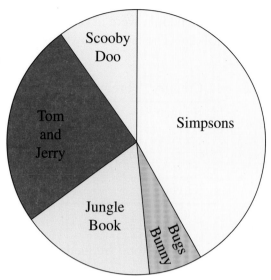

Measure the angles and complete the table.

Cartoon	Frequency	Angle
Simpsons	25	
Bugs Bunny		
Jungle Book	10	60°
Tom and Jerry		
Scooby Doo		
Total	60	

Reading from pie charts

Marilyn has £120 to spend each week. The pie chart shows what she spends her money on. How much does she spend on rent?

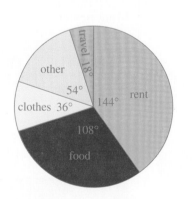

fraction of pie chart $= \dfrac{144}{360}$ ← angle for 'rent'
← total angle for pie chart

$= \dfrac{72}{180} = \dfrac{36}{90} = \dfrac{4}{10} = \dfrac{2}{5}$

money spent on rent $= \dfrac{2}{5}$ of £120

$= (120 \div 5) \times 2$

$= 24 \times 2$

$= £48$

1 The pie chart shows the 80 passengers travelling on a train. How many of the passengers were:

(a) men   (b) women

(c) girls   (d) boys

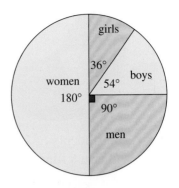

2 Jack Jones runs a pub. He makes his money from 3 main things: food, drink and hiring out rooms. The pie chart shows what fraction of his money he gets from each of these things.

If Jack makes £ 900 one week, how much did he make from:

(a) food

(b) hiring out a room

(c) drink

3

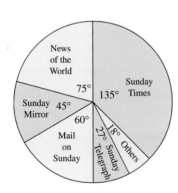

Penny delivers 240 newspapers each Sunday.

The pie chart shows the different newspapers which Penny delivers.

How many of the newspapers were:

(a) News of the World   (b) Sunday Mirror

(c) Sunday Telegraph   (d) Sunday Times

(e) Mail on Sunday   (f) Others

4 Neil draws a pie chart to show what he does during a typical day (24 hours).

How many hours does he do the following?

(a) exercise   (b) school

(c) sleep   (d) eat

(e) watch TV   (f) other things

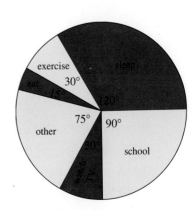

363

5

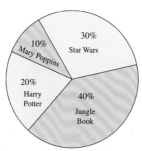

Some young people were asked who they would vote for at the next general election. The information is shown on the pie chart.

Find the angle on the pie chart for:

(a) Labour (b) the Green Party

(c) Conservative (d) the Liberal Democrats

6 The students of 2 different schools were asked to state their favourite children's film. Here are the results.

Holland Bank School

There were 800 students

Hatton Green School

There were 1000 students

(a) Carl says 'More students in Holland Bank School like Star Wars than the students in Hatton Green School.'

Use both charts to explain whether or not Carl is right.

(b) Yasmin says 'Less students in Holland Bank School like Harry Potter than the students in Hatton Green School,'

Use both charts to explain whether or not Yasmin is right.

7 People in the North and the South of England were asked how many hours of exercise they took each week. The information is shown in the pie charts below.

The North

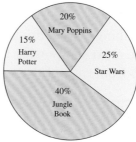

The South

Which of the statements below is correct?

(a) 'Less people in the North do some exercise than people in the South.'

(b) 'A smaller percentage of people in the North do some exercise than people in the South.'

(c) 'More people in the North do some exercise than people in the South.'
  Explain why you chose your answer.

8

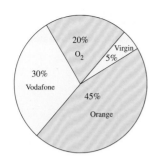

Over 2000 people were asked who their phone providers were. The results are shown in the pie chart.

Find the angle on the pie chart for:

(a) Vodafone   (b) O_2

(c) Virgin   (d) Orange

9 The pie charts below show the ages in years of people in the UK and Kenya.

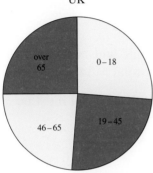
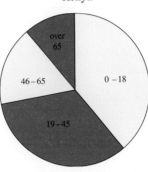

Which of the statements below are correct?

(a) 'There are more 0 to 18 year-olds in Kenya than in the UK.'

(b) 'There are less 0 to 18 year-olds in Kenya than in the UK.'

(c) A greater percentage of the people in Kenya are 0 to 18 year-olds than in the UK.'

Explain why you chose your answer.

Can you still?

(13C)   **Draw curves (see Unit 10)**

Can you still?

1. Draw an x-axis from -3 to 3 and a y-axis from 0 to 12
Complete the table below then draw the curve $y = x^2 + 2$

x	-3	-2	-1	0	1	2	3
y		6		3			

2. Draw an x-axis from -3 to 3 and a y-axis from -2 to 12
Complete the table below then draw the curve $y = x^2 - x$

x	-3	-2	-1	0	1	2	3
y			2				

Two-way tables

70 students from years 10 and 11 were asked what sport they played in their last games lesson.

The information is shown in the table below.

	Football	Rugby	Badminton	Total
Year 10	18	14	B	34
Year 11	14	E	6	C
Total	A	F	D	70

↕ A column is vertical.

↔ A row is horizontal.

(a) The 'Football' column total is 18 + 14 = 32

(b) The year 10 row total is 34. Year 10 'Football' and 'Rugby' is 18 + 14 = 32 so the 'Badminton' must be 2 to make the total = 34.

(c) The 'Total' column adds up to 70 so the year 11 Total must be 36 so that 34 + 36 = 70.

(d) The 'Badminton' column total is B + 6 = 2 + 6 = 8.

(e) The year 11 row total is C = 36. Year 11 'Football' and 'Badminton' is 14 + 6 = 20 so the 'Rugby' must be 16 to make the total = 36.

(f) The 'Rugby' column total is 14 + E = 14 + 16 = 30.

	Football	Rugby	Badminton	Total
Year 10	18	14	2	34
Year 11	14	16	6	36
Total	32	30	8	70

We can *check* our answers by adding the totals along the bottom row to make sure they add up to 70 (32 + 30 + 8 = 70 ✓).

M13.4

1 100 people were asked what their favourite kind of chocolate was. Copy and complete the two-way table below.

	Plain chocolate	Milk chocolate	White chocolate	Total
Female			5	43
Male	21			
Total		46	14	100

2 80 children were asked if they went to the cinema, swimming or cycling one day in the Easter holidays. The information is shown in the two-way table below.

	Cinema	Swimming	Cycling	Total
Boys	18	17		47
Girls	15		8	
Total				80

(a) Copy and complete the two-way table.

(b) How many children went swimming in total?

3 200 pupils were asked what their favourite school subjects were. The information is shown in the two-way table below.

	Art	PE	Maths	Science	Total
Boys		53	28		119
Girls		28		14	
Total	51			32	200

(a) Copy and complete the two-way table.

(b) One of these pupils is picked at random. Write down the *probability* that the pupil likes PE best.

4 400 students in years 10 and 11 were asked if they smoked or drank alcohol on a regular basis. The information is shown in the two-way table below.

	Smoke	Drink alcohol	Neither	Smoke and drink alcohol	Total
Year 10	21	40			
Year 11	23			38	227
Total			198	62	400

(a) Copy and complete the two-way table.

(b) One of these students is picked at random. Write down the *probability* that the student will not smoke or drink alcohol.

5 1000 people in Birmingham and Nottingham were asked how they travel to work. The information is shown in the two-way table below.

	Car	Walk	Bike	Train	Total
Birmingham	314	117		69	
Nottingham		175	41		
Total	530		72		1000

(a) Copy and complete the two-way table.

(b) One of the people from Birmingham *only* is chosen. What is the *probability* that this person travels to work by bike?

6 500 football fans from Liverpool and Manchester were asked which football team they supported. The two-way table below shows the information.

	Liverpool	Everton	Manchester United	Manchester City	Total
fans from Liverpool		83	15		210
fans from Manchester	12	16			
Total	119		156		500

(a) Copy and complete the two-way table.

(b) *Use a calculator* to find what percentage of the fans supported Manchester City (reminder: 'number of Manchester City fans ÷ 500 then multiply by 100').

7 1800 people were asked if they had been in a car accident. The information is shown in the two-way table according to different age groups.

	Car accident	No car accident	Total
17 to 25	123	481	
26 to 60	65		702
over 60			
Total	286		1800

(a) Copy and complete the two-way table.

(b) *Use a calculator* to find what percentage of the people had been in a car accident.

Alex and Kate own 9 days. They have worked out that it costs about £50 each week to deal with the dogs.

Use all the information provided to find out if Alex and Kate are correct. Make sure you show all your working out.

The dogs		
Breed	age (years)	weight (kg)
Scottish Terrier	3	9.1
Chihuahua	7	2.7
Labrador	6	29.5
Springer Spaniel	2	19.1
Beagle	2	15.9
Yorkshire Terrier	3	3.6
Labrador	11	31.8
Great Dane	6	50.9
Golden Retriever	9	31.4

Each dog must have a booster once each year which costs £32.

Each dog must be wormed and have flea drops which costs £11.45 each month.

Alex and Kate insure each dog against unexpected illness or injury. The total cost for all the dogs is £76 each month.

The dogs are fed either with dry food only or with dry food mixed with can food.

The amount of food given each day depends on the weight of the dog as shown in the table below.

Weight of dog (kg)	dry food	dry food mixed with can food
Up to 4.5	$\frac{1}{2}$ cup	$\frac{1}{4}$ can and $\frac{1}{2}$ cup
4.5 to 11	2 cups	$\frac{1}{2}$ can and $1\frac{1}{4}$ cups
11 to 23	$3\frac{1}{2}$ cups	1 can and 2 cups
23 to 34	$4\frac{1}{2}$ cups	$1\frac{1}{2}$ cans and 3 cups
Over 34	8 cups	2 cans and 5 cups

The Scottish Terrier, Yorkshire Terrier, Chihuahua, Beagle and Great Dane each have dry food only. The other four dogs have dry food mixed with can food.

The costs of the food are:

packet of
dry food
£4.50

(36 cups)

can
food
42 p

369

---

1. Finding the mean, median, mode and range for sets of numbers

(a) 9, 7, 3, 7, 4, 8, 2, 7, 1, 6, 1

For the set of numbers above, find the (i) mode (ii) median (iii) mean (iv) range

(b) 8, 6, 5, 9, 8, 6

For the set of numbers above, which is larger – the mean or the median?

---

2. Using charts and graphs

The chart below shows the percentage of people in the USA who are obese (*very* overweight).

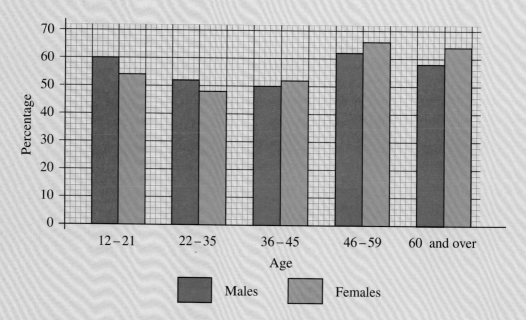

(a) In which age groups were the percentage of obese males greater than the percentage of obese females?

(b) What percentage of 46–59 year-old females are obese?

(c) What percentage of 22–35 year-old males are obese?

(d) What is the *difference* in the percentage of 46–59 year-old obese females compared to 46–59 year-old obese males?

3. Using stem and leaf diagrams

The ages of 25 people who work for a local newspaper are recorded below.

31	42	27	50	21
26	19	19	62	35
32	23	53	27	46
48	43	28	53	58
37	51	36	47	20

(a) Draw a stem and leaf diagram to show this data.

(b) What is the median age?

(c) Find the range of the ages.

4. Using pie charts

(a) In a list of the richest people in a country, their backgrounds are listed below.

Background	Number of people
inherited	15
business	28
music	20
sport	17
other	10

(i) Find the total number of people.

(ii) Work out the angle for each person to help draw a pie chart.

(iii) Work out the angle for each background and draw a pie chart.

(b)

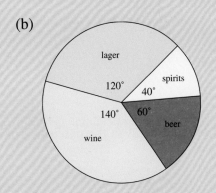

108 people were asked what their favourite drink is. The results are shown in the pie chart. How many people said:

(i) beer

(ii) lager

(iii) spirits

(iv) wine?

371

120 people were given the chance to go to Australia, India or the USA. The information showing their choices is in the two-way table.

	Australia	India	U.S.A	Total
Female		32		71
Male	24			
Total	47		33	120

(a) Copy and complete the two-way table.

(b) One of these people is picked at random. Write down the *probability* that the person has chosen India.

(c) *Use a calculator* to work out the *percentage* of the people who chose the USA.

Mixed examination questions

1   Here is a pictogram.
It shows the number of people who had a meal in a café on each of four days.

Monday	⊕ ⊕ ⊕
Tuesday	⊕ ⊕
Wednesday	⊕ ⊕ ◖
Thursday	⊕ ⊕ ⊕ ⊕ ⊕ ◿
Friday	

⊕ represents 20 people

(a) Write down the number of people who had a meal in the café on

(i) Monday,

(ii) Wednesday,

(iii) Thursday.

On Friday, 55 people had a meal in the café.

(b) Show this information on the pictogram.   (EDEXCEL)

2 John has a science test every week.
Here are John's scores in his last nine tests.

52, 59, 43, 49, 65, 68, 48, 53, 67

(a) Calculate his mean score.

(b) Find his median score.

(c) Find the range of his scores

3

2	3 7 8
3	0 2 3 6 6 9
4	1 4 5 6 7 8 8 9
5	0 0 0 0 3 6 7 7
6	1 2 2 4 5

Key: 2|7 represents 27 marks

The stem and leaf diagram shows the marks gained by 30 pupils in a test.

(a) Write down the highest mark.

(b) Find the median mark.

(c) Find the range of the marks.   (OCR)

4 Kim drew a pie chart to show the colours of the cars in the school car park.

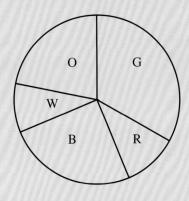

Key	
G	Green
R	Red
B	Blue
W	White
O	Other

(a) (i) Measure the angle for Green.

   (ii) What fraction of the cars was Green?

(b) What percentage of the cars was Blue?   (OCR)

373

5   60 British students each visited one foreign country last week.
    The two-way table shows some information about these students.

	France	Germany	Spain	Total
Female			9	34
Male	15			
Total		25	18	60

(a) Copy and complete the two-way table.

(b) One of these students is picked at random. Write down the probability that
    the student visited Germany last week.   (EDEXCEL)

6   Swimmers taking a survival test can achieve a gold, silver or bronze award.
    Last month 240 swimmers took the test.
    The results are shown in the table.

Award	Number of Swimmers
Gold	30
Silver	80
Bronze	120
Failed	10
Total	240

Draw a pie chart to illustrate this information.   (AQA)

In this unit we will explore two of the taxes that most people have to pay.

WATCH YOUR MONEY! – Income tax

Tim earns £900 each week. Before he gets his pay, he finds that £166.35 has been taken off his money already. This is *income tax*.

This does not make Tim happy but this money is used by the government to pay for things like hospitals, schools and defence.

Most people have income tax deducted from their pay *before* they receive it, by their employer, who then pays the tax to the government. This method of paying income tax is called *PAYE (Pay As You Earn)*

Tax allowance

An amount of money a person may earn before paying income tax (at the time of writing this is £6475 each year for a single person).

Taxable income

Taxable income = income – tax allowance
Income tax is worked out as a percentage of the taxable income.

Percentage rate of income tax

20% on first £37400 of taxable income.
40% on any other taxable income.

If Tim earns £900 each week, that will be £46800 in one year (assuming 52 weeks in one year).

     tax allowance = £6475

     taxable income = income – tax allowance

             = 46800 – 6475

             = £40325

Tim pays 20% of £37400 on first £37400 of taxable income.

This leaves 40325 – 37400 = £2925 of taxable income.

Tim must then pay 40% of £2925.

Income tax = 20% of £37400 = £7480

      and 40% of £2925 = £1170

Total income tax for the year = £8650 (this is £166.35 for each week if divided by 52 weeks)

1 Sophie earns £50000 each year. She has a tax allowance of £6475. Copy and complete the statement below to find out how much income tax Sophie must pay.

Taxable income = income – tax allowance

= 50000 – [   ]

= £43525

income tax = 20% of 37400 = £[   ]

and 40% of 'taxable income' – 37400

= 40% of [   ] = £[   ]

total income tax = £[   ] + £[   ] = £[   ]

2 Callum earns £13400 each year. He has a tax allowance of £6475. Copy and complete the statements below to find out how much income tax Callum must pay.

Taxable income = income – tax allowance

= [   ] – [   ]

= £[   ]

income tax = 20% of [   ]

total income tax = £[   ]

3 Wendy earns £28500 each year. She has a tax allowance of £6475.

(a) What is Wendy's taxable income?

(b) How much income tax will Wendy have to pay?

4 Alex earns £3950 each month. He has a tax allowance of £6475.

(a) What is his annual (yearly) taxable income?

(b) How much income tax will he pay for one year?

(c) How much income tax will he pay each month?

5 Angus earns £60000 each year. How much income tax will he pay? (He has a tax allowance of £6475)

6 Millie earns £320 each week. She has a tax allowance of £6475.

(a) Find her annual salary (assuming 52 weeks in one year).

(b) What is her taxable income?

(c) How much income tax will she pay for one year?

(d) How much income tax will she pay each week?

7 Dom earns £90 each week. His tax allowance is £6475. Assuming 52 weeks in one year, how much income tax will Dom pay each week?

8 Emma earns £896 each month from her work in a shop. She also works in a pub, earning £30 each week. Her tax allowance is £6475. Assuming 52 weeks in one year, how much income tax will Emma pay each week?

This is tax collected by local authorities. It is a tax on domestic property.
In general, the bigger the property is, the more tax will be charged.

Each property is put into a *valuation band*. At the time of writing the bands are as listed below.

Valuation band	Range of values
A	up to £40000
B	over £40000 and up to £52000
C	over £52000 and up to £68000
D	over £68000 and up to £88000
E	over £88000 and up to £120000
F	over £120000 and up to £160000
G	over £160000 and up to £320000
H	over £320000

The council tax is used to pay for local services such as rubbish collection, schools and the fire services.

Council tax is not paid on some properties, for example any property that only students live in or a property where all the people who live in it are aged under 18.

If only one person lives in a property they will get a 25% discount on the council tax bill.

Jack lives on his own in a flat worth £75000. This year's council tax rates in his area are shown in the table below:

Band	A	B	C	D	E	F	G	H
Annual council tax (£)	650	800	1000	1200	1350	1550	1900	2300

(a) How much council tax will Jack have to pay this year?

(b) If he spreads the council tax payment over 10 months, how much will he pay each month?

(c) Using the table at the start of this section, Jack's flat is in band D. The other table shows he must pay £1200 this year.

Jack lives on his own so gets a 25% discount.

25% of £1200 = £300

Jack pays £1200 – £300 = £900

For this exercise use the council tax rates shown in the table below.

Band	A	B	C	D	E	F	G	H
Annual council tax (£)	661	798	1109	1252	1420	1675	1910	2405

Use the table at the start of this section to find out which band each property belongs to in the following questions.

1. Harry and Erica Smith live in a house worth £105000. How much council tax will they have to pay?

2. Simon and Shanice live in a house worth £132000.

   (a) How much council tax will they have to pay?

   (b) If the council tax payment is spread over 10 months, how much will the monthly payments be?

3. Molly lives on her own in a bedsit valued at £50000. How much council tax will Molly have to pay this year?

4. The Jackson family live in a house valued at £210 000. If they spread their council tax payment over 10 months, what will the monthly payments be?

5. Jenny, David and Matt are all students. They live in a house valued at £90000. How much council tax will they have to pay this year?

6. Mr. and Mrs. Pickford live in a flat valued at £102,000. They are allowed to pay their council tax in 4 equal (quarterly) payments. How much will each quarterly payment be?

7. Rhys lives on his own in a bungalow valued at £110 000. If he spreads his council tax payment over 10 months, what will his monthly payments be?

8. Find out what the council tax bill for a band D property in *your area* is this year. Do you think council tax is a fair way of collecting money for local

GEOMETRY 3

In this unit you will learn how to:

– find perimeters of shapes

– find areas of triangles and rectangles

– find areas of trapeziums and parallelograms

– find circumferences of circles

– find areas of circles

– find surface areas and volumes of cuboids

– convert units of area and volume

– find volumes of prisms, particularly cylinders

– use similar triangles

– 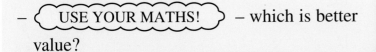 USE YOUR MATHS! – which is better value?

Perimeter

The perimeter of a shape is the distance around its edges.

It is a length and is measured in units of length such as metres or centimetres.

8 cm

3 cm

Perimeter = 8 + 3 + 8 + 3 = 22 cm

distance around
all its edges

1 Find the perimeter of each rectangle. All lengths are in cm.

(a)

9
4   4
9

(b)
3

6

(c)
8
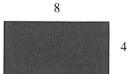
4

(d)
6

6

(e)
10
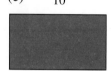
5

(f)
6

9

2 Draw 3 different rectangles with a perimeter of 18 cm.

3 Find the perimeter of a rectangle with a length of 12 cm and a width of 7 cm.

4 Find the perimeter of each triangle. All lengths are in cm.

(a)
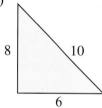
8   10
6

(b)
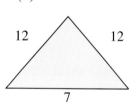
12   12
7

(c)
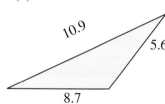
10.9   5.6
8.7

5 For each triangle below you are given the perimeter. Find the missing value x. All lengths are in cm.

(a)
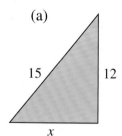
15   12
x
perimeter = 36 cm

(b)

8
13   x
perimeter = 40 cm

(c)
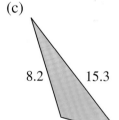
8.2   15.3
x
perimeter = 34 cm

6
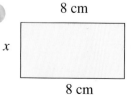
8 cm
x
8 cm

The perimeter of this rectangle is 26 cm.

Find the missing value x.

7 The perimeter of this rectangle is 44 cm.

Find the missing value x.

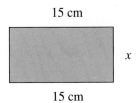

15 cm

x

15 cm

8

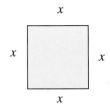

x

x x

x

The perimeter of this square is 36 cm.

Find the missing value x.

9 The perimeter of a square is 48 cm. How long is one of the sides of the square?

10

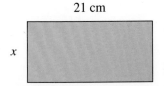

21 cm

x

The perimeter of this rectangle is 70 cm. Find the missing value x.

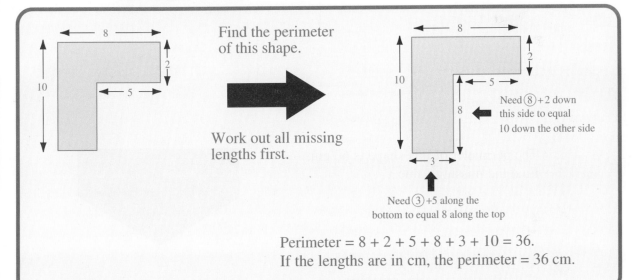

Find the perimeter of this shape.

Work out all missing lengths first.

8

2

5

10

8

2

5

10

8

3

Need ⑧+2 down this side to equal 10 down the other side

Need ③+5 along the bottom to equal 8 along the top

Perimeter = 8 + 2 + 5 + 8 + 3 + 10 = 36.
If the lengths are in cm, the perimeter = 36 cm.

E15.1

1

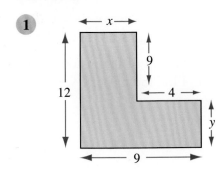

x

9

12

4

y

9

All lengths are in cm. Find the length of
(a) x

(b) y

(c) Find the perimeter of this shape.

In questions ②　to ⑦ , find the perimeter of each shape. All lengths are in cm.

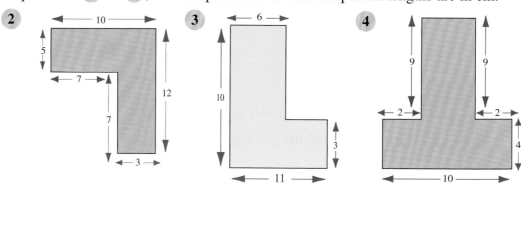

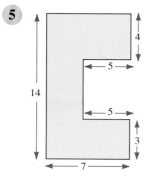

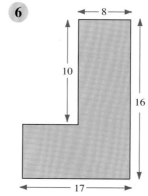

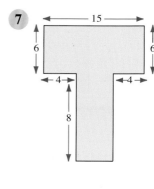

⑧

The perimeter of this shape is 60 cm.
Find the missing value x.

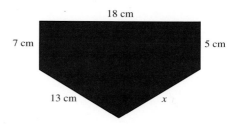

⑨

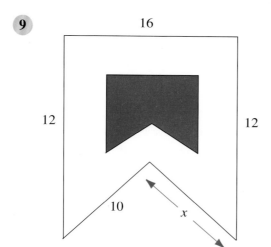

The perimeter of the large shape is
twice the perimeter of the inside
shape. All lengths are in cm.

The perimeter of the inside shape is
32 cm. Find the missing value x.

382

Area of triangles and rectangles

The area of a shape is the amount of surface it covers.

It is measured in squares, usually square metres (m²) or square centimetres (cm²).

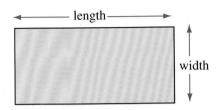

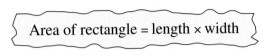

Area of rectangle = length × width

Area = 7 × 3
= 21 cm²

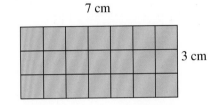

Area of triangle = $\frac{1}{2}$ area of rectangle

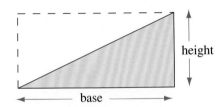

Area of triangle = $\frac{1}{2}$ (base × height)

Height = 7 cm   base = 8 cm

Area of triangle = $\frac{1}{2}$(base × height)

= $\frac{1}{2}$(8 × 7)

= $\frac{1}{2}$(56) = 28 cm²

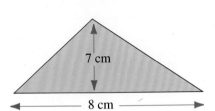

Find the area of this shape.

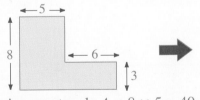

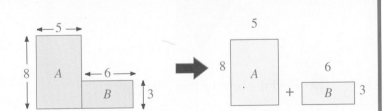

Area rectangle A = 8 × 5 = 40

Area rectangle B = 6 × 3 = 18

Total area   = 40 + 18 = 58

If each length is given in cm, the area of the shape is 58 cm².

Find the area of each shape below. All lengths are in cm.

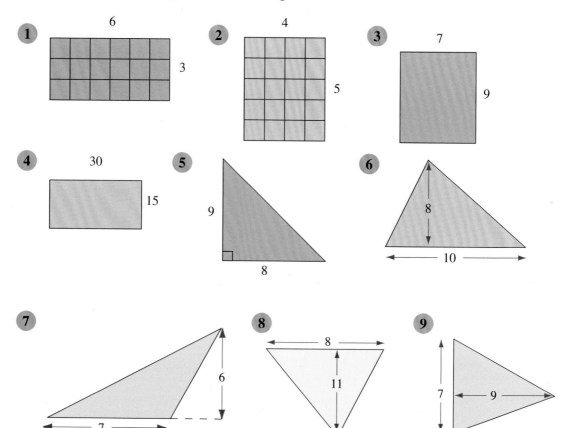

1 6 · 3

2 4 · 5

3 7 · 9

4 30 · 15

5 9 · 8

6 8 · 10

7 6 · 7

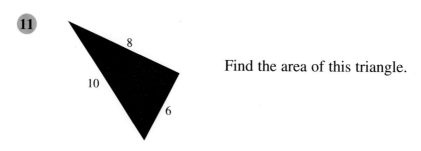

8 8 · 11

9 7 · 9

10 Find the area of a triangle with a base of 20 cm and a height of 9 cm

11 8 · 10 · 6

Find the area of this triangle.

12 Find the area of this triangle.

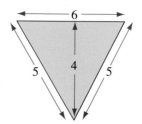

6 · 5 · 4 · 5

13 9 cm · Area = 54 cm² · x

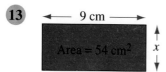

Find the missing value x.

14 Find the missing value x

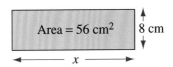

Area = 56 cm^2 8 cm

x

Find the area of each shape in questions **15** to **20** by splitting them into rectangles.

15

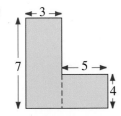

16

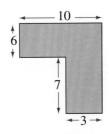

17

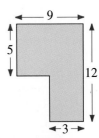

18

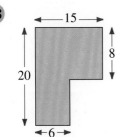

19

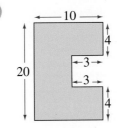

20

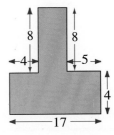

21 Find the shaded area.

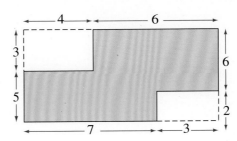

Find the area of each shape in questions **22** to **27** by splitting them into rectangles and triangles.

22

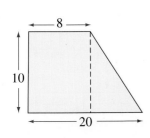

23

24

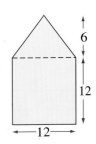

385

25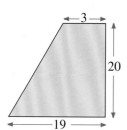

26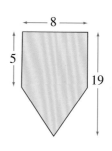

27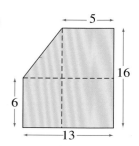

In questions **28** to **30**, find the pink area.

28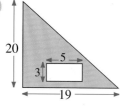

29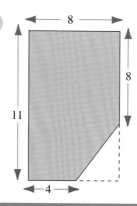

30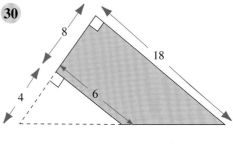

Areas of trapeziums and parallelograms

Parallelogram	**Trapezium** (2 parallel sides)
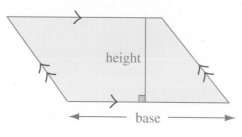	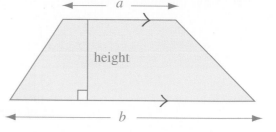

Area = base × height

Area = $b \times h$

Area = $\frac{1}{2}(a + b) \times h$

(a)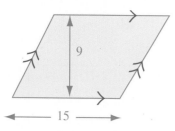

Area = base × height

    = 15 × 9

    = 135 cm²

(b)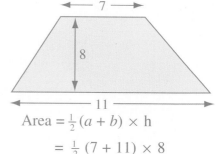

Area = $\frac{1}{2}(a + b) \times h$

    = $\frac{1}{2}(7 + 11) \times 8$

    = $\frac{1}{2}(18) \times 8$

    = 9 × 8 = 72 cm²

Find the area of each shape below. All lengths are in cm.

1

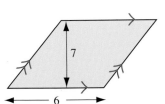

2

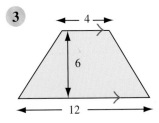

3

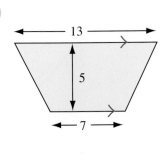

4

5

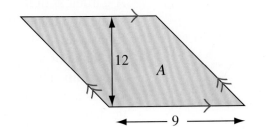

6

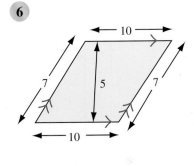

7 Which of the 2 shapes below has the larger area?

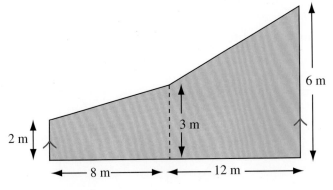

or

8

This is the plan of one end of a house. Find the area.

387

9 Find the pink area.

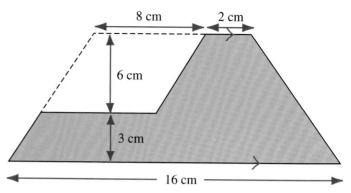

10 Find the area of the trapezium.

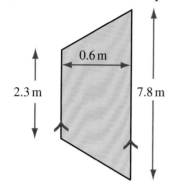

11 Find the area of the parallelogram.

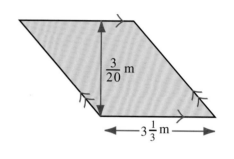

12

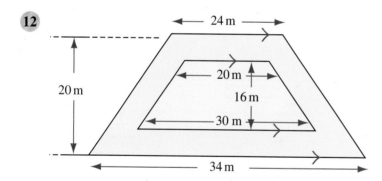

A garden is in the shape of a trapezium. It has a lawn also in the shape of a trapezium. The yellow area is a path around the lawn. Find the area of the path.

13 The area of the trapezium is equal to the area of the parallelogram. Find the missing value x

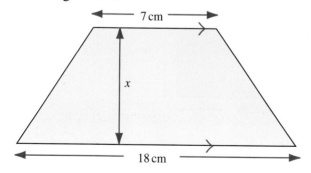

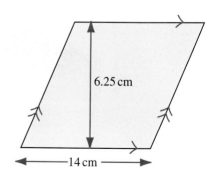

14 Wayne wants to grass an area in his garden (the green area). If it costs him £13 to grass every 30 m², how much will it cost him to grass the green area? (Give your answer to the nearest pound)

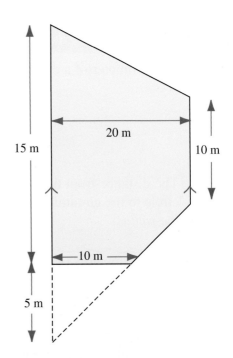

Can you still?

Can you still?

15A   **Percentages (see Unit 6)**

1. Which of the 3 questions below gives the largest answer?

   | 30% of £120 | or | 70% of £50 | or | 35% of £110 |

2. Sandeep gets a pay rise of 4%. If he used to earn £15000 each year, how much does he earn now?

3. Faye gets a 20% discount when she books a holiday to Spain. The holiday usually costs £650. How much does Faye pay for the holiday?

4. Beth scores 21 out of 35 in a science test. What percentage is this (to the nearest whole number)? *You may use a calculator.*

5. Kenny buys a digital radio for £190 + VAT. If VAT is 17.5%, how much will Kenny pay in total?

6. £6000 is invested in a bank at 4% per annum (year) compound interest. How much money will be in the bank after 2 years?

7. Sandra buys a caravan for £16000. Its value depreciates (goes down) each year by 5% of its value at the start of the year. How much is the caravan worth after 3 years?

Circumference of a circle

The perimeter of a circle is called the *circumference*.

The distance from the centre of a circle to the circumference is called the *radius*.

The distance across a circle through its centre is called the *diameter*.

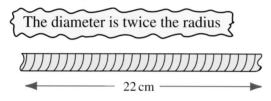

The diameter is twice the radius

← 22 cm →

A piece of string 22 cm long will make:

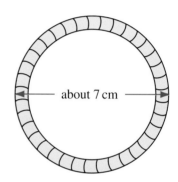

← about 7 cm →

A circle whose diameter is just over 7 cm.

If you divide the circumference of a circle by its diameter the number you obtain is always just over 3,

in fact   3.14159265.....

This number has many digits so it is more convenient to give the number a name.

We call it 'pi'.

This is the Greek letter π.

$$\pi = 3.14159265\dots$$

Most calculators have a $\boxed{\pi}$ button.

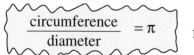

$$\frac{\text{circumference}}{\text{diameter}} = \pi$$ for any circle

so circumference = π × diameter

$C = \pi d$ *Learn* this formula.

Find the circumference of each of the circles below (Give your answer correct to 1 decimal place).

(a)

$C = \pi d$

$C = \pi \times 12 = 37.7$ cm.
(sometimes π is not worked out
and the answer is left as 12π)

(b)

radius is 3 cm so diameter = 6 cm

$C = \pi d$

$C = \pi \times 6 = 18.8$ cm.

M15.3

When necessary, give answers to 1 decimal place.

1 *Use a calculator* to find the circumference of each circle below.

(a)　　　　　　(b)　　　　　　(c)　　　　　　(d)

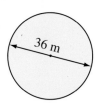

(e)　　　　　　(f)　　　　　　(g)　　　　　　(h)

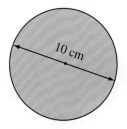

2 Which shape below has the larger perimeter – the square or the circle?

8 cm

10 cm

3 Kris walks around the edge of a circular lake of radius 250 m. If Kris walks once around the lake, how far does he walk? (Give your answer to the nearest metre)

391

(a) Find the perimeter of this shape (give the answer to 1 decimal place).

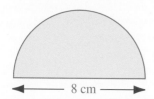

8 cm

The curved part is a semi-circle.

8 cm

$C = \pi d$ (whole circle)

$C = \pi \times 8 = 25.13$

We want half the circumference
= 25.13 ÷ 2 = 12.57

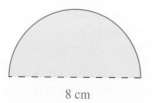

8 cm

Add on the straight line 8 cm

Perimeter of shape = 12.57 + 8 = 20.57

Perimeter = 20.6 cm (to 1 decimal place)

(b) A football of diameter 28 cm rolls in a straight line so that it makes 15 complete revolutions. How far does it roll? (Give your answer to the nearest cm).

$C = \pi d$

$C = \pi \times 28 = 87.96$

For one revolution (360° turn) the football rolls 87.96 cm (one circumference)

For 15 revolutions, the football rolls 15 × 87.96

= 1319.4 cm

= 1319 cm (to the nearest cm)

(ie. 13.19 m)

E15.3

Calculate the perimeter of each shape. All arcs are either semi-circles or quarter circles. Give answers correct to 1 decimal place.

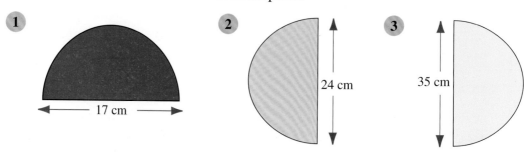

1   17 cm

2   24 cm

3   35 cm

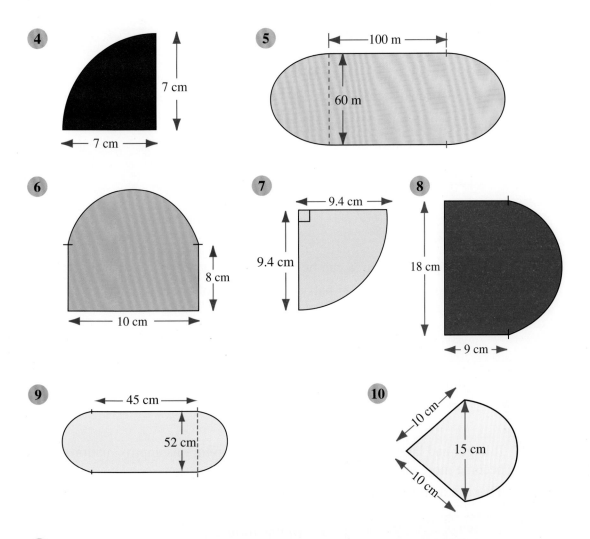

4 7 cm, 7 cm

5 100 m, 60 m

6 8 cm, 10 cm

7 9.4 cm, 9.4 cm

8 18 cm, 9 cm

9 45 cm, 52 cm

10 10 cm, 10 cm, 15 cm

11 The wheels on Inzaman's bike have a diameter of 65 cm. He travels so that the wheels go round completely 10 times. What distance does Inzaman travel? (Give your answer to the nearest cm).

12 Dan kicks a football down the side of a steep hill and it rolls 80 metres. If the diameter of the football is 27 cm, how many *complete* revolutions did the football make before it stopped?

13 A car tyre has a radius of 41 cm.

(a) How long is its circumference in cm?

(b) How many complete revolutions will the tyre make if the car travels 5 km?

14 The circumference of a circular plate is 91 cm. Calculate the diameter of the plate to the nearest cm.

15 A propeller rotates at 150 revolutions per minute. If the radius is 40 cm, how far does the end of the propeller travel in one hour? (Give your answer to the nearest kilometre).

(a) The circle below is divided into 12 equal sectors

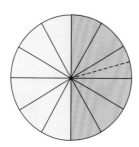

(b) The sectors are cut and arranged to make a shape which is nearly a rectangle. (one sector is cut in half).

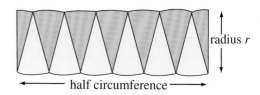

radius r

half circumference

(c) The approximate area can be found as follows:

length of rectangle $\approx$ half circumference of circle

$$\approx \frac{\pi \times 2r}{2} = \pi r^2$$

$$\approx \pi r^2$$

width of rectangle $\approx r$

$\therefore$ area of rectangle $\approx \pi r \times r$

$$\approx \pi r^2$$

If larger and larger numbers of sectors were used, this approximation would become more and more accurate.

This is a demonstration of an important result.

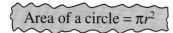

Area of a circle $= \pi r^2$ *Learn* this formula.

Note: πr^2 means 'r^2 then multiply by π'

Find the area of each of the circles below (give your answer correct to 1 decimal place).

(a)

8 cm

radius $= 8$ cm

area $= \pi r^2$

$= \pi \times 8^2$

$= \pi \times 64$

$= 201.1$ cm^2

(an 'exact' value of 64π could be given)

(b)

37 cm

diameter $= 37$ cm

so radius $= 37 \div 2 = 18.5$ cm

area $= \pi r^2$

$= \pi \times 18.5^2$

$= \pi \times 342.25$

$= 1075.2$ cm^2

In questions **1** to **9** , calculate the area of each circle correct to 1 decimal place.

1

9 cm

2

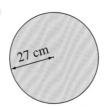

27 cm

3

3.7 cm

4

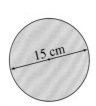

15 cm

5

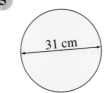

31 cm

6

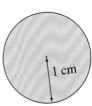

1 cm

7

50 cm

8

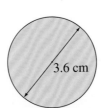

3.6 cm

9

8.7 cm

10 Tania creates a circular flower bed of radius 1.5 m. What is the area of this flower bed in m²?

11 Which shape below has the larger area – the rectangle or the circle?

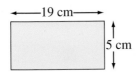

←—19 cm—→

5 cm

11.2 cm

12 Do *not* use a calculator in this question. Find the area of each circle, leaving π in your answer (for example, 18π).

(a)

2 cm

(b)

6 cm

(c)

20 cm

Find the area of this shape (give the answer correct to 1 decimal place).

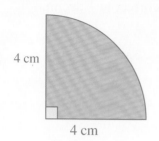

4 cm

4 cm

Area of circle $= \pi r^2$

$= \pi \times 4^2$

$= \pi \times 16 = 50.27$

Area of the quarter circle $= 50.27 \div 4$

$= 12.6 \text{ cm}^2$
(to 1 decimal place)

E15.4

In questions **1** to **6** find the area of each shape. All arcs are either semi-circles or quarter circles and the units are cm. Give answers correct to 1 decimal place.

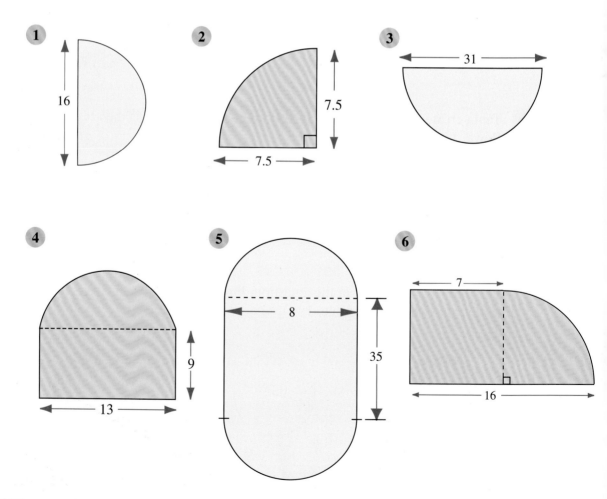

1

16

2

7.5

7.5

3

31

4

9

13

5

8

35

6

7

16

In questions ⑦ to ⑫ find the blue area. Lengths are in cm. Give answers correct to 1 decimal place.

7

8

9

10

11

12

Can you still?

Can you still?

15B   **Probability (see Unit 11)**

1. Jake has 11 cards as shown below:

S T I C K W I T H I T

   Jake picks a card at random. What is the probability that he picks the letter:

   (a) K?   (b) T?   (c) a letter in the first half of the alphabet?

2. Rena has 19 pencils. 9 are red, 3 are blue and the rest are black.

   Rena takes out a pencil at random. What is the probability that she takes out:

   (a) red?   (b) black?   (c) blue or black?

3. A dice is thrown 240 times. How many times would you expect to get:

   (a) a 5?   (b) an odd number?   (c) a square number?

4. The probability that Pat will remember to bring his textbook to his next maths lesson is 0.8. How many times would you expect him to bring his textbook in the next 30 lessons?

Key Facts

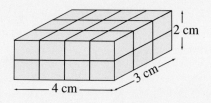

> Volume = length × width × height

Volume = 4 × 3 × 2
= 12 × 2
= 24 cm³

The cuboid has 6 faces.

Face		area (cm²)
Front	4 × 2 =	8
Back	4 × 2 =	8
Top	4 × 3 =	12
Bottom	4 × 3 =	12
Side 1	3 × 2 =	6
Side 2	3 × 2 =	6
Total		52

Total surface area = 52 cm²

M15.5

1

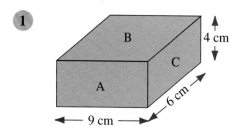

Write down the area of:

(a) the front face A

(b) the top face B

(c) the side face C

2 Copy and complete the tables below to find the total surface area of each cuboid.

(a)

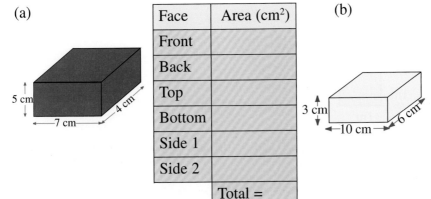

Face	Area (cm²)
Front	
Back	
Top	
Bottom	
Side 1	
Side 2	
Total =	

(b)

Face	Area (cm²)
Front	
Back	
Top	
Bottom	
Side 1	
Side 2	
Total =	

(c)

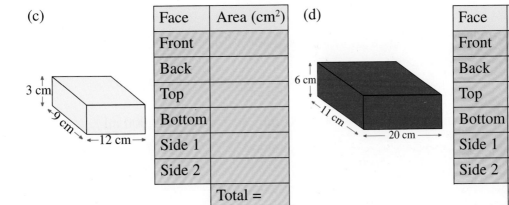

Face	Area (cm²)
Front	
Back	
Top	
Bottom	
Side 1	
Side 2	
Total =	

(d)

Face	Area (cm²)
Front	
Back	
Top	
Bottom	
Side 1	
Side 2	
Total =	

3 Find the volume of each cuboid in question **2** . (The units for each answer will be cm³)

4 Which of these 3 cuboids has the largest surface area?

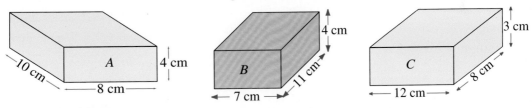

5

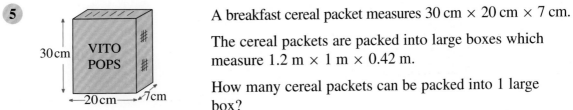

A breakfast cereal packet measures 30 cm × 20 cm × 7 cm.

The cereal packets are packed into large boxes which measure 1.2 m × 1 m × 0.42 m.

How many cereal packets can be packed into 1 large box?

6 How many 2 cm × 2 cm × 2 cm cubes will fit into a box which measures 30 cm × 12 cm × 18 cm?

Length: 1 m = 100 cm

Area: 1 m × 1 m = 100 cm × 100 cm

 1m / 1m

1 m² = 10000 cm²

100 cm / 100 cm

Volume: 1 m × 1 m × 1 m = 100 cm × 100 cm × 100 cm

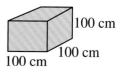 1m / 1m / 1m

1 m³ = 1000000 cm³

100 cm / 100 cm / 100 cm

Capacity:

1 litre = 1000 ml   1 ml is the same as 1cm³

From above, 1 m³ = 1000 000 cm³ so 1 m³ = 1000 000 ml

so   1 m³ = 1000 litres

(a) A rectangular tank measures 2 m by 1.2 m by 1.1 m. If the tank is completely full of water, how many litres of water does it contain?

Volume = 2 × 1.2 × 1.1

= 2.64 m³

= 2.64 × 1000 litres

= 2640 litres.

(b)

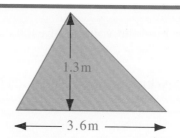

1.3 m

3.6 m

Find the area *in cm²*.

either

Area = $\frac{1}{2}$bh = $\frac{1}{2}$ × 3.6 × 1.3

= 2.34 m²

= 2.34 × 10000 cm²

= 23400 cm²

or change lengths first

Area = $\frac{1}{2}$bh = $\frac{1}{2}$ × 360 cm × 130 cm

= 23400 cm²

1 How many litres of water will each tank below contain when full.

(a)

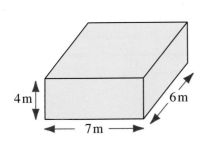

4m · 6m · 7m

(b)

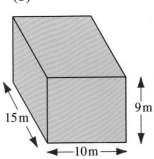

15m · 9m · 10m

(c)

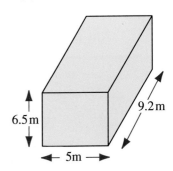

6.5m · 9.2m · 5m

2 Find the area of each shape below *in cm²*.

(a)

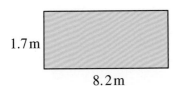

1.7m · 8.2m

(b)

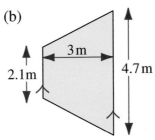

3m · 2.1m · 4.7m

(c)

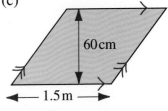

60cm · 1.5m

3 Copy and complete

(a) $1 \text{ m}^3 = \boxed{} \text{ cm}^3$

(b) $2 \text{ m}^3 = \boxed{} \text{ cm}^3$

(c) $4.7 \text{ m}^3 = \boxed{} \text{ cm}^3$

(d) $1 \text{ m}^2 = \boxed{} \text{ cm}^2$

(e) $3 \text{ m}^2 = \boxed{} \text{ cm}^2$

(f) $80000 \text{ cm}^2 = \boxed{} \text{ m}^2$

(g) $35000 \text{ cm}^2 = \boxed{} \text{ m}^2$

(h) $9.25 \text{ m}^2 = \boxed{} \text{ cm}^2$

(i) $1 \text{ m}^3 = \boxed{} \text{ litres}$

(j) $7 \text{ m}^3 = \boxed{} \text{ litres}$

(k) $5600 \text{ litres} = \boxed{} \text{ m}^3$

(l) $3.9 \text{ m}^3 = \boxed{} \text{ cm}^3$

4

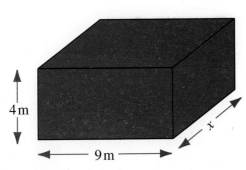

4m · 9m · x

The capacity of this rectangular tank is 72000 litres.

Find the missing value *x*.

Prisms

A prism has the same cross section throughout its length.

> Volume of prism = (Area of cross section) × (length)

Any cuboid is a prism since it has the same cross section throughout its length.

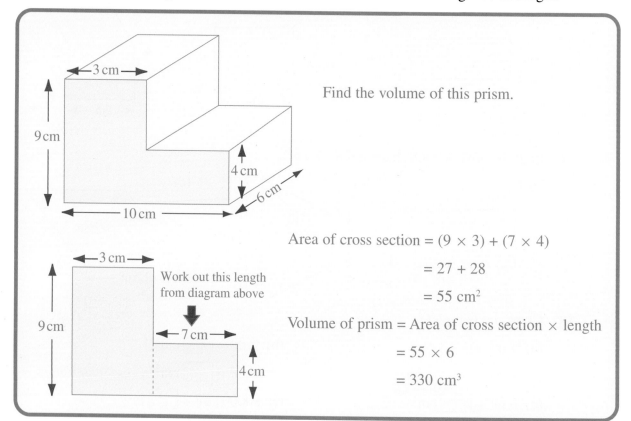

Find the volume of this prism.

Area of cross section = (9 × 3) + (7 × 4)

$$= 27 + 28$$

$$= 55 \text{ cm}^2$$

Volume of prism = Area of cross section × length

$$= 55 × 6$$

$$= 330 \text{ cm}^3$$

Work out this length from diagram above

M15.6

1 Which of the solids below are prisms?

(a)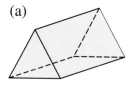

(b)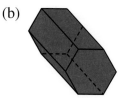

(c)

(d)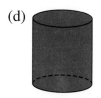

(e)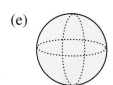

(f)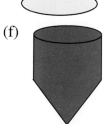

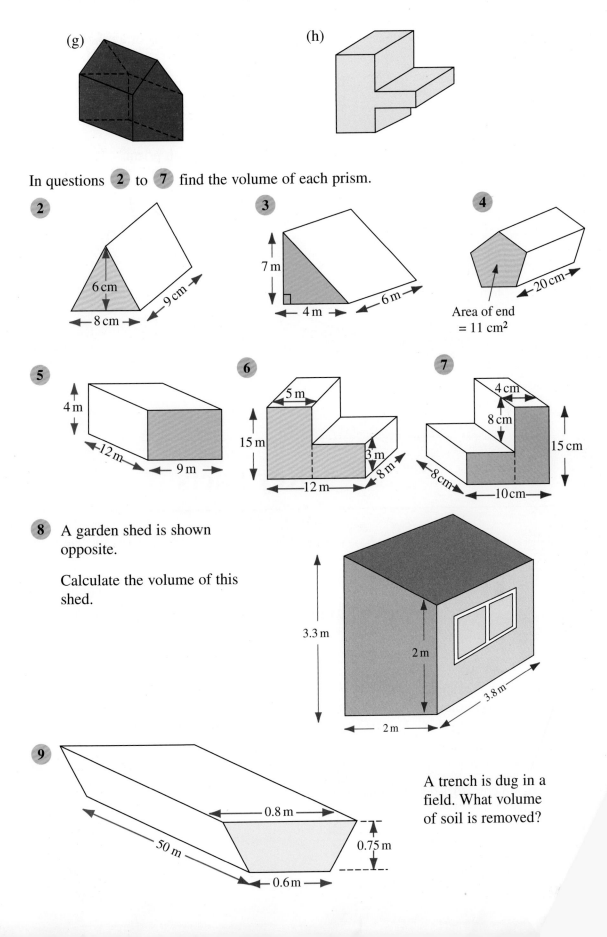

(g)

(h)

In questions **2** to **7** find the volume of each prism.

2

6 cm

8 cm

9 cm

3

7 m

4 m

6 m

4

20 cm

Area of end
= 11 cm²

5

4 m

12 m

9 m

6

5 m

15 m

12 m

3 m

8 m

7

4 cm

8 cm

15 cm

8 cm

10 cm

8 A garden shed is shown opposite.

Calculate the volume of this shed.

3.3 m

2 m

3.8 m

2 m

9

0.8 m

50 m

0.75 m

0.6 m

A trench is dug in a field. What volume of soil is removed?

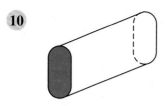

10 A piece of metal is in the shape of a prism. It has a volume of 6400 cm³.

If the area of the cross section is 32 cm², how long is the piece of metal?

In questions **11** and **12** find the *total surface area* of each prism.

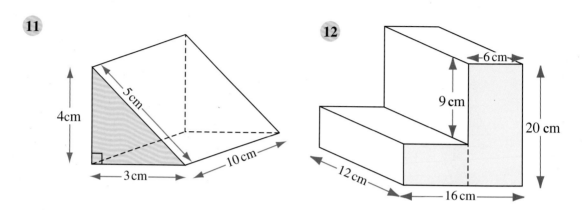

11 5 cm, 4 cm, 3 cm, 10 cm

12 6 cm, 9 cm, 20 cm, 12 cm, 16 cm

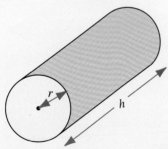

🔑 Key Facts

A cylinder is a prism because it has the same cross section throughout its length.

Volume = (area of cross section) × (length)

Volume = $\pi r^2 \times h$

$$V = \pi r^2 h$$

A cylinder has radius 5 cm and length 8 cm. Find the volume of the cylinder.

$V = \pi r^2 h$

$V = \pi \times 5^2 \times 8$

$V = 628.3$ cm³ (to 1 decimal place)

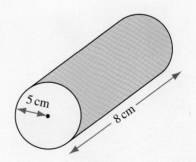

5 cm, 8 cm

Use a calculator and give answers to 1 decimal place where necessary.

In questions **1** to **6** find the volume of each cylinder.

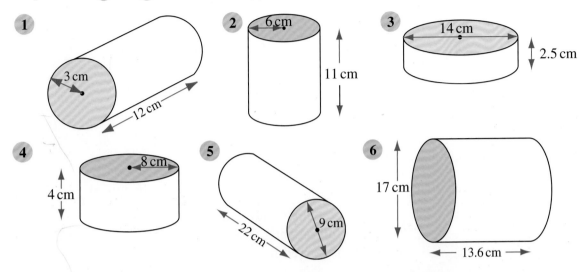

7 Find the volume of a cylindrical container of radius 2 m and height 10 m. Leave π in your answer (for example, 24π).

8 Find the volume in *litres* of a cylindrical tank of diameter 2.4 m and height 1.9 m.

9 Which of the cylinders below has the larger volume?

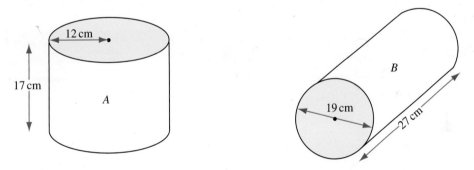

10 A cylindrical can of dog meat has a radius of 3.5 cm and a height of 11 cm. If the can contains 400 cm³ of dog meat, how much empty space is there inside the can? (Give your answer correct to 1 decimal place).

11 Cylinders are cut along the axis of symmetry. Find the volume of each object. (Give answers correct to 1 decimal place).

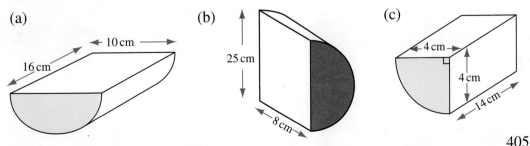

12  2 litres of lemonade is 2000 cm³.

How many glasses of radius 2.5 cm and height 10 cm can be completely filled from the bottle of lemonade?

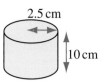

13 A 300 m tunnel is dug. It forms a prism with the cross section shown.

(a) Calculate the area of the cross section.

(b) Calculate the volume of earth which is dug out for the tunnel.

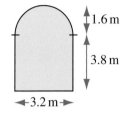

14 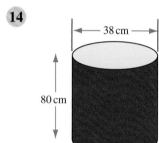 A cylindrical barrel is full of water. The water is poured into a trough as shown.

Will all the water go in without the trough overflowing?

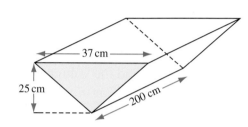

Similar triangles

Two triangles are *similar* if they have the same angles.

Corresponding sides must be in the same proportion.

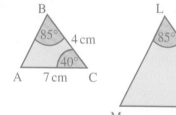

Find x

The triangles are similar because all 3 angles are the same.

Sides BC and LN correspond.

LN is $\frac{12}{4}$ times longer, ie. 3 times longer.

Each side in the larger triangle is 3 times longer than the corresponding side in the smaller triangle.

Sides MN and AC correspond so $x = 7 \times 3 = 21$ cm.

1 For each part of the Question below, the shapes are similar. Find x.

(a)

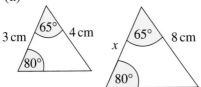

(b)

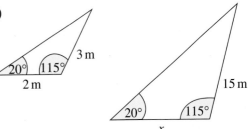

(c)

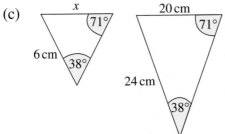

(d)

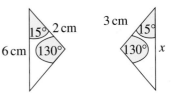

2

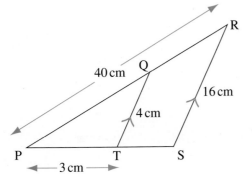

Triangles PQT and PRS are similar.

(a) Find PS

(b) Find PQ

3

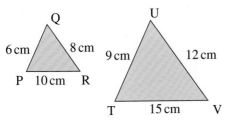

Explain why these triangles are similar.

4 Use similar triangles to find x in each diagram below.

(a)

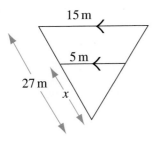

(b)

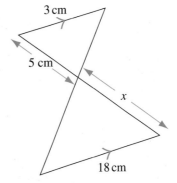

407

5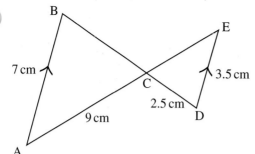

Triangles ABC and CDE are similar.

(a) Find BC

(b) Find CE

6 Use similar triangles to find *x*.

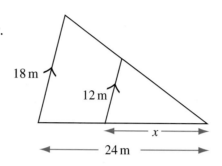

7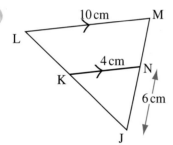

Use similar triangles to find the length of MN.

8 Use similar triangles to find *x* in each diagram below.

(a)

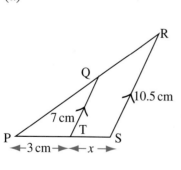

(b)

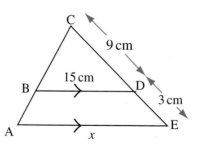

(c)

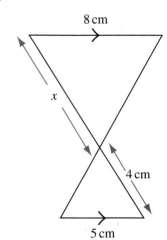

15C **General shape work (see units 3, 8 and 15)**

1. Each small square has a length of 1 cm.
   Find the perimeter of this shape.

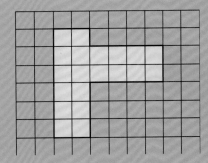

2.

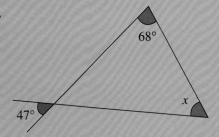

Find the size of angle *x*. Give reasons for your answer.

3.

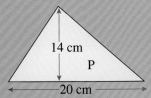

Which shape has the larger area and by how much?

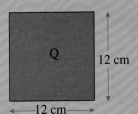

4.

Draw a different rectangle which has the same area as this rectangle.

5.

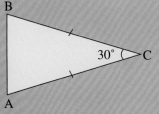

This is an isosceles triangle.
Work out the size of angle ABC.

(more questions on next page)

6.

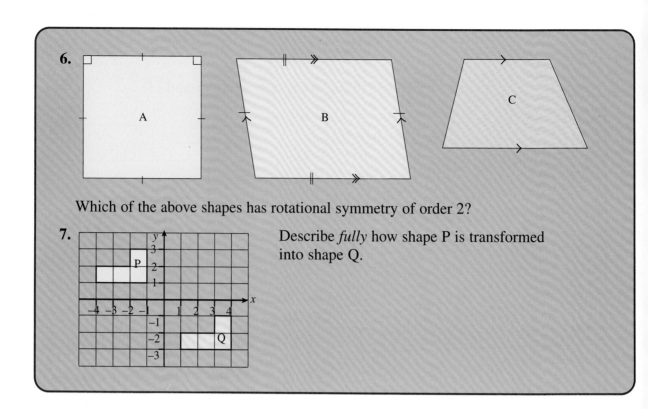

Which of the above shapes has rotational symmetry of order 2?

7.

Describe *fully* how shape P is transformed into shape Q.

How do you spot the best value in a shop?

A pack of 2 kitchen rolls £1.20

A pack of 3 kitchen rolls £1.71

To compare the cost, find the cost of 1 kitchen roll (the *unit* cost) for each pack.

2 rolls for £1.20 gives 60 p per roll

3 rolls for £1.71 gives 57 p per roll

The pack of 3 rolls is the *best value* (obviously you would only buy the pack of 3 kitchen rolls if you do not mind having that many rolls or have enough money to buy that pack at that particular moment).

Marshmallows £2.25 750 g	Which packet of Marshmallows is the best value?	Marshmallows £1.60 500 g

750 g costs 225 p, so 1g costs $\dfrac{225}{750} = 0.3$ p

500 g costs 160 p, so 1g costs $\dfrac{160}{500} = 0.32$ p

so the 750 g box is the best value.

OR

500 g costs 160 p so 250 g costs 80 p

At this price, 3×250 g = 750 g costs 3×80 p = £2.40

This is more expensive than the 750 g box.

Task

For each of questions **1** to **4**, decide which is the better value.

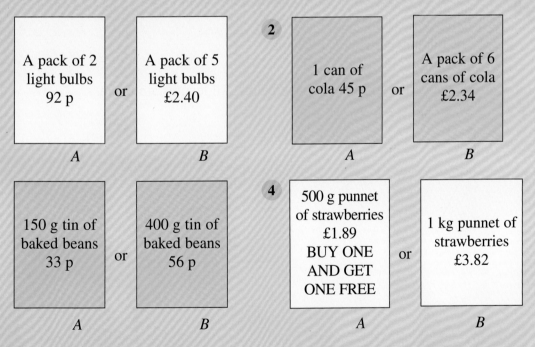

1

A pack of 2 light bulbs 92 p	or	A pack of 5 light bulbs £2.40
A		*B*

2

1 can of cola 45 p	or	A pack of 6 cans of cola £2.34
A		*B*

3

150 g tin of baked beans 33 p	or	400 g tin of baked beans 56 p
A		*B*

4

500 g punnet of strawberries £1.89 BUY ONE AND GET ONE FREE	or	1 kg punnet of strawberries £3.82
A		*B*

5 Carl is buying paper plates and plastic cups for a party. Paper plates cost 80 p for a pack of 20 or £1.50 for a pack of 50.

Plastic cups cost 78 p for a pack of 12 or £1.80 for a pack of 30.

Carl needs 60 plates and 75 cups. What is the cheapest way of buying them?

411

6 Jordan buys some tomato ketchup from the local supermarket. There are 3 different sized bottles.

| A | 600 g PLUS 20% EXTRA £1.26 | B | 750 g £1.50 | or C | 1 kg £1.90 |

Which bottle gives the best value for money?

7 Which box of washing powder below is the best value?

| A | 650 g £2.47 | B | 925 g £3.33 | or C | 1.2 kg £4.50 |

TEST YOURSELF ON UNIT 15

1. Finding perimeters of shapes

Find the perimeter of each shape below. All lengths are in cm.

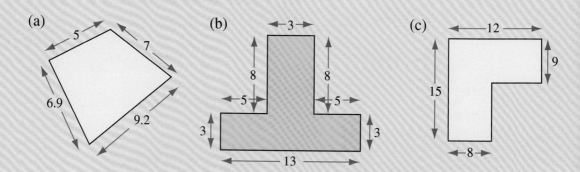

(a) 5, 7, 6.9, 9.2

(b) 3, 8, 8, 5, 5, 3, 3, 13

(c) 12, 9, 15, 8

(d)
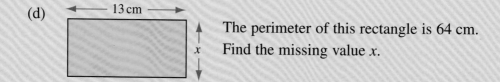
13 cm, x

The perimeter of this rectangle is 64 cm.
Find the missing value x.

2. Finding areas of triangles and rectangles

Find the area of each shape below. All lengths are in cm.

(a)   (b)   (c)

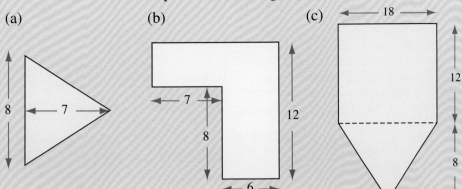

3. Finding areas of trapeziums and parallelograms

Find the area of each shape below. All lengths are in cm.

(a)   (b)   (c)

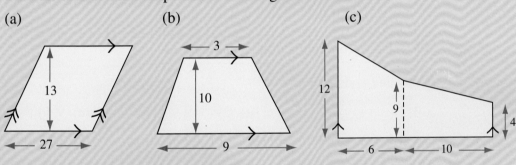

4. Finding circumferences of circles

Use a calculator to find the circumference or perimeter of each shape below. When necessary, give answers to 1 decimal place.

(a)   (b)   (c)

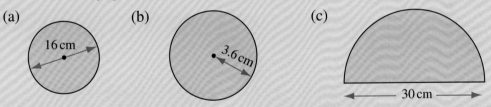

5. Finding areas of circles

Use a calculator to find the area of each shape below. When necessary, give answers to 1 decimal place.

(a)   (b)   (c)

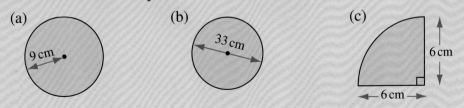

413

(d) Find the blue area.

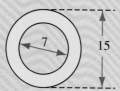

---

6. Finding surface areas and volumes of cuboids

Find (i) the volume and (ii) the total surface area of each cuboid below.

(a)

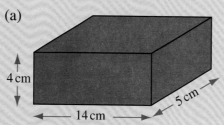

(b)

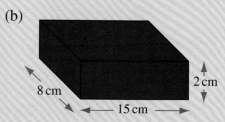

(c) A cuboid has a length of 20 cm and a width of 5 cm. What is the height of the cuboid if the volume is 320 cm³?

---

7. Converting units of area and volume

Copy and complete

(a) 1 m² = ☐ cm²

(b) 5 m³ = ☐ cm³

(c) 9.4 m³ = ☐ cm³

(d) 5.6 m² = ☐ cm²

(e) 2 m³ = ☐ litres

(f) 3.72 m³ = ☐ litres

(g) How many litres of water will this tank contain when full?

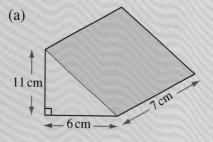

(h) Find the area of the shape below in cm².

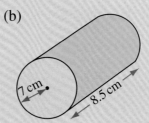

---

8. Finding volumes of prisms, particularly cylinders

Find the volume of each prism below. When necessary, give answers to 1 decimal place.

(a)

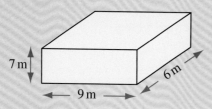

(b)

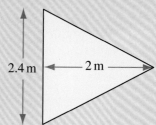

(c)

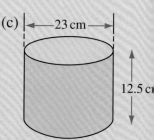

9. Using similar triangles

(a)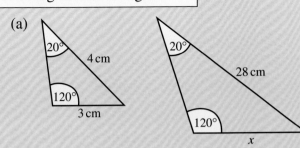

These 2 triangles are similar.

Find x.

(b)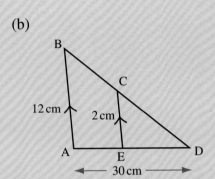

Find the length of DE.

(c)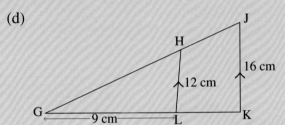

Find the length of QR.

(d)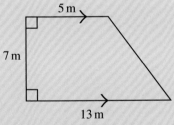

Find the length of LK.

Mixed examination questions

1

Work out the area of the shape.

(CCEA)

2 A circular pond has radius 8.2 metres.

(a) Calculate the circumference of the pond.

(b) Calculate the area of the pond.

(OCR)

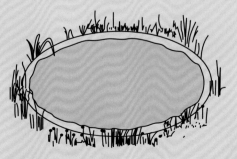

415

3 A photo frame is a square of side 20 cm.

It has a circular glass section and the rest is brass.

Work out the area of the brass part of the photo frame.
Take the value of π to be 3.142.

Give your answer to an appropriate degree of accuracy.　　(OCR)

4 Change 8 m³ to cm³.

5 The diagram shows a bale of straw.

The bale is a cylinder with radius 70 cm and
height 50 cm.

(a) Calculate the circumference of the bale.

Give your answer to an appropriate
degree of accuracy.

(b) Calculate the volume of the bale.

State your units.　　(AQA)

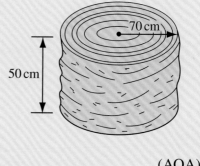

6 The diagram shows a right-angled
triangle *ABC* and a circle. *A, B* and *C*
are points on the circumference of
the circle. *AC* is a diameter of the
circle. The radius of the circle is
10 cm. *AB* = 16 cm and *BC* = 12 cm.
Work out the area of the shaded part
of the circle. Give your answer
correct to the nearest cm².

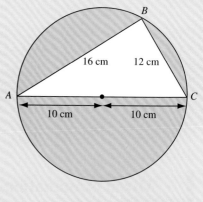

(EDEXCEL)

7 The area of a trapezium is 7430 mm².

Change 7430 mm² to cm².

8 The roof of a barn is a triangular prism as
shown in the diagram. The dimensions, in
metres, are given on the diagram.

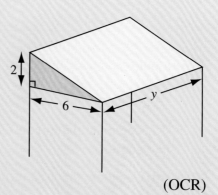

The volume of the roof space is 48 m³.
Work out the length of the roof, *y* metres.　　(OCR)

In this unit you will learn how to:

– draw scatter diagrams and describe correlation

– draw a line of best fit and use it to estimate values

– find the median and mode from tables of information

– find mean averages from tables of information (including grouped data)

– compare sets of data

– ⟨ USE YOUR MATHS! ⟩ – car insurance

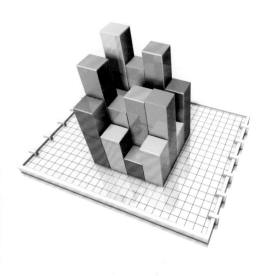

Scatter graphs

Sometimes it is important to find out if there is a connection between 2 sets of data.

Examples

• Do tall people weigh more?

• Do people who smoke die younger?

• Do people drink more when the weather is hot?

If there is a relationship, it will be easy to spot if the data is plotted on a scatter diagram – that is a graph in which one set of data is plotted on the horizontal axis and the other on the vertical axis.

• Here is a scatter diagram showing the number of hours without sleep for a group of people and their reaction time.

• We can see a connection. The longer people went without sleep, the greater their reaction time (ie. people reacted more slowly as they went without sleep).

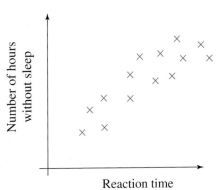

417

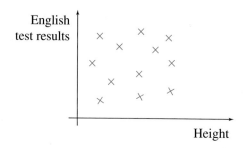

- This scatter graph shows the English test results for a group of students and their heights. We can see there is *no connection* between these 2 sets of data.

Correlation

The word 'correlation' describes how things *co-relate*. There is 'correlation' between 2 sets of data if there is a connection or relationship.

The correlation between 2 sets of data can be positive or negative and it can be strong or weak.

When the points are around a line which slopes *upwards* to the right, the *correlation* is *positive* (as the values for one set of data increases, the values for the other set of data also increases).

Strong correlation – the points are bunched close to a line through their midst.

Weak correlation – the points are more scattered.

No correlation

Points are completely spread out.

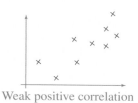

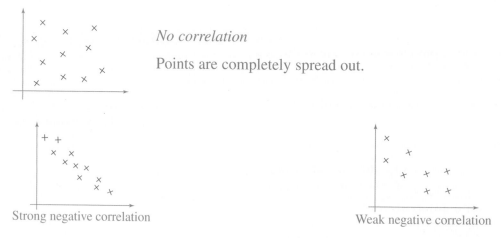

When the points are around a line which slopes *downwards* to the right, the *correlation* is *negative* (as the values for one set of data increases, the values for the other set of data decreases).

1 The table below shows the number of days absence for fifteen year 10 pupils and their maths test results.

Number of days absent	5	9	0	1	10	7	0	5	2	9	10	2	6	8	4
Test score	7	3	10	9	2	5	9	6	8	4	3	9	6	4	7

(a) Copy and complete this scatter graph to show the data in the table (the first point (5, 7) is done for you).

(b) Describe the correlation in this scatter graph.

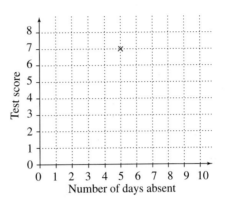

2 The table below shows the heights and weights of 12 people.

Weight (kg)	72	60	66	55	80	63	70	79	57	60	77	65
Height (cm)	175	167	177	168	184	173	180	188	171	173	178	170

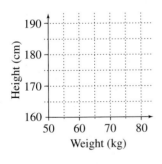

(a) Copy and complete this scatter graph to show the data in the table.

(b) Describe the correlation in this scatter graph.

3 Describe the correlation, if any, in these scatter graphs.

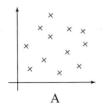

A

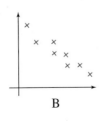

B

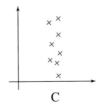

C

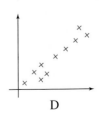

D

419

4 The table below shows the age and value of 12 used cars.

Age (years)	4	8	1	7	2	6	5	7	1	4	7	5
Value (£1000's)	7	2	8	3	7	2	6	5	9	5	4	4

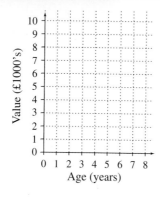

(a) Copy and complete this scatter diagram to show the data in the table.

(b) Describe the correlation in this scatter graph.

5 **Whole class activity**

(a) *If your teacher allows*, each person in your class must do as many step-ups onto a chair as possible in one minute. When a person finishes, that person must find his/her pulse rate by counting how many beats in one minute.

Also each person needs to find out his/her height (to the nearest cm) and record his/her shoe size.

Enter all the data in a table, either on the board or on a sheet of paper.

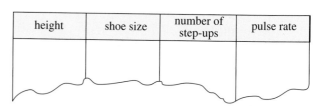

(b) Draw the scatter graphs shown below

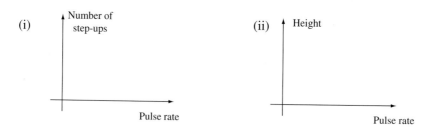

(c) Describe the correlation, if any, in the scatter graphs you drew in part (b).

(d) (i) Draw a scattergram of 2 sets of data where you think there might be positive correlation.

(ii) Was there indeed a positive correlation?

16A **Add, subtract, multiply and divide decimals**
(see Unit 9)

Do not use a calculator

1. Gary buys a magazine for £2.10 and spends £2.35 on the bus. How much change will he have left from £20?

2. Which calculation below gives the biggest answer?

   0.07×32 or 3.1×0.8 or 310×0.006

3. 5 friends go to a Premiership football game. The total cost is £167.50. How much does each friend pay if they split the cost equally?

4. Which sum below gives the larger answer?

   $2.7 + 9 + 1.36$ or $1.95 + 2.2 + 8$

5. Imran has £28.30 and spends £19.45. Terry has £41.65 and spends £32.90. Who has more money left?

6. A piece of wood 3.04 m long is cut into 8 equal pieces. How long will each short piece of wood be?

7. Copy the questions below and fill in the empty boxes.

   (a) $1.26 \div 0.3$ = ☐ ÷ 3 = ☐   (b) $2.76 \div 0.06$ = ☐ ÷ 6 = ☐

8. Copy and complete this number chain.

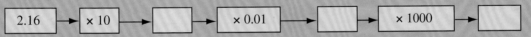

2.16 → × 10 → ☐ → × 0.01 → ☐ → × 1000 → ☐

Line of best fit

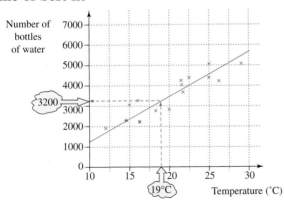

Number of bottles of water

7000
6000
5000
4000
3200
3000
2000
1000
0

10   15   19°C 20   25   30

Temperature (°C)

This scatter diagram shows the number of bottles of water sold by a supermarket each week and the average weekly temperature.

(a) A line of best fit is drawn (try to get the same number of points above the line as below).

(b) How many bottles of water are likely to be sold if the average weekly temperature is 19°C?

Draw a line up from the temperature axis to the line of best fit and then across to the vertical axis (as shown). We can estimate that 3200 bottles of water will be sold if the average weekly temperature is 19°C.

421

1 The table below shows the marks of 10 students in a Maths exam and a Science exam.

Maths	74	60	40	80	52	66	50	84	58	70
Science	70	62	44	76	54	56	46	70	56	64

(a) Copy and complete the scatter graph to show the data in the table.

(b) Draw the line of best fit.

(c) A student scored 72% in the Maths test but missed the Science test. Use your line of best fit to find out the Science mark that the student would have been most likely to get.

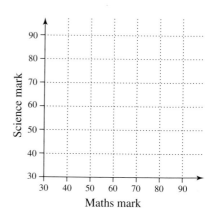

2 15 people were given a short term memory test where they could achieve a maximum score of 20. The table below shows their ages and marks.

Age	55	65	75	50	45	64	70	59	67	50	72	48	80	57	60
Score	17	12	10	16	18	13	15	15	15	17	12	19	10	15	12

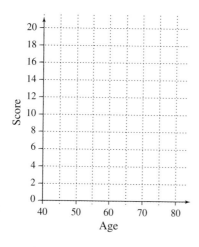

(a) Copy and complete the scatter diagram to show the data in the table.

(b) Draw the line of best fit.

(c) What score would you expect a 63 year-old to get?

3 In a certain area, 15 people are asked what their yearly household salary is and how much their house is worth. The information is shown in the table below.

Salary (£1000's)	47	70	23	40	32	55	15	49
Value of house (£1000's)	275	340	180	240	205	310	125	250

Salary (£1000's)	35	25	60	15	62	52	28
Value of house (£1000's)	250	210	130	300	290	275	190

(a) Draw a scatter diagram to show this data. Use the x-axis for salaries from 10 to 70. Use the y-axis for the values of the houses from 100 to 350.

(b) Draw the line of best fit.

(c) What would you expect the salary to be for the people living in a house worth £230,000?

(d) 2 points on the scatter diagram seem 'odd'. Give reasons why these points might have occurred.

4 A golfer records his weekly average score and how many hours be practises each week (in golf a score of 70 is *better* than a score of 80!). The information is shown in the table below.

Weekly average score	79	75	87	81	84	73	77	88	72	78	84	76
Weekly hours practising	22	24	19	21	22	23	24	17	26	22	19	21

(a) Draw a scatter graph to show this data. Use the x-axis for the weekly average score from 70 to 90. Use the y-axis for the weekly hours practising from 0 to 30.

(b) Describe the correlation in this scatter graph.

(c) Draw the line of best fit.

(d) If the golfer practised for 25 hours one week, what average score would you expect the golfer to get that week?

5 Information was recorded about 12 smokers. The table shows how many cigarettes they smoked each day and their age when they died.

Age	65	51	58	80	46	72	61	80	75	48	52	68
Number of cigarettes per day	37	42	40	10	44	23	35	20	26	49	44	32

(a) Draw a scatter graph to show this data. Use the x-axis for ages from 40 to 90. Use the y-axis for the number of cigarettes per day from 0 to 50.

(b) Describe the correlation in this scatter graph.

(c) Draw the line of best fit.

(d) If a person smoked 38 cigarettes each day, what age would you expect that person to live to?

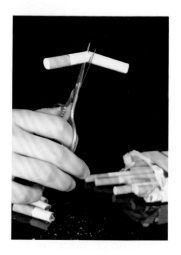

6 15 teenagers with part-time jobs were asked how much they earn each week and how much they spend on clothes/shoes on average each week. The information is shown in the table below.

Weekly earnings (£)	43	58	35	48	53	28	38	59	34	55	22	45	30	40	50
Weekly amount spent on clothes/shoes (£)	23	32	20	30	32	13	27	40	17	36	10	29	18	19	34

(a) Draw a scatter diagram to show this data. Use the x-axis for weekly earnings from 20 to 60. Use the y-axis for the weekly amount spent on clothes/shoes from 0 to 50.

(b) Describe the correlation in this scatter diagram.

(c) Draw the line of best fit.

(d) If a teenager earned £37 each week, how much would you expect the teenager to spend on clothes/shoes on average each week?

16B **Sequences (see Unit 12)**

1. For each sequence below, write down the *next 2 numbers*. What is the term-to-term rule for each sequence?

   (a) 29, 24, 19, 14,..

   (b) 48, 24, 12, 6,..

   (c) 2, 6, 12, 20,..

   (d) 64, 49, 36, 25,..

2. Sequence 8, 13, 18, 23,..

n	1	2	3	4
term	8	13	18	23
$5n$	5	10	15	20

   Use this table to find the nth term of the sequence.

3. Make a table like the one above to find the nth term of the sequence 6, 13, 20, 27,...

4. Here is a sequence of shapes made from sticks. Let n = shape number and s = number of sticks.

   $n = 1$
   $s = 6$

   $n = 2$
   $s = 10$

   $n = 3$
   $s = 14$

   (a) Draw the next shape in the sequence.

   (b) Find a formula for the number of sticks (s) for the shape number n.

   (c) Use the formula to find out how many sticks are in shape number 50.

Median and mode from tables of information

The table below shows the ages of some children.

Age	7	8	9	10
Frequency	4	2	1	2

Find (a) the modal age   (b) The median age

Answers

(a) 'frequency' is 'how many'. There are 4 ages of 7.
    7 occurs the most, so the mode = 7 (modal age)

425

(b) The table shows

7 7 7 7	8 8	9	10 10
4 lots	2 lots	1 lot	2 lots

The numbers are in order of size. The middle number is the median which is 8.

We do not want to have to write out all the numbers.
To find out the median directly from the table, add up the frequency row
$(4 + 2 + 1 + 2 = 9)$.

If you have n numbers, the middle number is always at position $\dfrac{n + 1}{2}$

M16.2

1 The table below shows the shoe sizes of some people.

Shoe size	6	7	8	9
Frequency	11	7	15	24

Find (a) the modal shoe size and (b) the median shoe size

2 The table below shows the heights of some children in year 11.

Height (cm)	171	172	173	174	175
Frequency	9	27	15	21	17

Find (a) the modal height and (b) the median height

3 Some people were asked how many holidays abroad they had taken in the last 2 years. The information is shown in the table below.

Number of holidays	0	1	2	3	4
Frequency	28	37	21	12	6

Find

(a) the modal number of holidays

(b) the median number of holidays

4 The 2 tables below show the number of visits made to the doctor during last year.

Number of visits	0	1	2	3	4
Frequency	32	29	15	9	3

14 to 21 year-olds

Number of visits	0	1	2	3	4
Frequency	8	19	42	35	31

Over 65 year-olds

(a) Find the median number of visits for *each* age group.

(b) Which age group has the higher median number of visits?

1 The table below shows how many days absence from school for some Year 10 pupils during the last term.

Number of days	0 to 2	3 to 5	6 to 8	over 8
Frequency	103	44	16	6

Find (a) the modal interval

(b) the interval which contains the median

2 The table below shows the weights of some newborn babies at the local hospital.

Weight (in pounds)	4 to 6	6 to 7	8 to 9	10 or more
Frequency	26	27	31	4

Find (a) the modal interval

(b) the interval which contains the median

3 The tables below show the salaries earned by workers in 2 firms,

EASITECH	
Salary (£1000's)	Frequency
4 to 6	7
7 to 10	15
11 to 15	29
16 to 25	36
26 or more	12

COMPFIX PLC	
Salary (£1000's)	Frequency
4 to 6	29
7 to 10	43
11 to 15	19
16 to 25	16
26 or more	13

(a) For each firm, find the interval which contains the median.

(b) For which firm do you think people generally earn more money? Explain why you think this.

4 This table shows how many goals were scored by the football teams in the Premiership one season.

Number of goals	Frequency
20 to 29	1
30 to 39	2
40 to 49	8
50 to 59	4
60 to 69	3
69 to 70	2

Find (a) the modal interval

(b) the interval which contains the median

427

Some students are asked how many pairs of shoes they have. The table shows the information.

Find the mean average.

$$\text{mean average} = \frac{\text{total number of pairs of shoes}}{\text{total number of people}}$$

Number of pairs of shoes	Frequency
1	5
2	3
3	3
4	5
5	4

total number of pairs of shoes
$$= (5 \times 1) + (3 \times 2) + (3 \times 3) + (4 \times 5) + (4 \times 5)$$
$$= 5 + 6 + 9 + 20 + 20 = 60$$

total number of people = total frequency = 5 + 3 + 3 + 5 + 4 = 20

so mean average $= \dfrac{60}{20} = 3$ pairs of shoes.

M16.3

Use a calculator if you need to.

1 This table shows the number of cars owned by people who live in Beech Grove.

(a) Find the total number of cars.

(b) Find the mean average.

Number of cars	Frequency
0	1
1	4
2	4
3	6

2 Some teenagers were asked how often they had been to the cinema in the last month. The information is shown in the table below.

Cinema trips	0	1	2	3	4	5
Frequency	98	42	34	15	8	3

(a) Find the total number of cinema trips.

(b) Find the mean average.

3

Number of children	Frequency
0	12
1	38
2	30
3	14
4	6

100 families are asked how many children they have. The information is recorded in this table.

(a) Find the total number of children.

(b) Find the mean average.

4 Some people were asked how many portions of fruit and vegetables they ate each day. The information is shown in the table below.

Number of portions	0	1	2	3	4	5	6	7
Frequency	17	20	16	28	11	4	3	1

(a) Find the total number of portions eaten.   (b) Find the mean average.

5 3 different hotels are rated by guests using a points score out of 20. The scores are shown in the table below.

HOTEL PARADISE	
Score	Frequency
14	21
15	38
16	33
17	49
18	17
19	24
20	6

HOTEL DE VERE	
Score	Frequency
14	31
15	21
16	49
17	42
18	21
19	17
20	9

TROPIC HOTEL	
Score	Frequency
14	86
15	91
16	33
17	75
18	61
19	47
20	18

(a) Work out the mean average for each hotel, giving your answers to 2 decimal places.

(b) Which hotel had the highest points score?

6 A group of young people visited Alton towers theme park. The number of major rides they had is shown in the table below.

Number of rides	2	3	4	5	6	7
Frequency	9	24	31	16	8	3

(a) Find the total number of rides.

(b) Find the mean average (give your answer to the nearest whole number).

Some year 11 students are asked how many CDs they have. The table shows the information.

Estimate the mean average.

We need to find the total number of CDs. The problem is we do not know *exactly* how many CDs each person has.

We will get a reasonable answer if we take the mid-value of each interval and assume that is how many CDs each person has.

Number of CDs	Frequency
0–9	28
10–19	18
20–29	33
30–39	21

To find the mid-value of an interval, add the first and last values then halve the answer.

For the 10–19 interval,

$$\text{mid-value} = \frac{10 + 19}{2} = 14.5$$

We now use the mid-value and the frequency to find the total number of CDs.

Number of CDs	Frequency	Mid-value
0–9	28	4.5
10–19	18	14.5
20–29	33	24.5
30–39	21	34.5

Total number of CDs = $(28 \times 4.5) + (18 \times 14.5) + (33 \times 24.5) + (21 \times 34.5)$

$$= 1920$$

Total number of people = total frequency = 28 + 18 + 33 + 21 = 100

$$\text{Mean average} = \frac{\text{total number of CDs}}{\text{total number of people}} = \frac{1920}{100} = 19.2 \text{ CDs.}$$

This is an *estimate* because we used the mid-values not the exact number of CDs.

Note

Sometimes the interval 10–19 might be written as $10 \leq n \leq 19$ where n is the number of CDs. ($n \leq 19$ means n is less than or equal to 19. See Unit 18 for more detail on inequalities.)

Examples

$20 \leq n \leq 29$ means n lies between 20 and 29 and can also equal 20 and 29.

$20 \leq n < 29$ means n lies between 20 and 29. It can equal 20 but it *cannot* equal 29.

1

Number of trips abroad	Frequency	Mid-value
0–2	6	
3–5	8	
6–10	5	8
11–15	1	

Some teenagers were asked how often they had been abroad in their lifetime. The information is shown in the table.

(a) Copy and complete the table.

(b) Estimate the total number of trips abroad.

(c) Estimate the mean average.

2 100 people were asked how many cups of tea they drank each week. The information is shown in the table.

(a) Copy and complete the table.

(b) Estimate the total number of cups of tea.

(c) Estimate the mean average.

Number of cups of tea (n)	Frequency	Mid-value
$0 \leq n < 10$	23	
$10 \leq n < 20$	29	15
$20 \leq n < 30$	38	
$30 \leq n < 40$	7	
$40 \leq n < 50$	3	45

3 The table below shows how many days off work were taken by staff at a hospital during the last year.

Number of days off work	0 to 9	10 to 19	20 to 29	30 to 39	40 to 59
Frequency	88	57	31	18	6
Mid-value					

(a) Copy and complete the table.

(b) Estimate the total number of days off work.

(c) Estimate the mean average.

4 The table below shows how many DVDs were owned by 250 families.

Number of DVD's (n)	$0 \leq n < 10$	$10 \leq n < 20$	$20 \leq n < 30$	$30 \leq n < 40$	$40 \leq n < 50$	$50 \leq n < 60$
Frequency	21	23	91	74	32	9
Mid-value						

(a) Estimate the total number of DVD's. (b) Estimate the mean average.

431

5 1000 people were asked how many hours of exercise they do during an average week. The information is shown in the table.

(a) Estimate the total number of hours of exercise.

(b) Estimate the mean average.

Number of hours of exercise (n)	Frequency
$0 \leq n < 1$	225
$1 \leq n < 3$	301
$3 \leq n < 5$	260
$5 \leq n < 7$	134
$7 \leq n < 9$	56
$9 \leq n < 12$	24

6 The tables below show the salaries earned by people in 3 different firms.

JETBUILD	
Salary(s) (£1000's)	Frequency
$4 \leq s < 6$	6
$6 \leq s < 10$	15
$10 \leq s < 15$	18
$15 \leq s < 25$	8
$25 \leq s < 70$	3

KABINSEAL	
Salary(s) (£1000's)	Frequency
$4 \leq s < 6$	8
$6 \leq s < 10$	21
$10 \leq s < 15$	24
$15 \leq s < 25$	17
$25 \leq s < 70$	5

(a) Which firm offers the higher mean average salary?

(b) Write down an estimate of this mean average salary.

7 The table below shows how many hours of TV were watched by 500 people last week.

Hours of TV (h)	$0 \leq h < 10$	$10 \leq h < 20$	$20 \leq h < 35$	$35 \leq h < 50$	$50 \leq h < 60$	$60 \leq h < 80$
Frequency	83	112	155	102	36	12

Estimate the mean average number of hours of TV watched.

8

Number of lengths swum (n)	Frequency
0 to 20	25
21 to 30	65
31 to 40	32
41 to 60	46
61 to 80	24
81 to 100	8

200 people took part in a sponsored swim. The table shows how many lengths they swam.

Estimate the mean number of lengths swum.

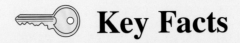

Key Facts

To compare 2 sets of data, always write at least 2 things:

1. Compare an *average* (i.e. mean, median or mode).

2. Compare the *range* of each set of data (this shows how spread out the data is).

---

6 members of the Harris family weigh 40 kg, 53 kg, 71 kg, 75 kg, 79 kg and 90 kg.

5 members of the Collins family weigh 61 kg, 62 kg, 84 kg, 86 kg and 87 kg.

Harris family: median = 73 kg (half way between 71 kg and 75 kg)
range = 90 – 40 = 50 kg

Collins family: median = 84 kg
range = 87 – 61 = 26 kg.

Compare the weights of the Harris family and the Collins family.

Answer

The *median* for the Harris family is less than the median for the Collins family but the *range* for the Harris family is greater than the range for the Collins family (i.e. the weights are more spread out).

M16.4

1 7 members of the Truman family weigh 46 kg, 51 kg, 52 kg, 67 kg, 74 kg, 79 kg and 82 kg.

4 members of the Jenkins family weigh 42 kg, 68 kg, 70 kg and 86 kg.

Copy and complete the statements below to compare the weights of the Truman family and the Jenkins family.

Truman family: median = _____ kg   range = _____ kg

Jenkins family: median = _____ kg   range = _____ kg

'The median for the Truman family is (*greater/smaller*) than the median for the Jenkins family and the range for the Truman family is (*greater/smaller*) than the range for the Jenkins family (i.e. weights for the Truman family are (*more/less*) spread out).'

433

2 Some 16 year-olds and 17 year-olds are asked how much they earn per hour in their part-time jobs. The information is shown below.

16 year-olds: £5	£4.50	£4.30	£4.80	£5.20		
	£5.75	£6.10	£5.15	£4.70	£4.60	
17 year-olds: £4.90	£5.30	£5	£5.25	£4.95	£6.20	£5.06 £5.50

Copy and complete the statements below to compare the hourly rate of pay for these 16 year-olds and 17 year-olds.

16 year-olds: mean = £ _____   range = £ _____

17 year-olds: mean = £ _____   range = £ _____

'The mean for the 16 year-olds is (*greater/smaller*) than the mean for the 17 year-olds and the range for the 16 year-olds is (*greater/smaller*) than the range for the 17 year-olds (i.e. the hourly rate of pay for the 16 year-olds is (*more/less*) spread out).'

3 The Wolves and the Sentinels are 2 basketball teams. The ages (in years) of the players in each team are listed below:

| The Wolves: | 23 | 18 | 19 | 25 | 20 | 27 | 23 | 22 | 20 | 26 |
| The Sentinels: | 22 | 28 | 19 | 27 | 21 | 21 | 29 | 21 | 25 | 22 |

Copy and complete the statements below to compare the ages of the players for the Wolves and the Sentinels.

The Wolves: median = _____   range = _____

The Sentinels: median = _____   range = _____

'The median for the Wolves is (*greater/smaller*) than the median for the Sentinels and the range for the Wolves is (*greater/smaller*) than the range for the Sentinels (i.e. the ages for the Wolves are (*more/less*) spread out).'

E16.4

1 The marks obtained by 2 classes in a maths test are shown in the back-to-back stem and leaf diagram.

Class 10A		Class 10B
9 6	4	3 3 7 8
7 7 7 3 2	5	0 1 4 6 6 6 8
9 9 8 8 4 1	6	2 5 5 8 9
6 6 5 2	7	4 5 7 7 9 9
8 7 4 0	8	1 3 6
1 1		2 4

(a) Find the median and range for each class.

(b) Write a sentence to compare the test marks for the two classes.

Key 4|6 = 64   Key 6|5 = 65

2 Ten students from year 10 and ten students from year 11 were asked how often they had their hair cut each year. The information is shown below:

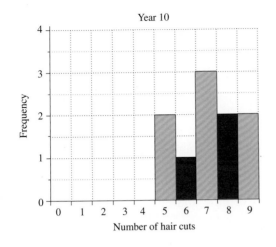

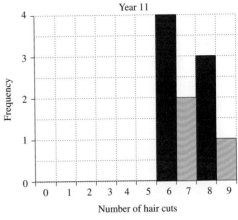

(a) Work out the mean and range for Year 10.

(b) Work out the mean and range for Year 11.

(c) Write a sentence to compare the number of hair cuts for the students in Year 10 and Year 11.

3 The tables below show how many televisions are owned by families living in 2 streets.

Ash Lane	
Number of TVs	Frequency
0	3
1	5
2	7
3	4
4	1

Tibbs Drive	
Number of TVs	Frequency
0	1
1	2
2	4
3	1
4	2

(a) Work out the mean and range for Ash Lane.

(b) Work out the mean and range for Tibbs Drive.

(c) Write a sentence to compare the number of televisions owned by families in Ash Lane and Tibbs Drive.

The law says you must have car insurance if you drive on public roads.

The car insurance will pay out money if you injure or kill somebody or damage another person's property.

The two main types of car insurance are:

Third party, fire and theft

This does not provide much cover for your own vehicle but will deal with the other person if you are responsible for the damage.

Fully comprehensive

This provides full cover for your own vehicle and any other vehicle involved.

Cost

The amount you pay for car insurance depends on several factors:

- the value of your car

- where your live

- your age

- if you have made a claim on the car insurance in recent years

No claims bonus

The amount you pay is reduced by 10% each year you do not claim on your car insurance. The biggest discount you can usually have is 60% which is a considerable saving. This percentage reduction is called the 'no claims bonus'.

The bonus is lost if you make a claim on your car insurance then you build up the bonus again over the next few years. Some people pay extra to protect their 'no claims bonus'.

Payments

Some people pay the annual (yearly) cost of their car insurance in one payment but many people spread the cost over 12 equal monthly instalments.

This year Karen's fully comprehensive car insurance quote is £700. She gets a 60% no claims bonus and wants to pay 12 equal monthly instalments. How much is each monthly payment (to the nearest penny)?

No claims bonus	= 60% of £700 = £420
Amount to pay	= £700 – £420 = £280
Monthly payment	= £ 280 ÷ 12 = £23.33 (to the nearest penny)

1   Warren is given a quote of £620 this year for third party, fire and theft insurance on his Nissan Micra. He gets a 60% no claims bonus and wants to pay 12 equal monthly instalments. How much is each monthly payment (to the nearest penny)?

2   Helen's fully comprehensive car insurance quote this year for her Astra is £1154. She has a 40% no claims bonus. If she pays 12 equal monthly instalments, how much is each payment (to the nearest penny)?

Copy and complete the table below to work out the monthly insurance payments for each car.

	Car	annual car insurance (£)	no claims bonus	annual insurance to pay (£)	monthly payment (£)
3	Corsa	950	60%	380	
4	Lexus	1260	60%		
5	Shogun	1530	30%		
6	Ford Escort	1125	50%		
7	Saab 900S	935	20%		
8	Ford Fiesta	870	60%		
9	VW Golf	1060	20%		

10 Sally bumps her car and has to claim on her car insurance. Her annual insurance is £1280. Before her claim she had a 60% no claims bonus. After the claim, her no claims bonus is reduced by 20% (ie. she has a 40% no claims bonus).

(a) What was her monthly payment before the claim?

(b) What is her monthly payment after the claim?

(c) How much more does she have to pay each month?

11 David is involved in a car accident and puts in a claim on his car insurance. His annual insurance is £1370. Before the accident he had a 50% no claims bonus. After the claim, his no claims bonus is reduced *to* 20%. How much more will he have to pay each month for his car insurance?

12 There are many other insurances that people are advised to take out, for example: life insurance, medical insurance, buildings insurance, contents insurance, critical illness insurance and income protection insurance.

(a) Find out what these insurances cover you for.

(b) **Discuss with your teacher** the advantages and disadvantages of taking out these types of insurance.

1. Drawing scatter diagrams and describing correlation

Describe the correlation, if any, in these scatter graphs.

(a)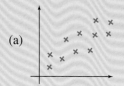

(b)

(c)

2. Drawing a line of best fit and using it to estimate values

The table below shows the engine sizes of 12 cars and how many miles per gallon they operate at.

Engine size (litres)	1.8	1.1	2	1.6	1	1.8	1.5	2.8	1.2	2	1.6	1.4	2.4	2.1
Miles per gallon	35	53	24	33	47	31	33	16	46	30	40	42	20	22

(a) Copy and complete the scatter diagram to show the data in the table.

(b) Draw the line of best fit.

(c) Use the line of best fit to estimate how many miles per gallon a 1.3 litre car would do.

(d) Roughly with what engine size would you expect the car to do 23 miles per gallon?

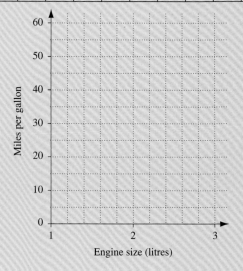

3. Finding the median and mode from tables of information

Some 16 year-olds were asked how many dental fillings they had been given during their lifetimes. The table shows the information.

Number of fillings	0	1	2	3	4	5
Frequency	12	17	24	18	7	3

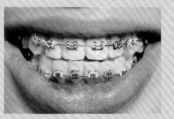

Find (a) the modal number of fillings

   (b) the median number of fillings

(a) This table shows the number of bicycles owned by families who live in Camden Terrace.

   (i) Find the total number of bicycles.

   (ii) Find the mean average.

Number of bicyles	Frequency
0	8
1	4
2	17
3	24
4	16
5	6

(b) The table below shows how many hours were spent using a computer by 200 people last week.

Hours using a computer(h)	$0 \le h < 5$	$5 \le h < 10$	$10 \le h < 20$	$20 \le h < 30$	$30 \le h < 40$	$40 \le h < 60$
Frequency	49	68	36	23	17	7

Estimate the mean number of hours spent using a computer.

5. Comparing sets of data

(a) 30 young people were asked how many cards they received on their last birthday (10 nine year-olds and 20 nineteen year-olds). The information is shown below:

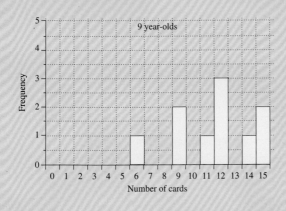
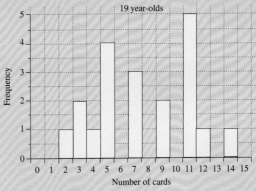

   (i) Work out the mean and range for the 9 year-olds.

   (ii) Work out the mean and range for the 19 year-olds.

   (iii) Use the means and ranges to *compare* the number of birthday cards received by 9 year-olds and 19 year-olds.

(b) The heights of 6 members of the Kallis family are 151 cm, 153 cm, 164 cm, 170 cm, 184 cm, and 186 cm.

The heights of 5 members of the Moore family are 162 cm, 169 cm, 175 cm, 177 cm and 180 cm.

(i) Find the median height and the range of the heights for each family.

(ii) Use the medians and ranges to *compare* the heights of the Kallis family and the Moore family.

Mixed examination questions

1 The table below shows the heights of a group of Year 7 pupils together with the height of each of their fathers. All measurements are in centimetres.

Pupil	A	B	C	D	E	F	G	H	I
Height of pupil	138	141	145	148	149	154	155	161	162
Height of father	151	155	153	170	161	176	185	186	192

(a) Draw a scatter graph to show this information.

The first three points are plotted for you.

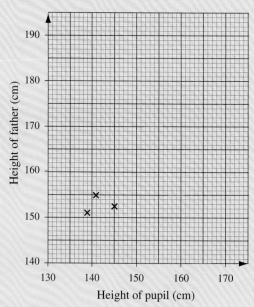

(b) Describe the correlation between the two sets of heights.

(c) Draw a line of best fit on the scatter diagram.

(d) A new pupil joins the group. His height is 151 cm. Use your line of best fit to estimate the height of his father.

(OCR)

2 Rosie had 10 boxes of drawing pins.

She counted the number of drawing pins in each box.

The table gives information about her results.

Number of drawing pins	Frequency	
29	2	
30	5	
31	2	
32	1	

(a) Write down the modal number of drawing pins in a box.

(b) Work out the range of the number of drawing pins in a box.

(c) Work out the mean number of drawing pins in a box.   (EDEXCEL)

3 One hundred batteries were tested to see how long they lasted.

The results are shown in the table below.

Time (t hours)	Frequency
$0 \leq t < 4$	12
$4 \leq t < 8$	20
$8 \leq t < 12$	34
$12 \leq t < 16$	25
$16 \leq t < 20$	9

Use the mid-points of the intervals to calculate an estimate of the mean time that a battery lasted.   (OCR)

4 The maximum load for a lift is 1200 kg.

The table shows the distribution of the weights of 22 people waiting for the lift.

Weight (w kg)	Frequency
$30 \leq w < 50$	8
$50 \leq w < 70$	10
$70 \leq w < 90$	4

Will the lift be overloaded if all of these people get in?

You must show working to support your answer.   (AQA)

441

In this unit you will learn how to:

– read scales

– use and convert metric units

– deal with 'time' problems

– use and convert imperial units

– convert between metric and imperial units

– find upper and lower bounds

– calculate with speed, density and other compound measures

– ⟨ USE YOUR MATHS! ⟩ – makeover

Reading scales

M17.1

For each of the scales work out:

    (a) the measurement indicated by each of the arrows.

    (b) the difference between the two arrows.

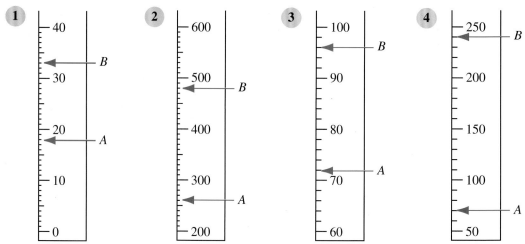

5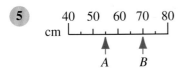

6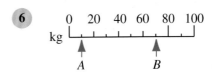

7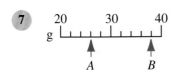

8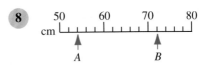

Write down the measurement shown by the arrow on each dial below.

9

10

11

12

13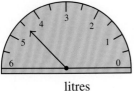

litres

14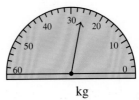

kg

Write down the time shown by each clock below:

15

16

17

18

19

20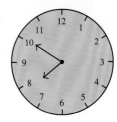

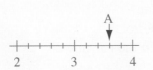

What number does *A* point to?

5 divisions cover 1 unit

so 1 division means $1 \div 5 = 0.2$

so *A* points to 3.6

For each of the scales work out:

(a) the measurement indicated by each of the arrows.

(b) the difference between the two arrows.

1

A   B

kg |++++++++|++++++++|
   7   8   9

2

A   B

cm |++++|++++|++++|
   4   5   6

3

A   B

litres |++++|++++|+|
       2   4   6

4

A   B

m |++++|++++|++++|
  16   17   18

5
- 0.6
← B
- 0.5

- 0.4

← A
- 0.3

litres

6
- 27

← B
- 26

- 25
← A
- 24

ml

7
- 47
← B
- 45

- 43
← A
- 41

ml

8
- 0.06
← B
- 0.05

- 0.04 ← A
- 0.03

kg

9

A   B

kg |+++|+++|+++|+++|
   6   7   8   9

10

A   B

cm |++|++|++++|++++|
   25   26   27   28

11

A   B

kg |++++|++++|++++|+|
   0.3   0.4   0.5   0.6

12

A   B

ml |++++|++++|++++|++|
   600   850   1100   1350

13
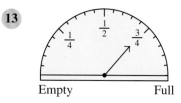

This is a fuel gauge on a car.
It is full with 50 litres of petrol.
How much petrol is there in the car now?

14 Here is another fuel gauge.
This is full with 60 litres of petrol.
How much petrol is there in the car now?

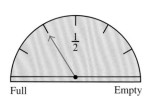

444

Write down the measurement shown by the arrow on each dial below.

15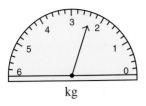
kg

16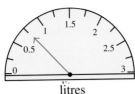
litres

17
kg

18
litres

19
ml

20
kg

Can you still?

17A **Draw graphs and find gradients (see Unit 10)**

Can you still?

1.

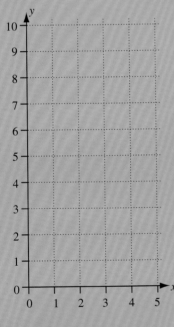

Draw these axes.

(a) Complete the table below then draw $y = 3x + 2$

x	0	1	2
y			

(b) Find the gradient of the line $y = 3x + 2$

(c) Complete the table below then draw $y = 5 - x$ on the same axes.

x	0	1	2
y			

(d) Find the gradient of the line $y = 5 - x$

2. Draw these axes.

Complete the table below then draw the curve $y = x^2 - 5$.

x	−3	−2	−1	0	1	2	3
y							

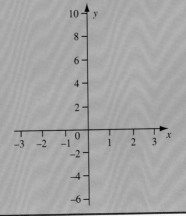

445

Key Facts

length	mass	volume
10 mm = 1 cm	1000 g = 1 kg	1000 ml = 1 litre or 1 l
100 cm = 1 m	1000 kg = 1 tonne	1 ml = 1 cm³
1000 m = 1 km		

Examples

Convert the following metric units.

(a) 7000 g into kg ⇨ ÷ 1000 ⇨ 7 kg

(b) 2.5 m into cm ⇨ × 100 ⇨ 250 cm

(c) 4.32 tonnes into kg ⇨ × 1000 ⇨ 4320 kg

(d) 400 ml into litres ⇨ ÷ 1000 ⇨ 0.4 l

M17.2

Write down which metric unit you would use to measure the following.

1. The distance from Bristol to London (m or km?)

2. The length of a pen (cm or mm?)

3. The mass of a dog (kg or tonnes?)

4. The length of a garden (cm or m?)

5. The contents of a full wine glass (litres or ml?)

6. The length of a submarine.

7. The mass of a tank.

8. The capacity of a bath full of water.

9. The mass of a nose stud.

10. The length of a CD case.

11 Write each length in cm.

(a) 7 m   (b) 4.5 m   (c) 1.62 m   (d) 50 mm   (e) 0.3 m

12 Write each mass in g.

(a) 5 kg   (b) 3.6 kg   (c) 9.2 kg   (d) 0.632 kg   (e) 6.42 kg

13 Write each volume in ml.

(a) 3 litres   (b) 24 cm^3 (c) 143 cm^3 (d) 9.6 litres   (e) 3.125 litres

14 Write each length in m.

(a) 8 km   (b) 300 cm   (c) 940 cm   (d) 6.3 km   (e) 8.092 km

15 Copy each sentence below and choose the most sensible estimate.

(a) A baby weighs (*400 g / 4 kg*).

(b) A bottle of wine contains (*7 ml / 0.7 l*).

(c) A woman weighs (*6 kg / 60 kg*).

(d) The height of the door is (*100 cm / 2 m*).

(e) The length of a toothbrush is (*16 mm / 16 cm*).

(f) A can of lemonade contains (*330 ml / 33 l*).

16 Write each mass in kg.

(a) 6000 g   (b) 5 tonnes   (c) 8.24 tonnes   (d) 9500 g   (e) 350 g

17 Write each length in km.

(a) 3000 m   (b) 9500 m   (c) 2471 m   (d) 4650 m   (e) 23000 m

18 Write each volume in litres.

(a) 2000 ml   (b) 60000 ml   (c) 8400 ml   (d) 670 ml   (e) 4 ml

19 Roy buys 1 kg of potatoes. 700 g are eaten. What is the weight of the potatoes that are left?

20 Gemma has a 2 litre bottle of cola. She pours out 4 glasses of cola each of 200 ml. What volume of cola is left in the bottle?

21 Nazim cuts 27 cm off a 2 m metal rod. What is the length of the metal rod now?

22 Lola runs one 1500 m race and one 800 m race. How many kilometres has she run in total?

23 A lorry and its load weigh 3.1 tonnes. If the load weighs 600 kg, how much does the lorry weigh?

Copy and complete the following:

1 6.35 m = ☐ cm   **2** 1.57 m = ☐ cm   **3** 8.1 m = ☐ cm

4 28 cm = ☐ m   **5** 1 cm = ☐ m   **6** 320 cm = ☐ m

7 9 cm = ☐ m   **8** 60 mm = ☐ cm   **9** 200 mm = ☐ cm

10 8 mm = ☐ cm   **11** 2500 m = ☐ km   **12** 350 m = ☐ km

13 9000 m = ☐ km   **14** 3 kg = ☐ g   **15** 9.5 kg = ☐ g

16 0.375 kg = ☐ g   **17** 575 g = ☐ kg   **18** 1849 g = ☐ kg

19 6 tonnes = ☐ kg   **20** 530 ml = ☐ litres   **21** 1832 ml = ☐ litres

22 5500 ml = ☐ litres   **23** 4.5 litres = ☐ ml   **24** 65 ml = ☐ litres

25 85 litres = ☐ ml   **26** 2.18 litres = ☐ ml   **27** 3.84 tonnes = ☐ kg

28 248 cm = ☐ m

29 A bag contains 2 kg of flour. 1350 g is used. What is the weight of the flour left in the bag?

30 One tin of baked beans weighs 270 g. How many *kilograms* do 9 tins weigh?

31 There are 48 tiles in a stack. Each tile is 7 mm thick. How high is the stack in centimetres?

32 How many 400 ml plastic beakers can be filled from an 88 litre barrel of beer?

33 Al has a 5.4 m piece of wood. He cuts it into small lengths of 45 cm. How many small pieces of wood will he have?

34 14 people have the following weights:

78 kg   69 kg   81 kg   83 kg   81 kg   77 kg   60 kg

52 kg   63 kg   50 kg   71 kg   51 kg   86 kg   81 kg

They get into a lift. The lift is *not* safe if the total weight of the people is more than 1 tonne. Will these 14 people be safe in this lift?

35 Write down the larger amount from each pair below.

(a) 19 m or 0.19 km

(b) 6 cm or 71 mm

(c) 2.3 tonnes or 285 kg

(d) 9200 ml or 9.4 litres

(e) 5.7 m or 569 cm

(f) 38 g or 0.04 kg

(g) 620 mm or 70 cm

(h) 9.6 kg or 9700 g

(i) 380 ml or 0.35 litres

(j) 3.2 km or 318000 cm.

17B **Solve equations by trial and improvement (see Unit 12)**

1.

x cm

$(x + 5)$ cm

The area of this rectangle is 73 cm².

area = $x(x + 5)$ = 73.

Copy the table below then carry it on to find x to *1 decimal place* by trial and improvement.

Trial	Calculation	Too large or too small?
$x = 5$	$5 \times 10 = 50$	too small
$x = 8$	$8 \times 13 = 104$	too large
$x = 6$	$6 \times 11 = 66$	too small
$x = 7$	$7 \times 12 = 84$	too large
$x = 6.5$	$\cdots$	$\cdots$

2. Solve this equation by trial and improvement. Give the answer to *1 decimal place*.

$$x^3 - x = 100$$

Try $x = 4$ and $x = 5$ first.

3. Solve $x^2 + 4x = 150$ by trial and improvement. Give the answer to *2 decimal places*.

Time

1 year = 12 months = 365 days = 52 weeks

3:20 a.m. (before midday) = 03:20 p.m. (after midday) = 15:20

M17.3

1 Change these times into 24-hour clock time.

(a) 11:15 a.m.   (b) 2:45 p.m.   (c) 5:30 p.m.   (d) 9:40 a.m.

(e) 6:50 p.m.   (f) 9:32 p.m.   (g) 8:24 a.m.   (h) 3:56 p.m.

2 Change these times into 12-hour clock time.

    (a) 10:40   (b) 16:20   (c) 19:35   (d) 21:10

    (e) 02:05   (f) 08:05   (g) 17:26   (h) 23:47

3 Calli gets on a bus at 08:20. The bus journey is 45 minutes. What time does Calli get off the bus?

4 Ravi leaves for work at 7:50 a.m. His journey to work takes 50 minutes. What time does he arrive at work?

5 Karen spends a day shopping in London. She leaves home at 08:10 and arrives home at 17:00. How many hours and minutes is she out shopping?

6 A meeting at work begins at 2:30 p.m. and ends at 4:15 p.m. How long did the meeting last for?

7 Copy and complete the following:

    (a) 1 year = ☐ weeks   (b) 5 years = ☐ weeks

    (c) 2 years = ☐ months   (d) 10 years = ☐ months

    (e) 2 years = ☐ days   (f) 3 years = ☐ days

8 Dom borrows some money from a bank. He must pay some money back each month for 3 years. For how many months must he pay back money?

9

Bus leaves   Bus arrives

How long was the Bus journey?

10

 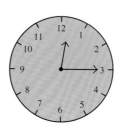

Train leaves   Train arrives

How long was the train journey?

11 Copy and complete the table below.

Old time	Add on	New time
16:30	25 minutes	16:55
13:50	30 minutes	
15:25	1 hour 40 minutes	
07:45	3 hours 30 minutes	
09:05	4 hours 50 minutes	
16:24	1 hour 45 minutes	
11:38	2 hours 50 minutes	

12

Film starts

A film lasts for 2 hours 40 minutes. At what time does the film end?

13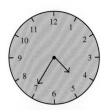

Plane leaves

A plane journey lasts for 3 hours 45 minutes. At what time does the plane journey end?

14 Simone arrives at the Gym at 16:25 and works out for 1 hour 40 minutes. At what time does she leave the Gym?

15 Phil drives from Reading up to Bromsgrove. He leaves at 08:45 and the journey takes 2 hours 45 minutes. When does he arrive at Bromsgrove?

16 Carol goes out to a party at 19:50. She arrives home 3 hours 35 minutes later. At what time does she arrive home?

17 Copy and complete this train timetable. Each train takes the same time between stations.

	Train 1	Train 2	Train 3	Train 4	Train 5	Train 6
Henton	09:00	09:57	10:30	11:23	12:15	13:12
Oldhill	09:08					
Eastham	09:23			11:46		
Colston	09:40					
Todwick	09:55		11:25			

451

Key Facts

Many people still 'think' using the old imperial units.

'Jack is 6 feet tall', 'Wendy weighs 10 stone'.

We have

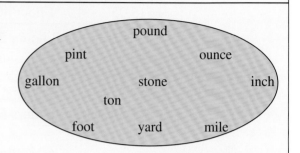

length	**volume**	**mass**
12 inches = 1 foot	8 pints = 1 gallon	16 ounces = 1 pound
3 feet = 1 yard		14 pounds = 1 stone
1760 yards = 1 mile		2240 pounds = 1 ton

Examples

Convert the following imperial units.

(a) 5 feet into inches ⇨ ×12 ⇨ 60 inches

(b) 6 stone 5 pounds into pounds.
    6 stone into pounds ⇨ ×14 ⇨ 84 pounds.
    so 6 stone 5 pounds = 84 + 5 = 89 pounds.

(c) 28 pints into gallons ⇨ ÷8 ⇨ 3.5 gallons.

E17.3

Write down which imperial unit you would use to measure the following.

(The key facts before the next Exercise may help you).

1. The length of a calculator (inches or yards?)

2. The mass of a cat (pounds or stones?)

3. The distance from London to York (yards or miles?)

4. The volume of a supermarket milk carton (pints or gallons?)

5. The length of a football pitch (yards or miles?)

6. The mass of a feather.

7 The length of a biro.

8 The capacity of a car petrol tank.

9 The capacity of a wine bottle.

10 The mass of a caravan.

11 Write each length in inches.

(a) 2 feet   (b) 6 feet   (c) 5 feet 2 inches   (d) 6 feet 5 inches

12 Write each mass in pounds.

(a) 3 stone   (b) 32 ounces   (c) 2 stone 4 pounds   (d) 5 stone 8 pounds

13 Write each volume in pints.

(a) 2 gallons   (b) 9 gallons   (c) 4½ gallons   (d) 7¼ gallons

14 Write each length in feet.

(a) 5 yards   (b) 7 yards 2 feet   (c) 48 inches   (d) 3 yards 1 foot

15 Copy each sentence below and choose the most sensible estimate.

(a) A bag of sugar weighs (*2 pounds / 2 ounces*).

(b) A teapot contains (*2 pints / 5 gallons*).

(c) A baby weighs (*7 stone / 7 pounds*).

(d) The length of a cricket pitch is (*22 inches / 22 yards*).

16 Copy and complete the following:

(a) 4 pounds = ☐ ounces   (b) 4 feet 10 inches = ☐ inches

(c) 2 miles = ☐ yards   (d) 9.5 gallons = ☐ pints

(e) 3 tons = ☐ pounds   (f) 2 stone 6 pounds = ☐ pounds

(g) 70 pounds = ☐ stone   (h) 7040 yards = ☐ miles

(i) 3 pounds 6 ounces = ☐ ounces   (j) 2½ tons = ☐ pounds

(k) 68 pints = ☐ gallons   (l) 3 stone 12 pounds = ☐ pounds

17 Henry weighs 15 stone 3 pounds. He goes on a diet and loses 1 stone 9 pounds. How much does Henry weigh now?

18 Ignes is 5 feet 4 inches tall. Nigel is 9 inches taller. How tall is Nigel?

19 During her lifetime Jackie gives 54 pints of blood. How many gallons is this?

20 Copy and complete the clues that go across. What word is shown going down the shaded boxes?

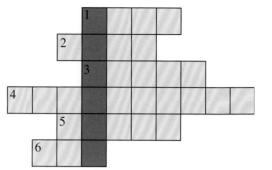

Clues

1. One thousand of these make a kilogram.

2. 3 feet.

3. 1000 millilitres.

4. Ten of these make a centimetre.

5. 16 ounces.

6. 2240 pounds.

Can you still?

Can you still?

17C **Find the mean, median, mode and range for sets of numbers (see Unit 13)**

1. For each set of numbers below find the

   (i) mode   (ii) median   (iii) mean   (iv) range

   (a) 9, 7, 1, 3, 8, 3, 4

   (b) 4, 4, 4, 8, 8, 8, 8, 4, 8

   (c) 0.9, 0.3, 0.7, 0.4, 0.7, 0.6

2. Write down 4 numbers with a mean of 5.

3. Write down 5 numbers which have a mean of 7 *and* a median of 10.

4. The mean weight of 50 people is 61 kg.

   (a) What is the total weight of all 50 people?

   (b) Another 30 people have a mean weight of 69 kg. What is the mean weight of all 80 people?

Converting between metric and imperial units

Key Facts

(The '≈' sign means 'is approximately equal to'.)

We have

length	mass	capacity
1 inch ≈ 2.5 cm	1 ounce ≈ 30 g	1 litre ≈ 1.8 pints
1 foot ≈ 30 cm	1 kg ≈ 2.2 pounds	1 gallon ≈ 4.5 litres
1 yard ≈ 90 cm		
1 mile ≈ 1.6 km		

To *change units*, use the values above and *multiply* or *divide*.

Examples

Convert the units shown.

(a) 2 yards into cm ⇨ ×90 ⇨ 180 cm

(b) 3 gallons into litres ⇨ ×4.5 ⇨ 13.5 litres

(c) 33 pounds into kg ⇨ ÷2.2 ⇨ 15 kg.

M17.4

You may use a calculator.

1 Write each length in cm.

(a) 4 inches   (b) 3 feet   (c) 5 yards   (d) 2.5 yards   (e) 1.5 feet

2 Write each mass in pounds.

(a) 3 kg   (b) 5 kg   (c) 3.5 kg   (d) 8.5 kg   (e) 6.2 kg

3 Write each capacity in litres.

(a) 2 gallons   (b) 9 gallons   (c) 20 gallons   (d) 5.5 gallons   (e) 4.6 gallons

4 On a journey, Tom's car used 6 gallons of petrol and Sarah's car used 26 litres of petrol. Which car used more petrol?

5 On a hiking holiday, Maggie walked 32 miles and Ed walked 53 km. Who walked further?

Copy and complete:

6 10 ounces ≈ ☐ g

7 5 litres ≈ ☐ pints

8 5 miles ≈ ☐ km

9 32 km ≈ ☐ miles

10 27 pints ≈ ☐ litres

11 4 kg ≈ ☐ pounds

12 66 pounds ≈ ☐ kg

13 31.5 litres ≈ ☐ gallons

14 19.2 km ≈ ☐ miles

15 7 yards ≈ ☐ cm

16 60 kg ≈ ☐ pounds

17 150 g ≈ ☐ ounces

18 6 feet ≈ ☐ cm

19 14 miles ≈ ☐ km

20 72 litres ≈ ☐ gallons

21 Which weighs more, A or B?

22 Which weighs more, C or D?

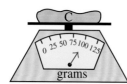 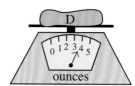

In questions **23** to **30**, which amount is the larger

23 5 kg or 12 pounds?

24 12 inches or 28 cm?

25 4 km or 3 miles?

26 35 pints or 21 litres?

27 250 g or 8 ounces?

28 8.5 feet or 250 cm?

29 2.5 gallons or 12 litres?

30 12 miles or 20 km?

31 Sandra fills up her car with 8 gallons of petrol.

How much will it cost if petrol costs 90 p per litre?

32 The distance from Leeds to York is about 24 miles.
How many km is this?

33 Jamie needs 6 ounces of bacon to put in a stew. He buys 170 g of bacon. Will he have enough?

34 Which is larger – a yard or a metre?

35 An exercise machine is only strong enough to take weights up to 16 stone. Arnie weighs 100 kg. Should he use the exercise machine?

(remember: 1 stone = 14 pounds).

36 On a building site, 50 kg of soil is moved every minute. How many tonnes of soil will be moved in 1 hour?

Measuring – upper and lower bounds

When you measure something, the measurement is never exact.

If you measure the diameter of a 5 pence coin with a ruler, you might read 1.7 cm. If you use a more accurate device for measuring you might read the diameter as 1.71 cm. An even more accurate device might give the diameter as 1.712 cm. None of these figures is precise.

They are all approximations to the actual diameter.

This means that there is always an error in making any kind of measurement such as length, weight, time, temperature and so on. This kind of error cannot be avoided.

Suppose the width of a book is measured at 16 cm to the nearest cm.

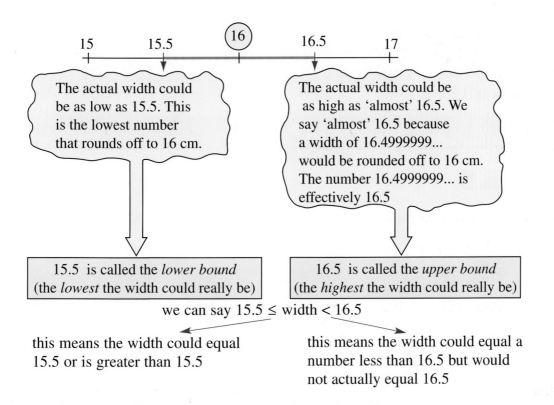

15   15.5   (16)   16.5   17

The actual width could be as low as 15.5. This is the lowest number that rounds off to 16 cm.

The actual width could be as high as 'almost' 16.5. We say 'almost' 16.5 because a width of 16.4999999... would be rounded off to 16 cm. The number 16.4999999... is effectively 16.5

15.5 is called the *lower bound* (the *lowest* the width could really be)

16.5 is called the *upper bound* (the *highest* the width could really be)

we can say 15.5 ≤ width < 16.5

this means the width could equal 15.5 or is greater than 15.5

this means the width could equal a number less than 16.5 but would not actually equal 16.5

457

The length of a nail is measured at 3.4 cm to the nearest *0.1 cm*.

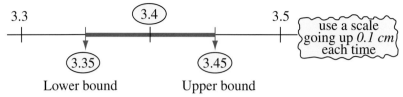

Lower bound   Upper bound

we can say 3.35 ≤ length < 3.45

The length of a park is measured at 3800 m to the nearest *100 m*.

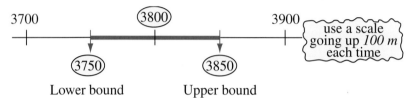

Lower bound   Upper bound

we can say 3750 ≤ length < 3850

(a) temperature of a room is 23.5°C to one decimal place.

23.4   23.5   23.6

23.45°C   23.55°C

Lower bound   Upper bound

(b) length of a table is 1430 mm to the nearest 10 mm.

1420   1430   1440

1425 mm   1435 mm

Lower bound   Upper bound

(c) weight of a lorry is 21000 kg to 2 significant figures.

20000   21000   22000

20500 kg   21500 kg

Lower bound   Upper bound

M17.4

1 The length of a pen is measured at 14 cm to the nearest cm.

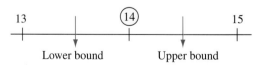

Lower bound   Upper bound

Write down   (a) the lower bound   (b) the upper bound

2 The height of a church tower is 42 m, measured to the nearest metre.

Write down   (a) the lower bound   (b) the upper bound

458

3 A man weighs 83 kg, measured to the nearest kg.

Write down (a) the lower bound   (b) the upper bound

4 The diameter of a one pound coin is 21.5 mm,

measured to the nearest 0.1 mm.

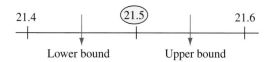

Write down   (a) the lower bound   (b) the upper bound

5 A baby weighs 3.6 kg, measured to the nearest 0.1 kg. Write down
(a) the lower bound (b) the upper bound

6 Copy and complete the table.

		Lower bound	Upper bound
(a)	length = 79 cm, to nearest cm		
(b)	mass = 32 kg, to nearest kg		
(c)	length = 6.3 m, to nearest 0.1 m		
(d)	volume = 15.7 m³, to nearest 0.1 m³		
(e)	width = 9.1 cm, to nearest 0.1 cm		

7 A coin weighs 10.3 g, correct to one decimal place. What is the least possible
weight of the coin?

8 A famous rock singer has a fortune of £24,712,000, correct to the nearest
£1000. What is the least amount of money the rock singer might have?

9 The width of a field is 530 m, correct to the nearest 10 m. What is the least
possible width of the field?

10 In a 100 m race a sprinter is timed at 10.12 seconds to the nearest
0.01 seconds. Write down the least possible time.

11 Copy and complete each statement. Part (a) is done as an example.

(a) A mass m is 48 g, to the nearest g, so $47.5 \leq m < 48.5$.

(b) A length l is 92.6 mm, to the nearest 0.1 mm, so $92.55 \leq l < \boxed{}$.

(c) A diameter d is 16.2 cm, to the nearest 0.1 cm, so $\boxed{} \leq d < \boxed{}$.

(d) A capacity C is 1200 litres, to the nearest 100 litres, so $\boxed{} \leq C < 1250$.

(e) A height h is 3.86 m, to the nearest 0.01 m, so $\boxed{} \leq h < \boxed{}$.

12

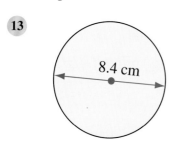

71.8 m

← 156.3 m →

The length and width of a field are measured to the nearest 0.1 m.

(a) Write down the lower bound for the length of the field.

(b) Write down the upper bound for the width of the field.

(c) The area of the field is length × width. Use a calculator to find the *lowest* possible value of the area of the field.

13

8.4 cm

The diameter of the circle is measured to the nearest 0.1 cm.

Circumference = π × diameter

Use a calculator to find the *greatest* possible value of the circumference of the circle. (Give the answer to 1 decimal place).

Can you still?

Can you still?

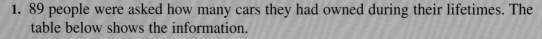

17D   **Find averages from tables of information (see Unit 16)**

1. 89 people were asked how many cars they had owned during their lifetimes. The table below shows the information.

Number of cars	0	1	2	3	4	5	6	7
Frequency	11	8	12	21	22	8	5	2

Find (a) the modal number of cars.   (b) the median number of cars.

(c) the total number of cars.   (d) the mean average number of cars.

2. 500 people were asked how much their houses were worth. The table below shows the information.

Value of house (£1000's)(v)	$50 \leq v < 100$	$100 \leq v < 200$	$200 \leq v < 300$	$300 \leq v < 400$	$400 \leq v < 500$	$500 \leq v < 700$
Frequency	75	184	112	72	41	16

Find (a) the modal interval.

(b) the interval which contains the median.

(c) estimate the mean average value of a house.

Speed

When Carl walks at a constant speed of 5 km per hour, it means he moves 5 km in 1 hour. In 2 hours he walks 10 km. In 3 hours he moves 15 km and so on. We see that the distance moved is equal to the speed multiplied by the time taken.

$$\text{Distance} = \text{speed} \times \text{time}$$

Speed can be measured in km per hour

$$\text{Speed} = \frac{\text{Distance}}{\text{Time}}$$

we also have

$$\text{Time} = \frac{\text{Distance}}{\text{Speed}}$$

These three important formulas can be remembered using a triangle as shown.

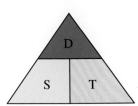

To find S: cover S and you have $\frac{D}{T}$

To find T: cover T and you have $\frac{D}{S}$

To find D: Cover D and you have $S \times T$

These formulas can only be used for objects moving at a *constant* speed.

Be careful!

- If the speed is in miles per hour, the distance must be in miles and the time must be in hours.

- If the speed is in metres per second, the distance must be in metres and the time must be in seconds.

(a) A car travels 100 miles in 2 hours 30 minutes.
Find the speed in mph

Time must be in hours only: 2 hours 30 minutes = 2.5 hours.

$$S = \frac{D}{T} = \frac{100}{2.5} = 40 \text{ mph.}$$

(b) Hazel runs at a steady speed of 8 m/s.

How far does she travel in 4.3 s?

$$D = S \times T = 8 \times 4.3 = 34.4 \text{ m.}$$

1 Find the speed of a car for each distance and time shown below.

(a) distance = 90 miles, time = 2 hours

(b) distance = 200 miles, time = 4 hours

(c) distance = 165 miles, time = 3 hours

(d) distance = 60 miles, time = 1.5 hours

2 Find how far a person runs for each speed and time below.

(a) speed = 7 m/s, time = 8 s   (b) speed = 5 m/s, time = 9 s

(c) speed = 6.5 m/s, time = 3 s   (d) speed = 4.9 m/s, time = 10 s

3 Find how long it takes a train to travel for each distance and speed below.

(a) distance = 160 km, speed = 80 km/hr

(b) distance = 210 km, speed = 70 km/hr

(c) distance = 250 km, speed = 100 km/hr

(d) distance = 100 km, speed = 80 km/hr

4 A plane flies 480 km at 320 km/hr. How long does the journey take?

5 A person cycles for 3 hours at a speed of 12 mph. How far does he travel?

6 Eurostar travels 420 km from London to Paris in 3 hours. Find the average speed of the train.

7 Charlie drives from Wells to Bristol at 40 mph in 30 minutes. How far is it from Wells to Bristol?

8 A hiker walks 28.5 miles at 3 mph. How long does the hiker walk for?

9 Find the speed in mph for each of the following.

Distance	Time	Speed (mph)
30 miles	30 minutes	
9 miles	15 minutes	
15 miles	20 minutes	
6 miles	5 minutes	
30 miles	45 minutes	

10 Terry cycles at 16 mph for 30 minutes then slows down to 12 mph for 15 minutes. How far does he travel in total?

11 Janine walks at 6 km/hr for 1 hour 30 minutes then 4 km/hr for 2 hours 15 minutes. How far does she walk in total?

12 A lorry leaves Cardiff at 09:30 and arrives in London at 12:00. The journey is 130 miles. What was the average speed of the lorry?

13 A magpie flies 2 miles in 10 minutes. What is its speed in mph?

14 Sima drives 50 miles from Leeds to Manchester at an average speed of 40 mph. If she left Leeds at 10:20, when did she arrive at Manchester?

15 The speed of light is 300,000,000 m/s. How long will it take light to travel 6,000,000 km? (Be careful with the units)

Density and other compound measures

If the density of a substance is 30 g/cm³, it means that 1 cm³ of the substance has a mass of 30 g.

Density = Mass per unit Volume so   Density = $\dfrac{\text{Mass}}{\text{Volume}}$

We can use a triangle again to remember the formulas.

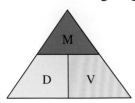

To find M: cover M and you have D × V

To find D: cover D and you have $\dfrac{M}{V}$

To find V: cover V and you have $\dfrac{M}{D}$

Note

There is a difference between 'mass' and 'weight' but in this book you may assume they have the same meaning.

(a) The density of silk is 1.3 g/cm³. What is the mass of 8 cm³ of silk?

M = D × V = 1.3 × 8 = 10.4 g.

(b) The density of copper is 8.9 g/cm³. The mass of a copper bar is 106.8 g. Find the volume of the copper bar.

$V = \dfrac{M}{D} = \dfrac{106.8}{8.9} = 12$ cm³.

Note

Speed and density are known as *compound measures*. Below is an example of different compound measures.

(c) A van can be hired at £45 per day. How much will it cost to hire the van for a fortnight (14 days)?

cost = 45 × 14 = £630

1. Copy and complete the table below:

Density (g/cm³)	Mass (g)	Volume (cm³)
	200	50
	80	5
13		8
24		36
10	150	
60		0.5
	36	9
16	320	
0.1	19	
	42	10

2. The density of brass is 8.2 g/cm³. The volume of a brass ring is 20 cm³. Find the mass of the brass ring.

3. A gold bar has a volume of 80 cm³ and a mass of 1544 g. Find the density of the gold.

4. A piece of cotton has a volume of 250 cm³ and a mass of 385 kg. Find the density of the cotton.

5. A liquid weighs 500 g and has a density of 2.5 g/cm³. Find the volume of the liquid.

6. Which has a greater mass – 30 cm³ of cast iron with density 7.4 g/cm³ or 25 cm³ of pure nickel with density 8.9 g/cm³? Write down by how much.

7. Find the volume of some lead weighing 3 kg. The density of lead is 11.4 g/cm³ (note: you must change 3 kg into grams first). Give your answer to the nearest whole number.

8. High alloy steel has a density of 8.3 g/cm³. Find the weight of some steel with a volume of 50 cm³.

9. Brass has a density of 8.2 g/cm³. Find the volume of a brass fitting which weighs 0.574 kg.

10. Find the volume of a piece of zinc alloy weighing 2 kg. The density of zinc alloy is 6 g/cm³. Give your answer to the nearest whole number.

11. 50 m   100 m

A farmer grows strawberries in this field. If the farmer makes £1.20 per m², how much money will the farmer make in total?

12. 40 m² of carpet costs £878. What is the cost per m² of the carpet?

13. A supermarket chain makes £900,000 profit per day. How much profit do they make in one year? Assume 365 days in one year.

Jenny has been given some money to do a bedroom makeover. A plan of her bedroom is shown below.

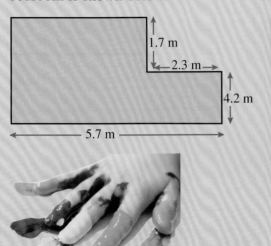

Task A

Jenny starts by painting her ceiling with acrylic matt paint. The paint will cover 11 to 13 square metres per litre. If Jenny gets the worst coverage of paint on her ceiling, how many litres of paint will she need for one coat?

Task B

Jenny wants to paint all her walls yellow. Each wall is shown below. Again, the paint will cover 11 to 13 square metres per litre but Jenny only gets the worst coverage.

1   How many litres of paint will Jenny need for one coat?

2   A 5 litre tin of paint costs £35.95. A 2.5 litre tin of paint costs £21.95. How much will Jenny need to spend on her yellow paint?

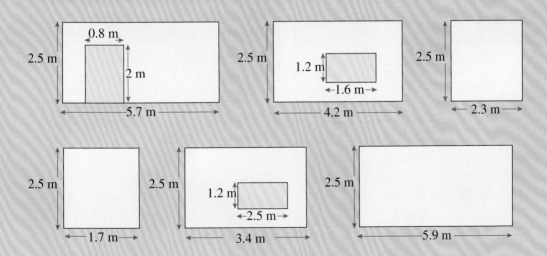

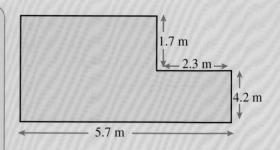

Task C

Jenny chooses a new carpet. She can only buy carpet which has a 4m width.

Each piece of carpet must be laid in the same direction.

1 What length of carpet must Jenny buy to cover her entire bedroom as cheaply as possible?

2 Multiply this length by the 4m width to find the area of carpet that Jenny must buy.

Single size beds	
Name	Price
Winchester	£178
Tamworth	£231
RDU	£155
Leonardo	£284
Paulton	£202
Relaxe	£301
Porter	£199
Memory foam	£324

Sofas	
Name	Price
Colston 2 Seater	£364
Mowbray 2 Seater	£473
Edwins 3 Seater	£719
Parkhead 2 Seater	£506
Canston Leather 3 Seater	£1120
Bintons Luxury 2 Seater	£790
Harrows Deluxe 2 Seater	£685
Tindwells Deluxe 3 Seater	£1065

Carpet	
Name	Price per m²
Howton Twist	£25.40
Palton Weave	£22.65
Cotswold Twist	£19.85
Mendip Supreme	£31.35
Classic Weave	£24.90
Winchester Pile	£28.30
Dalby Tuff Weave	£14.70
Cheasley Deluxe Twist	£37.40
Canton High Pile	£16.15
Paris Classic Twist	£38.25

Chest of Drawers	
Name	Price
Holton 3 Drawer	£173
Holton 5 Drawer	£256
Busby 3 Drawer	£206
Coventry 3 Drawer	£249
Chiltern Pine 4 Drawer	£186
Chiltern Pine 5 Drawer	£227
Parlton 4 Drawer	£284

Task D

Jenny has £1900 to do her bedroom makeover. A 5 litre pot of Brilliant White ceiling paint costs £27.95

1 Use your answers from parts A and B to find the total cost of her paint.

2 Choose a carpet from the table opposite and use your answer from part C to find the total cost of her carpet.

3 Jenny wants a new bed, sofa and chest of drawers. Choose one of each from the tables opposite.

   If she chooses all three, she gets a 20% discount. Find the total cost of the bed, sofa and chest of drawers.

4 Jenny must not spend more than £1900 on everything. Change your choices if you need to and show clearly how the total bill is less than £1900.

TEST YOURSELF ON UNIT 17

1. Reading scales

For each of the scales below, write down the measurement indicated by the arrow.

(a)
250
200
150
cm

(b)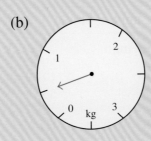

(c)
cm 30   40   50   60

(d)
1.6   1.7   1.8
kg

(e)
900
650
400
ml

(f)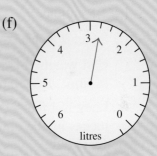

2. Using and converting metric units

Copy and complete the following:

(a) 9.5 m = ☐ cm   (b) 7.5 kg = ☐ g   (c) 6.12 kg = ☐ g

(d) 2000 ml = ☐ litres   (e) 3200 g = ☐ kg   (f) 2.6 km = ☐ m

(g) 850 m = ☐ km   (h) 5.9 litres = ☐ ml   (i) 46 ml = ☐ litres

(j) 4 tonnes = ☐ kg   (k) 6 g = ☐ kg   (l) 85 mm = ☐ cm

(m) Chas has 1.4 kg of flour and uses 638 g. How much flour does he have left?

(n) Sarah knocks over a 2 litre bottle of water and spills 735 ml. How much water is left in the bottle?

467

3. Dealing with 'time' problems

(a) Shanta catches a train at 14:45. Is this in the morning or the afternoon?

(b)

Plane leaves   Plane arrives

How long was the plane journey?

(c) Ravi and Bella start watching a DVD at 7:40 p.m. The DVD lasts for 2 hours 25 minutes. At what time do they stop watching the DVD?

(d) A game of football starts at 12:30. The game finishes 1 hour 40 minutes later. At what time does the game finish?

(e) Joey gets up at 07:45 and goes to bed at 23:30. How long is he up for?

4. Using and converting imperial units

Copy and complete the following:

(a) 5 stone = ☐ pounds   (b) 7 yards = ☐ feet

(c) 3 gallons = ☐ pints   (d) 24 inches = ☐ feet

(e) 48 ounces = ☐ pounds   (f) 12 feet = ☐ yards

(g) 3.5 gallons = ☐ pints   (h) 2 stone 3 pounds = ☐ pounds

(i) 5 feet 9 inches = ☐ inches

(j) Carl weighs 11 stone 10 pounds. He has a wonderful holiday and puts on a ½ stone. How much does Carl now weigh?

(k) Lucy is 4 feet 11 inches tall when she is 11 years old. She grows another 7 inches by the time she is 16 years old. How tall is Lucy when she is 16 years old?

5. Converting between metric and imperial units

Copy and complete the following:

(a) 10 inches ≈ ☐ cm   (b) 100 cm ≈ ☐ inches

(c) 10 miles ≈ ☐ km   (d) 25 miles ≈ ☐ km

(e) 32 km ≈ ☐ miles   (f) 4 gallons ≈ ☐ litres

(g) 5 kg ≈ ☐ pounds   (h) 88 pounds ≈ ☐ kg

(i) 90 litres ≈ ☐ gallons   (j) Which is further – 6 miles or 10 km?

(k) A barrel contains 30 litres of beer. How many whole pints of beer would this provide?

6. Finding upper and lower bounds

(a) The diameter of a 10 pence coin is 2.4 cm, measured to the nearest 0.1 cm.

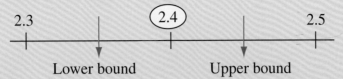

2.3   2.4   2.5

Lower bound   Upper bound

Write down   (i) the lower bound   (ii) the upper bound

(b) The length of a road is 364 m, measured to the nearest metre.
Write down   (i) the lower bound   (ii) the upper bound

(c) A woman weighs 65 kg, measured to the nearest kg.
Write down   (i) the lower bound   (ii) the upper bound

(d) The width of a book is 18.8 cm, measured to the nearest 0.1 cm.
Write down   (i) the lower bound   (ii) the upper bound

7. Calculating with speed, density and other compound measures

(a) Sharon walks for 3 hours at a speed of 5 km/hr. How far does Sharon walk?

(b) Greg cycles 63 km at a speed of 14 km/hr. How long does the journey take him?

(c) 12 cm^3 of gold weighs 231.6 g. Find the density of gold.

(d) A steel bar has a volume of 600 cm^3. If the density of steel is 8.3 g/cm^3, find the mass of the steel bar.

(e) A car costs £39 per day to hire. How much will it cost to hire the car for 12 days?

(f) A lorry travels at 51 mph for 20 minutes. How far does the lorry travel?

Mixed examination questions

1   (a) How many grams are there in 1½ kilograms?

(b) How many centimetres are there in 2 metres?

(c) How many millilitres are there in 3 litres?

(d) Which **metric** unit would be the most useful to measure

(i) the area of a football pitch

(ii) the capacity of a car's petrol tank?   (OCR)

2 What is the reading on each of these scales?

(i)

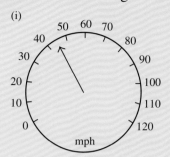

(ii)

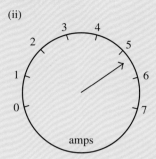

(EDEXCEL)

3 Two villages are 40 km apart.

(a) Change 40 km into metres.

(b) How many miles are the same as 40 km?

(AQA)

4 Here is part of a train timetable from Crewe to London.

Station	Time of Leaving
Crewe	08:00
Wolverhampton	08:40
Birmingham	09:00
Coventry	09:30
Rugby	09:40
Milton Keynes	10:10

(a) At what time should the train leave Coventry?

The train should arrive in London at 10:45

(b) How long should the train take to travel from Crewe to London?

Verity arrived at Milton Keynes station at 09:53

(c) How many minutes should she have to wait before the 10:10 train leaves?

(EDEXCEL)

5 The speed limit in London is 30 miles per hour. In Paris the speed limit is 50 kilometres per hour.

Which of these two speeds is slower?
Show clear working to support your answer.

(OCR)

6 The mass of 5 m³ of copper is 44 800 kg.

(a) Work out the density of copper.

The density of zinc is 7130 kg/m³.

(b) Work out the mass of 5 m³ of zinc.

(EDEXCEL)

7 Each side of a regular pentagon has a length of 101 mm, correct to the nearest millimetre.

(i) Write down the **least** possible length of each side.

(ii) Write down the **greatest** possible length of each side.

(EDEXCEL)

ALGEBRA 4

In this unit you will learn how to:

– change the subject of a formula

– deal with inequalities

– use the laws of indices

– review algebra

– ⟨ USE YOUR MATHS! ⟩ – buying a house

Changing the subject of a formula

(a) $a = 3b$

Make b the subject of the formula.

$a = 3 \times b$

$\dfrac{a}{3} = \dfrac{\cancel{3} \times b}{\cancel{3}}$

$\dfrac{a}{3} = b$ we say that $b = \dfrac{a}{3}$

(b) $p = 5q + 8$ Make q the subject of the formula.

$\boxed{p} = \boxed{5q} \boxed{+8}$

$\boxed{p} - 8 = \boxed{5q} \boxed{+8} - 8$

$p - 8 = 5q$

$\dfrac{p - 8}{5} = \dfrac{\cancel{5}q}{\cancel{5}}$

$\dfrac{p - 8}{5} = q$ we say that $q = \dfrac{p - 8}{5}$

M18.1

Copy and complete each statement below:

1 If $x = y + 5$ then $x \ \square\ 5 = y$

2 If $x = y + 8$ then $x \ \square\ 8 = y$

3 If $a = b - 3$ then $a \ \square\ 3 = b$

4 If $a = b + 9$ then $a \ \square\ 9 = b$

5 If $a = 6b$ then $\dfrac{a}{\square} = b$

6 If $x = y - 2$ then $x \ \square\ 2 = y$

7 $p = 3q$ Make q the subject of the formula.

8 $a = 7b$ Make b the subject of the formula.

9 $x = \dfrac{y}{9}$ Make y the subject of the formula.

10 Make x the subject of each formula given below:

(a) $y = x - 9$ (b) $y = \dfrac{x}{12}$ (c) $y = x + 6$ (d) $y = x + 20$

(e) $y = 8x$ (f) $y = 10x$ (g) $y = x - 4$ (h) $y = x - 25$

(i) $y = \dfrac{x}{3}$ (j) $y = \dfrac{x}{15}$ (k) $y = x + 100$ (l) $y = 18x$

11 Match up pairs of formulas which are the same. There will be one odd formula left over.

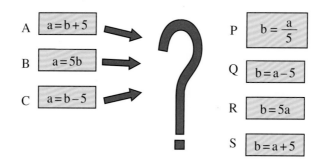

A $a = b + 5$ P $b = \dfrac{a}{5}$

B $a = 5b$ Q $b = a - 5$

C $a = b - 5$ R $b = 5a$

S $b = a + 5$

12 Copy and fill each box below:

(a) $x = 3y + 2$

$x - \square = 3y + 2 - \square$

$x - \square = 3y$

$\dfrac{x - \square}{\square} = y$

(b) $x = 4y - 9$

$x + \square = 4y - 9 + \square$

$x + \square = 4y$

$\dfrac{x + \square}{\square} = y$

13 $a = 2b - 5$ Make b the subject of the formula.

14 $p = 9q + 7$ Make q the subject of the formula.

15 $a = 7b + 1$ Make b the subject of the formula.

16 $x = 3y - 10$ Make y the subject of the formula.

17 Make x the subject of each formula given below:

(a) $y = 2x + 8$ (b) $y = 6x - 5$ (c) $y = 8x - 10$

(d) $y = \dfrac{x}{3} + 2$ (e) $y = \dfrac{x}{5} - 6$ (f) $y = \dfrac{x}{2} - 4$

$c(x - d) = y$ Make x the subject of the formula

$c(x - d) = y$ *multiply out the bracket first*

$\boxed{cx} \; \boxed{-cd} = \boxed{y}$ add cd onto *both* sides of the equation

$\boxed{cx} \; \boxed{-cd} + cd = \boxed{y} + cd$

$cx = y + cd$ divide *both* sides of the equation by c

$\dfrac{\cancel{c}x}{\cancel{c}} = \dfrac{y + cd}{c}$ the c cancels down

$x = \dfrac{y + cd}{c}$

E18.1

1 Copy and fill each box below:

(a) $y = ax - b$

$y + \square = ax - b + \square$

$y + \square = ax$

$\dfrac{y + \square}{\square} = x$

(b) $v = at + u$

$v - \square = at + u - \square$

$v - \square = at$

$\dfrac{v - \square}{\square} = t$

2 Make x the subject of each formula given below:

(a) $y = px + q$ (b) $y = cx - h$ (c) $y = rx - 2p$

(d) $q = cx + 3s$ (e) $bx + 5c = 2f$ (f) $y = ax + b - c$

3 Copy and fill each box below:

(a) $y = \dfrac{fx - g}{h}$

$\square = fx - g$

$\square + g = fx - g + g$

$\square + g = fx$

$\dfrac{\square + g}{\square} = x$

(b) $\dfrac{px + 2h}{c} = y$

$px + 2h = \square$

$px + 2h - 2h = \square - \square$

$px = \square - \square$

$x = \dfrac{\square - \square}{\square}$

4 Make x the subject of each formula given below:

(a) $c(x + d) = y$ 　　　　(b) $m(x - n) = q$ 　　　　(c) $r(x + 5) = y$

(d) $a(x + 7) = 3b$ 　　　　(e) $y = f(x - g)$ 　　　　(f) $4b = s(x - t)$

5 Make x the subject of each formula given below:

(a) $\dfrac{ax + d}{4} = e$ 　　　　(b) $\dfrac{bx + 3c}{y} = p$ 　　　　(c) $\dfrac{ax - r}{5} = q$

(d) $y = \dfrac{cx - 2d}{7}$ 　　　　(e) $y = \dfrac{ax - 3c}{b}$ 　　　　(f) $\dfrac{px + qr}{8} = y$

6 $h = 3g + m$ Make g the subject of the formula.

7 $v = u + fy$ Make y the subject of the formula.

Can you still? 　　　　　　　　　　　　　　　　　　　　　　　　*Can you still?*

18A **Find the circumference and area of circles (see Unit 15)**

1. *Use a calculator* to find (i) the perimeter (ii) the area of each shape below. When necessary, give answers to 1 decimal place.

(a)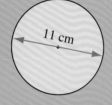
11 cm

(b)
9 cm

(c)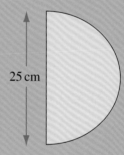
25 cm

2. Find the total distance around this running track.

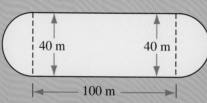
40 m　　40 m
100 m

3. Find the *area* of this shape.

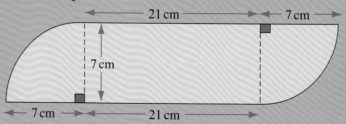
21 cm　　7 cm
7 cm
7 cm　　21 cm

Show on a number line the range of values of x for the inequalities shown.

(a) $x > 2$

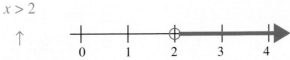

The circle at the left hand end of the range is open. This means x *cannot* equal 2.

'x is greater than 2'

(b) $x \leq -1$

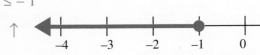

The circle at -1 is filled in. This means x *can* equal -1.

'x is less than or equal to -1'

(c) $-2 \leq x < 1$

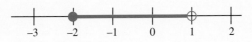

x is greater than -2 and *can equal* -2.

x is also less than 1 but *cannot equal* 1.

M18.2

1 Write down the inequalities shown below:

(a)

(b)

(c)

(d)

(e)

(f)

(g)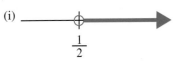

(h)

(i)

(j)

(k)

(l)

2 Draw a number line to show the following inequalities.

(a) $x \geq 3$

(b) $x < 6$

(c) $x \leq -3$

(d) $3 < x < 8$

(e) $-6 < x \leq 2$

(f) $n > -1$

(g) $-7 \leq n < -3$

(h) $2 \leq t \leq 4$

(i) $-2 < p \leq 0$

3 If $\square < 120$, write a possible number for $\square$

4 If $\square > 50$, write a possible number for $\square$

5 Write a possible number for $\square$ in each of the following:

   (a) $\square > 820$ (b) $\square < 175$ (c) $300 < \square$

   (d) $1100 < \square$ (e) $185 < \square$ (f) $\square < 362$

6 Write a possible number for $\square$ in each of the following:

   (a) $150 < \square < 250$ (b) $730 < \square < 750$ (c) $1241 < \square < 1243$

   (d) $428 < \square < 430$ (e) $-6 < \square < 0$ (f) $-8 < \square < -4$

7 Copy and fill each box below with $<$ or $>$

   (a) $17 \; \square \; 13$ (b) $228 \; \square \; 241$ (c) $7.5 \; \square \; 7.05$ (d) $-6 \; \square \; -5$

8 Answer true or false:

   (a) $-4 > 3$ (b) $3.6 < 3.17$ (c) $5.23 > 5.1$ (d) $6\frac{1}{4} < 6.5$

Solve the inequalities:

(a) $x + 6 > 14$ (b) $x - 3 \leq 6$ (c) $4x < 320$ (d) $\frac{x}{7} \geq -3$

    $x > 8$ $x \leq 9$ $x < \dfrac{320}{4}$ $x \geq -3 \times 7$

                                    $x < 80$ $x \geq -21$

E18.2

1 Copy and fill in the boxes below:

   (a) $x - 5 > 3$ (b) $\frac{x}{4} \leq 9$ (c) $2x + 4 < 10$

     $x > 3 + \square$ $x \leq 9 \times \square$ $2x < 10 - \square$

     $x > \square$ $x \leq \square$ $2x < \square$

                                     $x < \square$

Solve the inequalities in Questions **2** to **13**.

2 $x + 8 < 15$ **3** $x - 2 \geq 9$ **4** $n - 8 < 1$

5 $n + 6 \geq -2$ **6** $a - 7 > -2$ **7** $b - 6 \geq -4$

8 $5 + x \leq 17$ **9** $4n \leq 20$ **10** $6y > 42$

11 $\frac{b}{3} \geq 8$ **12** $\frac{x}{5} < -9$ **13** $3x \geq -12$

Find the range of values of x which satisfy each inequality in Questions **14** to **19** and show each answer on a number line.

14 $5x \leq 30$

15 $9x > -27$

16 $2 + x \geq 6$

17 $\dfrac{x}{2} \geq 1$

18 $x + 3 < 0$

19 $\dfrac{x}{4} \leq -2$

In Questions **20** to **25** write down all the *integer* values (*whole numbers*) of x which satisfy the given inequalities.

20 $0 < x < 4$

21 $2 \leq x \leq 4$

22 $1 \leq x < 7$

23 $-2 \leq x \leq 2$

24 $-4 < x \leq 0$

25 $-5 \leq x < 4$

26 Write down the smallest integer x for which $2x > 5$.

27 Write down the largest integer x for which $10x < 56$.

Solve the inequalities in Questions **28** to **39** .

28 $2x + 7 > 19$

29 $3x - 1 \leq 14$

30 $6n - 5 \geq 43$

31 $4b + 12 \leq 28$

32 $3 + 7x > -4$

33 $4n - 8 < 0$

34 $3(a - 2) < 15$

35 $4(x + 3) \leq 20$

36 $\dfrac{a}{6} - 4 \geq 2$

37 $5x + 3 \geq 2x + 21$

38 $8n - 2 > 3n + 33$

39 $6x + 8 < 38 - 4x$

Can you still?

Can you still?

18B   **Find surface areas and volumes of cuboids (see Unit 15)**

1.   Which of these 3 cuboids has the *smallest* surface area?

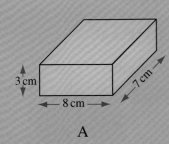

A

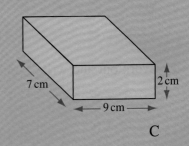

B

C

2.   Which of the 3 cuboids in Question 1 has the *largest volume*?

3.   The *volume* of this cuboid is 420 cm³.

What is the length l of the cuboid?

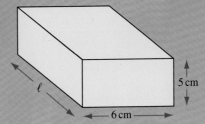

Key Facts

$3^4 \Leftarrow$ the 'power' 4 is also called the 'index' ('indices' for more than one index)

⇧

this number is called the 'base'

To *multiply* numbers with indices, *add the indices*. The base numbers must be the same.

$$a^m \times a^n = a^{m+n}$$

To *divide* numbers with indices, *subtract the indices*. The base numbers must be the same.

$$a^m \div a^n = a^{m-n}$$

M18.3

1 Copy and complete. Write the answer as a number in index form.

(a) $3^3 \times 3^4 =$

(b) $5^2 \times 5^4 =$

(c) $8^3 \times 8^3 =$

(d) $7^2 \times 7^3 =$

(e) $4^6 \times 4 =$

(f) $6^5 \times 6^2 =$

2 Copy and complete. Write the answer as a number in index form.

(a) $7^6 \div 7^2$

(b) $4^7 \div 4^4$

(c) $3^9 \div 3$

(d) $5^8 \div 5^5$

(e) $6^{10} \div 6^7$

(f) $4^6 \div 4^5$

3 Work out and write each answer as a number in index form.

(a) $8^6 \times 8^2$

(b) $4^7 \times 4^3$

(c) $9^8 \div 9^5$

(d) $6^4 \times 6^4$

(e) $8^7 \div 8$

(f) $5^5 \div 5^2$

(g) $3^3 \times 3^2 \times 3^4$

(h) $2^6 \times 2 \times 2^3$

(i) $(4^3)^2$

4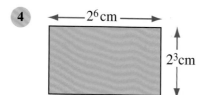

Write down the area of this rectangle in index form.

2^6 cm

2^3 cm

478

5 Copy and complete

(a) $3^4 \times 3^2 = \square$

(b) $\square \times 6^4 = 6^6$

(c) $\square \times 9^4 = 9^7$

(d) $4^6 \times \square = 4^8$

(e) $9^3 \times \square = 9^4$

(f) $4^8 \div 4^2 = \square$

(g) $3^8 \div \square = 3^2$

(h) $8^{10} \div \square = 8^5$

(i) $\square \div 4^5 = 4^7$

6 Write down the area of this square in index form.

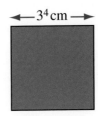

← 3^4 cm →

7 Work out and write each answer as a number in index form.

(a) $5^3 \times 5^9 \times 5^2$

(b) $8^7 \times 8^2 \times 8^4$

(c) $\dfrac{4^8 \times 4^3}{4^7}$

(d) $\dfrac{7^6 \times 7^8}{7^4}$

(e) $\dfrac{8^9}{8^2 \times 8^3}$

(f) $\dfrac{6^8}{6^3 \times 6^3}$

8 Which statements below are true?

(a) $4^3 \times 4^2 = 4^5$

(b) $7^9 \div 7^3 = 7^6$

(c) $2^8 \times 2 = 2^9$

(d) $3^6 \times 3 = 3^6$

(e) $5^6 \div 5^3 = 5^2$

(f) $8^7 \div 8 = 8^6$

🔑 Key Facts

To raise an index number to another power, multiply the indices.

$$(a^m)^n = a^{mn}$$

(a) $\dfrac{a^2 \times a^7}{(a^2)^2} = \dfrac{a^9}{a^4} = a^5$

(b) $\dfrac{n^4 \times n^6}{(n^4)^2} = \dfrac{n^{10}}{n^8} = n^2$

$4^2 \div 4^2 = 4^{2-2} = 4^0$

$4^2 \div 4^2 = 16 \div 16 = 1$

so $4^0 = 1$

LEARN! $a^0 = 1$ for any number a (apart from $a = 0$)

1 Copy and complete. Write the number in index form.

(a) $(3^2)^4$ (b) $(5^3)^2$ (c) $(6^3)^4$ (d) $(7^4)^2$

(e) $(5^6)^3$ (f) $(8^2)^5$ (g) $(3^5)^3$ (h) $(6^3)^5$

2 Which is larger? $\boxed{10^0}$ or $\boxed{3^0}$

3 Copy and complete. Write the number in index form.

(a) $(3^4)^2 \times 3^3$ (b) $(2^3)^4 \times 2^6$ (c) $6^5 \times (6^2)^2$

(d) $\dfrac{7^3}{7^0}$ (e) $\dfrac{(5^2)^4}{(5^3)^2}$ (f) $\dfrac{9 \times (9^3)^3}{9^7}$

(g) $\dfrac{8^2 \times 8^6}{(8^2)^3}$ (h) $\dfrac{4^3 \times (4^5)^2}{4^7}$ (i) $\dfrac{(2^3)^2 \times (2^3)^2}{2^4 \times 2^3}$

4 What is the value of $(4^0)^6$?

5 Simplify the expressions below.

(a) $a^4 \times a^3$ (b) $x^7 \times x^4$ (c) $x^9 \div x^4$

(d) $(n^3)^2$ (e) $a^{10} \div a^6$ (f) $(x^3)^3$

(g) n^0 (h) $p^8 \times p$ (i) $m^{14} \div m^8$

(j) $(x^2)^0$ (k) $(a^2)^4 \times a^5$ (l) $x^p \div x^p$

6

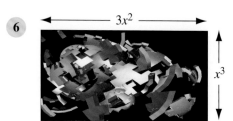

$3x^2$

x^3

Write down the area of this picture in index form.

7 Simplify the expressions below.

(a) $5x^3 \times x^6$ (b) $4x^2 \times 4x^2$ (c) $5p^3 \times 2p^2$

(d) $8a^2 \times 3a^4$ (e) $\dfrac{8a^5}{a^2}$ (f) $\dfrac{10x^6}{2x^4}$

8 Which is larger? $\dfrac{(3^3)^2 \times 3^2}{3^3 \times (3^2)^2}$ or $\dfrac{(3^2)^3 \times 3^3}{3^5 \times 3^2}$

  A B

9 Simplify the expressions below.

(a) $\dfrac{x^5 \times x^3}{x^6}$

(b) $\dfrac{a^2 \times a^6}{(a^2)^2}$

(c) $\dfrac{(m^3)^2 \times m^4}{(m^3)^3}$

(d) $\dfrac{a^8}{a^3 \times a}$

(e) $\dfrac{n^9 \times (n^2)^4}{(n^3)^5}$

(f) $\dfrac{x^8 \times x^4}{(x^3)^2 \times x^2}$

(g) $\dfrac{(x^3)^6}{x^2 \times (x^2)^5}$

(h) $\dfrac{a^{20}}{(a^3)^4 \times (a^2)^2}$

(i) $\dfrac{n^2 \times (n^4)^2}{(n^2)^3 \times n}$

10 Multiply out the brackets below, leaving each answer in index form.

(a) $x^3(x^3 + x^2)$

(b) $n^4(n^5 - n)$

(c) $x^7(x^2 + x^5)$

Can you still?

18C   **Find volumes of prisms (see Unit 15)**

Can you still?

Find the volume of each prism below. When necessary, give answers to 1 decimal place.

1.

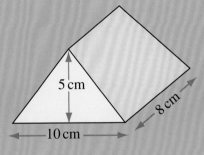

5 cm   8 cm   10 cm

2.

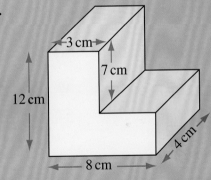

3 cm   7 cm   12 cm   8 cm   4 cm

3.

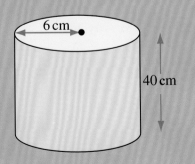

6 cm   40 cm

4.

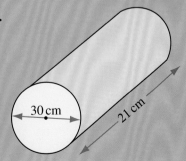

30 cm   21 cm

Key Facts

Remember:

mn means $m \times n$

$\dfrac{m}{n}$ means $m \div n$

m^2 means $m \times m$

$4(m - 3)$ means '$m - 3$ then multiply by 4'

$m + n$ cannot be added together because the term m is not like the term n

$6m + m = 7m$ because $6m$ and m are like terms

M18.4

In questions ① to ⑯ find the value of each expression when $m = 7$

$n = 4$

$p = 9$

① $3m$

② $5n - p$

③ np

④ $4m + 3n$

⑤ n^2

⑥ $p^2 - m^2$

⑦ $6(p - m)$

⑧ $8(m + n)$

⑨ $2m + 3p$

⑩ $m(p - n)$

⑪ $m^2 + 4p$

⑫ $5(n^2 - 3n)$

⑬ $\dfrac{8m}{2n}$

⑭ $\dfrac{4m + 2n}{p}$

⑮ $\dfrac{p^2 - 3m}{n}$

⑯ $m^2 + n^2 + p^2$

Collect the like terms in questions ⑰ to ㉒

⑰ $6x + 4x - 3x$

⑱ $15y - 6y - y$

⑲ $6x + 3y + 2x$

⑳ $5x + 7y + 3x - x$

㉑ $4x + 3 - 2x$

㉒ $9y + 3x - 4y + 5$

㉓

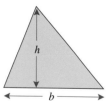

The area A of a triangle can be found using the formula

$A = \dfrac{1}{2}\, bh$

Find the area of a triangle when $b = 12$ and $h = 7$.

㉔ $m = 6n - 5$ Find m when $n = 5$.

㉕ $y = 3(x + 2)$ Find y when $x = 6$.

In questions **1** to **16** find the value of each expression when $a = -3$
$b = 6$
$c = -5$

1 $6a$

2 $5b + 3c$

3 $b - c$

4 a^2

5 ac

6 $a + c$

7 $2b - c$

8 $3b - 4a$

9 $b + c$

10 $5a + 2c$

11 $a^2 + b^2$

12 abc

13 $a(b - a)$

14 $4(a - c)$

15 $15 + 2a$

16 $a + 2b + c$

Simplify the following expressions

17 $4ab + a + 3ab$

18 $6xy - 4xy + 5x - x$

19 $6pq + 3pq - p$

20 $5ab + a + b - 3ab$

21 $7xy + 3y - xy + y$

22 $6p + pq - 5p + 4pq$

23 Write down an expression for the perimeter of this shape. Simplify your answer as much as possible.

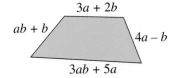

$3a + 2b$
$ab + b$
$4a - b$
$3ab + 5a$

24 $v = u + at$ Find v when $u = 8$, $a = 3$ and $t = 9$.

25 $s = \frac{1}{2} t (u + v)$ Find s when $t = 6$, $u = 3.5$ and $v = 7.5$

Remember:

$4m \times 2n = 8mn$ multiply numbers first then the letters

$12m \div 3 = 4m$

Multiply out $6(m + 3)$ gives $6m + 18$

Expand $m(m + n)$ gives $m^2 + mn$ ('expand' means 'multiply out')

Expand $a(2b + a)$ gives $2ab + a^2$

Simplify the following:

1 $9y \times 3$ **2** $4 \times 3m$ **3** $6p \times 2$ **4** $16n \div 8$

5 $15q \div 5$ **6** $7m \times 3n$ **7** $4a \times 6b$ **8** $5a \times 3a$

9 $8m \times m$ **10** $12n \div 6$ **11** $m \times 7n$ **12** $m \times 7m$

Multiply out

13 $5(m + 5)$ **14** $3(2n + 3)$ **15** $2(3x - 7)$ **16** $7(2a + 9)$

17 $4(2x + 3)$ **18** $6(1 - 4y)$ **19** $3(5p - 2)$ **20** $m(3m + 2)$

21 $a(5 + 4b)$ **22** $n(n + 5)$ **23** $a(4 + 3b)$ **24** $p(p - q)$

25 $y(x + y)$ **26** $3(2m - 3)$ **27** $n(4n + 1)$ **28** $6(3a - 2b)$

Remember:

factorise $4x + 4y$ 4 is the common factor of $4x$ and $4y$

so take out the common factor 4 and write $4(x + y)$

$3a - 3b = 3(a - b)$ common factor 3

$a^2 - ab = a(a - b)$ common factor a

$4a + 8b = 4(a + 2b)$ common factor 4

Copy and complete

1 $5m + 20 = 5\left(m + \boxed{}\right)$ **2** $8x + 6 = 2\left(\boxed{} + 3\right)$

3 $6y - 24 = 6\left(y - \boxed{}\right)$ **4** $7n - 42 = 7\left(\boxed{} - \boxed{}\right)$

5 $20a - 12 = 4\left(\boxed{} - \boxed{}\right)$ **6** $30y + 18 = \boxed{}\left(\boxed{} + \boxed{}\right)$

Factorise the expressions below:

7 $10n + 4$ **8** $6y + 15$ **9** $8x - 18$

10 $14m + 6n$ **11** $10x - 15y$ **12** $ab + ac$

13 $a^2 + an$ **14** $m^2 - 3m$ **15** $pq + p^2$

16 $5mn - 35mp$ **17** $8a^2 + 10ab$ **18** $15mn - 6n^2$

For questions **1** to **3**, you will need to draw axes like these:

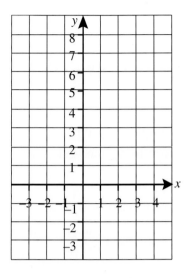

1 Complete the table below then draw the straight line $y = x + 3$

x	0	1	2	3	4
y					

2 Complete the table below then draw the straight line $y = 2x + 1$

x	−2	−1	0	1	2	3
y						

3 Complete the table below then draw the curve $y = x^2 - 3$

x	−3	−2	−1	0	1	2	3
y							

Remember:

Solve $3n + 2 = 23$
$3n = 23 - 2$
$3n = 21$
$n = \dfrac{21}{3}$
$n = 7$

Solve $5n - 3 = 42$
$5n = 42 + 3$
$5n = 45$
$n = \dfrac{45}{5}$
$n = 9$

Solve these equations:

1 $8n = 32$

2 $\dfrac{n}{3} = 9$

3 $4n + 3 = 39$

4 $5n - 4 = 36$

5 $6n - 11 = 19$

6 $3n + 7 = 25$

7 $7n + 8 = 43$

8 $10n - 4 = 26$

9 $4n + 28 = 68$

10 $4n - 2 = 3n + 5$

11 $6n + 3 = 4n + 11$

12 $5n - 1 = 3n + 13$

Now solve these:

13 $8n - 3 = 4n + 17$

14 $5n + 6 = 3n + 24$

15 $10n + 16 = 5n + 46$

16 $12n + 7 = 9n + 22$

17 $6n - 9 = 2n + 19$

18 $22 = 5n - 18$

19 $17 = 3n + 5$

20 $7n - 4 = 4n + 17$

21 $31 = 8n - 17$

Solve these equations (remember to multiply out the brackets first):

1 $4(n + 5) = 32$

2 $6(n - 2) = 36$

3 $3(n + 4) = 30$

4 $2(2n + 1) = 22$

5 $5(2n - 4) = 20$

6 $3(3n - 7) = 15$

7 $6(2n - 5) = 42$

8 $8(n + 7) = 72$

9 $5(9 + n) = 60$

10

$4n + 3$

$2n + 1$

The perimeter of this rectangle is 56 cm.
(a) Write down an equation using the perimeter.
(b) Find n.

11 Solve $3(n - 2) = 2(n + 3)$

12 Solve $3(2n + 6) = 4(n + 7)$

■ USE YOUR MATHS! – Buying a house

Although house prices may seem very expensive at the moment, you may one day in the future wish to buy a house.

Mortgages

Most people need to take out a mortgage which they usually pay back over 25 years. Interest has to be paid on the mortgage so it is important to shop around for the best deal.

Repayment mortgage

An amount is paid each month to pay the interest and some of the borrowed money. The monthly amount is worked out so that all the money is paid back after 25 years.

Interest – only mortgage

This costs less than a repayment mortgage because only the interest is paid back each month. This means that after 25 years you will still owe the same amount of money as you borrowed at the start.

You would have to save money to pay back the mortgage at the end or have another plan. If not, you would have to sell your home to pay back the mortgage at the end.

Deposit

If you save some money towards your new home before you buy it, your mortgage payments will be smaller. Often if you have at least a 5% deposit you will get a better deal on the mortgage interest rate.

Hidden costs

Stamp Duty

Money paid to the government when a property is bought.

If you buy a flat for £90000, you have to pay stamp duty of 1% of £90000 to the government. That is £900.

At the time of writing,	stamp duty
property worth up to £60000	– no stamp duty
£60001 to £250000	– 1% of the cost of the property
£250001 to £500000	– 3% of the cost of the property
more than £500000	– 4% of the cost of the property

Solicitor

You have to pay a solicitor to make sure there are no legal problems with your new property.

Surveyor

You need a surveyor to check that your new property is safe and will not cost you expensive repairs in the future.

Task

1   Dan wants to buy a house for £140,000. He earns £35,000 each year. A building society will give him a mortgage of 3.5 times his annual (yearly) salary.

   (a) How much mortgage can Dan get?

   (b) How much more money does he need to buy the house?

   (c) Stamp duty is 1% of £140,000. The solicitor and surveyor bills amount to £2000. How much money will he really need to have saved to buy this house if he takes the full mortgage?

2   Jim and Hannah have saved £40,000. They earn £30,000 between them each year. A bank will give them a mortgage of 4 times their joint annual salary.

   (a) How much mortgage can they get?

   (b) They want to buy a house for £155,000. Stamp duty is 1%. The solicitor and surveyor bills amount to £2800. Can they afford this house? How much money will be left over if they take out the full mortgage?

3   Donna sells her flat and makes £73,000 profit. She earns £27,000 each year. A bank will give her a mortgage of 3.5 times her annual salary.

   (a) What is the most money she will have available to buy a new property?

   (b) If she bought a house for this amount of money, how much stamp duty would be payable at 1%?

4   4 friends want to buy a house together. They can jointly raise a mortgage of £240,000 and have a total deposit of £41,000.

   They buy a house costing £268,000. Stamp duty is 3%. The solicitor and surveyor bills amount to £3420.

   How much money will they have left over if they take out the full mortgage?

5   Laura earns £26,000 each year and Bruce earns £19,000. They can both get a mortgage of 3.5 times their salary.

   (a) How much mortgage can Laura get?

   (b) How much mortgage can Bruce get?

   (c) They have a joint deposit of £33,000. They buy a property costing £182,000. Stamp duty is 1%. The solicitor and surveyor bills amount to £2950. What is the *lowest* joint mortgage they would need to take out?

6   Peter and Sonia can *rent* a flat for £560 each month. They could *buy* a similar flat and the monthly mortgage payments would be £560. *Discuss with your teacher* the advantages and disadvantages of buying the flat compared to renting the flat.

---

1. Changing the subject of a formula

Make x the subject of each formula given below:

(a) $y = x + 3$ (b) $y = 4x$ (c) $y = x - 9$ (d) $y = 2x + 1$

(e) $y = 5x - 2$ (f) $y = ax - b$ (g) $a(x + b) = y$ (h) $\dfrac{x}{a} - b = y$

---

2. Dealing with inequalities

Write down the inequalities shown below:

(a)

(b)

(c)

Draw a number line to show the following inequalities:

(d) $x < -2$ (e) $4 < x < 7$ (f) $-6 \leq x < 1$

Solve the inequalities below:

(g) $x + 3 \geq 7$ (h) $x - 4 > 8$ (i) $5x \leq 35$

(j) $\dfrac{x}{9} \geq 6$ (k) $3x + 5 < 29$ (l) $2(x - 3) > 14$

(m) Write down all the integer values (whole numbers) of x which satisfy the inequality

$$-4 \leq x < 2$$

---

3. Using the laws of indices

Work out and write each answer as a number in index form.

(a) $5^3 \times 5^4$ (b) $6^7 \div 6^5$ (c) $8^9 \div 8^4$

(d) $\dfrac{3^7 \times 3^4}{3^6}$ (e) 4^0 (f) $(3^2)^3$

(g) $\dfrac{4^2 \times 4^6}{(4^3)^2}$ (h) $\dfrac{(2^4)^3 \times 2^3}{2^9}$ (i) $\dfrac{5^7 \times 5^0}{(5^2)^3}$

Simplify the expressions below.

(j) $a^8 \div a^2$ (k) $(x^4)^5$ (l) $y^6 \times y^3 \times y^4$

(m) $m^3 \times m$ (n) $\dfrac{x^4 \times x^5}{x^7}$ (o) $\dfrac{x^3 \times (x^2)^4}{(x^3)^3}$

(a) If $p = 4n + 7$, find p when $n = 6$.

(b) If $a = \dfrac{2b + 4}{c}$, find a when $b = 25$ and $c = 9$.

(c) If $w = 4(y - m)$, find w when $y = 8$ and $m = 3$.

Expand (multiply out):

(d) $5(4n + 3)$ (e) $8(2y - 3)$ (f) $n(n - p)$

(g)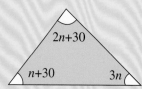

Write down an equation involving the angles in this triangle then solve it to find n.

Solve these equations:

(h) $8n - 6 = 26$ (i) $5n - 3 = 2n + 18$

(j) $4(2n + 1) = 36$ (k) $2(n + 6) = 13$

(l) Draw the straight line $y = 2x - 1$ by completing this table first.

x	0	1	2	3	4
y					

Mixed examination questions

1 Evaluate $7^6 \div 7^4$ (CCEA)

2 Write each of these expressions as a single power of y.

(i) $y^2 \times y^3$ (ii) $\dfrac{y^8}{y^2}$ (iii) $(y^4)^2$ (OCR)

3 Make t the subject of the formula

$v = u + 8t$

4 Rearrange the following formula to make L the subject.

P = 2L + 2W   (OCR)

5 Multiply out $n^2(n - n^4)$

6 Simplify $\dfrac{5^4 \times 5^6}{5^3}$ Give your answer as a single power of 5   (OCR)

7 Solve the inequality $3 + 4x > 9$ (AQA)

8 (i) Write down the integer values of n for which $1 < 3n \leq 12$

(ii) Solve the inequality $5x - 2 \geq 1$ (OCR)

9 Simplify $2a^5 \times 3a^2$ (AQA)

10 (a) Solve $n + 3 = 7$ (b) Solve $6m - 14 = 16$

(c) Solve $3p - 7 = p + 8$ (d) Solve $4(2q + 3) = 84$

11 List the values of x, where x is an integer, such that $-1 < x - 2 \leq 1$ (AQA)

12 Rearrange the formula $y = r + 3x$ to make x the subject.   (EDEXCEL)

13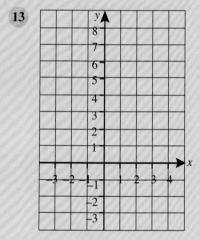

(a) Complete the table below for $y = x^2 - 2$

x	-4	-3	-2	-1	0	1	2	3	4
y		7				-1			

(b) Copy these axes and draw the graph of $y = x^2 - 2$

(c) Use your graph to find the value of y when $x = 2.5$

In this unit you will learn how to:

– measure lengths and angles

– construct triangles

– construct perpendicular bisectors, angle bisectors and angles without using a protractor

– make scale drawings

– use map scales

– draw loci

– ⟨ USE YOUR MATHS! ⟩ – handle the food

Measuring lengths and angles

M19.1

1 Read the measurements shown on the ruler.

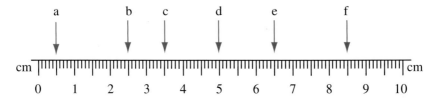

Measure these lines to the nearest tenth of a centimetre.

2 _____

3 _____   **4** _____

5 _____   **6** _____

7

8

9 Measure the perimeter of each shape below to the nearest tenth of a centimetre.

(a)

(b)

(c)

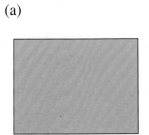
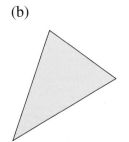
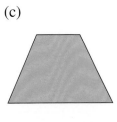

E19.1

Using a protractor, measure the following angles.

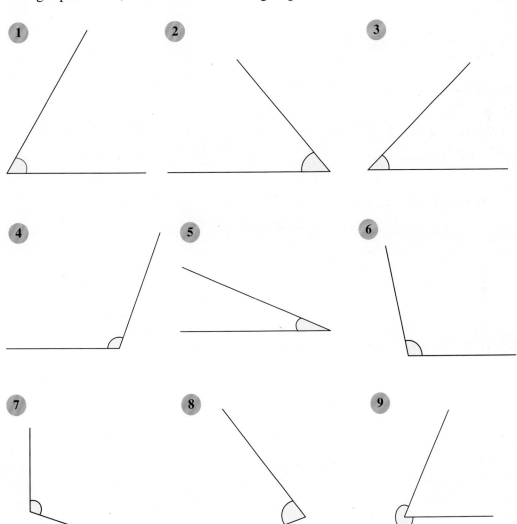

1

2

3

4

5

6

7

8

9

10 Use a protractor to draw the following angles. Label each angle acute, obtuse or reflex.

(a) 70°   (b) 25°   (c) 54°   (d) 31°

(e) 165°   (f) 108°   (g) 172°   (h) 15°

(i) 310°   (j) 230°   (k) 126°   (l) 283°

Can you still?

Can you still?

19A   **Use fractions (see Unit 5)**

1. Which fraction is larger – 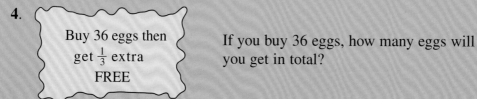 $\dfrac{2}{5}$ or $\dfrac{2}{3}$?

2. How many quarters make $5\dfrac{3}{4}$?

3. Work out   (a) $\dfrac{5}{9} - \dfrac{1}{9}$ (b) $\dfrac{5}{8} + \dfrac{2}{9}$

4.

> Buy 36 eggs then get $\frac{1}{3}$ extra FREE

If you buy 36 eggs, how many eggs will you get in total?

5. Work out $\dfrac{2}{5}$ of £40.

6. Marie has £40. She spends $\frac{3}{5}$ of her money on Saturday. How much money does she have left?

7. Work out   (a) $\dfrac{3}{7} \times \dfrac{2}{9}$ (b) $2\dfrac{2}{3} \times 1\dfrac{1}{5}$

8. 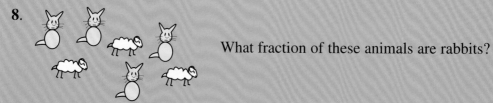   What fraction of these animals are rabbits?

9. $4\frac{1}{2}$ bars of chocolate are shared equally between 5 children. What fraction of a bar of chocolate does each child get?

10. Work out   (a) $\dfrac{2}{9} \div \dfrac{5}{6}$ (b) $3\dfrac{3}{4} \div \dfrac{5}{12}$

494

M19.2

This Exercise deals with triangles where 2 sides and an angle are known or 2 angles and a side are known.

Use a ruler and protractor to draw:

1

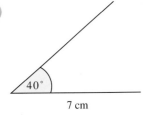

40°

7 cm

2

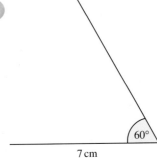

60°

7 cm

Now draw both of these on the same diagram like below:

3

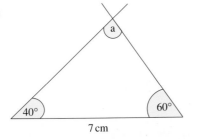

a

40° 60°

7 cm

Measure angle *a*. It should be 80°.

4 Use a ruler and protractor to draw:

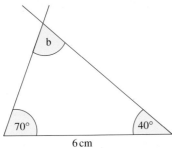

b

70° 40°

6 cm

Measure and write down angle *b*.

5 Draw accurately:

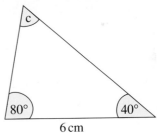

c

80° 40°

6 cm

Measure and write down angle *c*.

6 Use a ruler and protractor to draw:

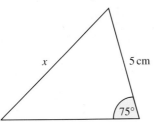

x 5 cm

75°

6 cm

Measure the length of the side marked *x*.

495

In questions ⑦ to ⑫, construct the triangles and measure the lengths of the sides marked *x*.

7
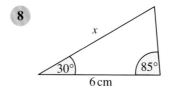

8

9
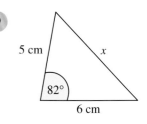

10
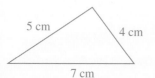

11
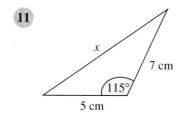

12
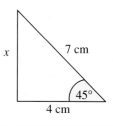

If we know all 3 sides, a triangle can be drawn with a ruler and a pair of compasses only.

Draw accurately

(a) Draw one side with a ruler

(b) Set your pair of compasses to 5 cm. Put the point of the pair of compasses on one end of the line and draw an arc of radius 5 cm.

(c) Set your pair of compasses to 4 cm. Put the point of the pair of compasses on the other end of the line and draw an arc of radius 4 cm.

Join the point where the 2 arcs cross to each end of the 7 cm line to make a *perfect* triangle.

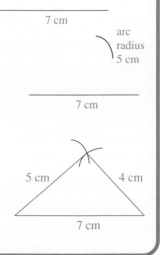

E19.2

In questions ① to ⑥, use a ruler and compasses only to draw each triangle. Use a protractor to measure each angle *x*.

1
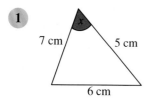

2
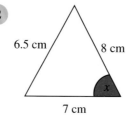

3
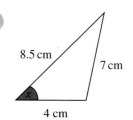

4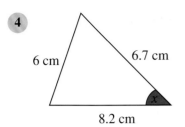

5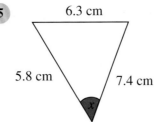

6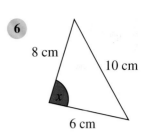

7 Construct an equilateral triangle with each side equal to 6 cm. Measure the angles to check that each one is 60°.

8 Draw a right-angled triangle with shorter sides equal to 4.5 cm and 6 cm. Measure the longest side of the triangle.

9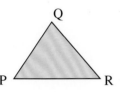

Draw a triangle PQR, where PR = 7.5 cm, QP̂R = 55° and PQ = 5 cm.

Measure the length of QR.

10 Draw a triangle XYZ, where XY = 4.8 cm, YZ = 6.1 cm and XZ = 7 cm. Measure XŶZ, YẐX and ZX̂Y.

Draw accurately the diagrams in questions **11** to **14** .

11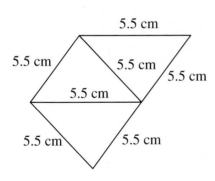

12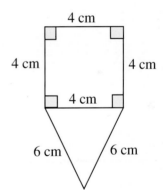

13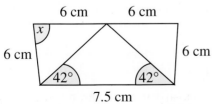

Measure x.

14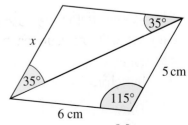

Measure x.

497

Perpendicular bisector

Draw a line AB 8 cm long.

Set the pair of compasses to more than 4 cm (half the line AB). Put the compass point on A and draw an arc as shown.

Put the compass point on B (**Do not let the compasses slip**). Draw another arc as shown.

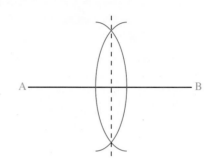

This broken line cuts line AB in half (*bisects*) and is at right angles to line AB (*perpendicular*).

The broken line is called the *perpendicular* bisector of line AB.

Bisector of an angle

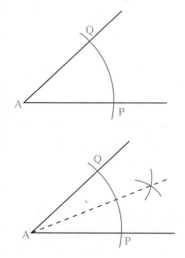

Put the compass point on A and draw an arc as shown.

Put the compass point on P and draw an arc as shown.

Put the compass point on Q and draw an arc as shown.

This broken line cuts the angle in half (*bisects*).

This broken line is called the *angle bisector*.

M19.3

1. Draw a horizontal line AB of length 9 cm. Construct the perpendicular bisector of AB. Check that each half of the line measures 4.5 cm exactly.

2. Draw a horizontal line CD of length 6 cm. Construct the perpendicular bisector of CD. Check that each half of the line measures 3 cm exactly.

3. Draw a *vertical* line EF of length 10 cm. Construct the perpendicular bisector of EF.

4. Draw an angle of 80°. Construct the bisector of the angle. Use a protractor to check that each half of the angle now measures 40°.

5 Draw an angle of 110°. Construct the bisector of the angle.

6 (a) Use a pencil, ruler and a pair of compasses *only* to *construct* the triangle ABC shown opposite.

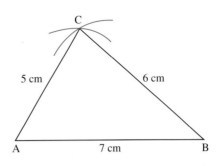

(b) Construct the perpendicular bisector of line AB.

(c) Construct the perpendicular bisector of line BC.

(d) Construct the perpendicular bisector of line AC. The 3 perpendicular bisectors should cross at the same point.

7 Draw any triangle XYZ and construct:

(a) the perpendicular bisector of XY.

(b) the perpendicular bisector of XZ.

Mark the point of intersection M.

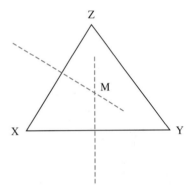

(c) Take a pair of compasses and, with centre at M and radius MX, draw a circle through the points X, Y and Z. This is the *circumcircle of triangle XYZ*.

(d) Repeat this construction for another triangle with different sides.

8 Draw any triangle ABC and then construct the bisectors of angles A, B and C. If done accurately the three bisectors should all pass through one point.

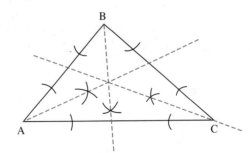

9 Draw any triangle XYZ and construct the bisectors of angles X and Y to meet at point M.

With centre at M draw a circle which just touches the sides of the triangle. This is the *inscribed circle of the triangle*.

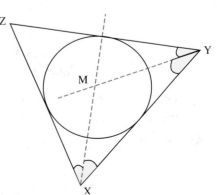

Repeat the construction for a different triangle.

499

Constructing a 60° angle

Draw a line 6 cm long.

Set the pair of compasses to less than 6 cm. Put the compass point on A and draw an arc as shown.

Put the compass point on B (**Do not let the compasses slip**). Draw another arc as shown.

Join C to the end of the line. The two lines make an angle of 60°. BÂC = 60°

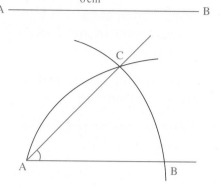

Constructing a 90° angle at a point on a line

Draw any line and mark a point on that line.

Set the pair of compasses to around 3 cm. Put the compass point on A and draw 2 small arcs which cross the line on each side of A. (If necessary, make the line longer)

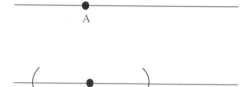

Put the compass point on B and set the compasses longer than BA. Draw an arc above the line.

Put the compass point on C (**Do not let the compasses slip**). Draw another arc as shown.

Join D and A with a straight line.

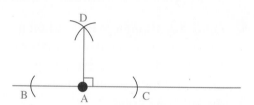

The two lines make an angle of 90°.
CÂD = 90°

E19.3

1 (a) Draw a line 9 cm long and mark the point A on the line as shown.

4 cm   A   5 cm

(b) Construct an angle of 90° at A.

2 Construct an angle of 60°.

3 (a) Draw a line 7 cm long and mark the point B on the line as shown.

(b) Construct an angle of 45° at B.

4 Construct an angle of 30°.

5 Construct an equilateral triangle with each side equal to 5 cm.

6 Construct these triangles (only use a protractor to *check* at the end).

(a)

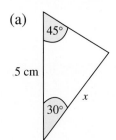

Measure x.

(b)

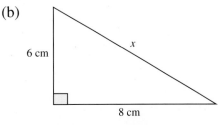

Measure x.

7 Construct each shape below and measure x.

(a)

(b)

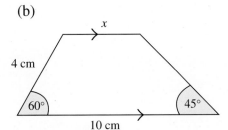

(c)

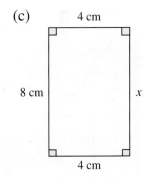

8 (a) Draw any line and any point as shown opposite.

A •

A •

(b) Put the compass point on A and set the compasses so that an arc can be drawn as shown.

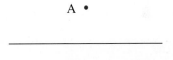

(c) Now draw the perpendicular bisector of the line BC.

The line AD is described as the *perpendicular from the point A to the line*.

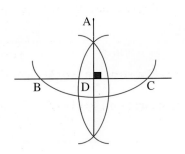

501

9 Construct an angle of 15°.

10 Construct a right-angled triangle ABC, where AB = 7 cm, AB̂C = 90° and BÂC = 45°. Measure the length of BC.

11 Construct an angle of 22.5°.

12 Draw any vertical line and any point as shown opposite.

Construct the perpendicular from the point to the line.

Can you still?

Can you still?

19B **Round off to decimal places and significant figures**
(see Unit 9)

1. Which numbers below round to 6.8 (to 1 decimal place)?

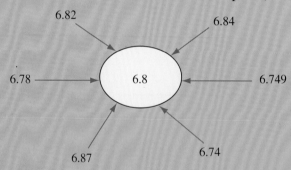

2. Round these numbers to 2 decimal places.

    (a) 4.138   (b) 8.216   (c) 9.462

3. Round these numbers to 3 significant figures.

    (a) 4.176   (b) 2381   (c) 51635

4. 0.06028 = 0.0603 to 3 significant figures. Is this true or false?

5. Round off 52.516 to 2 significant figures.

6. Use a calculator to work out each question below giving each answer to 3 significant figures.

    (a) 5.86 × 2.7   (b) 9.86²   (c) 17 ÷ 0.18

    (d) 281 – 2.1983   (e) $\sqrt{(28.5 - 9.1)}$ (f) $\dfrac{5.12 \times 3.9}{6.75}$

Scale drawings

Draw an accurate scale drawing of each shape below using the scale shown.

1

12 m
8 m

Scale: 1 cm for every 4 m

2

15 m
20 m
25 m

Scale: 1 cm for every 5 m.

3

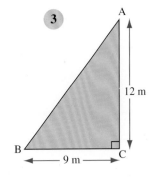

A
12 m
B
9 m
C

Scale: 1 cm for every 3 m. Measure (in cm) then write down the actual length of AB (in m).

4

1.5 m
3 m

Scale: 2 cm for every 1 m.

5

32 m
20 cm
16 cm
24 m
4 m
8 m

Scale: 1 cm for every 8 m.

6

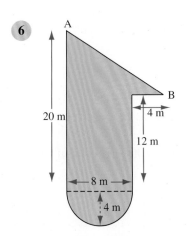

A
20 m
B
4 m
12 m
8 m
4 m

Scale: 1 cm for every 4 m. Measure in cm the length of AB.

503

Map scales

On a map of scale 1:3000 000, Leeds and Manchester are 2 cm apart. What is the actual distance between the cities?

1 cm on map   = 3000 000 cm for real

2 cm on map   = 2 × 3000 000 cm for real

                     = 6000 000 cm   (÷ 100 to change cm into m)

                     = 60000 m   (÷ 1000 to change m into km)

                     = 60 km

The actual distance between Leeds and Manchester is 60 km.

E19.4

You may use a calculator.

1 A model of a ship is made using a scale of 1:50. The model is 16 cm long. How long is the real ship? (give your answer in metres)

2

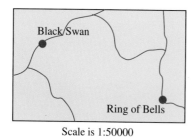

Scale is 1:50000

Measure the shortest distance between the Black Swan and the Ring of Bells (give your answer in km).

3 Two towns are 3 cm apart on a map whose scale is 1:5000 000. Find the actual distance (in km) between the two towns.

4 A lake is 5 cm long on a map whose scale is 1:50000. Find the actual length (in km) of the lake.

5 Copy and complete the table below.

Map length	Scale	Real length
6 cm	1:80	m
4 cm	1:5000	m
9 cm	1:200 000	km
cm	1:2000	160 m
cm	1:3000 000	120 km
cm	1:1000 000	35 km

6 The length of part of a railway track is 18 km. How long will it be on a map of scale 1:200 000?

7

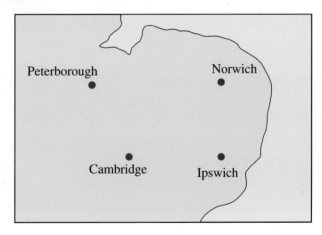

Scale is 1:3000000

Measure then write down the actual distances (in km) between:

(a) Norwich and Ipswich

(b) Peterborough and Norwich

(c) Cambridge and Ipswich

8 The distance between two cities is 110 km. How far apart will they be on a map of scale 1:2000 000?

9 The length of a house is 8.4 m. A plan of the house is drawn using a scale of 1:70. How long will the house be on the plan?

19C **Using ratios (see Unit 6)**

1. 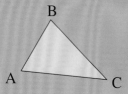 Write down the ratio of black squares to white squares.

2. In Hatton High School there are 120 girls and 150 boys in year 11. Find the ratio of girls to boys, giving your answer in its *simplest form*.

3. Divide £240 in the ratio 5:7.

4. A shandy is made by mixing beer and lemonade in the ratio 2:7. If 100 ml of beer is used, how much shandy is made in total?

5. A small firm makes £40000 profit which is to be shared between 3 people (Tom, Gus and Mel) in the ratio 8:11:6. How much money does Mel get?

6. The sides AB and BC in a triangle are in the ratio 2:3. If AB = 12 cm, how long is BC?

7. 8 magazines cost £24. How much do 7 magazines cost?

8. 14 packets of crisps cost £3.78. How much will 9 packets of crisps cost?

9. 4 new car tyres cost £168. How much will 3 new car tyres cost?

Locus

Sarah walks so that she is always 2 km from a point A.

She ends up walking in a circle. She walks in a circle because she is following the rule that she is always 2 km from point A. The circle is called a '*locus*'.

A *locus* is the *set of points* which fit a given rule.

The plural of locus is '*loci*'.

For Sarah walking above, the circle is the *locus* of points 2 km from point A.

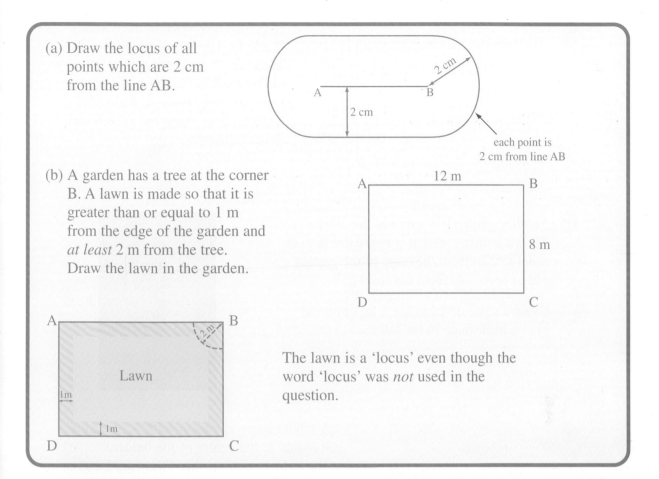

(a) Draw the locus of all points which are 2 cm from the line AB.

each point is 2 cm from line AB

(b) A garden has a tree at the corner B. A lawn is made so that it is greater than or equal to 1 m from the edge of the garden and *at least* 2 m from the tree. Draw the lawn in the garden.

Lawn

The lawn is a 'locus' even though the word 'locus' was *not* used in the question.

M19.5

You will need a ruler and a pair of compasses.

1. Draw the locus of all points which are 4 cm from a point A.

2. Draw the locus of all points which are 3 cm from the line AB.

   A ————— 6 cm ————— B

3. A goat is tied by a 5 m rope to a peg in the middle of a large field. Using a scale of 1 cm for 1 m, shade the area that the goat can graze in.

4. Draw the locus of all points which are less than or equal to 1.5 cm from the line PQ.

   P ————— 5 cm ————— Q

5. A wild headteacher is placed in a cage. The pupils are not allowed to be within one metre of the cage. Using a scale of 1 cm for 1 m, sketch the cage and show the locus of points where the pupils are *not* allowed.

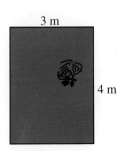

507

6

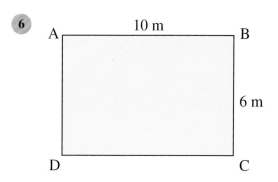

A garden has a tree at the corners C and D. The whole garden is made into a lawn except for anywhere less than or equal to 4 m from any tree. Using a scale of 1 cm for 2 m, draw the garden and shade in the lawn.

7 Another garden has a tree at the corner A. A lawn is made so that it is greater than or equal to 2 m from the edge of the garden and *at least* 5 m from the tree.

Using a scale of 1 cm for 2 m, draw the garden and shade in the lawn.

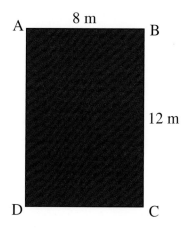

8

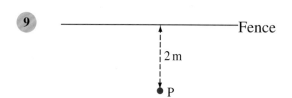

A ladder leans against a wall. A person is standing at the centre of the ladder. The ladder starts to slip! Draw the locus of the person as the ladder falls (make sure in your drawing, the ladder stays the same length!).

9

A goat is tied by a 3 m rope to a peg P as shown. Using a scale of 1 cm for 1 m, copy the diagram then shade the area that the goat can graze in.

10

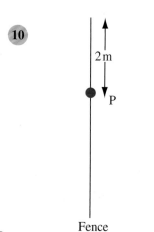

The goat is moved so that it is tied by a 3 m rope to a peg P as shown. Using a scale of 1 cm for 1 m, copy the diagram then shade the area that the goat can graze in.

You will need a ruler and a pair of compasses.

1 Draw the locus of points which are the same distance from P and Q below.

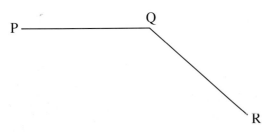
P •– – – – – – – – – – – –• Q
6 cm

2

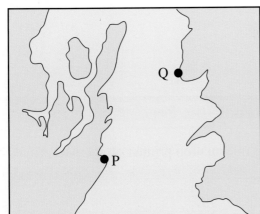

Draw the locus of points which are the same distance from the lines PQ and QR.

3

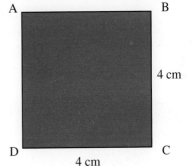

A ship sails so that it is *equidistant* from ports P and Q. Using a scale of 1 cm for 1 km, draw a rough copy of this diagram with P and Q 4 km apart.

Construct the path taken by the ship.

4 Draw this square.

Show the locus of points inside the square which are nearer to A than to C *and* are more than 3 cm from B.

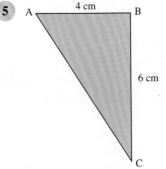

A ———— B
4 cm
4 cm
D ———— C
4 cm

5 Draw one copy of triangle ABC and show on it:

(a) the locus of points equidistant from A and B

(b) the locus of points equidistant from lines AB and AC

(c) the locus of points nearer to AC than to AB

A —4 cm— B
6 cm
C

509

6 A transmitter at Redford has a range of 80 km and another transmitter at Hatton has a range of 60 km. The 2 transmitters are 120 km apart.

Using a scale of 1 cm for 20 km, draw the 2 transmitters then shade the area where a signal can be received from both transmitters.

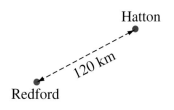

7 A child's block is rolled along the floor by rotating about its corners.

Draw the locus of B.

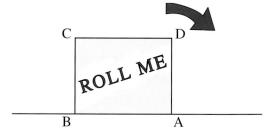

USE YOUR MATHS! – Handle the Food

Some bread rolls have the following information printed on the packet.

How to store and bake	
❄	**Freezable** If freezing, freeze on the day of purchase and consume within 1 month. Defrost thoroughly and use within 24 hours. Once thawed do not re-freeze.
♥	Oven bake | Electric	200°C
Gas	6 | 10 mins
♥	Oven bake from frozen | Electric	190°C
Gas	5 | 13 mins

Nutrition information			
Typical values	Per 100 g	Per roll	% of GDA for women
Energy	975 kJ 230 kcal	487 kJ 115 kcal	– 5.8 %
Protein	8.3g	4.2g	9.3%
Carbohydrate of which sugars of which starch	49.4g 3.2g 46.2g	24.7g 1.6g 23.1g	10.7% 1.8% –
Fat of which saturates	1.4g 0.4g	0.7g 0.2g	1.0% 1.0%
Fibre	3.0g	1.5g	6.3%
Salt	1.08g	0.54g	9.0%

Guideline daily amounts (GDA)		
Women	Men	Children (5–10 years)
– 2000 kcal	– 2500 kcal	– 1800 kcal
45g	55g	24g
230g 90g –	300g 120g –	220g 85g –
70g 20g	95g 30g	70g 20g
24g	24g	15g
6g	6g	4g

Task A

1. Gary needs to bake two bread rolls from frozen. What setting must he use on his gas cooker?

2. Gary puts his frozen bread rolls in the cooker at 13:55. At what time must he take the rolls out of the oven?

3. There are 30 days in June. If Gary freezes bread rolls on Tuesday, 9th June, by what date must he eat the rolls and on what day of the week would this be?

4. Sandy buys bread rolls and wants to eat them on the same day. At what time must she put the rolls in the oven if she wants to take them out at 6:35 p.m?

5. Sandy eats two rolls. How much protein has she eaten?

6. Gary eats rolls and works out that he has eaten 2.1g of fat. How many rolls does he eat?

7. How much fibre is in 250g of these bread rolls?

Task B

1. What is the guideline daily amount (GDA) of energy kcals for men?

2. Gary eats two bread rolls. Is this more or less than 10% of his energy GDA?

3. What is the *least* number of bread rolls that would give a woman more than her GDA of carbohydrate?

4. Sandy eats four bread rolls. What percentage of the GDA of fat for women has she eaten?

5. Gary eats three bread rolls in total. How much more fibre must he eat on that day if he is to reach his GDA for fibre?

TEST YOURSELF ON UNIT 19

1. Measuring lengths and angles

(a) Measure AB to the nearest tenth of a centimetre.

A ————————————————— B

(b) Measure the perimeter of this trapezium to the nearest tenth of a centimetre.

(c) Using a protractor, measure each angle stated below:

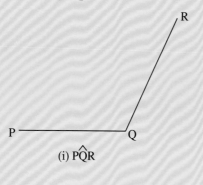

(i) PQ̂R

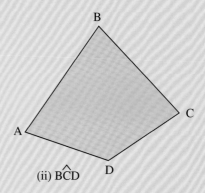

(ii) BĈD

2. Constructing triangles

(a) Use a ruler and protractor to draw:

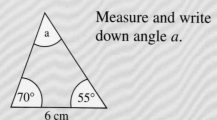

Measure and write down angle *a*.

(b) Use a ruler and compasses only to construct:

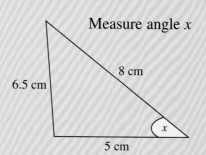

Measure angle *x*

3. Constructing perpendicular bisectors, angle bisectors and angles

(a) Draw a *vertical* line PQ of length 8 cm.

Construct the perpendicular bisector of PQ.

(b) Draw an angle of 70°. Construct the bisector of the angle.

(c) Construct this triangle.

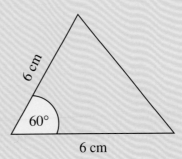

(d) Construct an angle of 30°.

4. Making scale drawings

Draw an accurate scale drawing of each shape below using the scale shown.

(a)

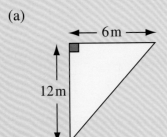

Scale: 1 cm for every 3 m

(b)

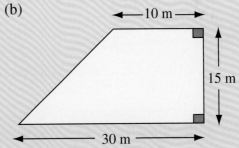

Scale: 1 cm for every 5 m

5. Using map scales

(a) A model of a building is made using a scale of 1:200. The model length of the building is 15 cm. How long is the real building (give your answer in metres)?

(b) Cara is making a scale drawing of her garden using a scale of 1:50. If her pond has a diameter of 3 m, what is the diameter of the pond on the scale drawing (give the answer in cm)?

(c) The distance between two villages is 7.5 km. How far apart will they be (in cm) on a map of scale 1:300 000?

6. Drawing loci

(a) Draw the locus of all points which are 3.5 cm from the line PQ.

P ———————————— Q
  7 cm

(b) The diagram shows a rectangular room ABCD. Draw *three* diagrams using a scale at 1 cm for every 1 m. Use a separate diagram to show each locus below:

(i) Points in the room less than or equal to 3 m from B.

(ii) Points in the room which are an equal distance from both B and C. (*'equidistant'* from B and C).

(iii) Points in the room which are greater than or equal to 2 m from D.

Mixed examination questions

1

55°   38°
  12 cm

Use your ruler, compasses and protractor to make an accurate construction of this triangle.

(WJEC)

2 Copy the line AB. Draw the locus of all points which are 3 cm away from the line AB.

(EDEXCEL)

3 Make an accurate drawing of a triangle with sides 5 cm, 7 cm and 8 cm long.

4 The diagram represents a triangular garden *ABC*. The scale of the diagram is 1 cm represents 1 m. A tree is to be planted in the garden so that it is nearer to *AB* than to *AC*, within 5 m of point *A*.

Copy the diagram and shade the region where the tree may be planted.

(EDEXCEL)

5

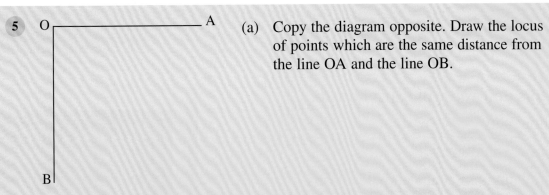

(a) Copy the diagram opposite. Draw the locus of points which are the same distance from the line OA and the line OB.

Some points are the same distance from the line OA and the line OB and are also 4 cm from the point B.

(b) Mark the positions of these points with crosses.   (EDEXCEL)

6 Copy the diagram below.

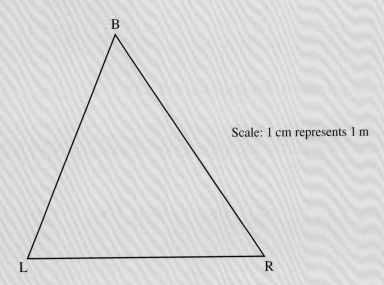

Scale: 1 cm represents 1 m

Triangle LRB is the plan of a garden drawn to a scale of 1 cm to 1 m.

A lime tree (*L*), a rowan tree (*R*) and a beech tree (*B*) are at the corners of the garden.

(a) Construct the perpendicular bisector of *LR*. Show your construction lines clearly.

(b) Diana wants to put a bird table in the garden.

   The bird table must be nearer the rowan tree than the lime tree.

   It must also be within 4 metres of the beech tree.

   Shade the region on the plan where the bird table may be placed.   (OCR)

In this unit you will learn how to:

– draw nets

– draw 3-D objects

– draw and use plans and elevations

– use bearings

– use Pythagoras' theorem

– solve problems with shapes and lines using co-ordinates

– find reciprocals

– ⟨ USE YOUR MATHS! ⟩ – the real cost

Nets

🗝 Key Facts

A shape which folds up to make a solid is called a *net*.

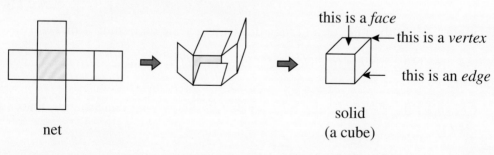

this is a *face*

this is a *vertex*

this is an *edge*

net → → solid (a cube)

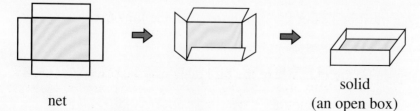

net → → solid (an open box)

1

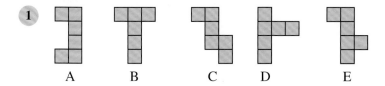

A   B   C   D   E

Which of these nets will fold to make a cube?
If your teacher wants you to, draw the nets on squared paper, cut them out and fold them to see which ones do make cubes.

2 Draw an accurate *net* for this cube.

3

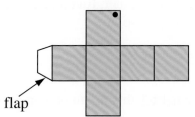

This net makes a cuboid.
Each small square is 1 cm long.

(a) How long will the cuboid be?

(b) How wide will it be?

(c) How high will it be?

(d) What is the volume of the cuboid?

4 Draw an accurate net for this cuboid.

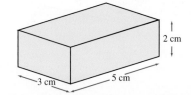

5

(a) Sketch this net.

(b) Which edge will the flap be stuck to? Put a ✓ on this edge.

(c) Two other corners will meet the corner with a •
Put a • in each corner that meets the corner with a •

flap

6 Draw a net for this *open* box.
If your teacher wants you to, cut out the net and fold it to check it is right.

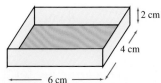

7

The dots on opposite faces of a die add up to seven. There must be 4 dots on the bottom face of this die.

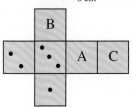

This is a net of a die. How many dots are on faces A, B and C?

517

8 Which of the nets below will make a closed box?

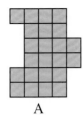

A

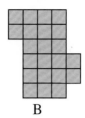

B

1 This diagram shows the net of a solid.

(a) Use *compasses* and a *ruler* to draw the net accurately on paper or card.

(b) Draw on some flaps.

(c) Cut out the net, fold and glue it to make the solid.

(d) What is the name of the solid?

6 cm

5 cm
5 cm

6 cm

2 The diagram shows a triangular prism.

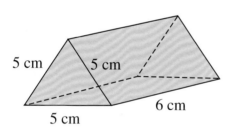

5 cm   5 cm

5 cm   6 cm

(a) Use *compasses* and a *ruler* to construct the net for this prism on paper or card.

(b) Draw on some flaps.

(c) Cut out the net, fold and glue it to make the solid.

3 Here is another triangular prism (a wedge).

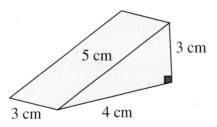

5 cm   3 cm

3 cm   4 cm

(a) Use *compasses* and a *ruler* to construct the net for this prism on paper or card.

(b) Draw on some flaps.

(c) Cut out the net, fold and glue it to make the solid.

4 Draw an *accurate net* for this square-based pyramid.

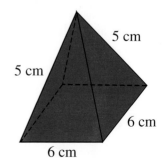

5 cm

5 cm

6 cm

6 cm

20A **Use metric units (see Unit 17)**

1. Which of the amounts below are the same as 30 cm?

   (3 m)   (300 mm)   (0.3 m)   (30 m)

2. Which of the amounts below are the same as 40 kg?

   (4000 g)   (40000 g)   (400 g)   (4 tonnes)

3. Copy and complete the following:

   (a) 7.5 kg = ☐ g   (b) 8 litres = ☐ ml   (c) 300 ml = ☐ litres

   (d) 0.6 m = ☐ cm   (e) 4200 g = ☐ kg   (f) 2.8 km = ☐ m

4. Mary has a 1.5 litre bottle of ginger beer. She and a friend drink 860 ml. How much ginger beer is left in the bottle?

5. Sandra runs in a 40 km race. She has to stop 2700 m *before* the end of the race.

3-D objects

M20.2

You will need isometric dot paper.

1

Here is a cube made from eight 1 cm cubes.

Draw a cuboid with a volume of 18 cm³.

2 Draw a cuboid with a volume of 20 cm³.

3 Make a copy of each object below. For each drawing state the number of 'multilink' cubes needed to make the object.

(a)

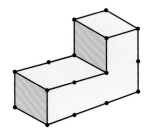

(b)

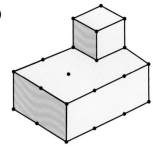

519

4 Using four cubes, you can make several different shapes. A and B are different shapes but C is the same as A.

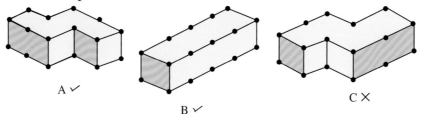

A ✓

B ✓

C ✗

Make as many *different* shapes as possible, using four cubes, and draw them all (including shapes A and B above) on isometric paper.

5

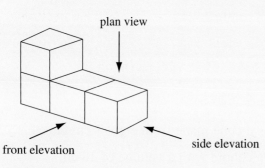

This shape falls over onto the shaded face.

Draw the shape after it has fallen over.

🔑 # Key Facts

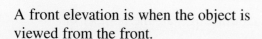

plan view

front elevation

side elevation

Here is a 3-D object made from centimetre cubes.

A plan view is when the object is looked at from above.

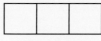

plan view

A front elevation is when the object is viewed from the front.

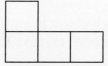

front elevation

A side elevation is when the object is viewed from the side.

side elevation

In Questions ① to ⑥ draw (a) the plan view, (b) the front view and (c) the side view of the object.

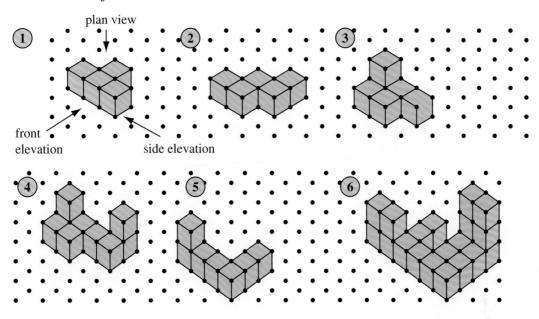

In Questions ⑦ to ⑩ you are given the plan and two elevations of an object.
Use the information to make the shape using centimetre cubes. Draw the object on isometric paper if you can.

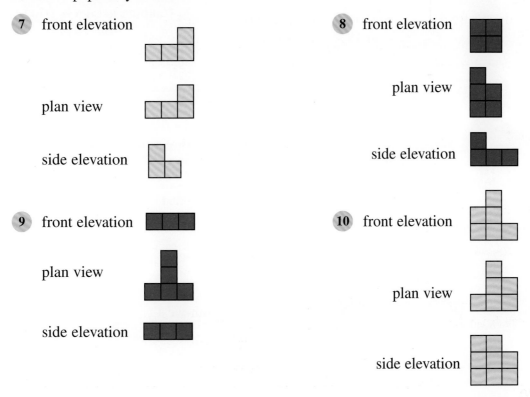

Key Facts

Bearings are used by navigators on ships and aircraft and by people travelling in open country.

Bearings are measured from the *North* line in a *clockwise* direction.
A bearing is always given as a *three-figure number*.

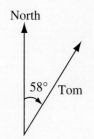

Tom is walking on a bearing of 058°.

3-figures used

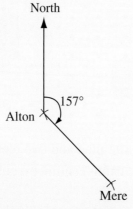

Mere is on a bearing of 157° *from Alton*.

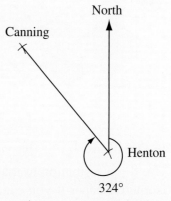

Canning is on a bearing of 324° *from Henton*.

M20.3

1

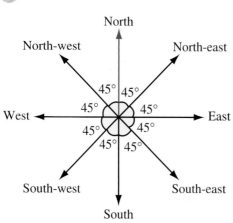

Write down the bearing for each compass direction below:

(a) East

(b) South-east

(c) West

(d) North-east

(e) South-west

(f) North-west

(g) South

(h) North

2 Peter hits 6 golf balls, aiming north, with his usual precision. The golf balls travel in the directions shown. On what bearing does each golf ball fly?

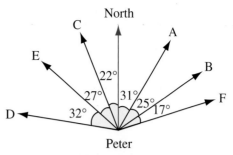

Write down the bearing of:

(a) Henly *from Dinder*

(b) Dinder *from Weare*

(c) Weare *from Dinder*

(d) Weare *from Henly*

(e) Dinder *from Henly*

(f) Henly *from Weare*

3

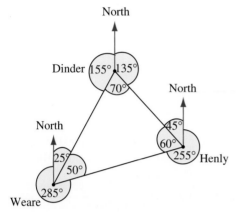

4 Seven travellers head off from camp on their search for the 'meaning of life'. They begin walking in the directions shown. On what bearing is each traveller walking?

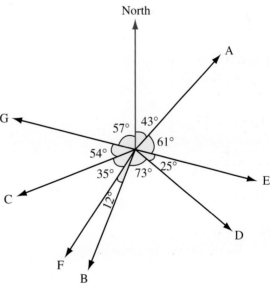

E20.3

1

 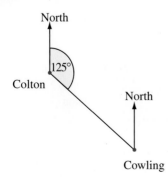

Find the bearing of:

(a) Cowling *from Colton*

(b) Colton *from Cowling*

2

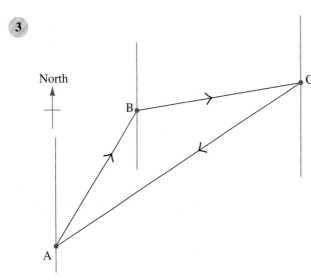

Use a protractor to measure the bearing of:

(a) Carling *from Pinton*

(b) Otley *from Carling*

(c) Pinton *from Otley*

(d) Carling *from Otley*

3

A hiker walks from A to B then B to C and finally from C to A.

Use a protractor to measure the bearing of the walk from

(a) *A to B*

(b) *B to C*

(c) *C to A*

4 Yasmin goes on a sponsored walk. Her route is shown opposite.

Work out the bearing of the journey from:

(a) Start to Jam Hill

(b) Jam Hill to Pilling Mount

(c) Pilling Mount to the White Swan

(d) The White Swan back to the Finish

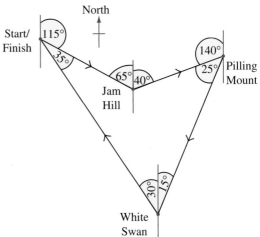

5 A ship sails 6 km due north and then a further 8 km on a bearing of 070°.

Use a scale of 1 cm for every 1 km to show the ship's journey. How far is the ship now from its starting point?

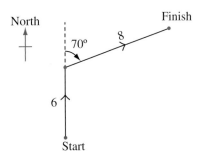

6 A ship sails 7 km due south and then a further 5 km on a bearing of 120°. Use a scale of 1 cm for every 1 km to show the ship's journey. How far is the ship from its starting point?

7 A ship sails 6 km on a bearing of 065° and then a further 7 km on a bearing of 165°. Use a scale of 1 cm for every 1 km to show the ship's journey. Find the distance of the ship from its starting point?

20B   **Use percentages (see Unit 6)**

1. Which 2 numbers below are equal to each other?

$\frac{7}{25}$ 2.8   28% $\frac{1}{28}$

2. At a local garage, 8 out of 40 cars fail their MOT. What *percentage* of the cars fail their MOT?

3. 9 out of 36 children say that their favourite film is 'Star Wars'. What *percentage* of children say that their favourite film is *not* 'Star Wars'?

4. Which 2 answers below are the same?

 20% of £80   15% of £60   5% of £180

5. A computer costs £780 + VAT. If VAT is 17.5%, work out how much the computer costs altogether.

6. In June, Rebecca earns £160 each week. After a pay rise she earns £168 each week. What is the *percentage increase* in her pay?

7. £3000 is invested at 5% per annum (year) compound interest. How much money will there be after 2 years?

8. There are 5000 fish in a lake. Each year, the lake loses 4% of its fish at the start of the year. How many fish are in the lake after 2 years?

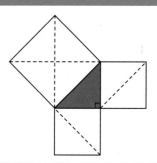

Here is a dissection which demonstrates a result called Pythagoras' theorem. Pythagoras was a famous Greek mathematician who proved the result in about 550 B.C. The dissection works only for isosceles right angled triangles.

 Key Facts

Pythagoras' theorem

In a *right angled* triangle, the square on the hypotenuse is equal to the sum of the squares on the other two sides.

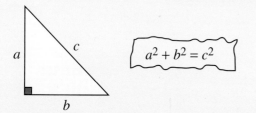

$$a^2 + b^2 = c^2$$

The 'hypotenuse' is the *longest* side in a right angled triangle.

To find the *hypotenuse*, square the known sides, *add* then square root. To find one of the *shorter sides*, square the known sides, *subtract* then square root.

(a) Find the length x.

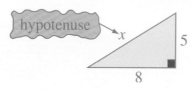

$x^2 = 5^2 + 8^2$

$x^2 = 25 + 64$

$x^2 = 89$

$x = \sqrt{89}$

$x = 9.43$ (to 2 decimal places)

(b) Find the length y.

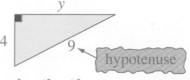

$y^2 + 4^2 = 9^2$

$y^2 + 16 = 81$

$y^2 = 81 - 16$

$y^2 = 65$

$y = \sqrt{65}$

$y = 8.06$ (to 2 decimal places)

You will need a calculator. Give your answers correct to 2 decimal places where necessary. The units are cm.

1 Find the length x. (x is the hypotenuse)

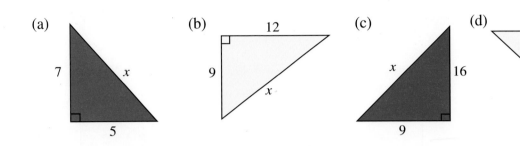

(a)   (b)   (c)   (d)

2 Find the length x. x is one of the shorter sides.

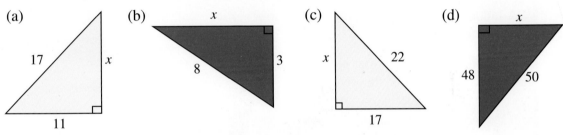

(a)   (b)   (c)   (d)

3 Find the length x.

Be careful! Check whether x is the hypotenuse or one of the shorter sides.

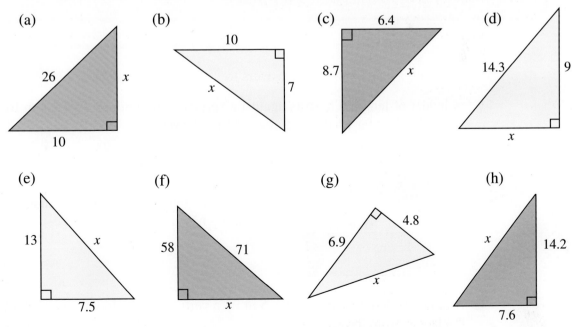

(a)   (b)   (c)   (d)

(e)   (f)   (g)   (h)

4 Find the length AB.

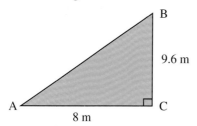

5 Find the length PQ.

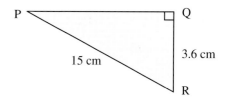

6 Find the length MN.

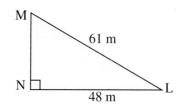

7 Find the length YZ.

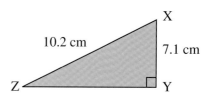

A ladder of length 6 m reaches 4.8 m up a vertical wall. How far is the foot of the ladder from the wall?

x is one of the shorter sides in a right angled triangle. Use Pythagoras' theorem.

$x^2 + 4.8^2 = 6^2$

$x^2 + 23.04 = 36$

$x^2 = 12.96$

$x = \sqrt{12.96}$

$x = 3.6$ m

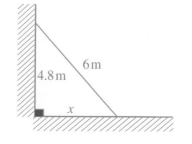

E20.4

You will need a calculator (give answers to 2 decimal places)

1 A ladder of length 6 m rests against a vertical wall, with its foot 2.4 m from the wall. How far up the wall does the ladder reach?

2

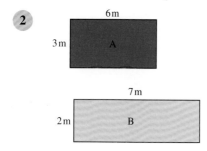

Which rectangle has the longer diagonal and by how much?

3 A ladder of length 7 m reaches 5 m up a vertical wall. How far is the foot of the ladder from the wall?

4

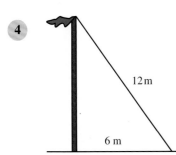

A rope attached to a flagpole is 12 m long. The rope is fixed to the ground 6 m from the foot of the flagpole. How tall is the flagpole?

5 Towley is 8 km due east of Hapton. Castleton is 12 km due south of Hapton. How far is Towley from Castleton?

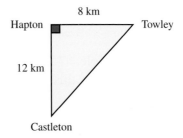

6 Redford is 9 km due north of Hagshed. Peltsham is 7 km due west of Hagshed. How far is Redford from Peltsham?

7 A ship sails 50 km due north and then a further 62 km due east. How far is the ship from its starting point?

8

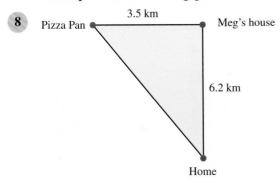

Kat and Holly are sisters. They are meeting friends at Pizza Pan. Kat drives *directly* to Pizza Pan. Holly has to pick up Meg on the way to Pizza Pan. How much further does Holly drive than Kat?

9 A clothes line is attached to 2 vertical walls as shown. How long is the clothes line?

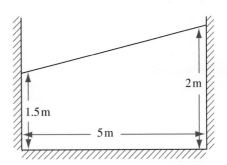

10

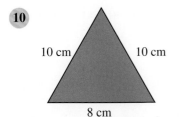

An *isosceles* triangle has a line of symmetry which divides the triangle into two right-angled triangles as shown.

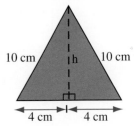

Use Pythagoras' theorem to find the height h of the triangle.

11 Find the height of each isosceles triangle below.

(a)
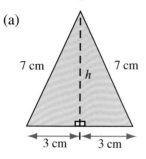
7 cm   7 cm
h
3 cm   3 cm

(b)
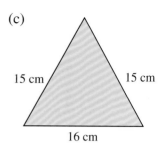
12 cm   12 cm
h
10 cm

(c)
15 cm   15 cm
16 cm

12 Area of triangle $= \frac{1}{2}bh$
Find the area of this isosceles triangle.

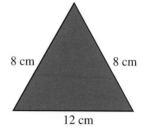
8 cm   8 cm
12 cm

13 Calculate the vertical height and hence the area of an equilateral triangle of side 16 cm.

14 Find the length x. The units are cm.

(a)
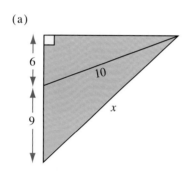
6
10
9
x

(b)
13
12
10
x

(c)
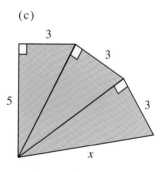
3
3
5
3
x

Shapes and lines using co-ordinates

M20.5

You may use a calculator.

1
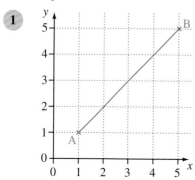

(a) Find the co-ordinates of the midpoint of line AB.

(b) Calculate the length AB, using Pythagoras' theorem.

2 Draw an *x*-axis from –5 to 5 and a *y*-axis from –5 to 5.

ABCD is a square. A is (– 3, 2), B is (– 3, – 4), C is (3, – 4).

(a) Draw the square.

(b) Write down the co-ordinates of D.

(c) Write down the co-ordinates of the centre of the square.

(d) Calculate the length of the diagonal AC.

3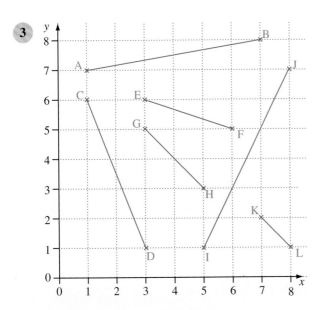

Calculate the length of each line *and* write down the co-ordinates of the midpoint of each line.

4 Calculate the length of the line joining (2, 1) to (8, 9).

5 Draw an *x*-axis from 0 to 7 and a *y*-axis from – 3 to 3.

PQRS is a parallelogram. P is (4, 1), Q is (2, – 2), R is (6, – 2).

(a) Draw the parallelogram.

(b) Write down the co-ordinates of S.

(c) Write down the co-ordinates of the midpoint of diagonal QS.

(d) Calculate the length of the diagonal QS.

6 Draw an *x*-axis from –5 to 5 and a *y*-axis from –5 to 5.

ABCD is a rhombus. A is (– 4, 2), B is (1, 2), C is (4, – 2).

(a) Draw the rhombus.

(b) Write down the co-ordinates of D.

(c) Write down the co-ordinates of the midpoint of diagonal BD.

(d) Calculate the length of the diagonal AC.

ReYreecal Reciprocals

Key Facts

The *reciprocal* of a number n is $\dfrac{1}{n}$

where n can never equal zero.

A calculator usually has a reciprocal button $\boxed{\dfrac{1}{x}}$

The reciprocal of 3 is $\dfrac{1}{3}$ (note: $3 \times \dfrac{1}{3} = 1$)

The reciprocal of 0.25 is $\dfrac{1}{0.25}$ which equals 4 (note: $0.25 \times 4 = 1$)

The reciprocal of $\dfrac{1}{6}$ is $\dfrac{1}{1/6}$ which means $1 \div \dfrac{1}{6}$ which equals 6 (note: $\dfrac{1}{6} \times 6 = 1$)

E20.5

1 Write down the reciprocal of each number below:

     (a) 5   (b) 8   (c) $\dfrac{1}{2}$ (d) 0.2   (e) $\dfrac{1}{9}$ (f) 0.1

2 $0.8 \times 1.25 = 1$ and $0.8 \times 1.5 = 1.2$
Write down the reciprocal of 0.8

3 What number needs to be multiplied by $\dfrac{1}{7}$ to give an answer of 1?

4 What number needs to be multiplied by $\dfrac{1}{16}$ to give an answer of 1?

5 What is the reciprocal of $\dfrac{1}{n}$?

6 If $\dfrac{2}{3} \times \dfrac{3}{2} = 1$, write down the reciprocal of $\dfrac{2}{3}$.

7 Write down the reciprocal of:

     (a) $\dfrac{3}{5}$ (b) $\dfrac{4}{9}$ (c) $\dfrac{2}{13}$ (d) $2\dfrac{1}{2}$

532

Task A

Choose any regular activity that you like to do, eg: swim, play football, climb, play computer games, watch TV, play in a band and so on.

Your task is to calculate the real weekly cost of your chosen activity. All your calculations must be shown very clearly.

RESEARCH EVERY ASPECT!

• if you travel to do your activity, what is the real cost of this?

• what are the initial costs like buying a television or a pair of football boots?

• have you considered the cost of electricity when you are using a computer, etc at home? The real cost must be worked out even if adults pay for it!

Task B

Could your chosen activity be done more cheaply?

Research the options using the internet or other sources of information.

Task C

Look at a partner's calculations for a different activity. Does the information seem sensible? Are the calculations correct? Has anything been missed out in your opinion?

1. Drawing nets

(a)

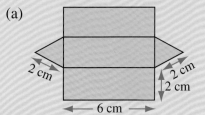

This diagram shows the net of a solid.

Name the solid.

(b)

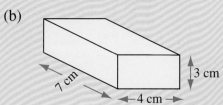

Draw an accurate net for this cuboid.

2. Drawing 3-D objects

(a) On isometric dot paper, draw any solid with a volume of 10 cm³.

(b)

This shape falls over onto the red face.

Draw the shape after it has fallen over.

(c) Draw a hexagonal prism.

3. Drawing and using plans and elevations

(a)   front elevation

Draw this object on isometric paper.

plan view

side elevation

(b) Draw and label the plan and a side elevation for this solid (called a frustum).

(c)

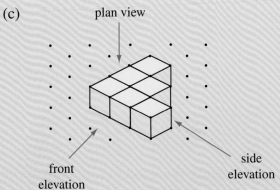

Draw the plan view, the front view and the side view of this object.

---

4. Using bearings

(a)

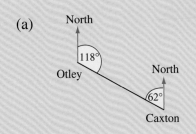

(i) Write down the bearing of Caxton from Otley.

(ii) Write down the bearing of Otley from Caxton.

(b) *Use a protractor* to measure the bearing of:

   (i) Ambleford from Cayton

   (ii) Berwick from Cayton

   (iii) Berwick from Ambleford

   (iv) Cayton from Ambleford

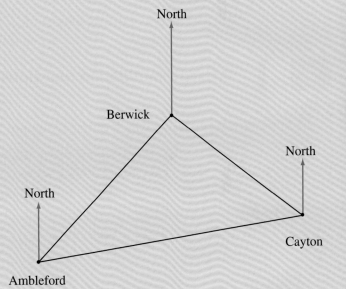

---

5. Using Pythagoras' theorem

(a)

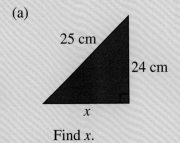

Find x.

(b)

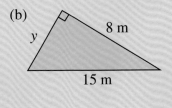

Find y.

(c)

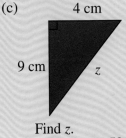

Find z.

535

6. Solving problems with shapes and lines using co-ordinates

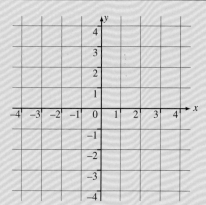

(a) Copy this grid.

(b) ABCD is a rectangle. A is (–3, 2), B is (3, 2), C is (3, –3).

Draw the rectangle.

(c) Write down the co-ordinates of D.

(d) Write down the co-ordinates of the midpoint of diagonal BD.

(e) Calculate the length of the diagonal BD.

(f) Calculate the length of the line joining (3, 1) to (7, 6).

7. Finding reciprocals

(a) Write down the reciprocal of 10.

(b) What is the reciprocal of 0.5?

(c) $\frac{3}{4} \times \frac{4}{3} = 1$ and $\frac{3}{4} \times \frac{4}{5} = \frac{3}{5}$

Write down the reciprocal of $\frac{3}{4}$.

Mixed examination questions

1 Write down which of the following are nets of a cube.

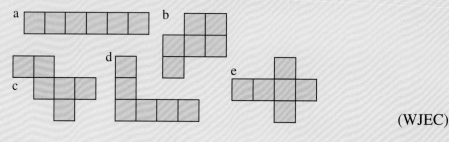

(WJEC)

2

XYZ is a right-angled triangle.
XY = 3.2 cm.
XZ = 1.7 cm.

Calculate the length of YZ.

Give your answer correct to 3 significant figures.

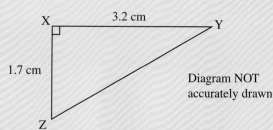

Diagram NOT accurately drawn

(EDEXCEL)

3 These drawings show two views of the same solid made with centimetre cubes. The base of the solid is horizontal.

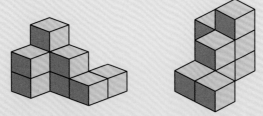

(a) How many centimetre cubes are there in the solid?

(b) Draw an accurate full-sized plan view of the solid on a centimetre grid.

(OCR)

4 The diagram shows three villages. Abshelf (A), Grasston (G) and Haswell (H).

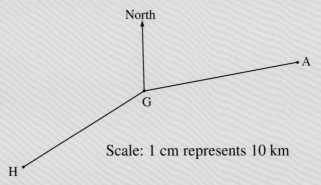

North

A

G

Scale: 1 cm represents 10 km

H

The North line through Grasston is shown.

(a) What is the distance, in kilometres, between Abshelf and Grasston?

(b) Measure and write down the bearing of Abshelf from Grasston.

(c) Measure and write down the bearing of Haswell from Grasston.   (OCR)

5 A lift at the seaside takes people from sea level to the top of a cliff, as shown.

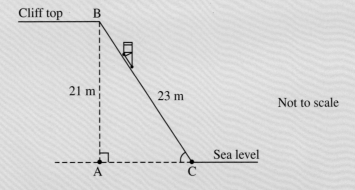

Cliff top   B

21 m   23 m

Not to scale

Sea level

A   C

From sea level to the top of the cliff, the lift travels 23 m and rises a height of 21 m.

Calculate the distance AC.   (AQA)

Page 527   M20.4

1. (a) 8.60   (b) 15   (c) 18.36   (d) 25

2. (a) 12.96   (b) 7.42   (c) 13.96   (d) 14

3. (a) 24   (b) 12.21   (c) 10.80   (d) 11.11

(e) 15.01   (f) 40.95   (g) 8.41   (h) 16.11

4. 12.50 m   **5.** 14.56 cm   **6.** 37.64 m   **7.** 7.32 cm

Page 528   E20.4

1. 5.50 m   **2.** B by 0.57 m   **3.** 4.90 m   **4.** 10.39 m

5. 14.42 km   **6.** 11.40 km   **7.** 79.65 km   **8.** 2.58 km

9. 5.02 m   **10.** 9.17 cm   **11.** (a) 6.32   (b) 10.91   (c) 12.69

12. 31.75 cm^2 **13.** 110.85 cm^2 **14.** (a) 17   (b) 11.18   (c) 7.21

Page 530   M20.5

1. (a) (3, 3)   (b) 5.66   **2.** (b) (3, 2)   (c) (0, −1)   (d) 8.49

3. AB$\left(4, 7\frac{1}{2}\right)$, 6.08; CD$\left(2, 3\frac{1}{2}\right)$, 5.39, EF$\left(4\frac{1}{2}, 5\frac{1}{2}\right)$, 3.16

GH(4, 4), 2.83, IJ$\left(6\frac{1}{2}, 4\right)$, 6.71, KL$\left(7\frac{1}{2}, 1\frac{1}{2}\right)$, 1.41

4. 10   **5.** (b) (8, 1)   (c) $\left(5, -\frac{1}{2}\right)$ (d) 6.71

6. (b) (−1, −2)   (c) (0, 0)   (d) 8.94

Page 532   E20.5

1. (a) 0.2 or $\frac{1}{5}$ (b) 0.125 or $\frac{1}{8}$ (c) 2   (d) 5   (e) 9   (f) 10

2. 1.25   **3.** 7   **4.** 16   **5.** n **6.** $\frac{3}{2}$ or 1.5

7. (a) $\frac{5}{3}$ (b) $\frac{9}{4}$ or 2.25   (c) $\frac{13}{2}$ or 6.5   (d) $\frac{2}{5}$ or 0.4

Page 534   Test yourself on Unit 20

1. (a) prism (triangular based)

3. (b) 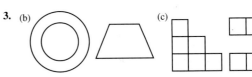 (c)

4. (a) (i) 118°   (ii) 298°

(b) (i) 260°   (ii) 307°   (iii) 043°   (iv) 080°

5. (a) 7 cm   (b) 12.69 m   (c) 9.85 cm

6. (c) D (−3, −3)   (d) $\left(0, -\frac{1}{2}\right)$ (e) 7.81

7. (a) $\frac{1}{10}$ or 0.1   (b) 2   (c) $\frac{4}{3}$

Page 536   Mixed examination questions

1. c, e   **2.** 3.62 cm

3. (a) 9   (b)

4. (a) 39 km   (b) 080°   (c) 240°

5. 9.4 m

Index